Shojo Beat

ORESAMA TEACHER

Vol. **2**

& Art by

Tsubaki

ORESAMA TEACHER

Volume 2
CONTENTS

Chapter 6 ---------------------4

Chapter 7 ---------------------37

Chapter 8 ---------------------67

Chapter 9 ---------------------97

Chapter 10 ------------------129

Chapter 11 ------------------159

End Notes --------------------189

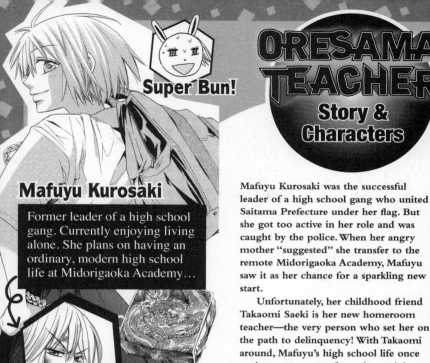

ORESAMA TEACHER
Story & Characters

Mafuyu Kurosaki was the successful leader of a high school gang who united Saitama Prefecture under her flag. But she got too active in her role and was caught by the police. When her angry mother "suggested" she transfer to the remote Midorigaoka Academy, Mafuyu saw it as her chance for a sparkling new start.

Unfortunately, her childhood friend Takaomi Saeki is her new homeroom teacher—the very person who set her on the path to delinquency! With Takaomi around, Mafuyu's high school life once again starts to stray from the straight and narrow.

Mafuyu fights to save her first new friend, Hayasaka, from his troubles. But in order to hide her identity, she wears a rabbit mask and becomes **Super Bun**...

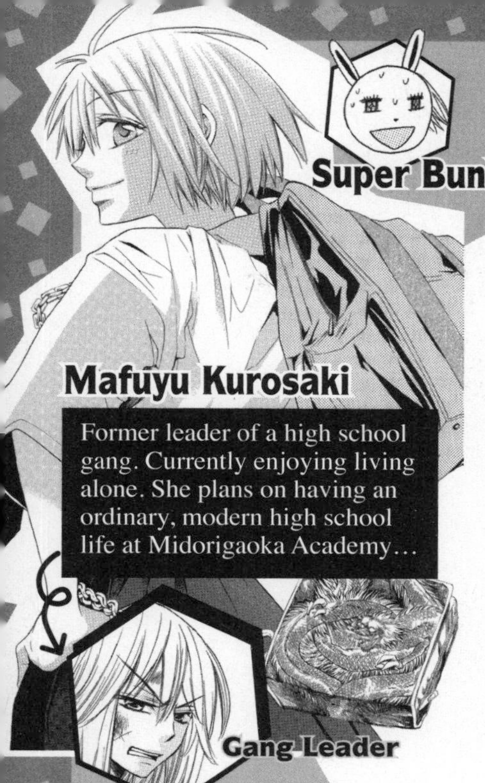

Super Bun!
Gang Leader

Mafuyu Kurosaki

Former leader of a high school gang. Currently enjoying living alone. She plans on having an ordinary, modern high school life at Midorigaoka Academy...

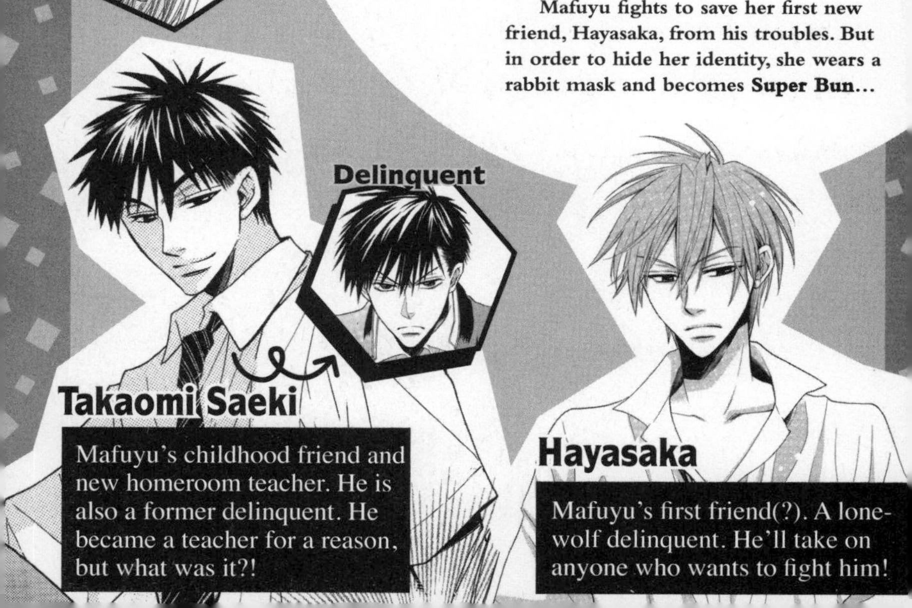

Delinquent

Takaomi Saeki

Mafuyu's childhood friend and new homeroom teacher. He is also a former delinquent. He became a teacher for a reason, but what was it?!

Hayasaka

Mafuyu's first friend(?). A lone-wolf delinquent. He'll take on anyone who wants to fight him!

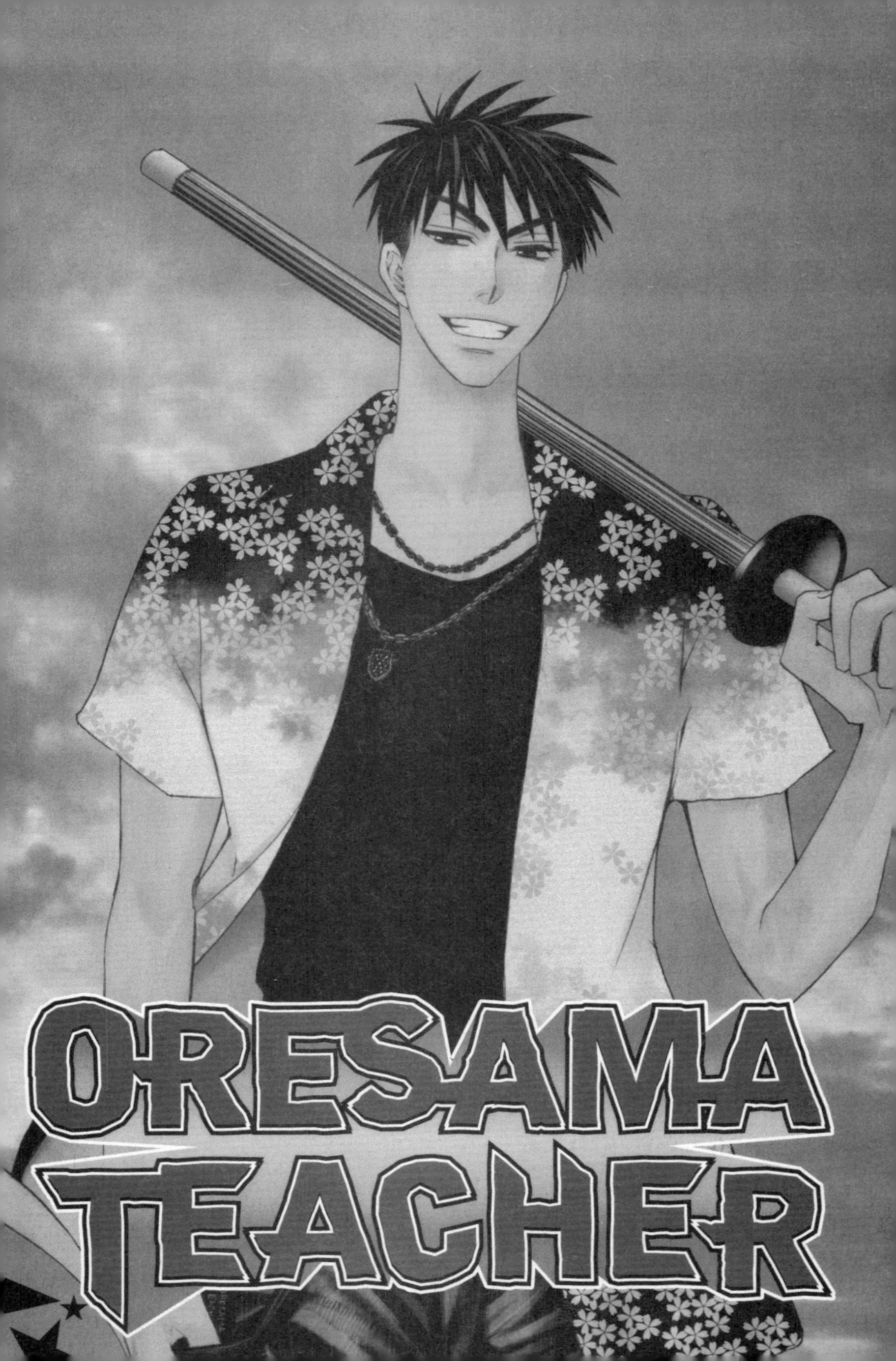
ORESAMA
TEACHER

Chapter 6

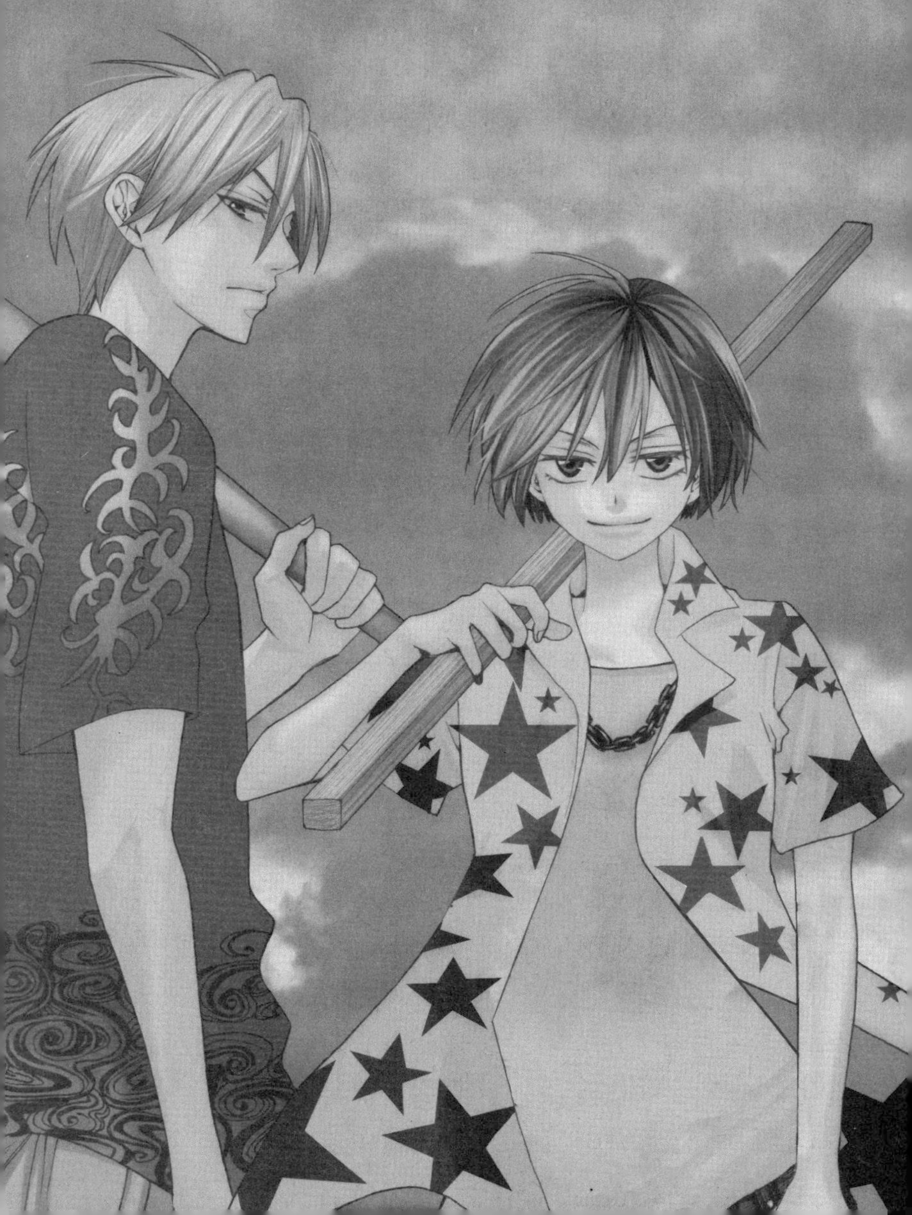

IT'S THE SECOND VOLUME OF ORESAMA TEACHER!

This time there wasn't enough room for bonus pages, so the only extra is the cover.

I hope you enjoy it.

SPECIAL THANKS

My sister, my family, my editor. Tooya-san, Pochi-san, Shiina-san, Kana-yan And you, the reader.

To those who came to my autograph session: Thank you so very much! I was deeply moved by your taking time out of your busy schedule to come. I was so surprised at the number of elementary and middle school children.

YAY!

And you even gave me hand-made gifts. I was so happy!

TELL ME, HAYASAKA!

HAYASAKA, YOU REALLY HAVE A HUNDRED PHONE NUMBERS?
YEAH ...
That's right.
HOW CAN I GET LOTS LIKE YOU...?
HUH?
IT'S EASY TO GET THAT MANY.
I ADD EVERY-ONE FROM CLASS.
AND THE STORES I GO TO A LOT.
Like my salon.
...
OH...
SO, ZERO NUMBERS THAT COUNT...

Hayasaka doesn't have friends either.

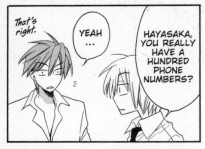

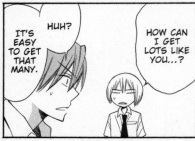

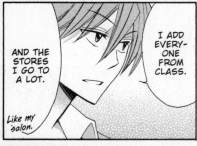

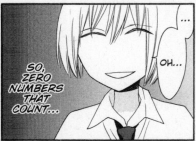

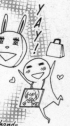

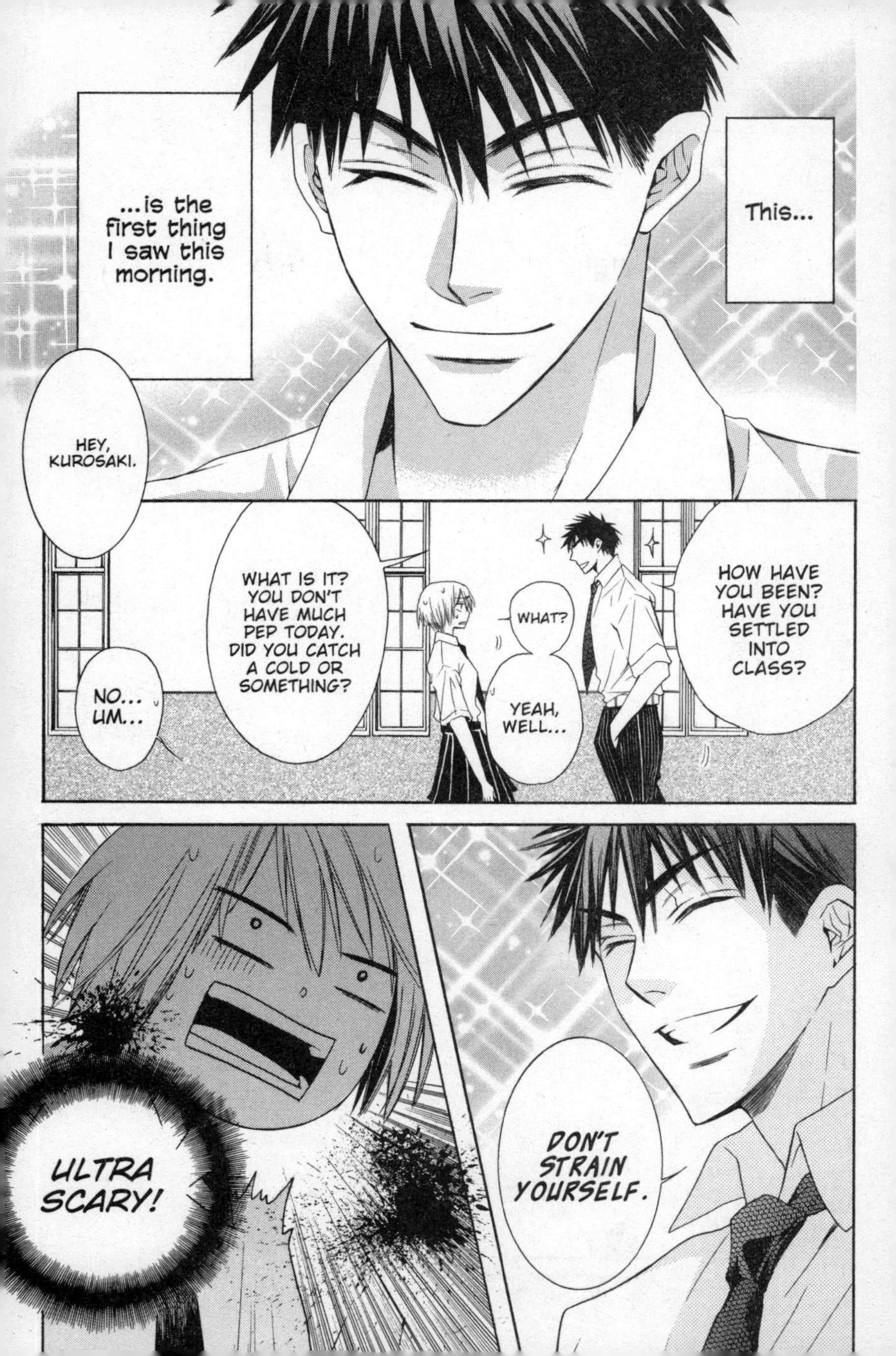
This...
...is the first thing I saw this morning.
HEY, KUROSAKI.
HOW HAVE YOU BEEN? HAVE YOU SETTLED INTO CLASS?
WHAT?
YEAH, WELL...
WHAT IS IT? YOU DON'T HAVE MUCH PEP TODAY. DID YOU CATCH A COLD OR SOMETHING?
NO... UM...
DON'T STRAIN YOURSELF.
ULTRA SCARY!

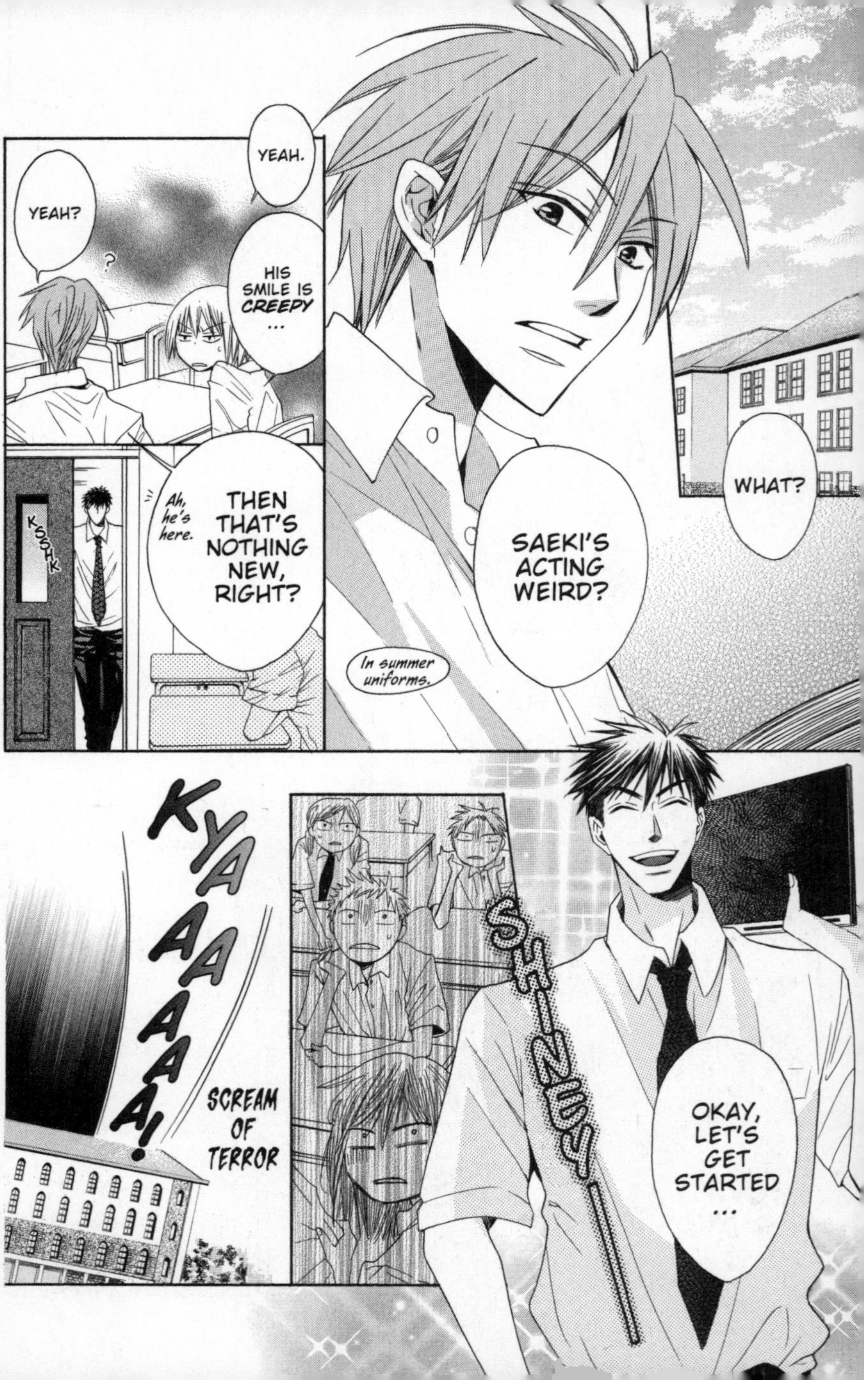
WHAT?
SAEKI'S ACTING WEIRD?
In summer uniforms.
YEAH.
HIS SMILE IS *CREEPY*...
YEAH?
?
THEN THAT'S NOTHING NEW, RIGHT?
Ah, he's here.
KSSHK
SHINEY
OKAY, LET'S GET STARTED...
KYAAAAAAA!
SCREAM OF TERROR

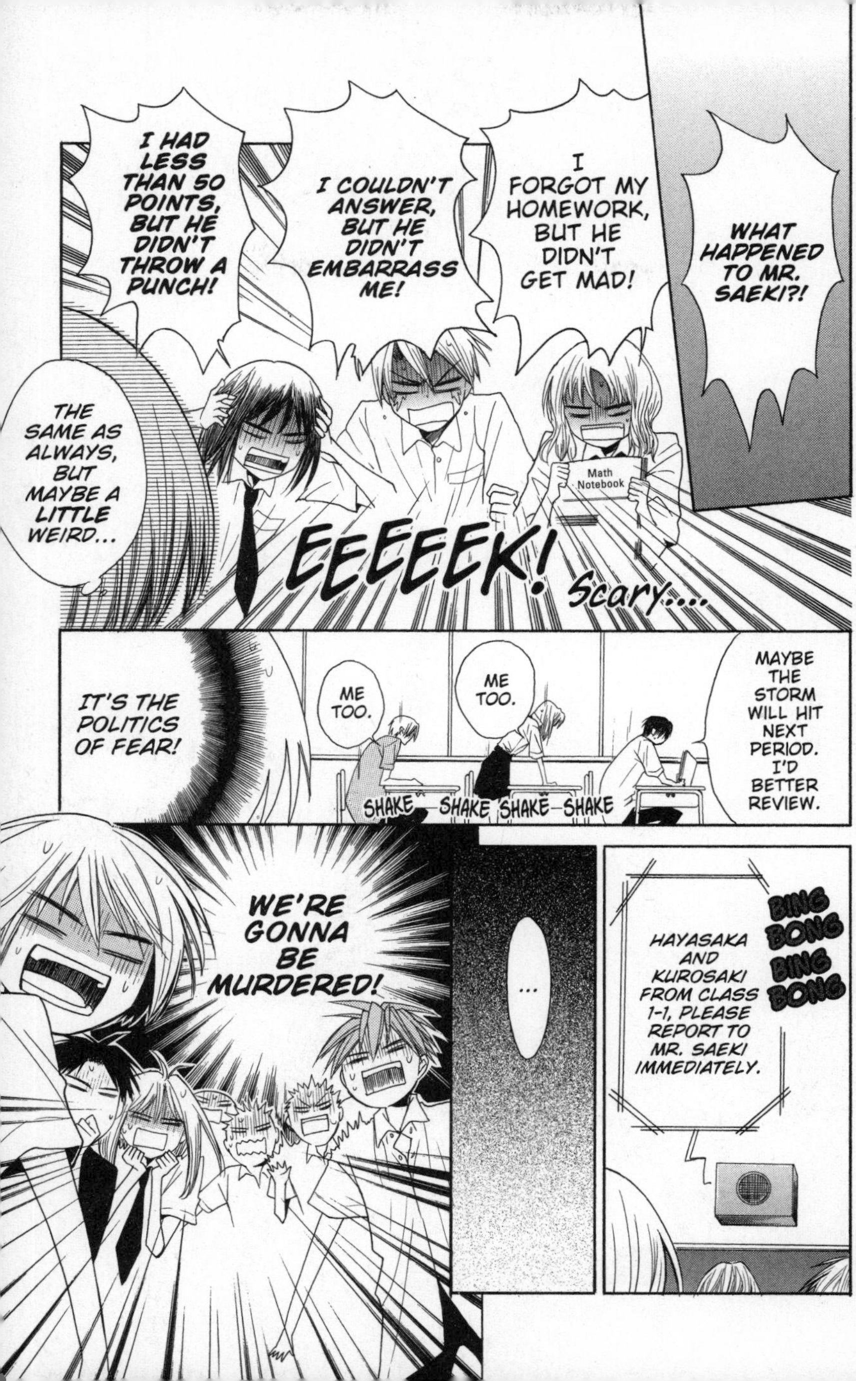
WHAT HAPPENED TO MR. SAEKI?!
I FORGOT MY HOMEWORK, BUT HE DIDN'T GET MAD!
I COULDN'T ANSWER, BUT HE DIDN'T EMBARRASS ME!
I HAD LESS THAN 50 POINTS, BUT HE DIDN'T THROW A PUNCH!
THE SAME AS ALWAYS, BUT MAYBE A LITTLE WEIRD...
Math Notebook
EEEEEK!
Scary....
MAYBE THE STORM WILL HIT NEXT PERIOD. I'D BETTER REVIEW.
ME TOO.
ME TOO.
IT'S THE POLITICS OF FEAR!
SHAKE SHAKE SHAKE SHAKE
BING BONG BING BONG
HAYASAKA AND KUROSAKI FROM CLASS 1-1, PLEASE REPORT TO MR. SAEKI IMMEDIATELY.
...
WE'RE GONNA BE MURDERED!

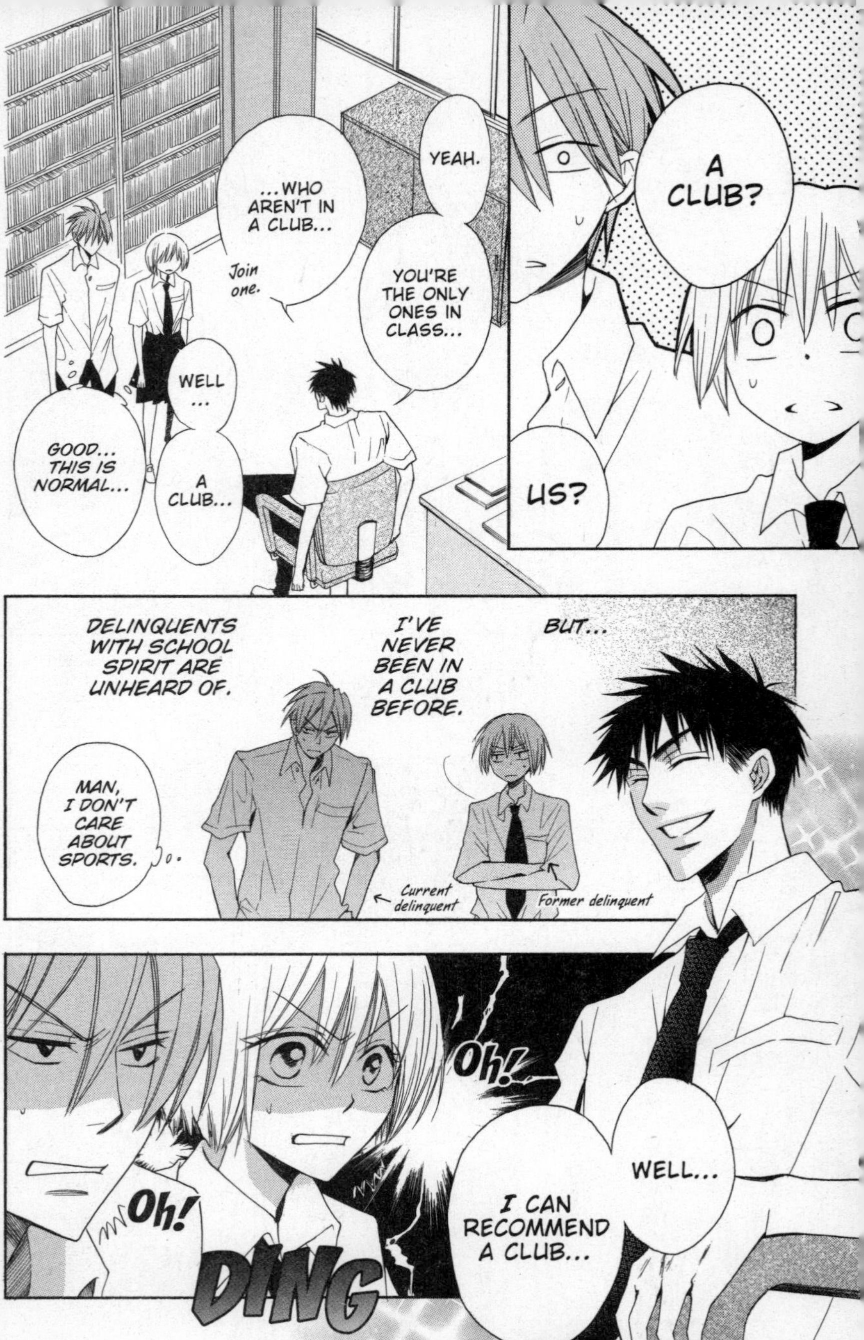

A CLUB?
US?
YEAH.
YOU'RE THE ONLY ONES IN CLASS...
...WHO AREN'T IN A CLUB...
Join one.
WELL...
A CLUB...
GOOD... THIS IS NORMAL...
BUT...
I'VE NEVER BEEN IN A CLUB BEFORE.
DELINQUENTS WITH SCHOOL SPIRIT ARE UNHEARD OF.
MAN, I DON'T CARE ABOUT SPORTS.
Former delinquent
Current delinquent
WELL...
I CAN RECOMMEND A CLUB...
Oh!
Oh!
DING

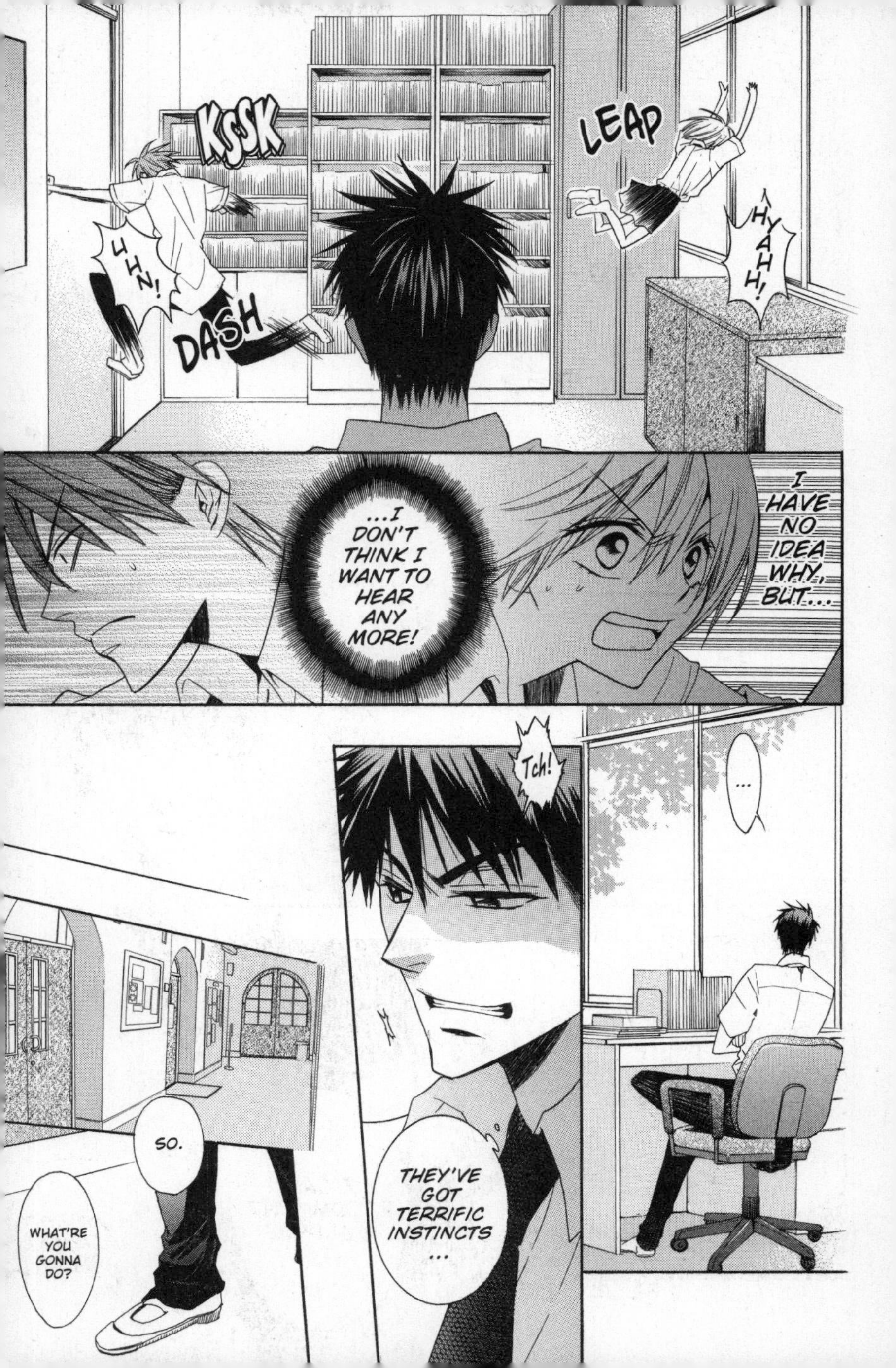
LEAP
HYAHH!
KSSK
UHN!
DASH
I HAVE NO IDEA WHY, BUT...
...I DON'T THINK I WANT TO HEAR ANY MORE!
...
Tch!
THEY'VE GOT TERRIFIC INSTINCTS...
SO.
WHAT'RE YOU GONNA DO?

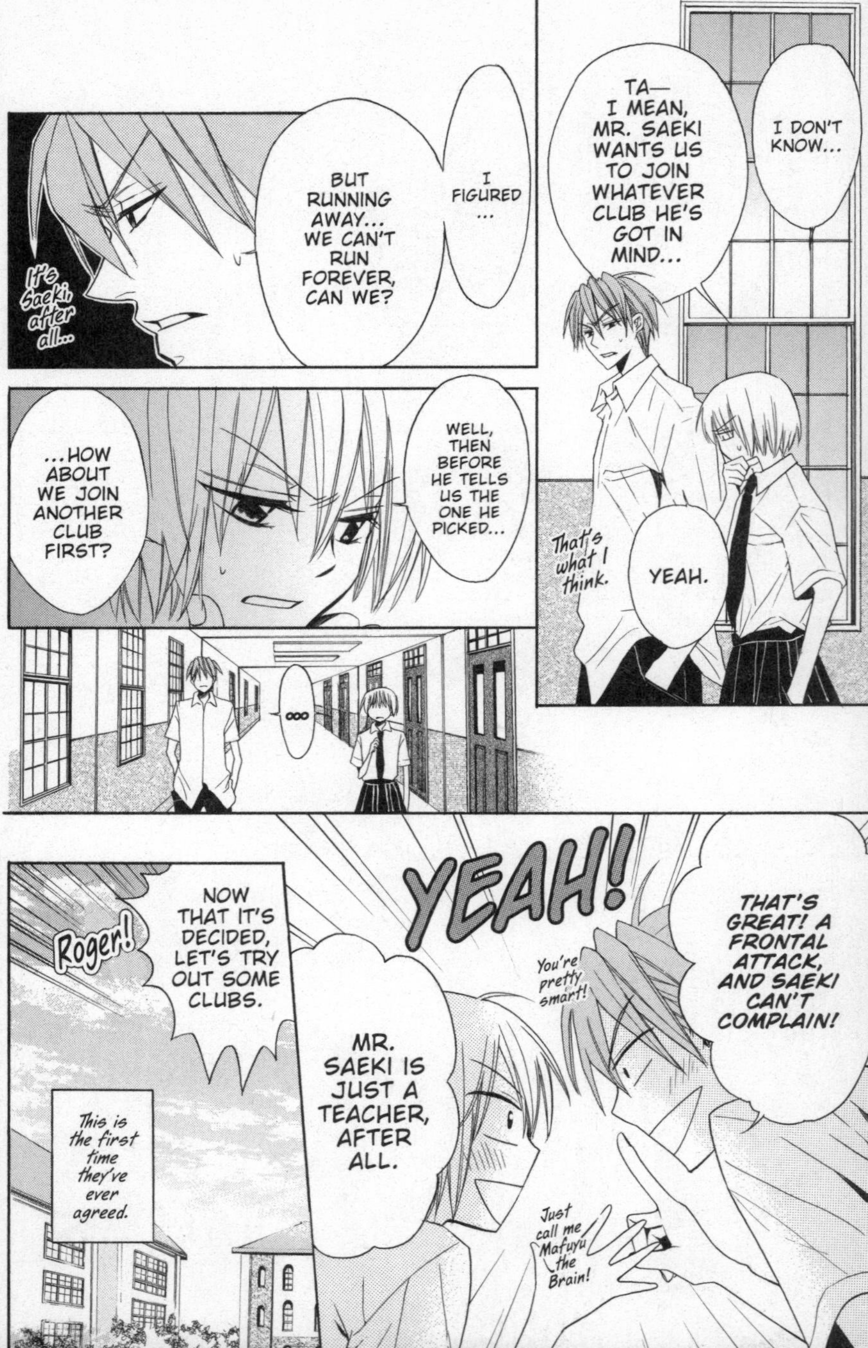
I DON'T KNOW...
TA— I MEAN, MR. SAEKI WANTS US TO JOIN WHATEVER CLUB HE'S GOT IN MIND...
YEAH.
That's what I think.
I FIGURED...
BUT RUNNING AWAY... WE CAN'T RUN FOREVER, CAN WE?
It's Saeki, after all...
WELL, THEN BEFORE HE TELLS US THE ONE HE PICKED...
...HOW ABOUT WE JOIN ANOTHER CLUB FIRST?
...
THAT'S GREAT! A FRONTAL ATTACK, AND SAEKI CAN'T COMPLAIN!
YEAH!
You're pretty smart!
MR. SAEKI IS JUST A TEACHER, AFTER ALL.
Just call me Mafuyu the Brain!
NOW THAT IT'S DECIDED, LET'S TRY OUT SOME CLUBS.
Roger!
This is the first time they've ever agreed.

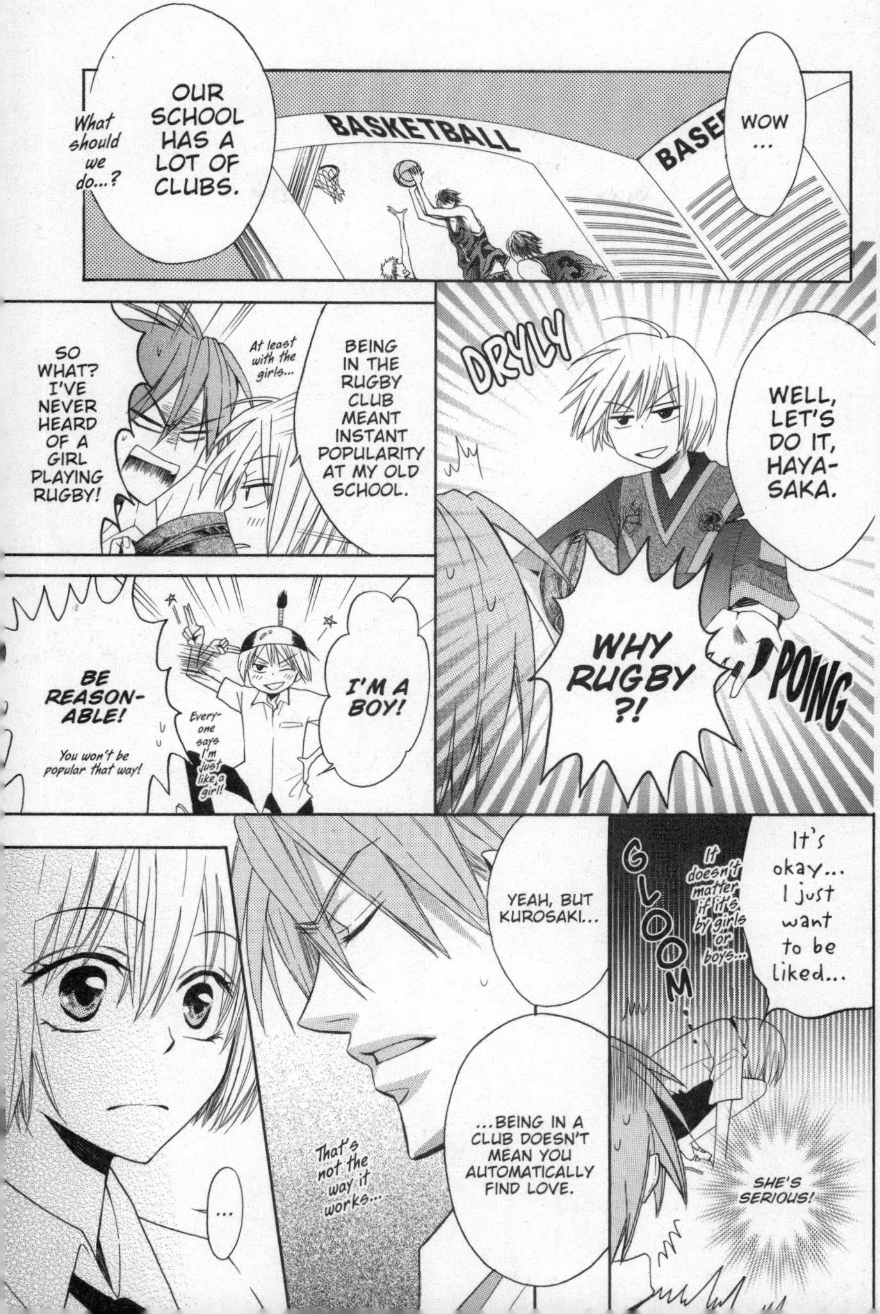
OUR SCHOOL HAS A LOT OF CLUBS.
WOW...
BASEB
BASKETBALL
What should we do...?
DRYLY
WELL, LET'S DO IT, HAYA-SAKA.
WHY RUGBY ?!
POING
BEING IN THE RUGBY CLUB MEANT INSTANT POPULARITY AT MY OLD SCHOOL.
At least with the girls...
SO WHAT? I'VE NEVER HEARD OF A GIRL PLAYING RUGBY!
I'M A BOY!
Every-one says I'm just like a girl!
BE REASON-ABLE!
You won't be popular that way!
It's okay... I just want to be liked...
It doesn't matter if it's by girls or boys...
GLOOM...
SHE'S SERIOUS!
YEAH, BUT KUROSAKI...
...BEING IN A CLUB DOESN'T MEAN YOU AUTOMATICALLY FIND LOVE.
That's not the way it works...
...

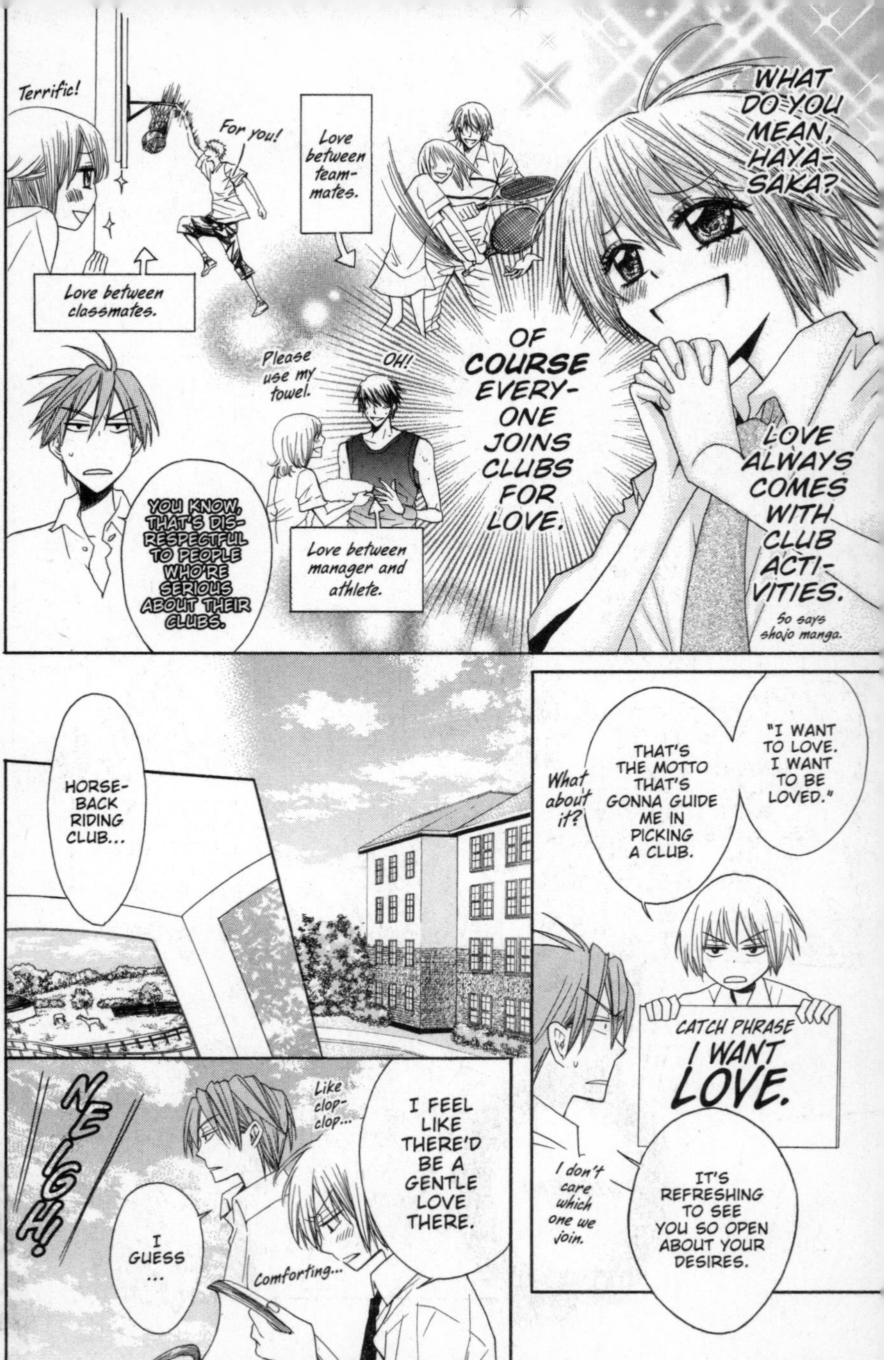
WHAT DO YOU MEAN, HAYA-SAKA?
LOVE ALWAYS COMES WITH CLUB ACTI-VITIES.
So says shojo manga.
OF COURSE EVERY-ONE JOINS CLUBS FOR LOVE.
Love between team-mates.
For you!
Terrific!
Love between classmates.
OH!
Please use my towel.
Love between manager and athlete.
YOU KNOW, THAT'S DIS-RESPECTFUL TO PEOPLE WHO'RE SERIOUS ABOUT THEIR CLUBS.
"I WANT TO LOVE. I WANT TO BE LOVED."
THAT'S THE MOTTO THAT'S GONNA GUIDE ME IN PICKING A CLUB.
What about it?
CATCH PHRASE I WANT LOVE.
IT'S REFRESHING TO SEE YOU SO OPEN ABOUT YOUR DESIRES.
I don't care which one we join.
HORSE-BACK RIDING CLUB...
I FEEL LIKE THERE'D BE A GENTLE LOVE THERE.
Like clop-clop...
NEIGH!
I GUESS...
Comforting...

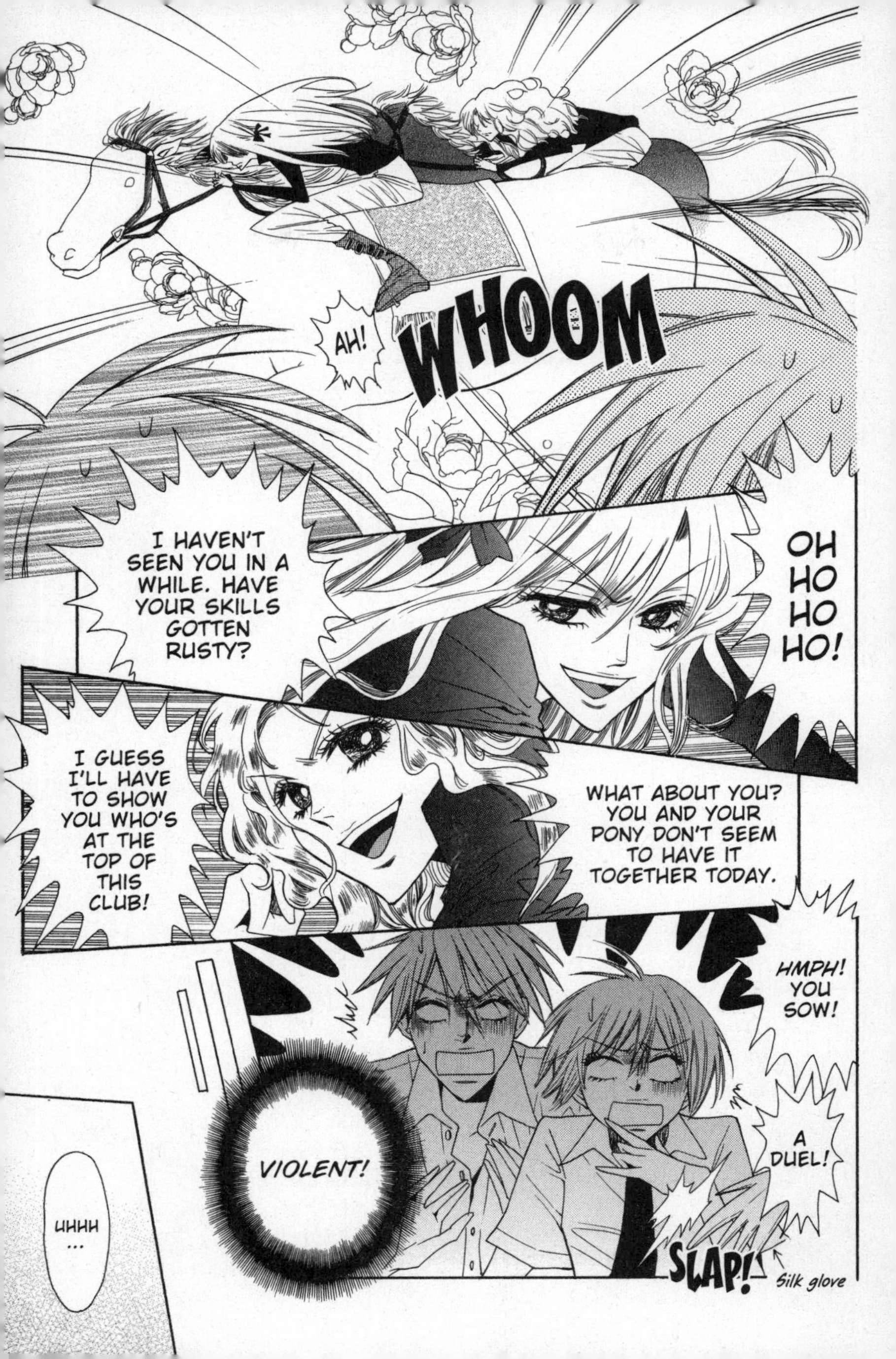
WHOOM
AH!
OH HO HO HO!
I HAVEN'T SEEN YOU IN A WHILE. HAVE YOUR SKILLS GOTTEN RUSTY?
WHAT ABOUT YOU? YOU AND YOUR PONY DON'T SEEM TO HAVE IT TOGETHER TODAY.
I GUESS I'LL HAVE TO SHOW YOU WHO'S AT THE TOP OF THIS CLUB!
HMPH! YOU SOW!
A DUEL!
SLAP!
Silk glove
VIOLENT!
UHHH ...

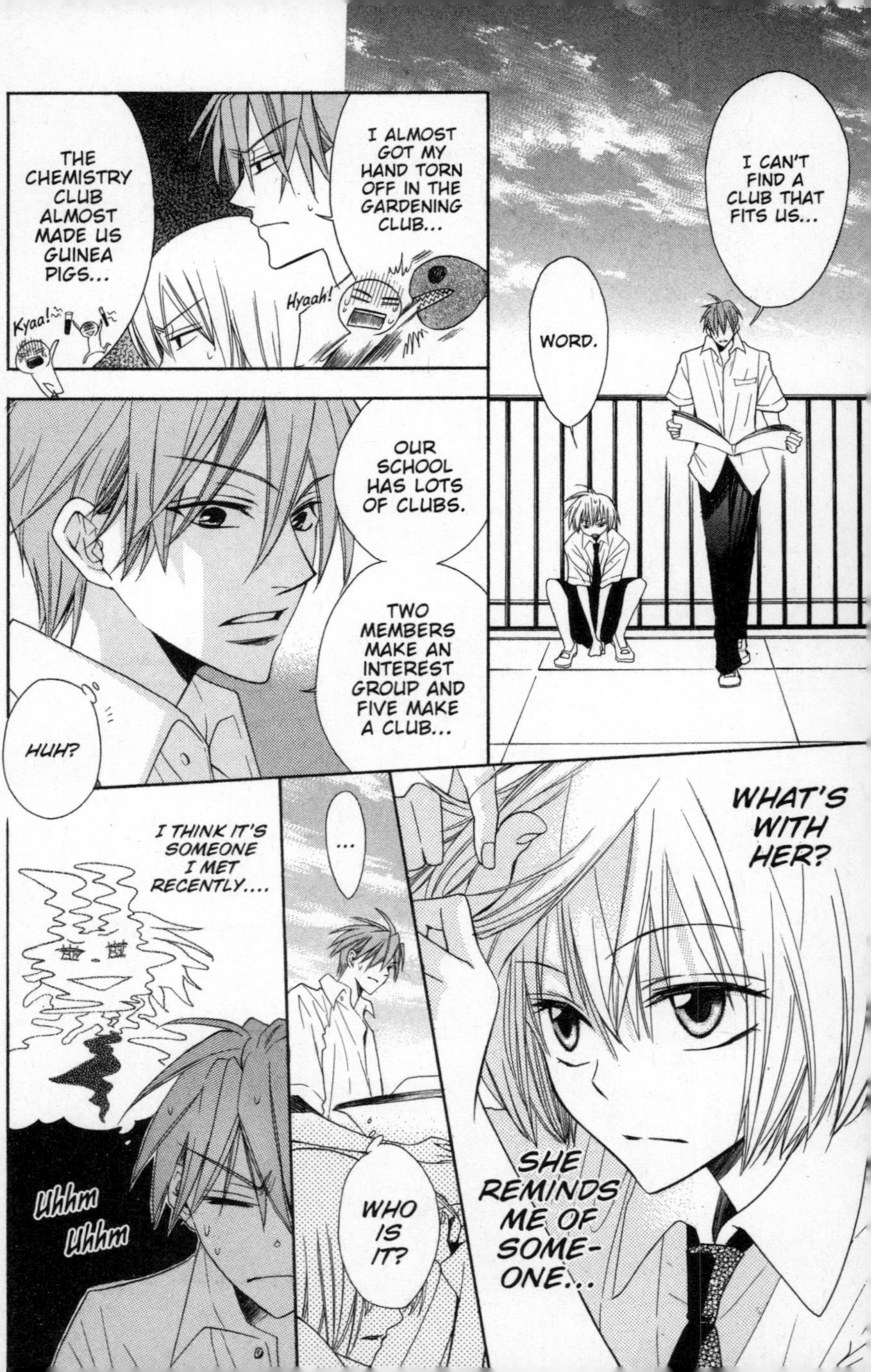
I CAN'T FIND A CLUB THAT FITS US...
WORD.
I ALMOST GOT MY HAND TORN OFF IN THE GARDENING CLUB...
Hyaah!
THE CHEMISTRY CLUB ALMOST MADE US GUINEA PIGS...
Kyaa!
OUR SCHOOL HAS LOTS OF CLUBS.
TWO MEMBERS MAKE AN INTEREST GROUP AND FIVE MAKE A CLUB...
HUH?
WHAT'S WITH HER?
SHE REMINDS ME OF SOME-ONE...
...
WHO IS IT?
I THINK IT'S SOMEONE I MET RECENTLY....
Uhhm Uhhm

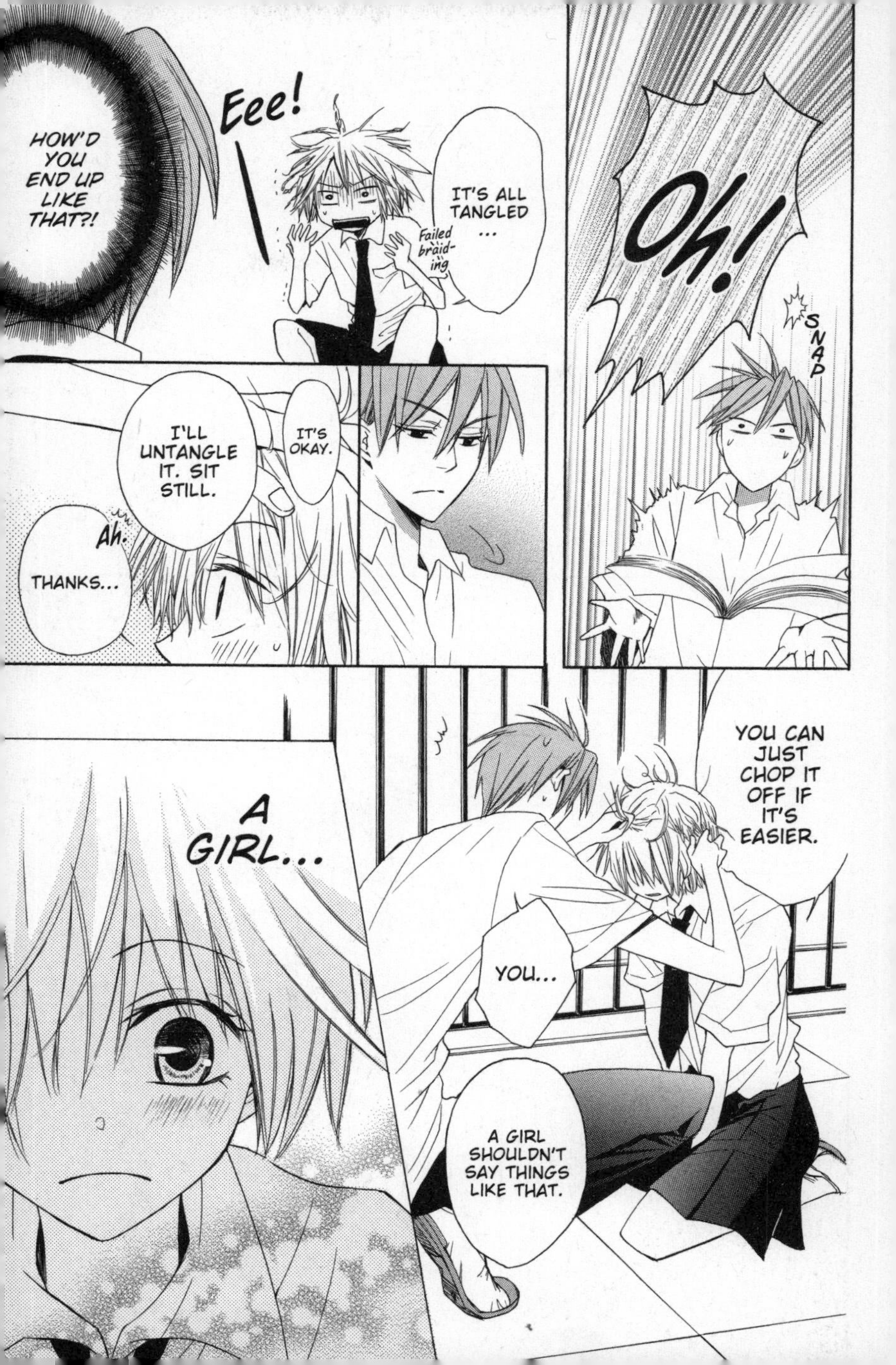
Oh!
SNAP
Eee!
IT'S ALL TANGLED ...
Failed braiding
HOW'D YOU END UP LIKE THAT?!
IT'S OKAY.
I'LL UNTANGLE IT. SIT STILL.
Ah. THANKS...
YOU CAN JUST CHOP IT OFF IF IT'S EASIER.
YOU...
A GIRL SHOULDN'T SAY THINGS LIKE THAT.
A GIRL...

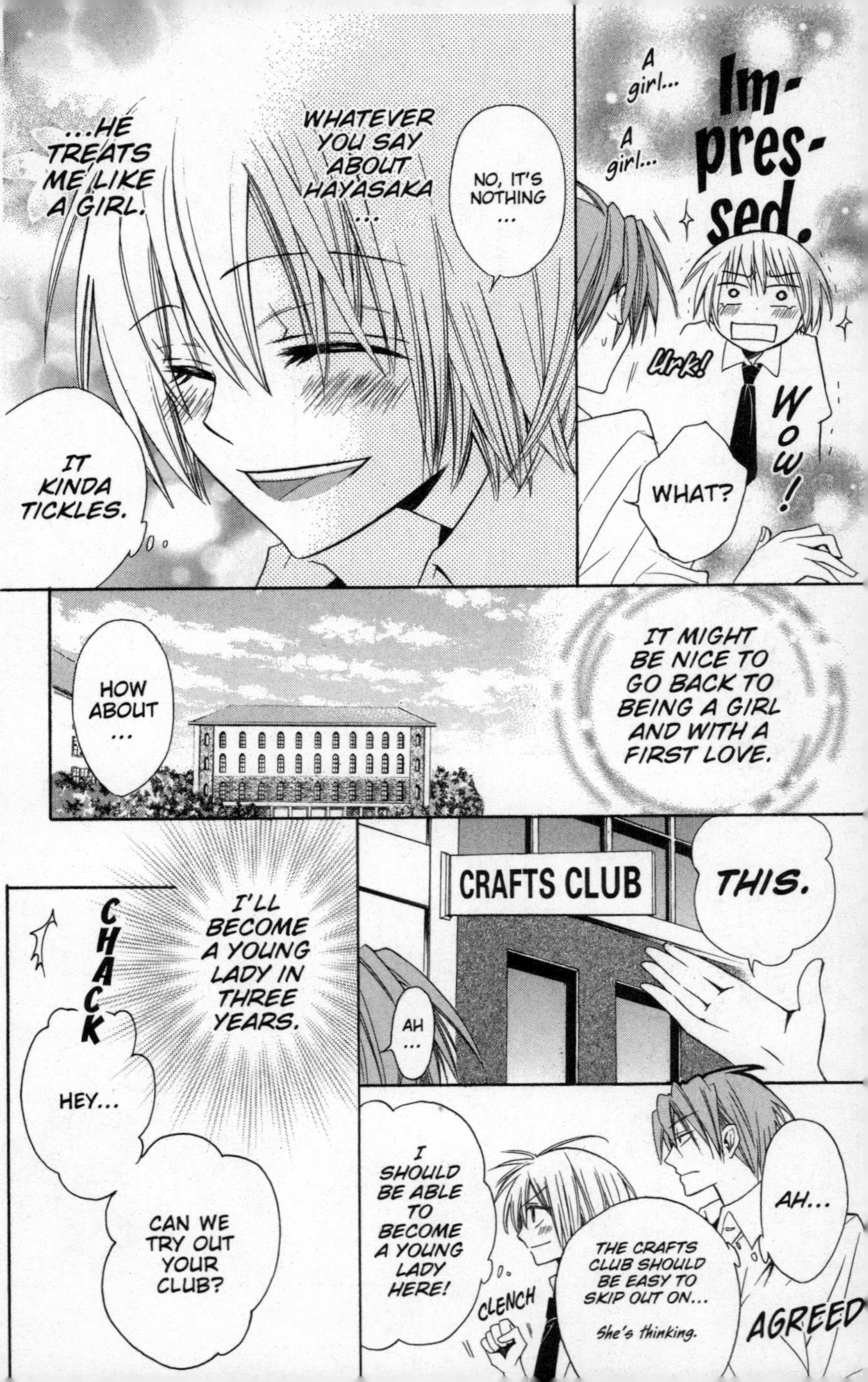
A girl... A girl...
Im-pres-sed.
Urk!
Wow!
WHAT?
NO, IT'S NOTHING ...
WHATEVER YOU SAY ABOUT HAYASAKA ...
...HE TREATS ME LIKE A GIRL.
IT KINDA TICKLES.
IT MIGHT BE NICE TO GO BACK TO BEING A GIRL AND WITH A FIRST LOVE.
HOW ABOUT ...
THIS.
CRAFTS CLUB
AH ...
AH...
THE CRAFTS CLUB SHOULD BE EASY TO SKIP OUT ON...
She's thinking.
AGREED
I SHOULD BE ABLE TO BECOME A YOUNG LADY HERE!
CLENCH
I'LL BECOME A YOUNG LADY IN THREE YEARS.
CHACK
HEY...
CAN WE TRY OUT YOUR CLUB?

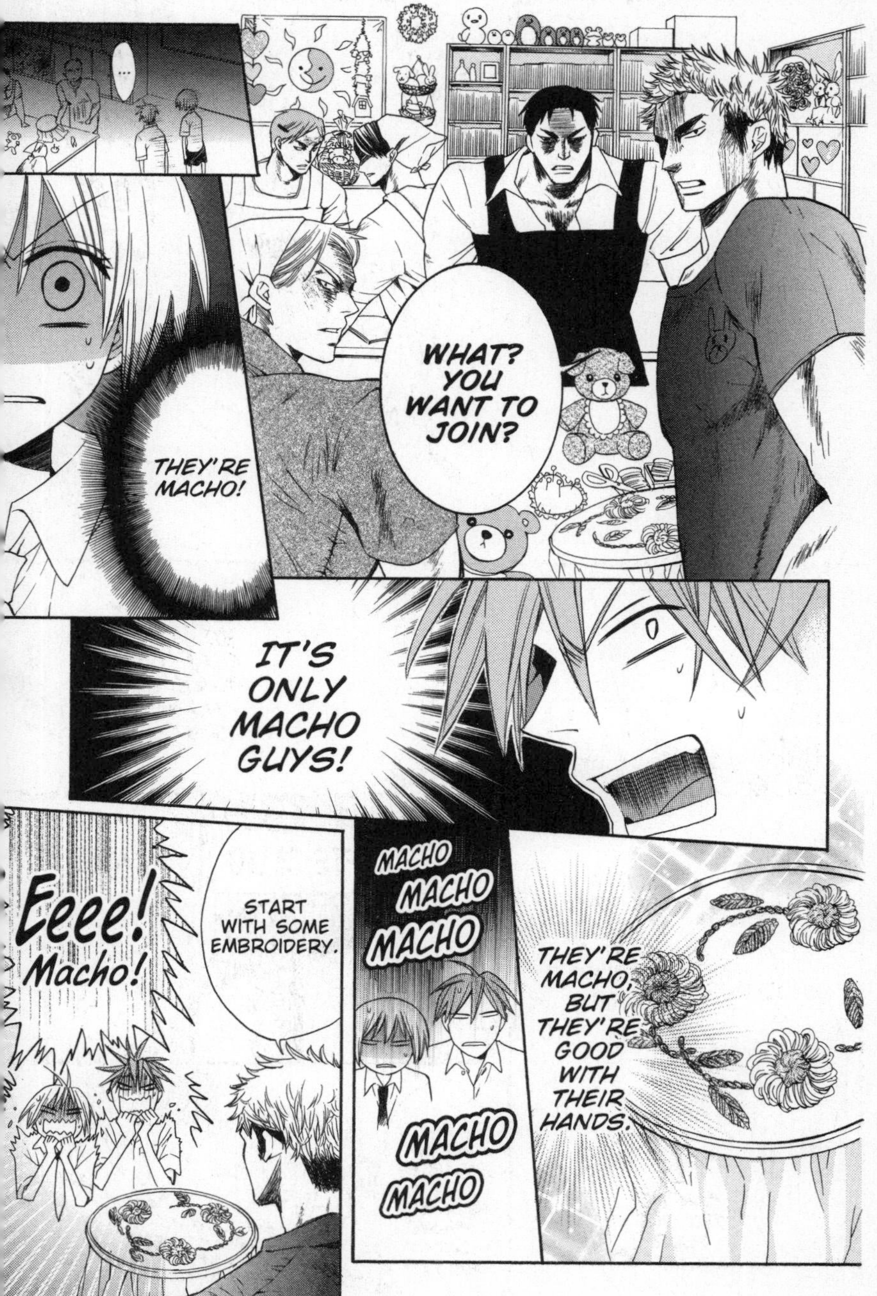
WHAT? YOU WANT TO JOIN?
...
THEY'RE MACHO!
IT'S ONLY MACHO GUYS!
THEY'RE MACHO, BUT THEY'RE GOOD WITH THEIR HANDS.
MACHO MACHO MACHO
MACHO MACHO
START WITH SOME EMBROIDERY.
Eeee! Macho!

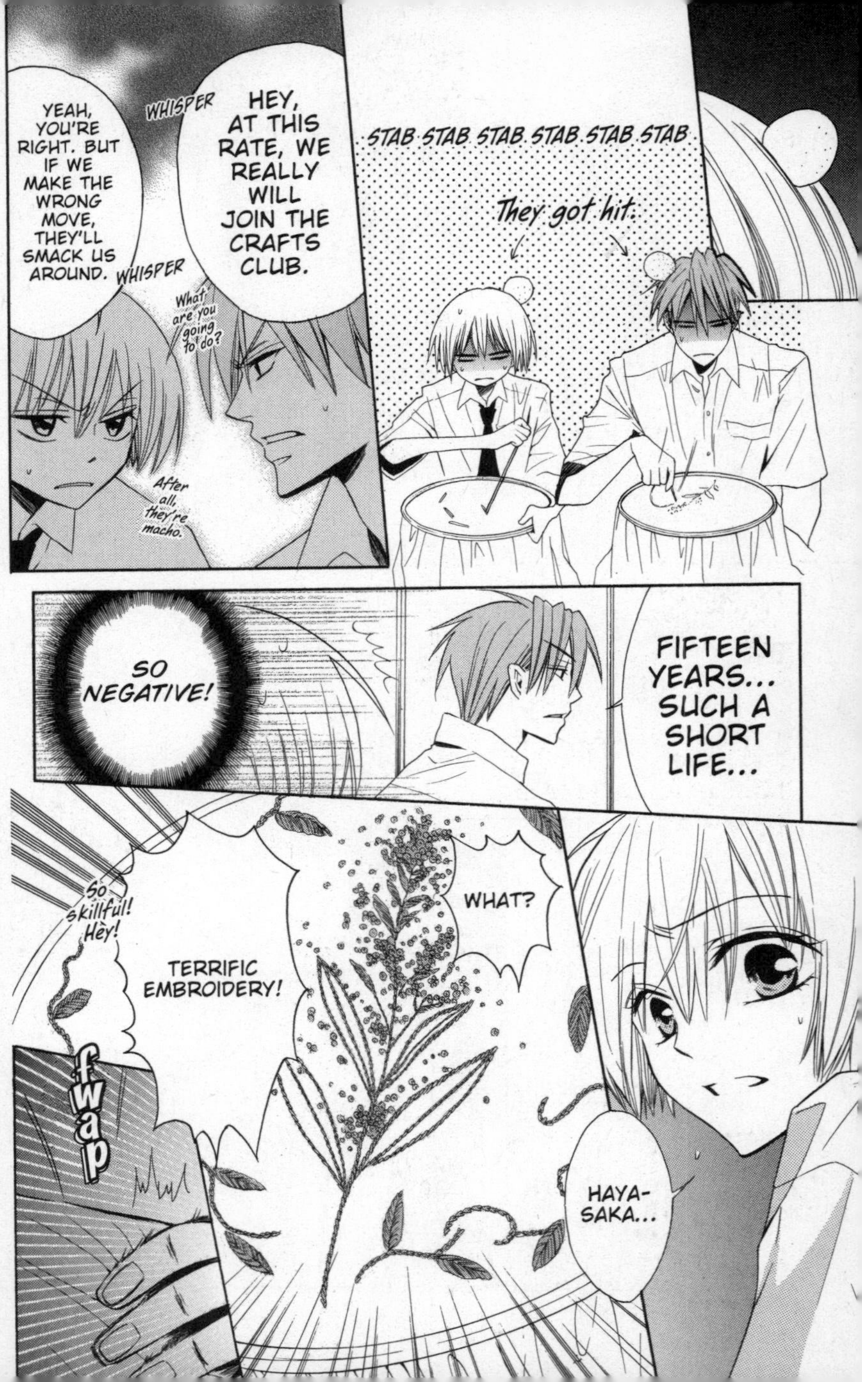
STAB STAB STAB STAB STAB STAB
They got hit.
HEY, AT THIS RATE, WE REALLY WILL JOIN THE CRAFTS CLUB.
WHISPER
YEAH, YOU'RE RIGHT. BUT IF WE MAKE THE WRONG MOVE, THEY'LL SMACK US AROUND.
WHISPER
What are you going to do?
After all, they're macho.
FIFTEEN YEARS... SUCH A SHORT LIFE...
SO NEGATIVE!
HAYA-SAKA...
WHAT?
TERRIFIC EMBROIDERY!
So skillful! Hey!
fwap

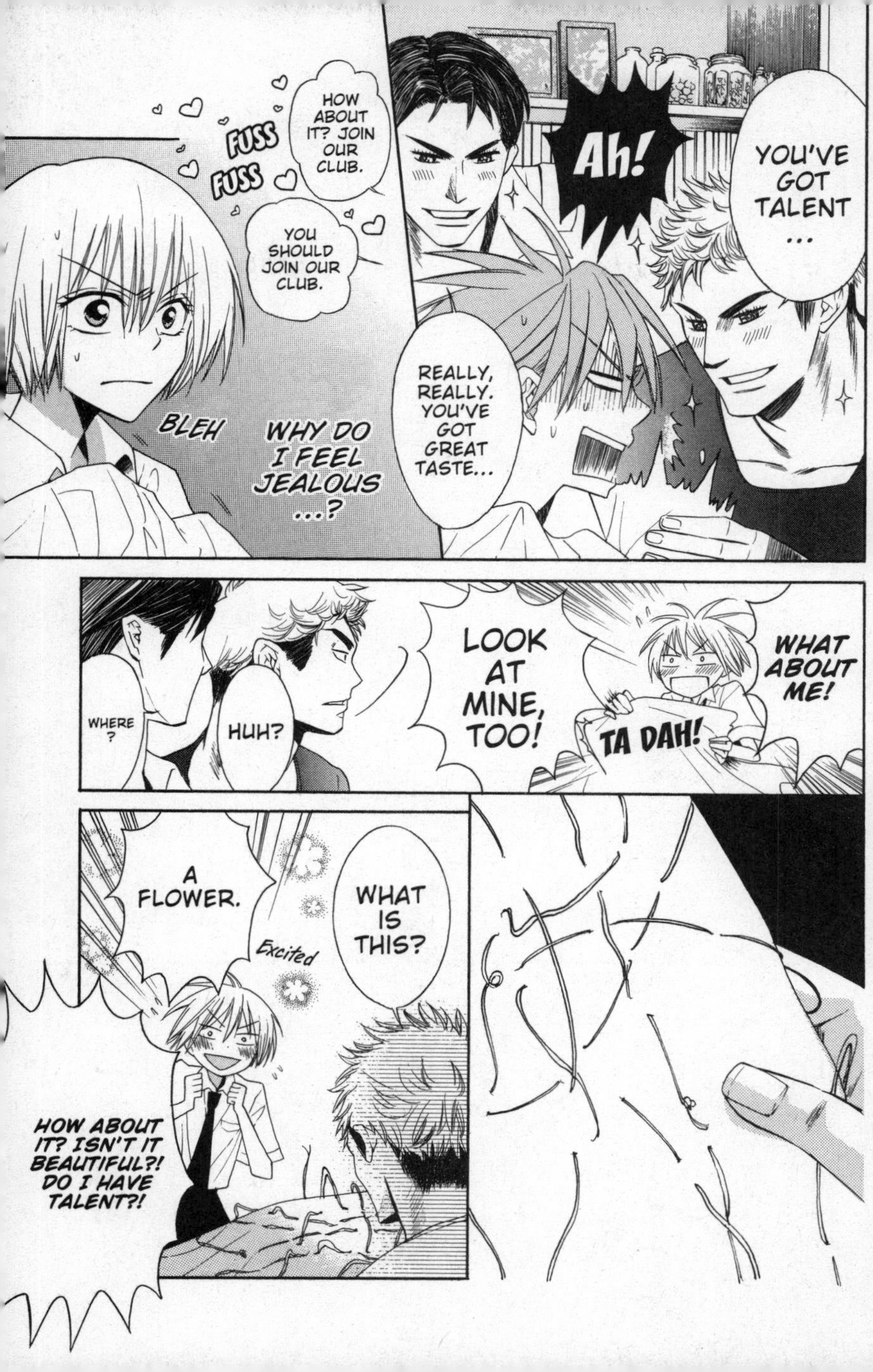
Ah!
YOU'VE GOT TALENT ...
REALLY, REALLY. YOU'VE GOT GREAT TASTE...
HOW ABOUT IT? JOIN OUR CLUB.
FUSS FUSS
YOU SHOULD JOIN OUR CLUB.
WHY DO I FEEL JEALOUS ...?
BLEH
WHAT ABOUT ME!
TA DAH!
LOOK AT MINE, TOO!
HUH?
WHERE?
WHAT IS THIS?
Excited
A FLOWER.
HOW ABOUT IT? ISN'T IT BEAUTIFUL?! DO I HAVE TALENT?!

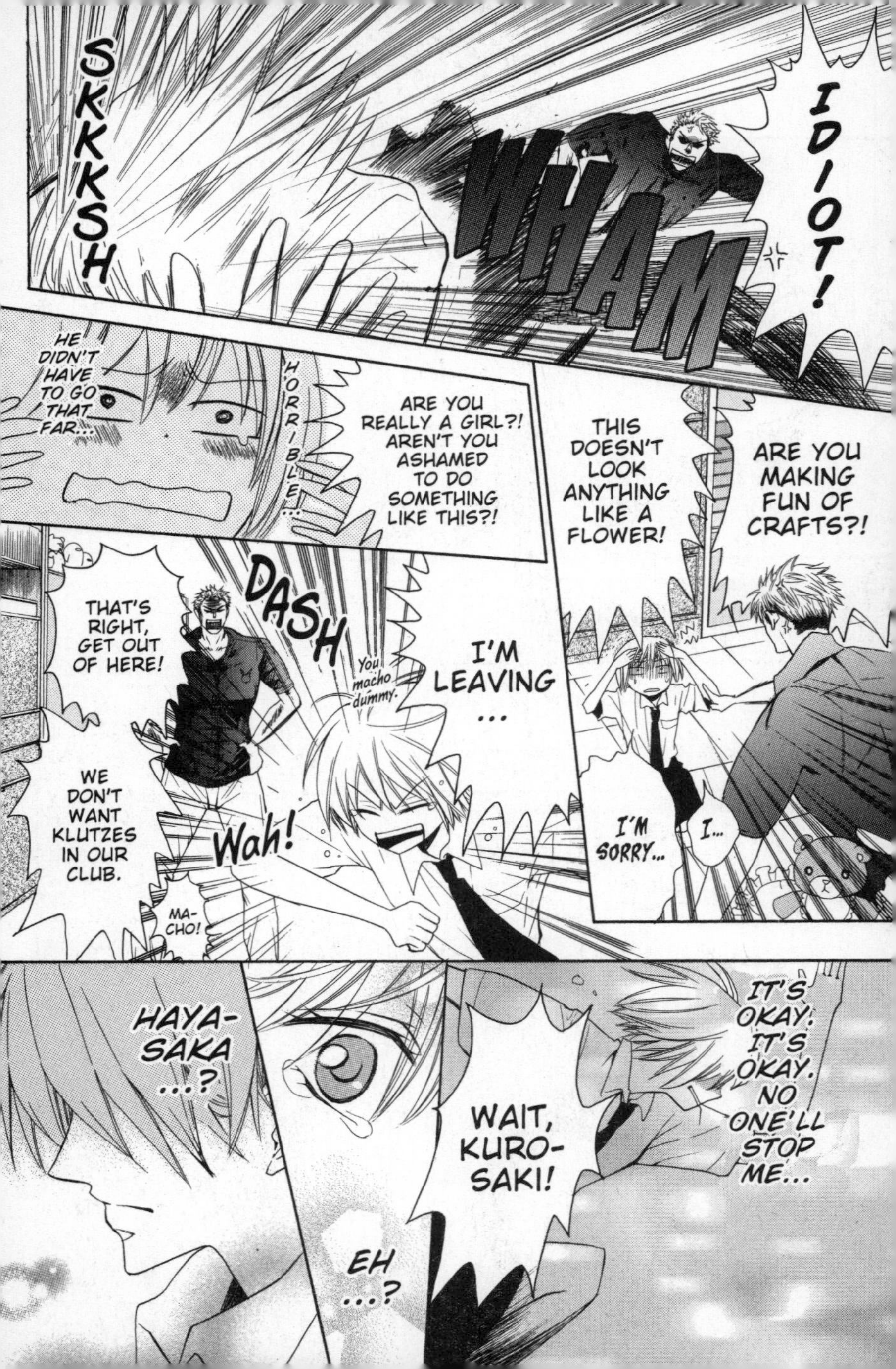
IDIOT!
WHAM
SKKKSH
ARE YOU MAKING FUN OF CRAFTS?!
THIS DOESN'T LOOK ANYTHING LIKE A FLOWER!
I...
I'M SORRY...
ARE YOU REALLY A GIRL?! AREN'T YOU ASHAMED TO DO SOMETHING LIKE THIS?!
HORRIBLE...
HE DIDN'T HAVE TO GO THAT FAR...
I'M LEAVING...
You macho dummy.
DASH
THAT'S RIGHT, GET OUT OF HERE!
WE DON'T WANT KLUTZES IN OUR CLUB.
Wah!
MA-CHO!
IT'S OKAY. IT'S OKAY. NO ONE'LL STOP ME...
WAIT, KURO-SAKI!
EH...?
HAYA-SAKA...?

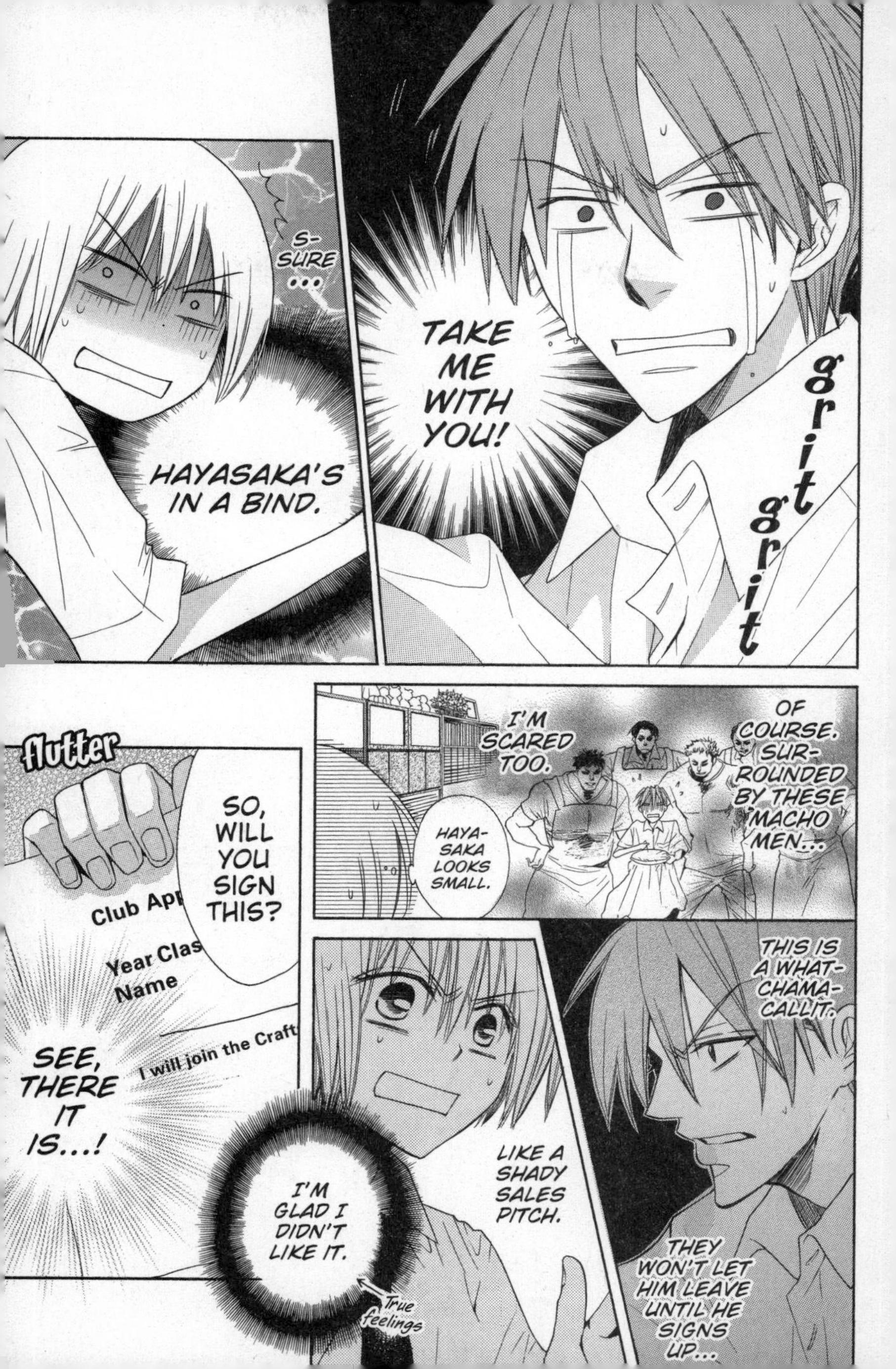
TAKE ME WITH YOU!
grit grit
S-SURE...
HAYASAKA'S IN A BIND.
OF COURSE. SURROUNDED BY THESE MACHO MEN...
I'M SCARED TOO.
HAYASAKA LOOKS SMALL.
THIS IS A WHATCHAMACALLIT.
LIKE A SHADY SALES PITCH.
THEY WON'T LET HIM LEAVE UNTIL HE SIGNS UP...
I'M GLAD I DIDN'T LIKE IT.
True feelings
flutter
SO, WILL YOU SIGN THIS?
Club App
Year Clas
Name
I will join the Craft
SEE, THERE IT IS...!

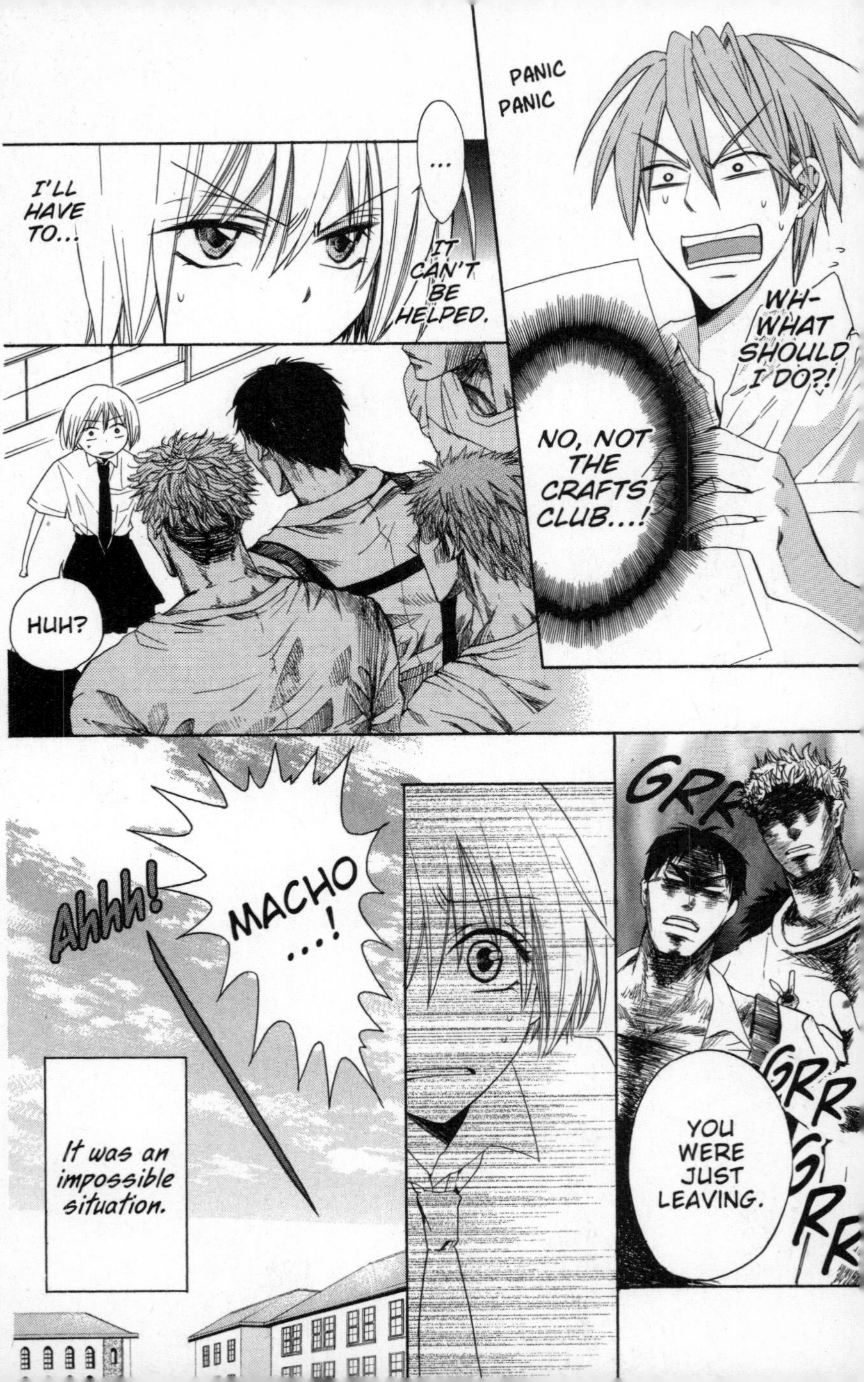
PANIC
PANIC
WH-WHAT SHOULD I DO?!
NO, NOT THE CRAFTS CLUB...!
...
IT CAN'T BE HELPED.
I'LL HAVE TO...
HUH?
GRR
YOU WERE JUST LEAVING.
GRR
GRRR
MACHO ...!
Ahhh!
It was an impossible situation.

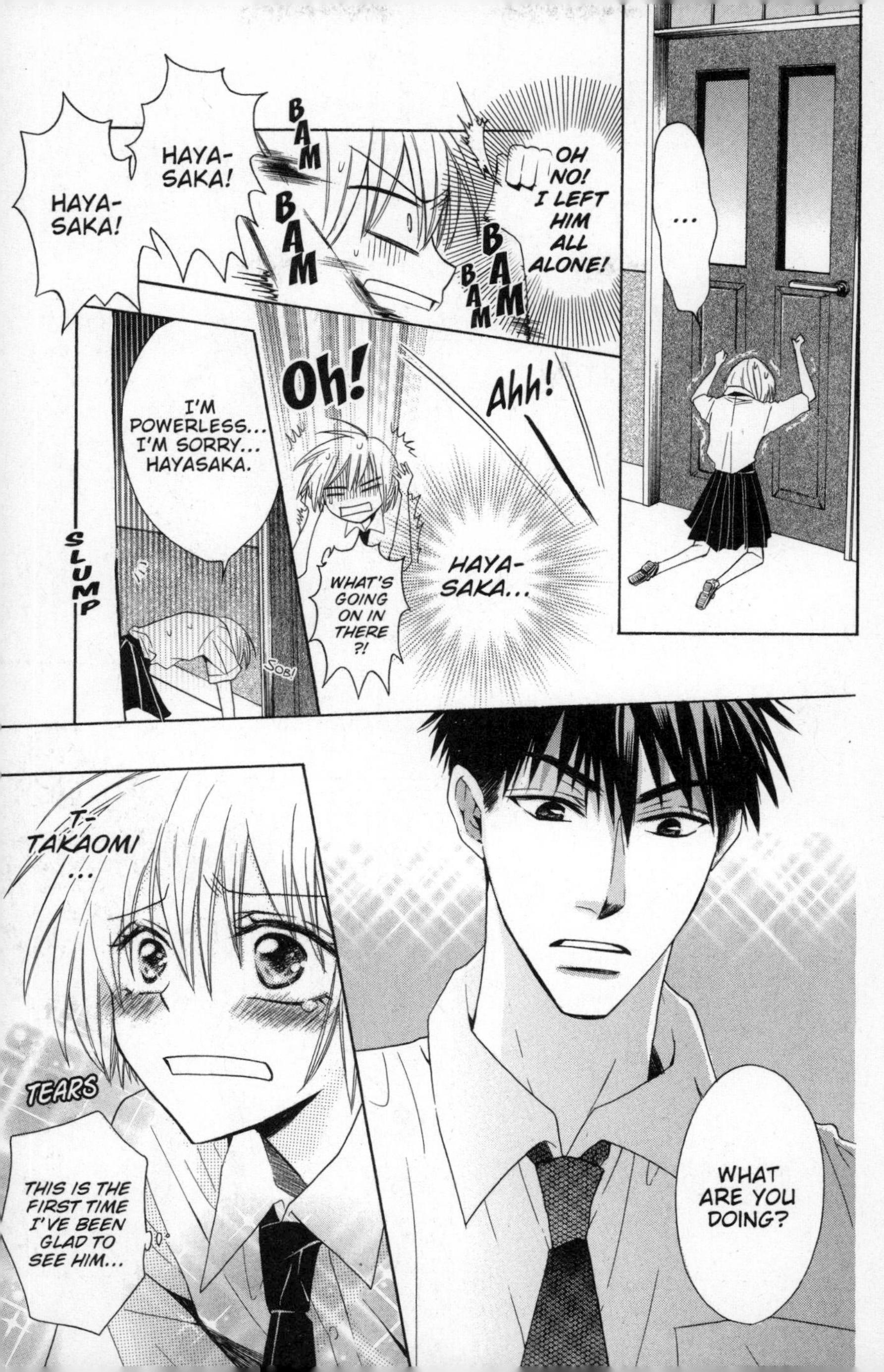
...
OH NO! I LEFT HIM ALL ALONE!
BAM BAM
BAM
BAM
BAM BAM
HAYA-SAKA!
HAYA-SAKA!
Ahh!
HAYA-SAKA...
Oh!
WHAT'S GOING ON IN THERE?!
I'M POWERLESS... I'M SORRY... HAYASAKA.
SLUMP
SOB!
WHAT ARE YOU DOING?
T-TAKAOMI...
TEARS
THIS IS THE FIRST TIME I'VE BEEN GLAD TO SEE HIM...

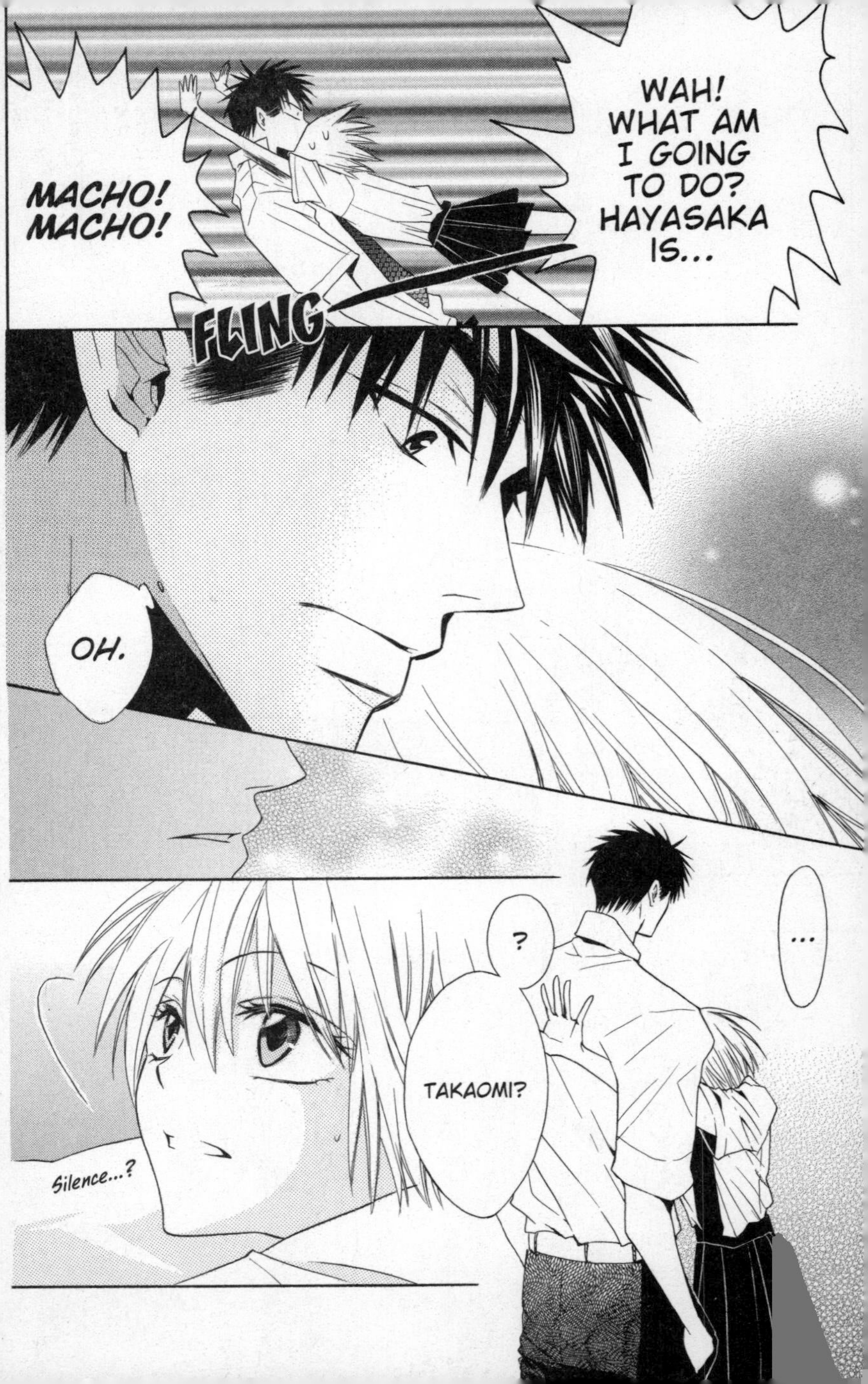
WAH! WHAT AM I GOING TO DO? HAYASAKA IS...
MACHO! MACHO!
FLING
OH.
...
?
TAKAOMI?
Silence...?

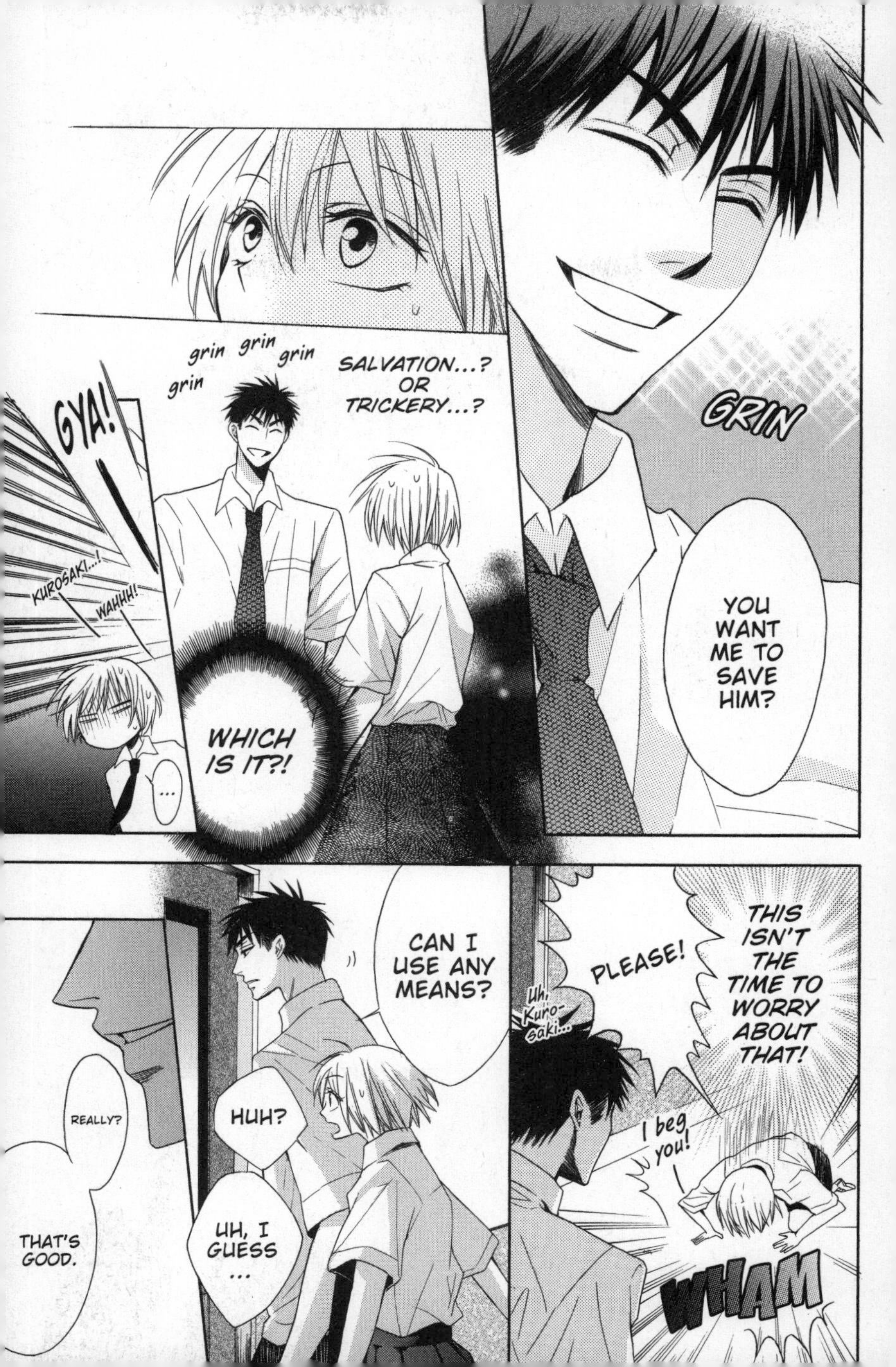
GRIN
YOU WANT ME TO SAVE HIM?
grin grin grin grin
SALVATION...? OR TRICKERY...?
WHICH IS IT?!
GYA!
KUROSAKI...!
WAHHH!
...
THIS ISN'T THE TIME TO WORRY ABOUT THAT!
PLEASE!
Uh, Kuro-saki...
I beg you!
WHAM
CAN I USE ANY MEANS?
HUH?
UH, I GUESS ...
REALLY?
THAT'S GOOD.

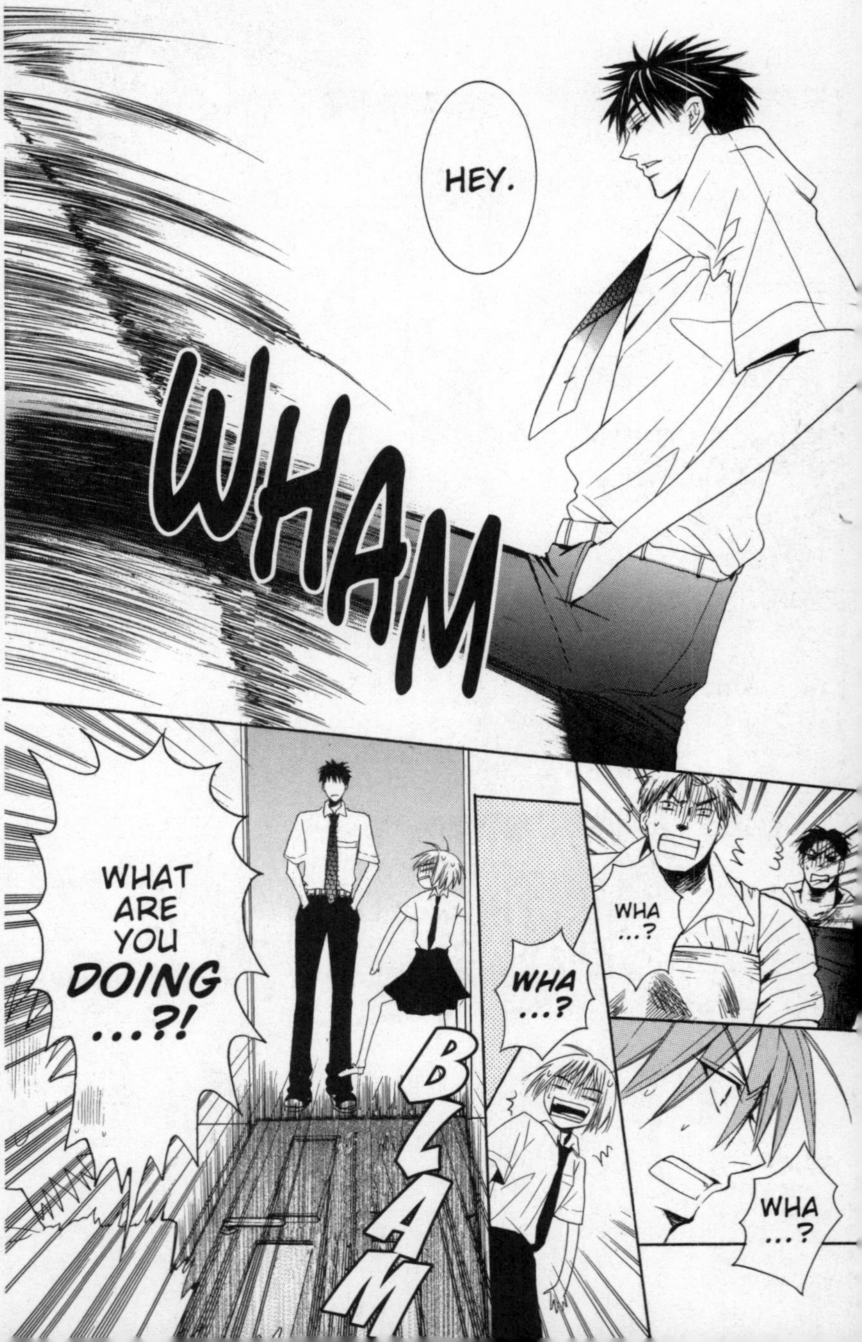
HEY.
WHAM
WHA ...?
WHA ...?
WHA ...?
BLAM
WHAT ARE YOU DOING ...?!

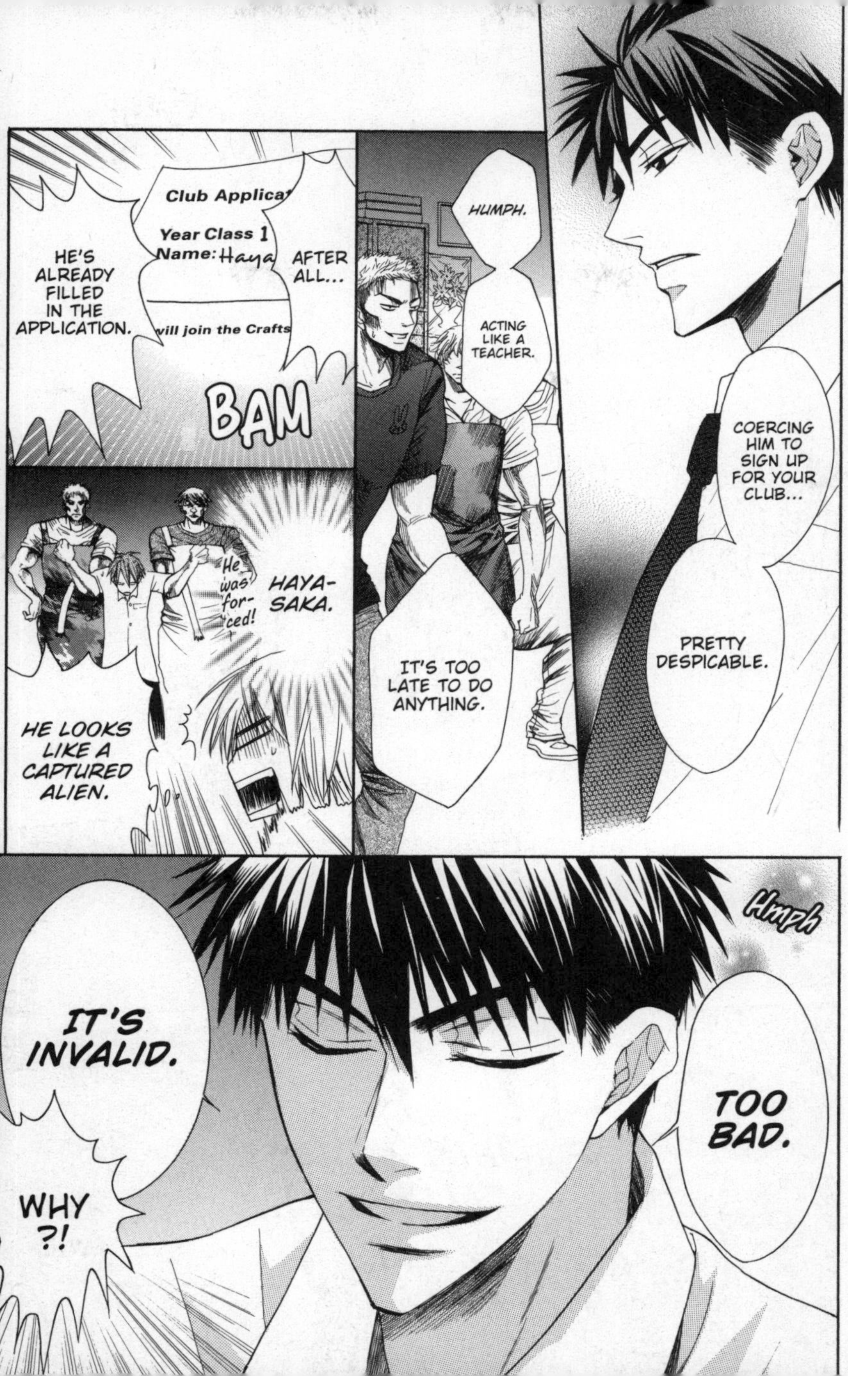
COERCING HIM TO SIGN UP FOR YOUR CLUB...
PRETTY DESPICABLE.
HUMPH.
ACTING LIKE A TEACHER.
IT'S TOO LATE TO DO ANYTHING.
AFTER ALL...
HE'S ALREADY FILLED IN THE APPLICATION.
Club Applicat
Year Class 1
Name: Haya
will join the Crafts
BAM
HAYA-SAKA.
He was for-ced!
HE LOOKS LIKE A CAPTURED ALIEN.
Hmph
TOO BAD.
IT'S INVALID.
WHY ?!

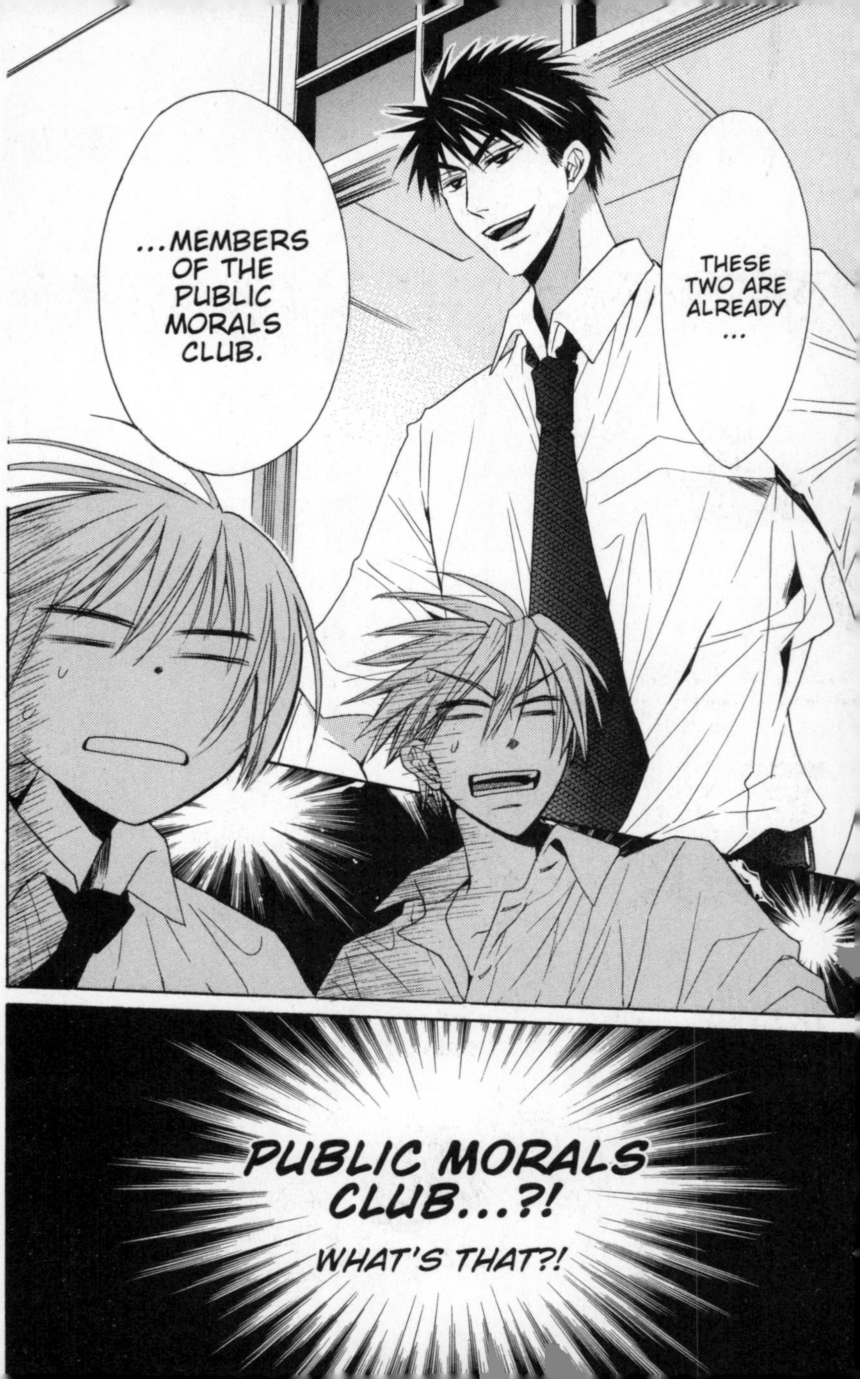
THESE TWO ARE ALREADY ...
...MEMBERS OF THE PUBLIC MORALS CLUB.
PUBLIC MORALS CLUB...?!
WHAT'S THAT?!

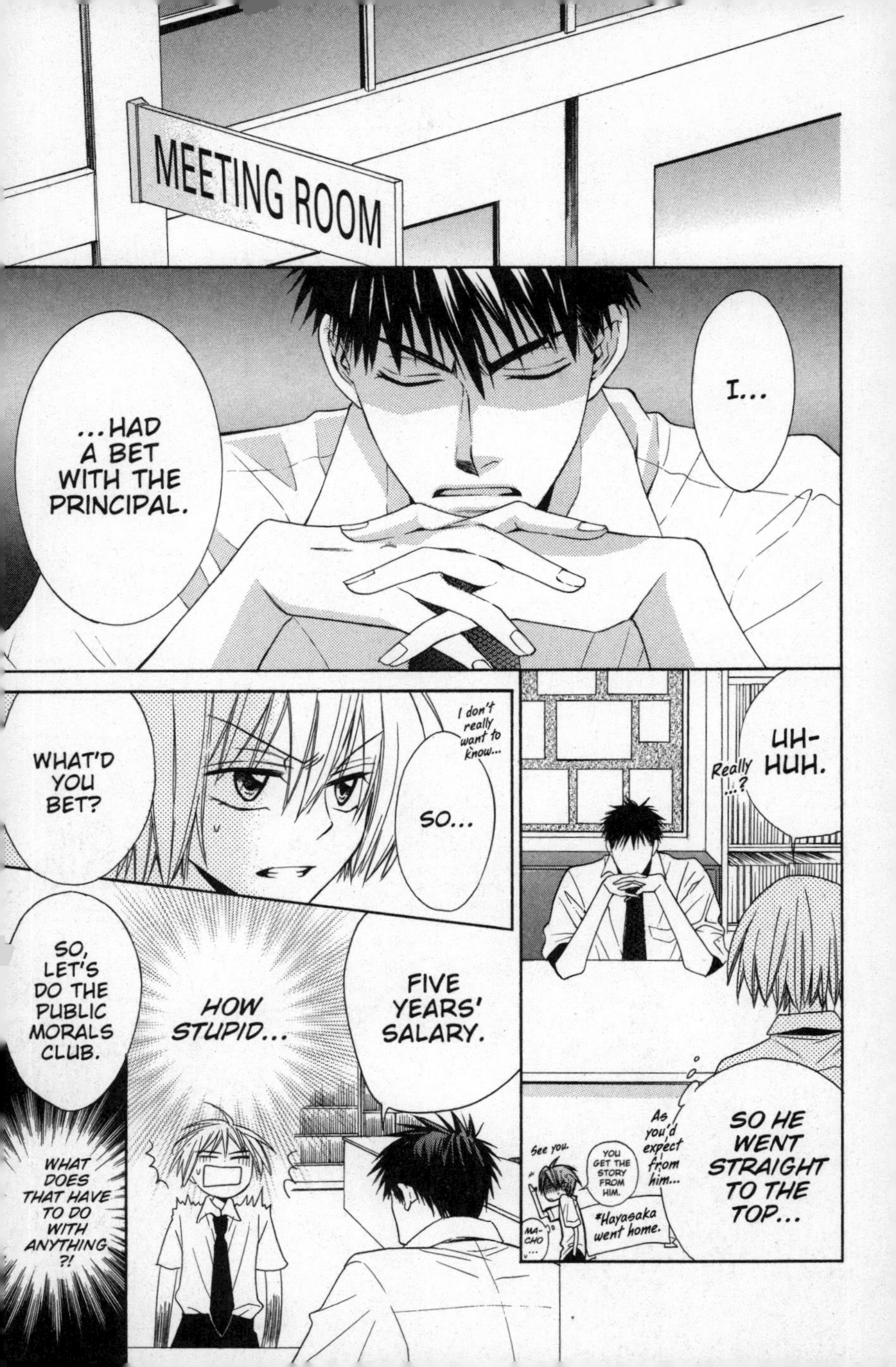
MEETING ROOM
I...
...HAD A BET WITH THE PRINCIPAL.
UH-HUH.
Really...?
SO...
I don't really want to know...
WHAT'D YOU BET?
SO HE WENT STRAIGHT TO THE TOP...
As you'd expect from him...
YOU GET THE STORY FROM HIM.
See you.
MA-CHO...
*Hayasaka went home.
FIVE YEARS' SALARY.
HOW STUPID...
SO, LET'S DO THE PUBLIC MORALS CLUB.
WHAT DOES THAT HAVE TO DO WITH ANYTHING?!

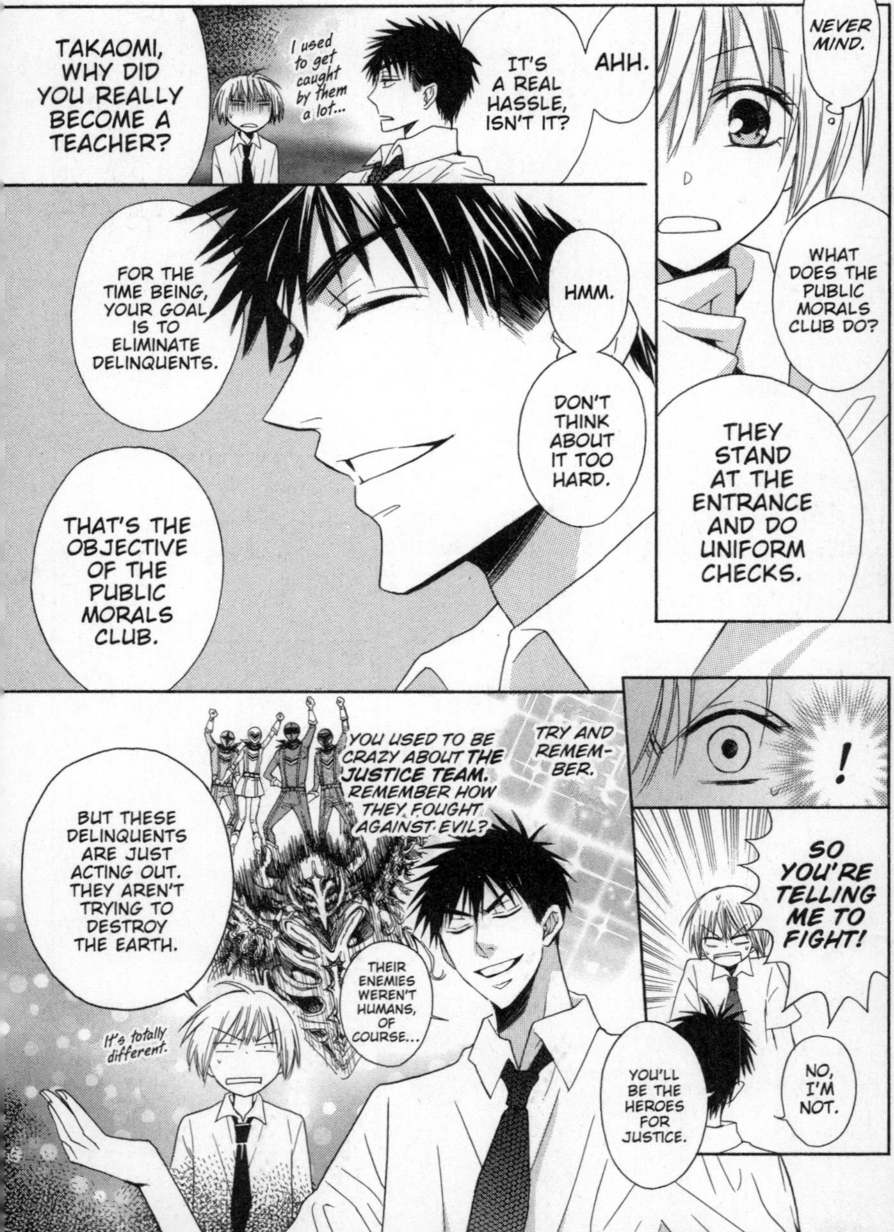
NEVER MIND.
WHAT DOES THE PUBLIC MORALS CLUB DO?
THEY STAND AT THE ENTRANCE AND DO UNIFORM CHECKS.
AHH.
IT'S A REAL HASSLE, ISN'T IT?
I used to get caught by them a lot...
TAKAOMI, WHY DID YOU REALLY BECOME A TEACHER?
HMM.
DON'T THINK ABOUT IT TOO HARD.
FOR THE TIME BEING, YOUR GOAL IS TO ELIMINATE DELINQUENTS.
THAT'S THE OBJECTIVE OF THE PUBLIC MORALS CLUB.
!
SO YOU'RE TELLING ME TO FIGHT!
NO, I'M NOT.
YOU'LL BE THE HEROES FOR JUSTICE.
TRY AND REMEMBER.
YOU USED TO BE CRAZY ABOUT THE JUSTICE TEAM. REMEMBER HOW THEY FOUGHT AGAINST EVIL?
THEIR ENEMIES WEREN'T HUMANS, OF COURSE...
BUT THESE DELINQUENTS ARE JUST ACTING OUT. THEY AREN'T TRYING TO DESTROY THE EARTH.
It's totally different.

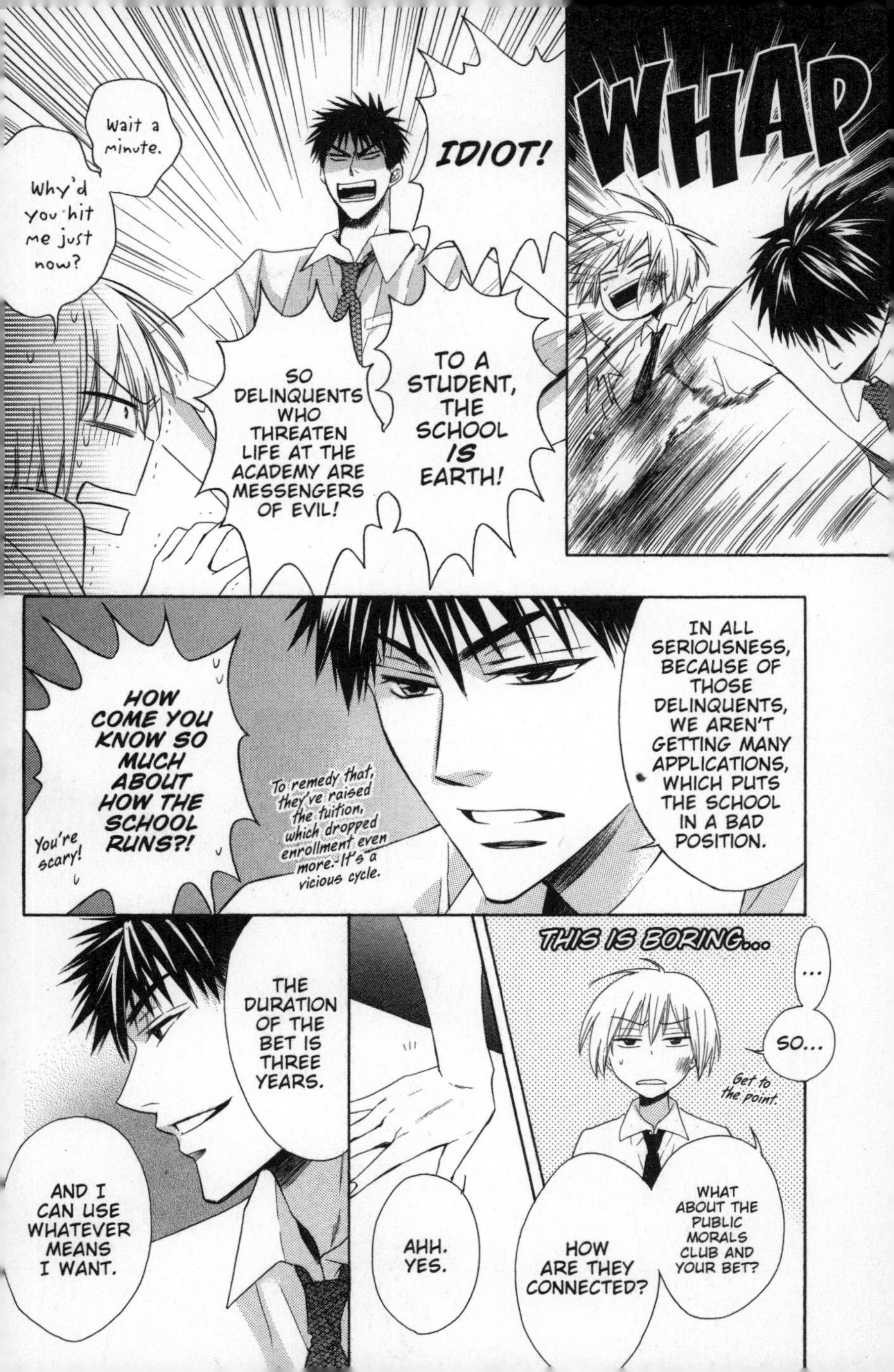
WHAP
IDIOT!
TO A STUDENT, THE SCHOOL IS EARTH!
SO DELINQUENTS WHO THREATEN LIFE AT THE ACADEMY ARE MESSENGERS OF EVIL!
Wait a minute.
Why'd you hit me just now?
IN ALL SERIOUSNESS, BECAUSE OF THOSE DELINQUENTS, WE AREN'T GETTING MANY APPLICATIONS, WHICH PUTS THE SCHOOL IN A BAD POSITION.
To remedy that, they've raised the tuition, which dropped enrollment even more. It's a vicious cycle.
HOW COME YOU KNOW SO MUCH ABOUT HOW THE SCHOOL RUNS?!
You're scary!
THIS IS BORING...
...
SO...
Get to the point.
WHAT ABOUT THE PUBLIC MORALS CLUB AND YOUR BET?
HOW ARE THEY CONNECTED?
AHH. YES.
THE DURATION OF THE BET IS THREE YEARS.
AND I CAN USE WHATEVER MEANS I WANT.

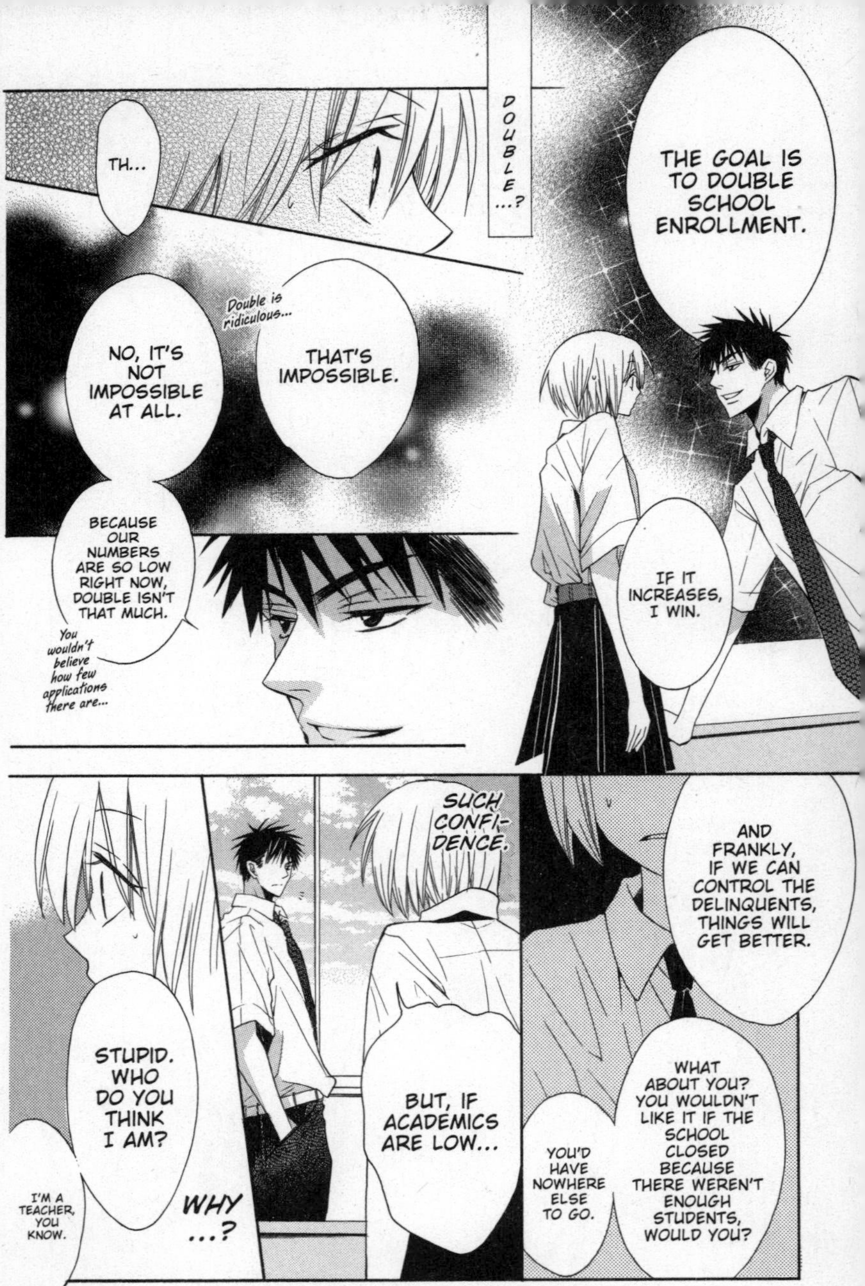
THE GOAL IS TO DOUBLE SCHOOL ENROLLMENT.
IF IT INCREASES, I WIN.
DOUBLE...?
TH...
Double is ridiculous...
THAT'S IMPOSSIBLE.
NO, IT'S NOT IMPOSSIBLE AT ALL.
BECAUSE OUR NUMBERS ARE SO LOW RIGHT NOW, DOUBLE ISN'T THAT MUCH.
You wouldn't believe how few applications there are...
AND FRANKLY, IF WE CAN CONTROL THE DELINQUENTS, THINGS WILL GET BETTER.
WHAT ABOUT YOU? YOU WOULDN'T LIKE IT IF THE SCHOOL CLOSED BECAUSE THERE WEREN'T ENOUGH STUDENTS, WOULD YOU?
YOU'D HAVE NOWHERE ELSE TO GO.
SUCH CONFIDENCE.
BUT, IF ACADEMICS ARE LOW...
WHY ...?
STUPID. WHO DO YOU THINK I AM?
I'M A TEACHER, YOU KNOW.

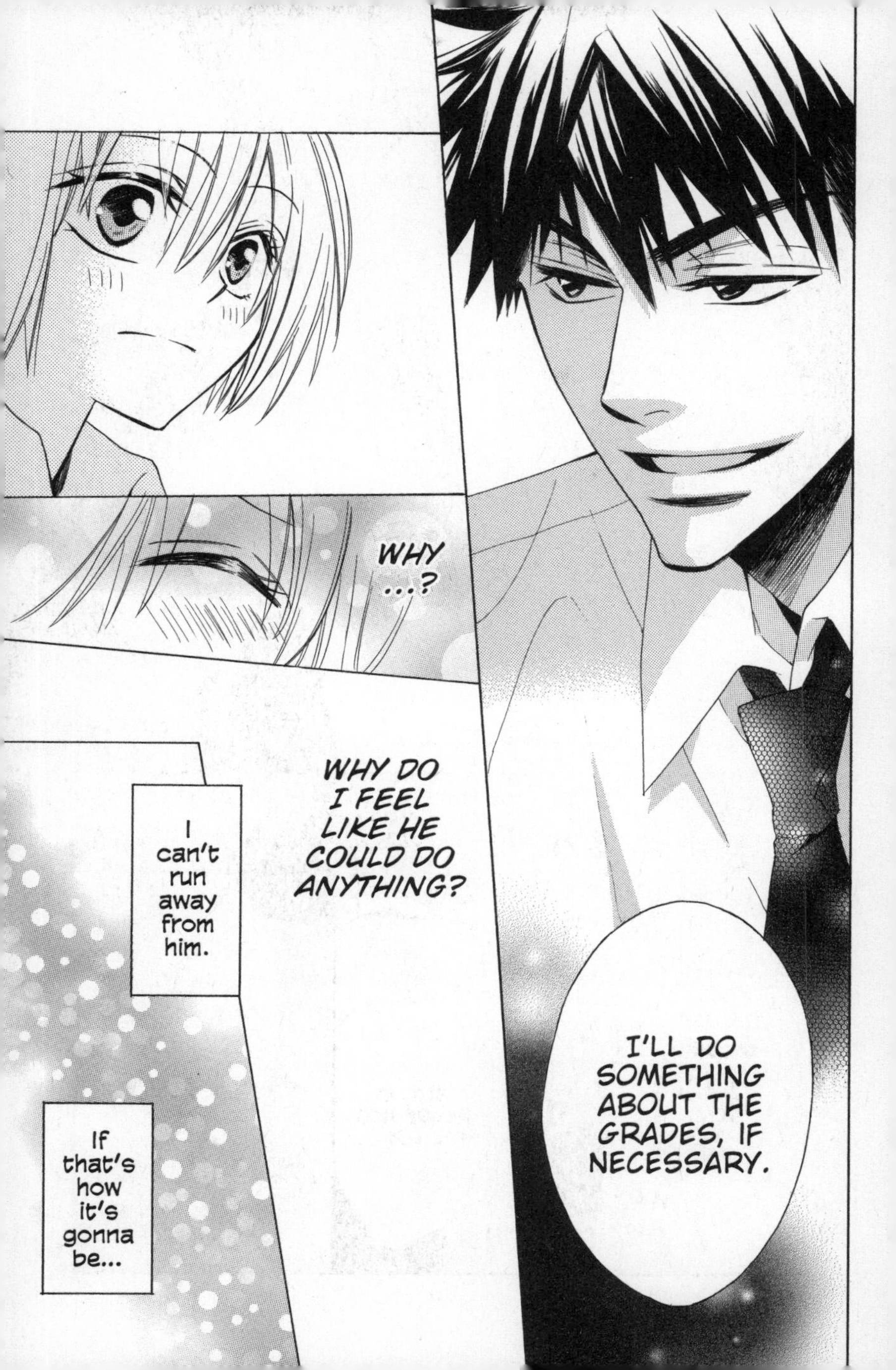
I'LL DO SOMETHING ABOUT THE GRADES, IF NECESSARY.
WHY ...?
WHY DO I FEEL LIKE HE COULD DO ANYTHING?
I can't run away from him.
If that's how it's gonna be...

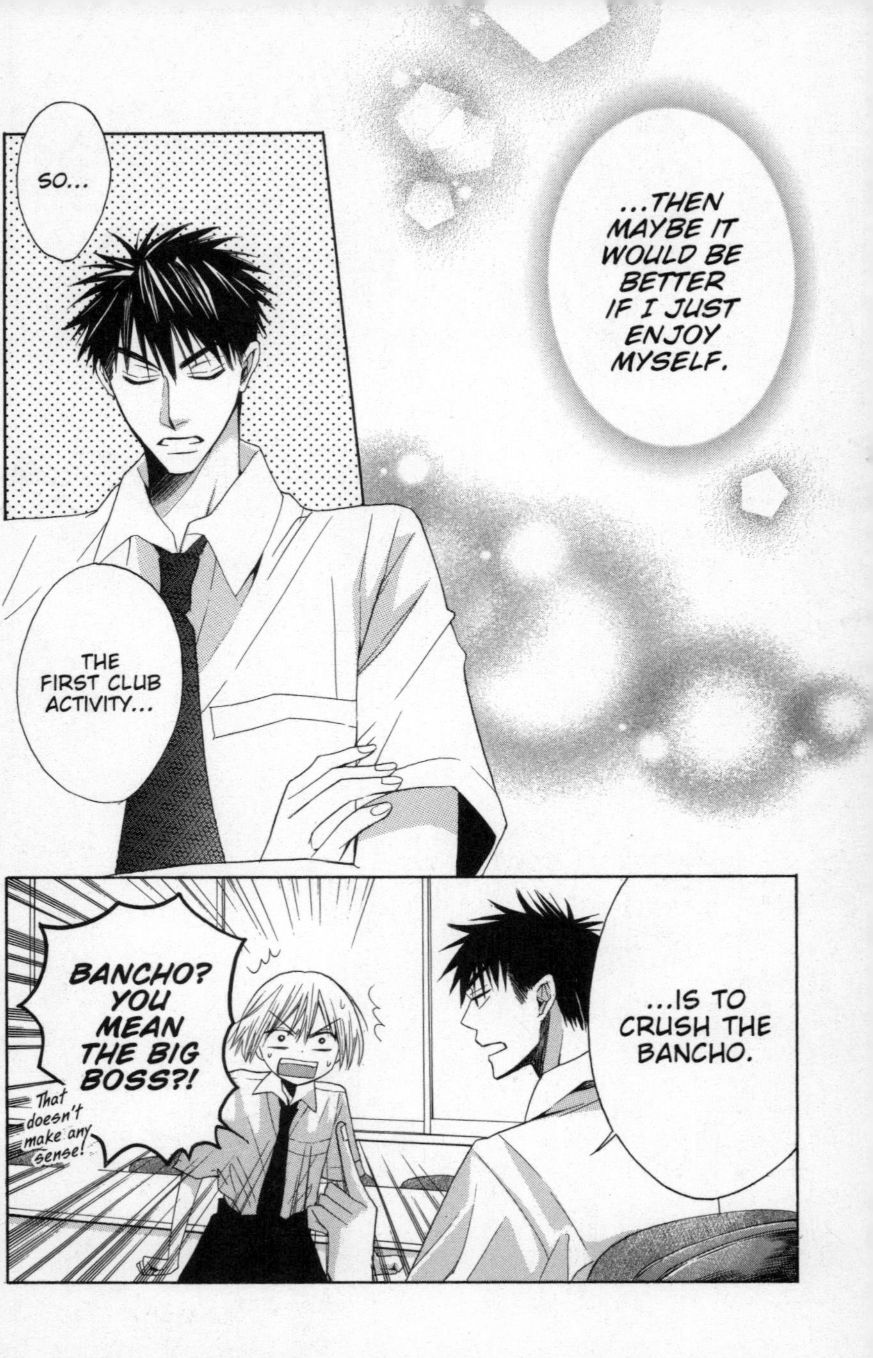
...THEN MAYBE IT WOULD BE BETTER IF I JUST ENJOY MYSELF.
SO...
THE FIRST CLUB ACTIVITY...
...IS TO CRUSH THE BANCHO.
BANCHO? YOU MEAN THE BIG BOSS?!
That doesn't make any sense!

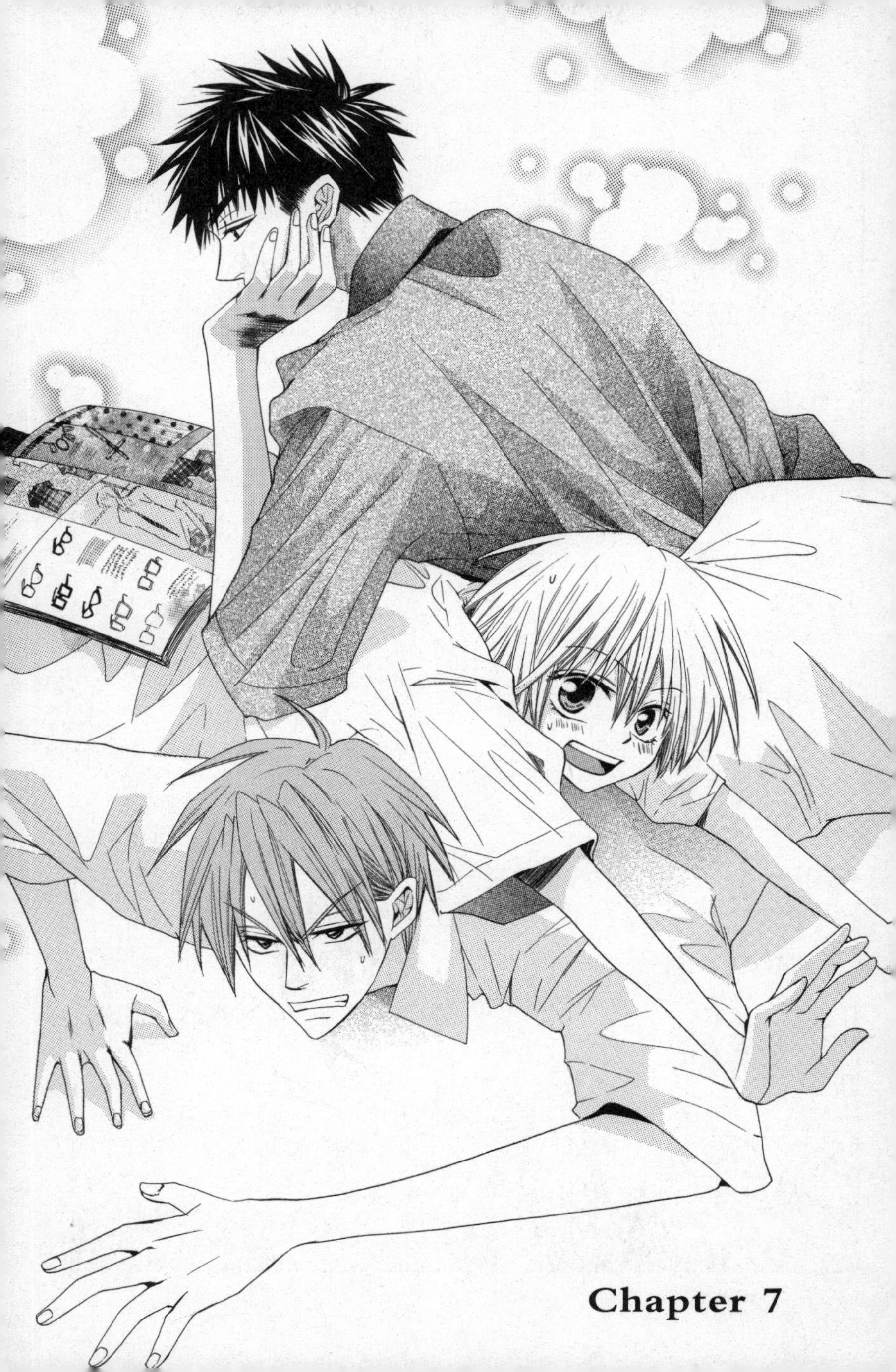

Chapter 7

What Is a Bancho?

① It used to mean "ruler." When shift work was instituted, the leader or commander of a shift was known as the bancho.

Historically, managed the lower ranks of government guards or employees. First appeared in the ancient East Asian system of centralized governance... Etc.

THIS ONE. → ② The leader of delinquent boys and/or girls in a school.

From the *Kojien* dictionary.

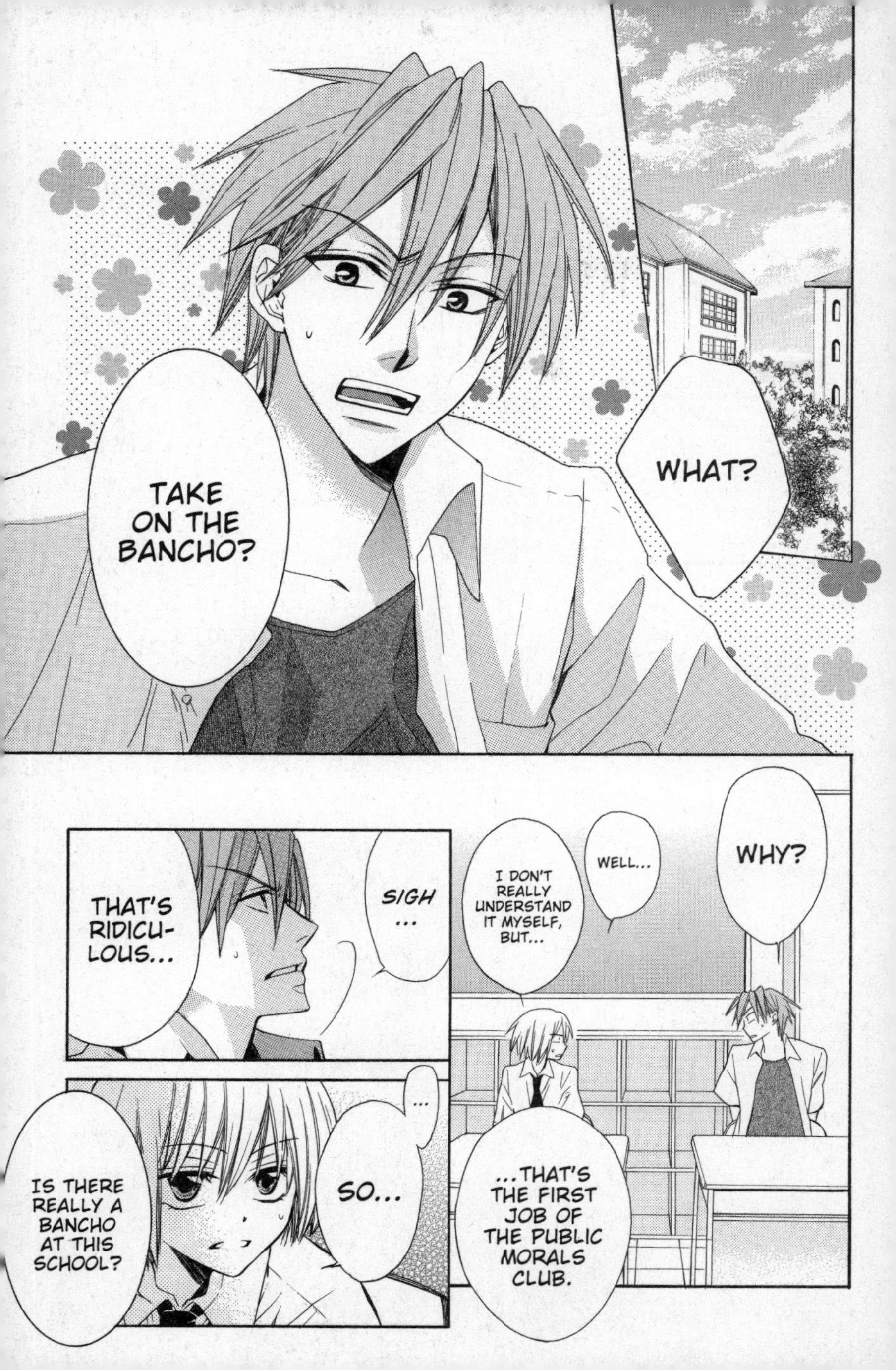
WHAT?
TAKE ON THE BANCHO?
WHY?
WELL...
I DON'T REALLY UNDERSTAND IT MYSELF, BUT...
...THAT'S THE FIRST JOB OF THE PUBLIC MORALS CLUB.
SIGH...
THAT'S RIDICULOUS...
...
SO...
IS THERE REALLY A BANCHO AT THIS SCHOOL?

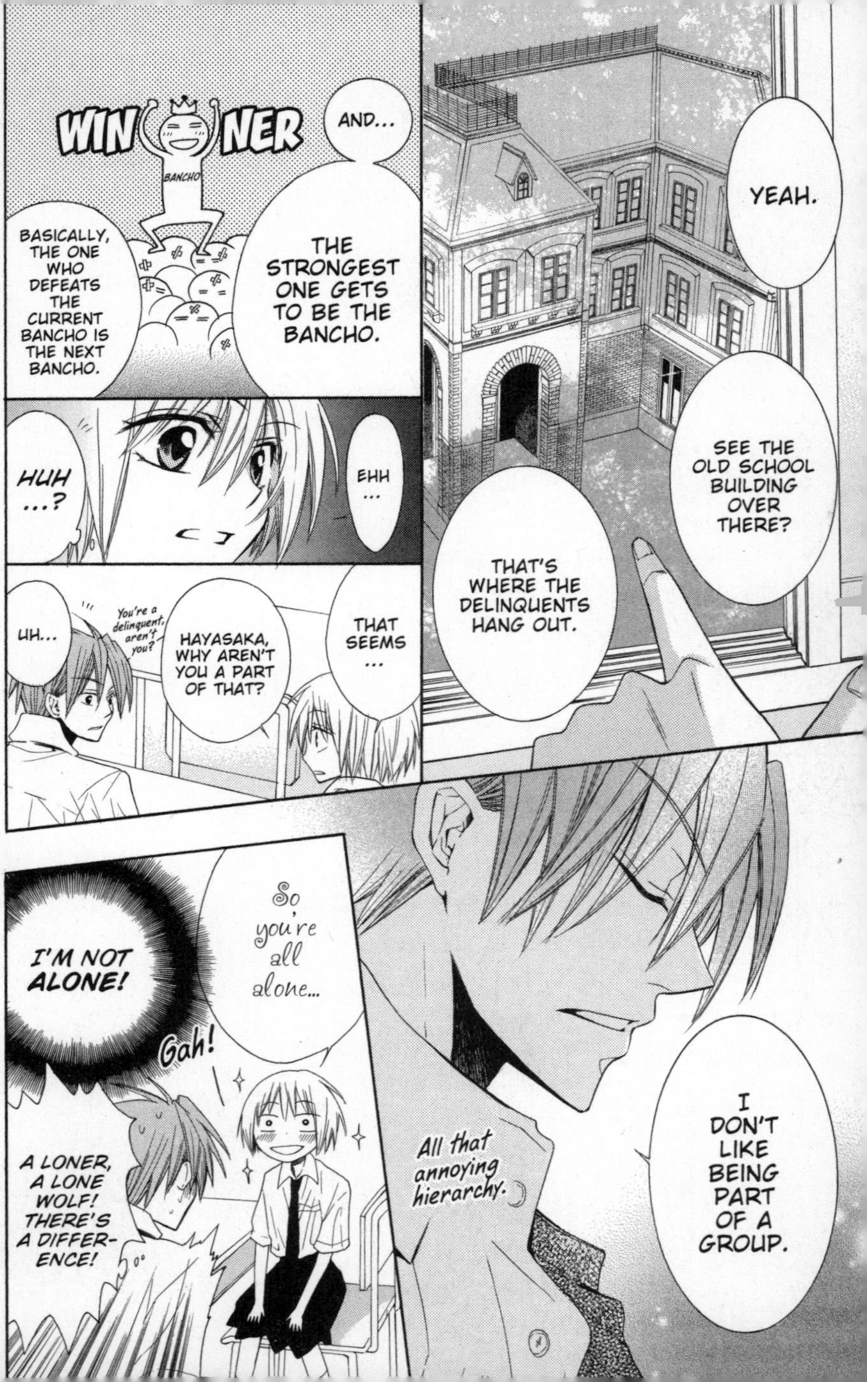
YEAH.
SEE THE OLD SCHOOL BUILDING OVER THERE?
THAT'S WHERE THE DELINQUENTS HANG OUT.
AND...
THE STRONGEST ONE GETS TO BE THE BANCHO.
WINNER
BANCHO
BASICALLY, THE ONE WHO DEFEATS THE CURRENT BANCHO IS THE NEXT BANCHO.
EHH...
HUH...?
THAT SEEMS...
HAYASAKA, WHY AREN'T YOU A PART OF THAT?
You're a delinquent, aren't you?
UH...
I DON'T LIKE BEING PART OF A GROUP.
All that annoying hierarchy.
So, you're all alone...
Gah!
I'M NOT ALONE!
A LONER, A LONE WOLF! THERE'S A DIFFERENCE!

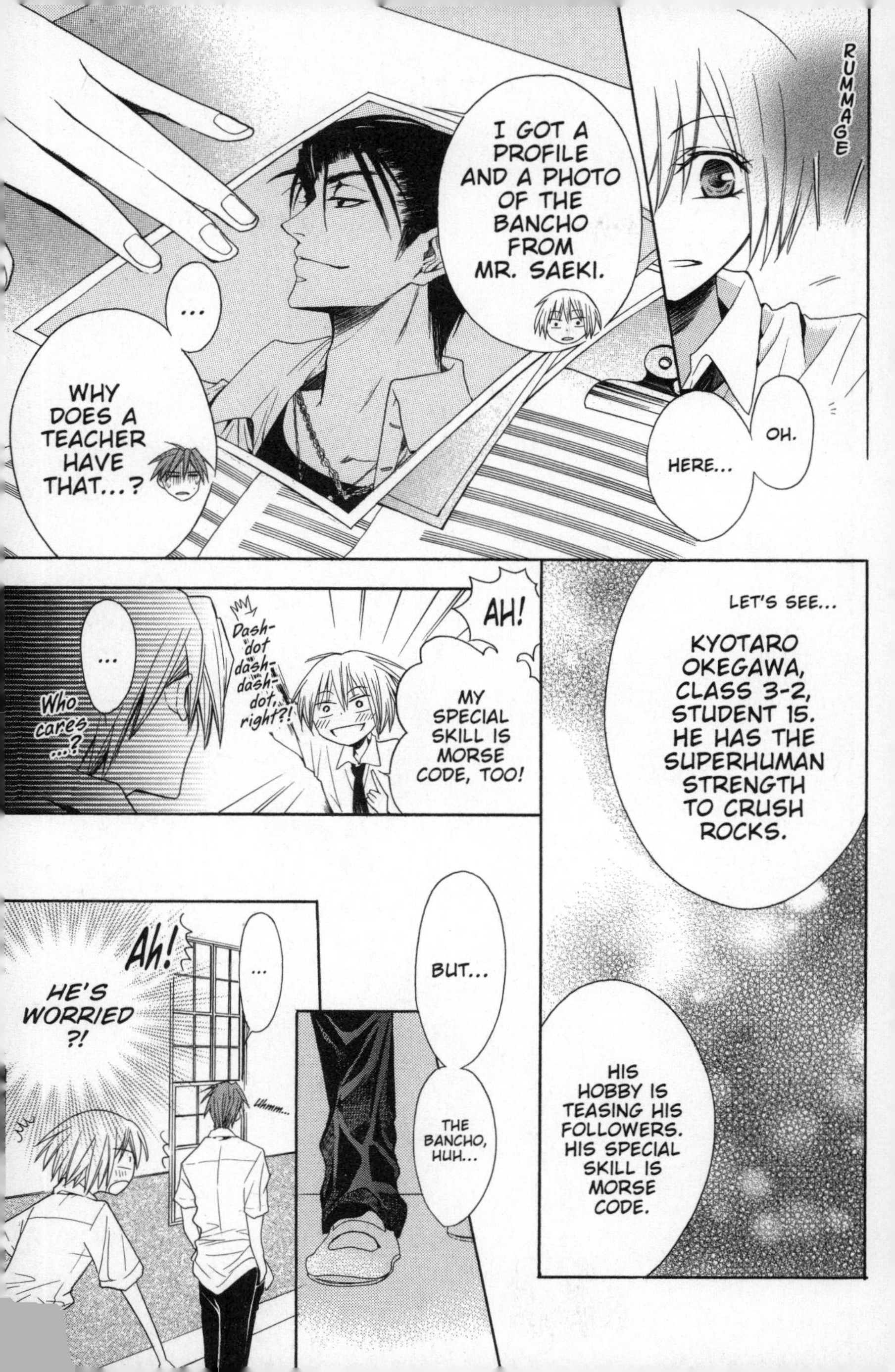
RUMMAGE
OH.
HERE...
I GOT A PROFILE AND A PHOTO OF THE BANCHO FROM MR. SAEKI.
...
WHY DOES A TEACHER HAVE THAT...?
LET'S SEE...
KYOTARO OKEGAWA, CLASS 3-2, STUDENT 15. HE HAS THE SUPERHUMAN STRENGTH TO CRUSH ROCKS.
HIS HOBBY IS TEASING HIS FOLLOWERS. HIS SPECIAL SKILL IS MORSE CODE.
AH!
MY SPECIAL SKILL IS MORSE CODE, TOO!
Dash-dot dash-dash-dot, right?!
...
Who cares...?
BUT...
THE BANCHO, HUH...
...
Ah!
HE'S WORRIED?!
Uhmm...

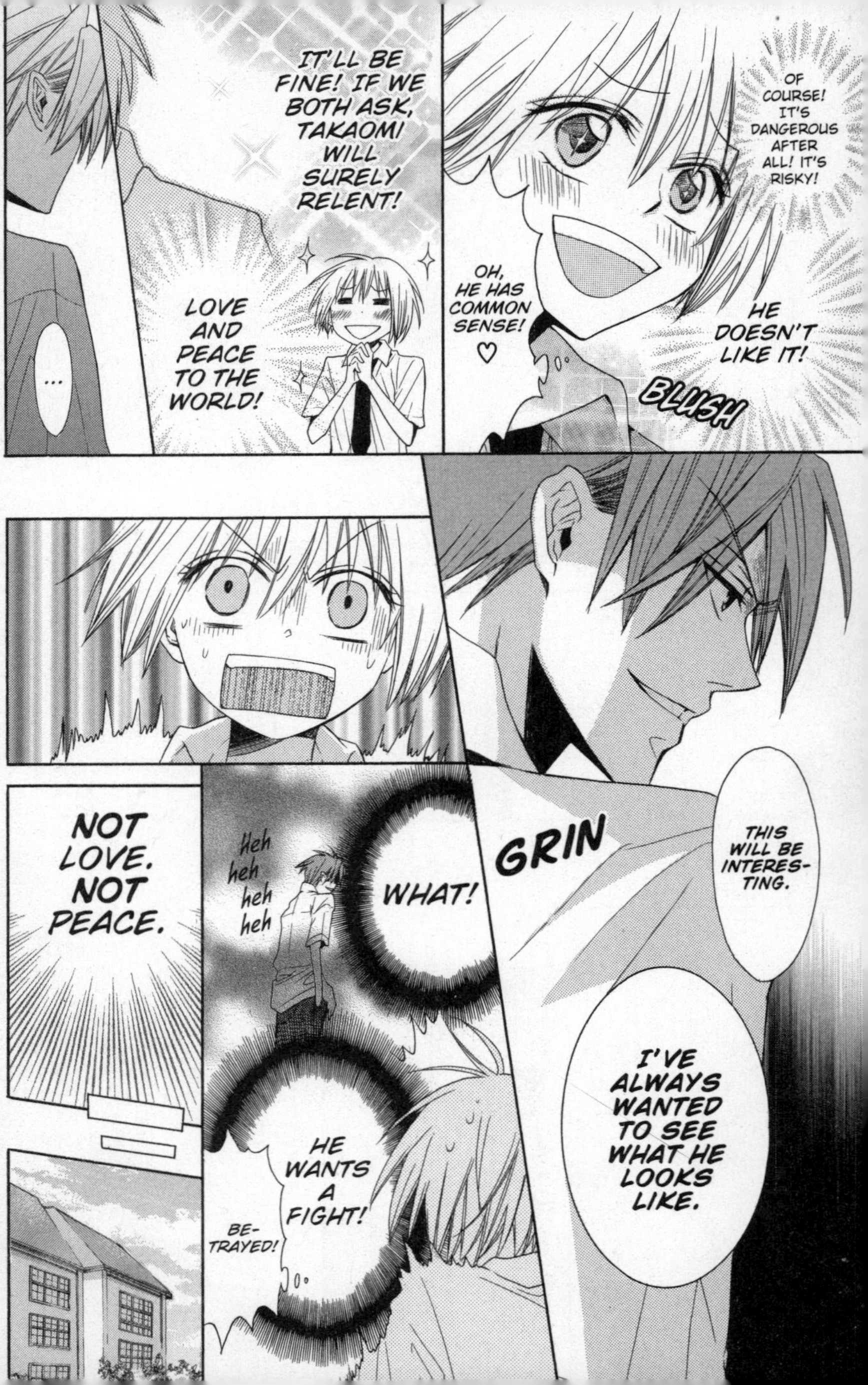
OF COURSE! IT'S DANGEROUS AFTER ALL! IT'S RISKY!
HE DOESN'T LIKE IT!
OH, HE HAS COMMON SENSE! ♡
BLUSH
IT'LL BE FINE! IF WE BOTH ASK, TAKAOMI WILL SURELY RELENT!
LOVE AND PEACE TO THE WORLD!
...
THIS WILL BE INTERES-TING.
GRIN
I'VE ALWAYS WANTED TO SEE WHAT HE LOOKS LIKE.
WHAT!
heh heh heh heh
HE WANTS A FIGHT!
BE-TRAYED!
NOT LOVE. NOT PEACE.

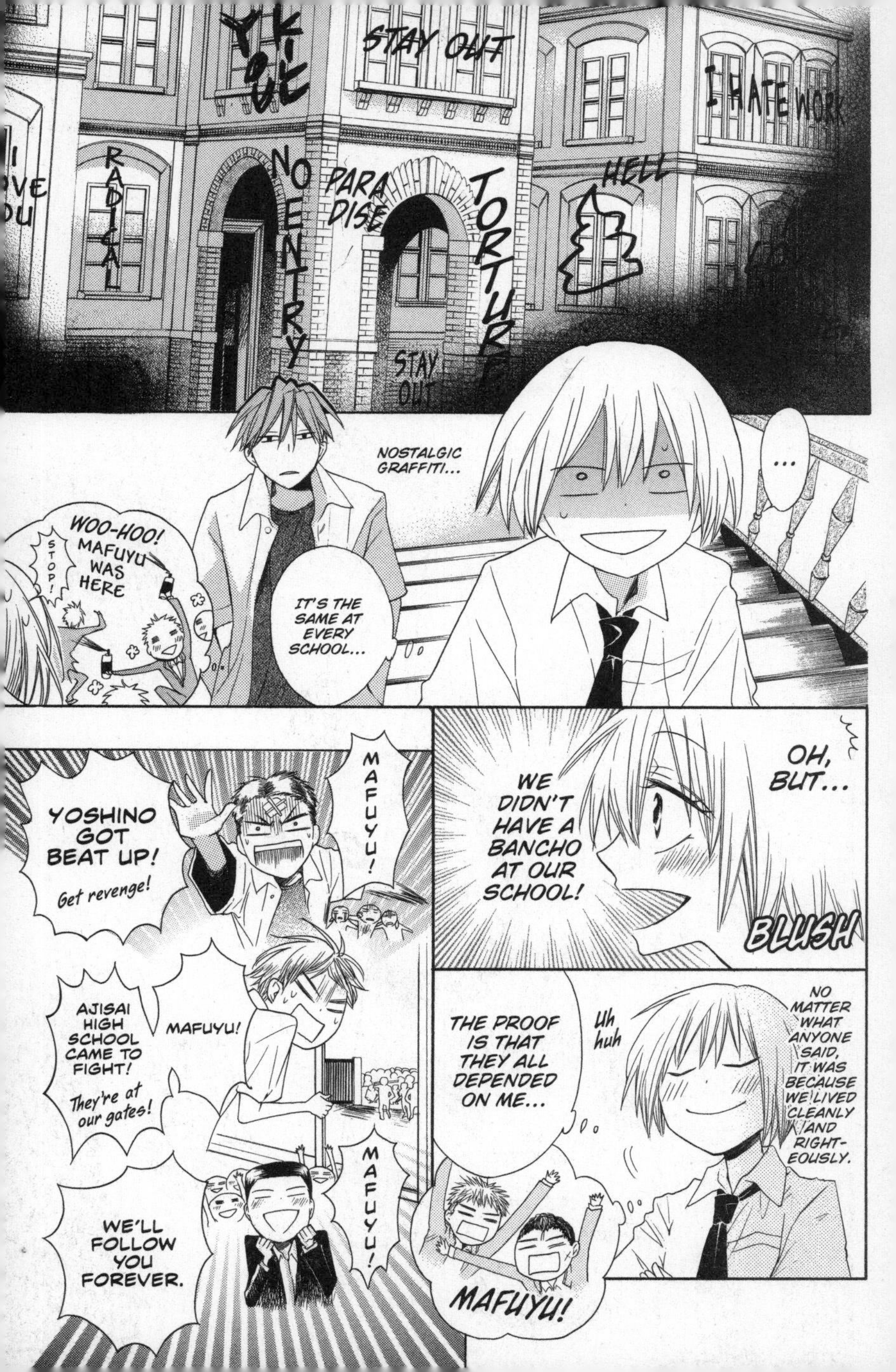
STAY OUT
I HATE WORK
TORTURE
HELL
PARADISE
NO ENTRY
RADICAL
STAY OUT
...
NOSTALGIC GRAFFITI...
IT'S THE SAME AT EVERY SCHOOL...
WOO-HOO! MAFUYU WAS HERE
STOP!
OH, BUT...
WE DIDN'T HAVE A BANCHO AT OUR SCHOOL!
BLUSH
NO MATTER WHAT ANYONE SAID, IT WAS BECAUSE WE LIVED CLEANLY AND RIGHTEOUSLY.
Uh huh
THE PROOF IS THAT THEY ALL DEPENDED ON ME...
MAFUYU!
MAFUYU!
YOSHINO GOT BEAT UP! Get revenge!
MAFUYU!
AJISAI HIGH SCHOOL CAME TO FIGHT! They're at our gates!
MAFUYU!
WE'LL FOLLOW YOU FOREVER.

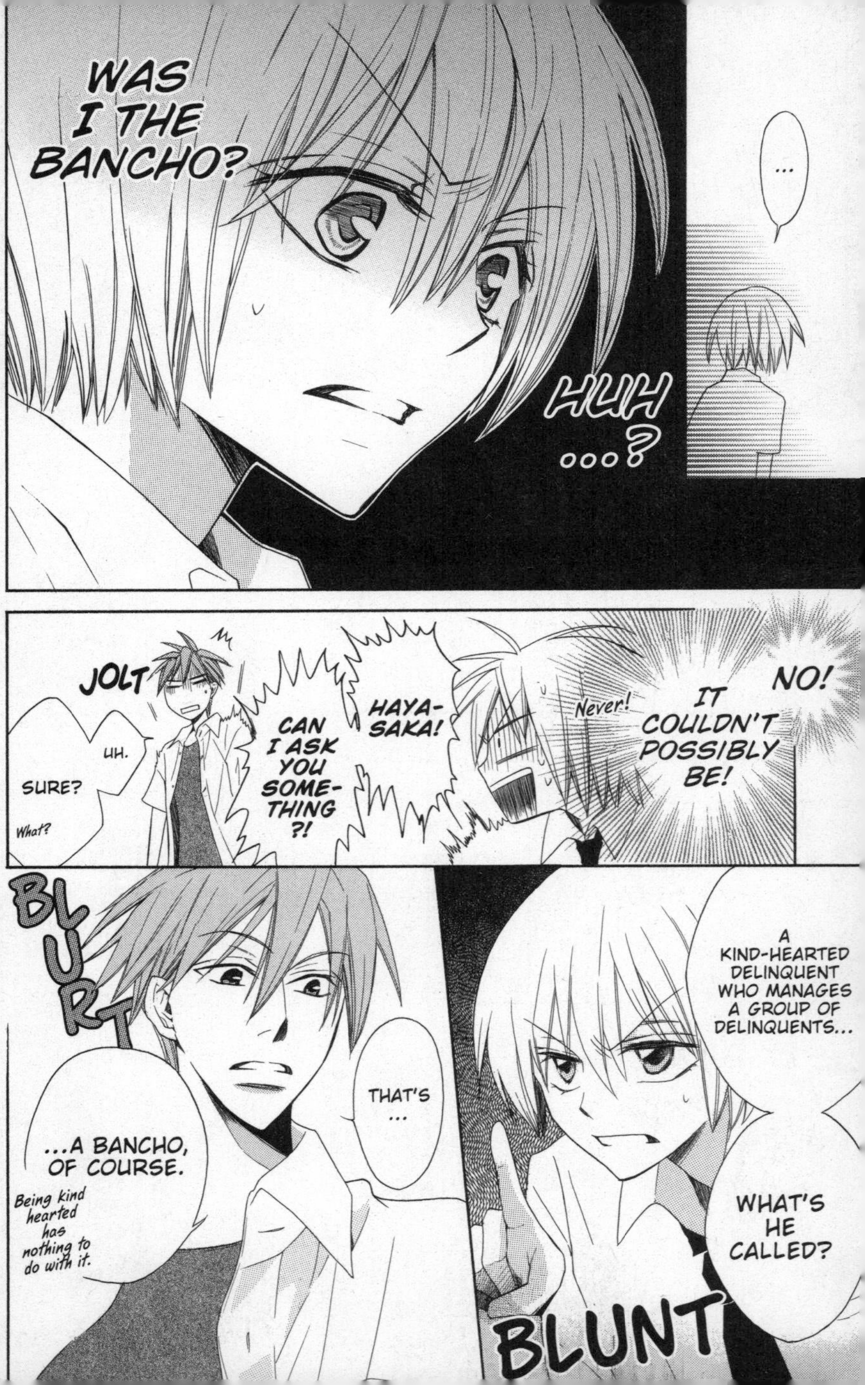
...
HUH ...?
WAS I THE BANCHO?
NO! IT COULDN'T POSSIBLY BE!
Never!
HAYA-SAKA! CAN I ASK YOU SOMETHING?!
JOLT
UH. SURE?
What?
A KIND-HEARTED DELINQUENT WHO MANAGES A GROUP OF DELINQUENTS...
WHAT'S HE CALLED?
BLUNT
THAT'S ...
BLURT
...A BANCHO, OF COURSE.
Being kind hearted has nothing to do with it.

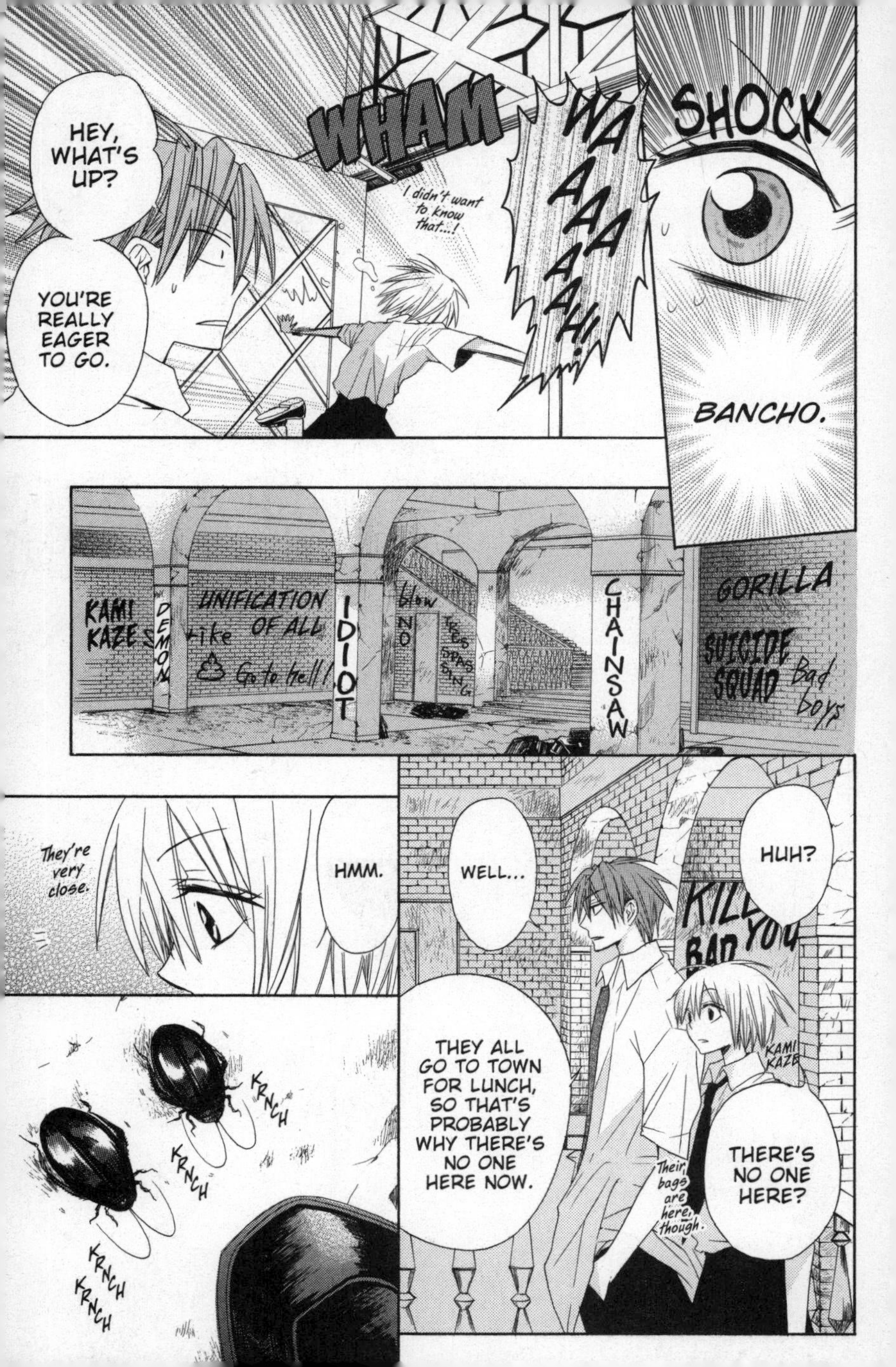
SHOCK
BANCHO.
WAAAAAAAH!
WHAM
I didn't want to know that...!
HEY, WHAT'S UP?
YOU'RE REALLY EAGER TO GO.
GORILLA
SUICIDE SQUAD
Bad boys
CHAINSAW
TRESPASSING
NO
blow
IDIOT
UNIFICATION OF ALL
Go to hell!
DEMON
KAMIKAZE
HUH?
KILL YOU
WELL...
THERE'S NO ONE HERE?
Their bags are here, though.
KAMIKAZE
THEY ALL GO TO TOWN FOR LUNCH, SO THAT'S PROBABLY WHY THERE'S NO ONE HERE NOW.
HMM.
They're very close.
KRNCH
KRNCH
KRNCH
KRNCH

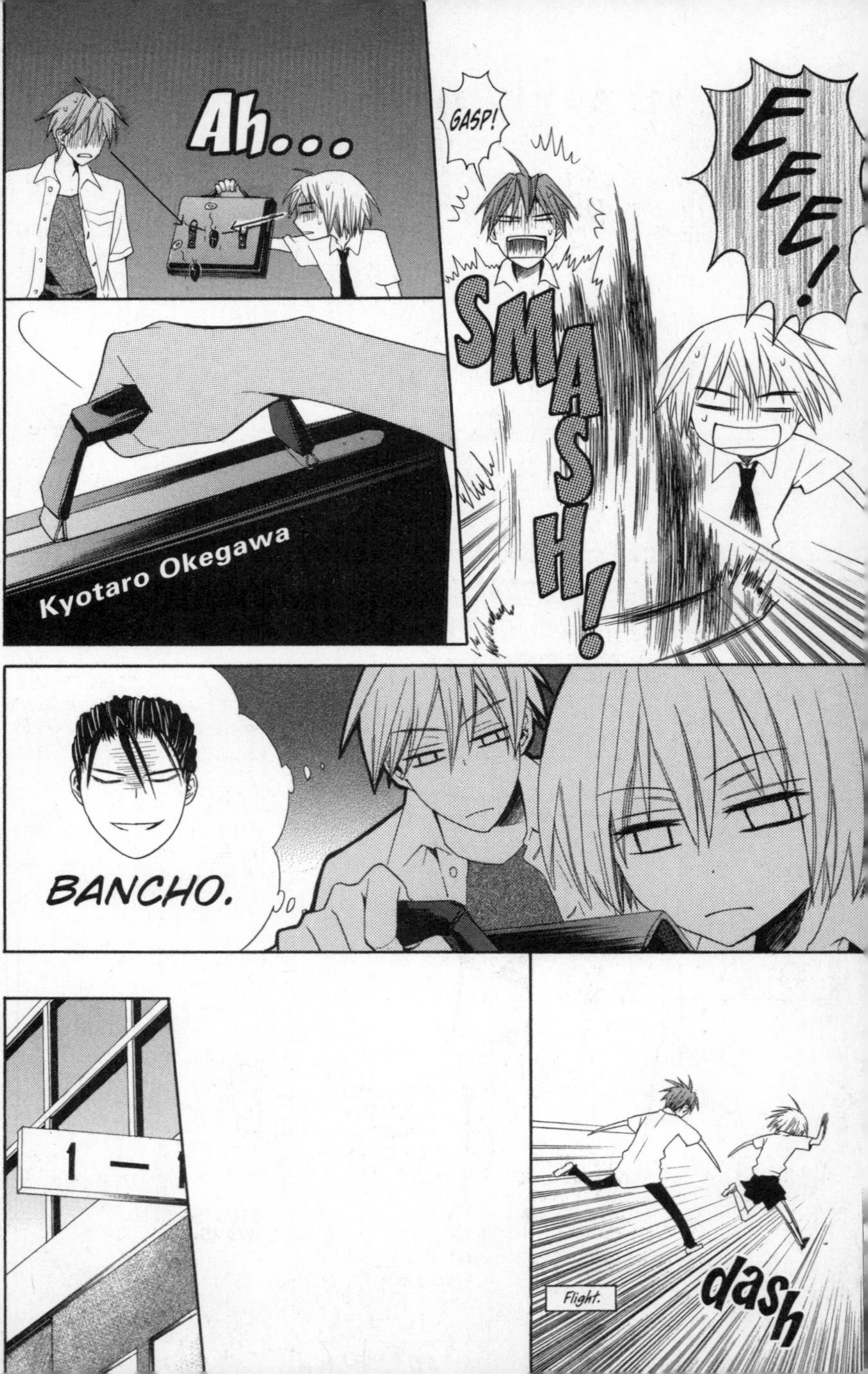
GASP!
EEE!
SMASH!
Ah...
Kyotaro Okegawa
BANCHO.
Flight.
dash
1-1

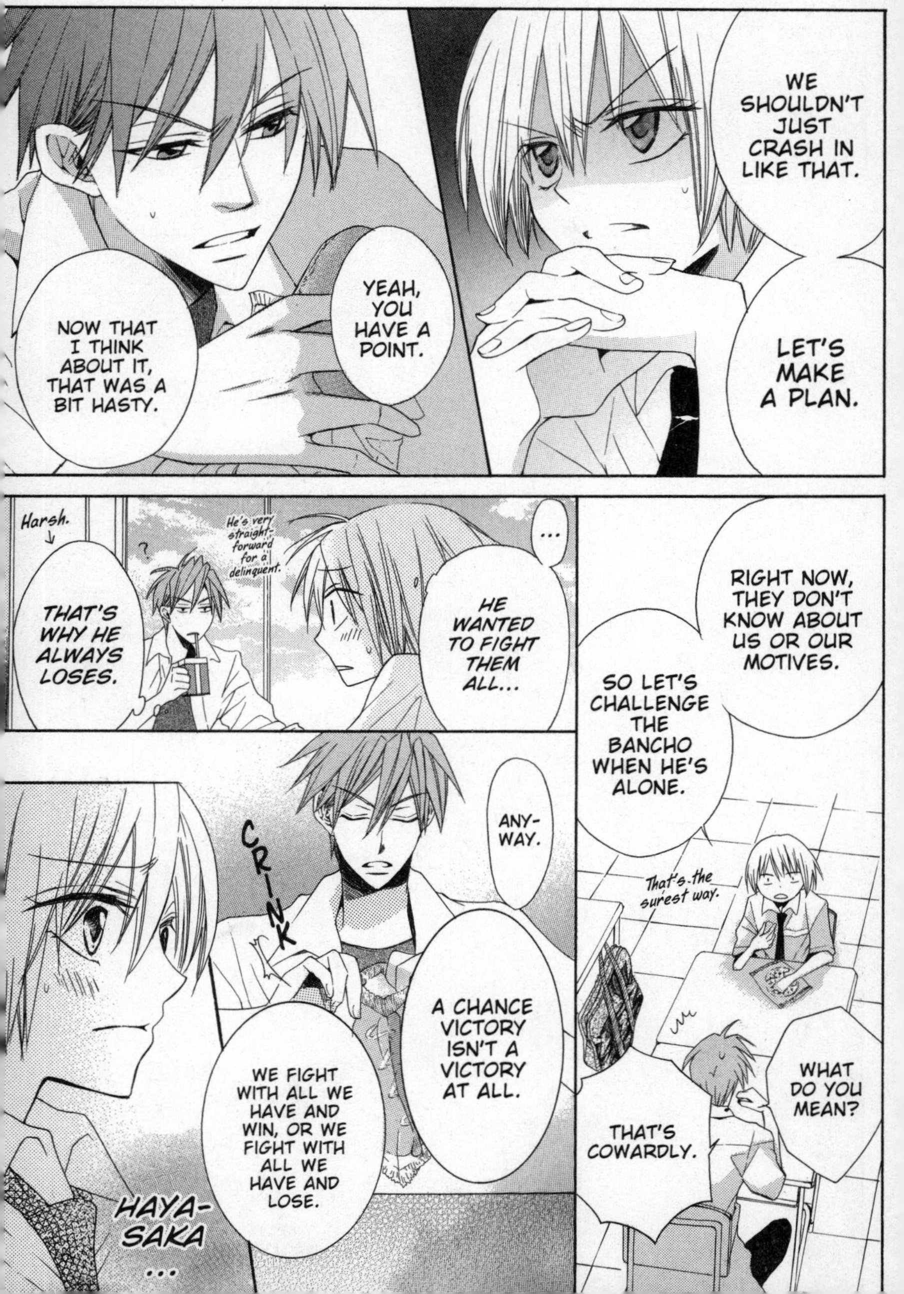
WE SHOULDN'T JUST CRASH IN LIKE THAT.
LET'S MAKE A PLAN.
YEAH, YOU HAVE A POINT.
NOW THAT I THINK ABOUT IT, THAT WAS A BIT HASTY.
RIGHT NOW, THEY DON'T KNOW ABOUT US OR OUR MOTIVES.
SO LET'S CHALLENGE THE BANCHO WHEN HE'S ALONE.
That's the surest way.
WHAT DO YOU MEAN?
THAT'S COWARDLY.
...
HE WANTED TO FIGHT THEM ALL...
He's very straightforward for a delinquent.
Harsh.
THAT'S WHY HE ALWAYS LOSES.
ANY-WAY.
CRINK
A CHANCE VICTORY ISN'T A VICTORY AT ALL.
WE FIGHT WITH ALL WE HAVE AND WIN, OR WE FIGHT WITH ALL WE HAVE AND LOSE.
HAYA-SAKA...

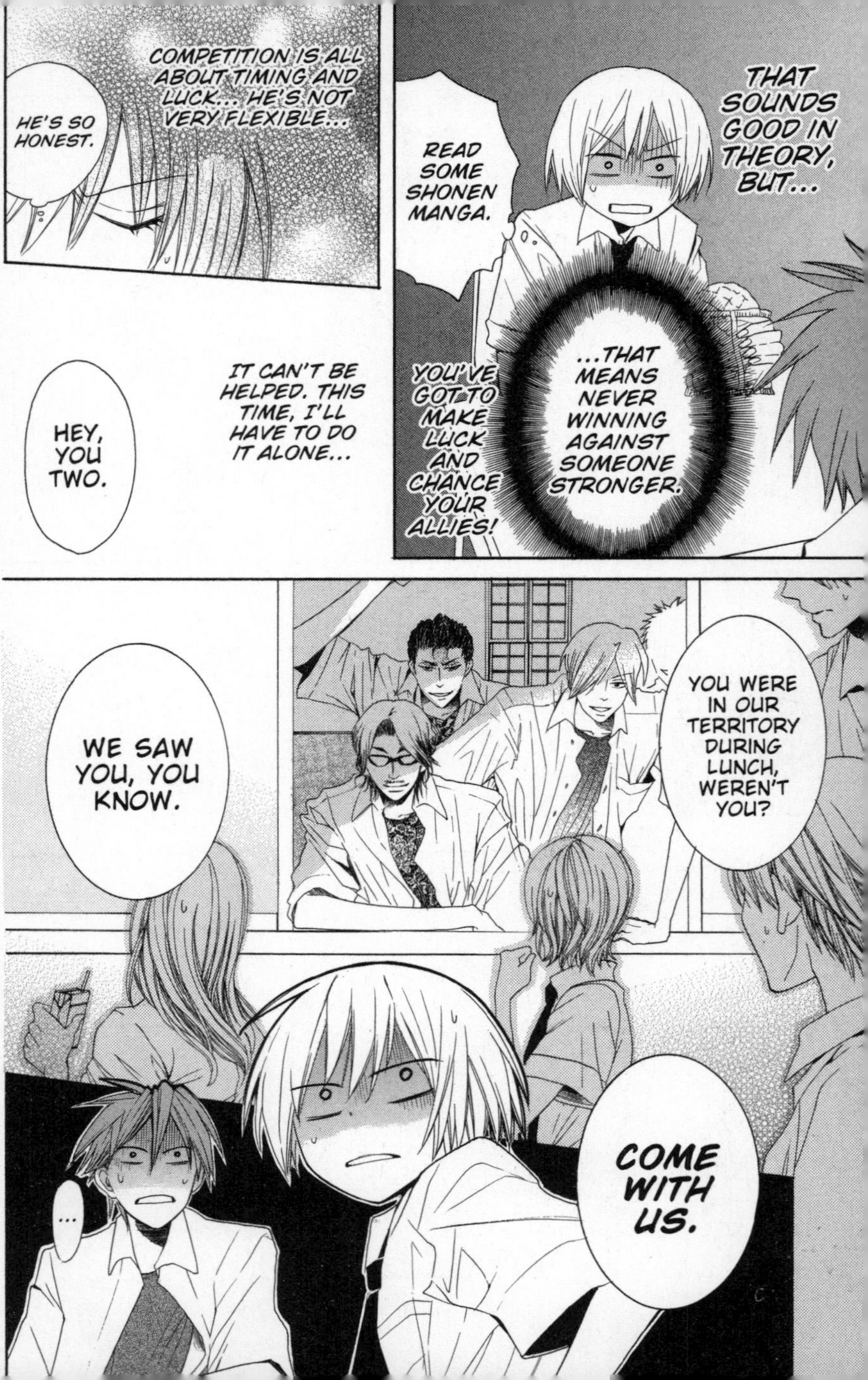
THAT SOUNDS GOOD IN THEORY, BUT...
READ SOME SHONEN MANGA.
...THAT MEANS NEVER WINNING AGAINST SOMEONE STRONGER.
YOU'VE GOT TO MAKE LUCK AND CHANCE YOUR ALLIES!
COMPETITION IS ALL ABOUT TIMING AND LUCK... HE'S NOT VERY FLEXIBLE...
HE'S SO HONEST.
IT CAN'T BE HELPED. THIS TIME, I'LL HAVE TO DO IT ALONE...
HEY, YOU TWO.
YOU WERE IN OUR TERRITORY DURING LUNCH, WEREN'T YOU?
WE SAW YOU, YOU KNOW.
COME WITH US.
...

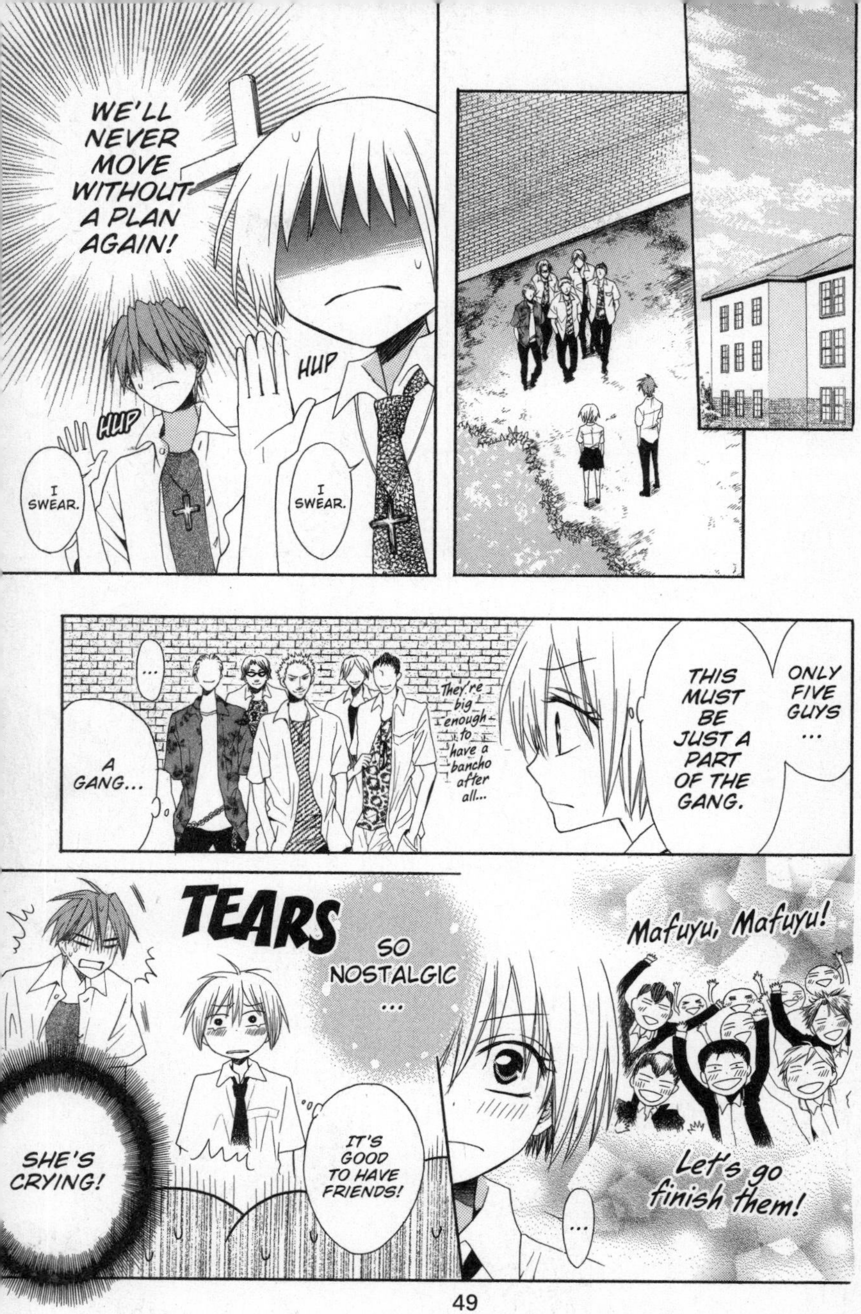
WE'LL NEVER MOVE WITHOUT A PLAN AGAIN!
HUP
I SWEAR.
HUP
I SWEAR.
ONLY FIVE GUYS ...
THIS MUST BE JUST A PART OF THE GANG.
They're big enough to have a bancho after all...
...
A GANG...
Mafuyu, Mafuyu!
Let's go finish them!
...
TEARS
SO NOSTALGIC ...
IT'S GOOD TO HAVE FRIENDS!
SHE'S CRYING!

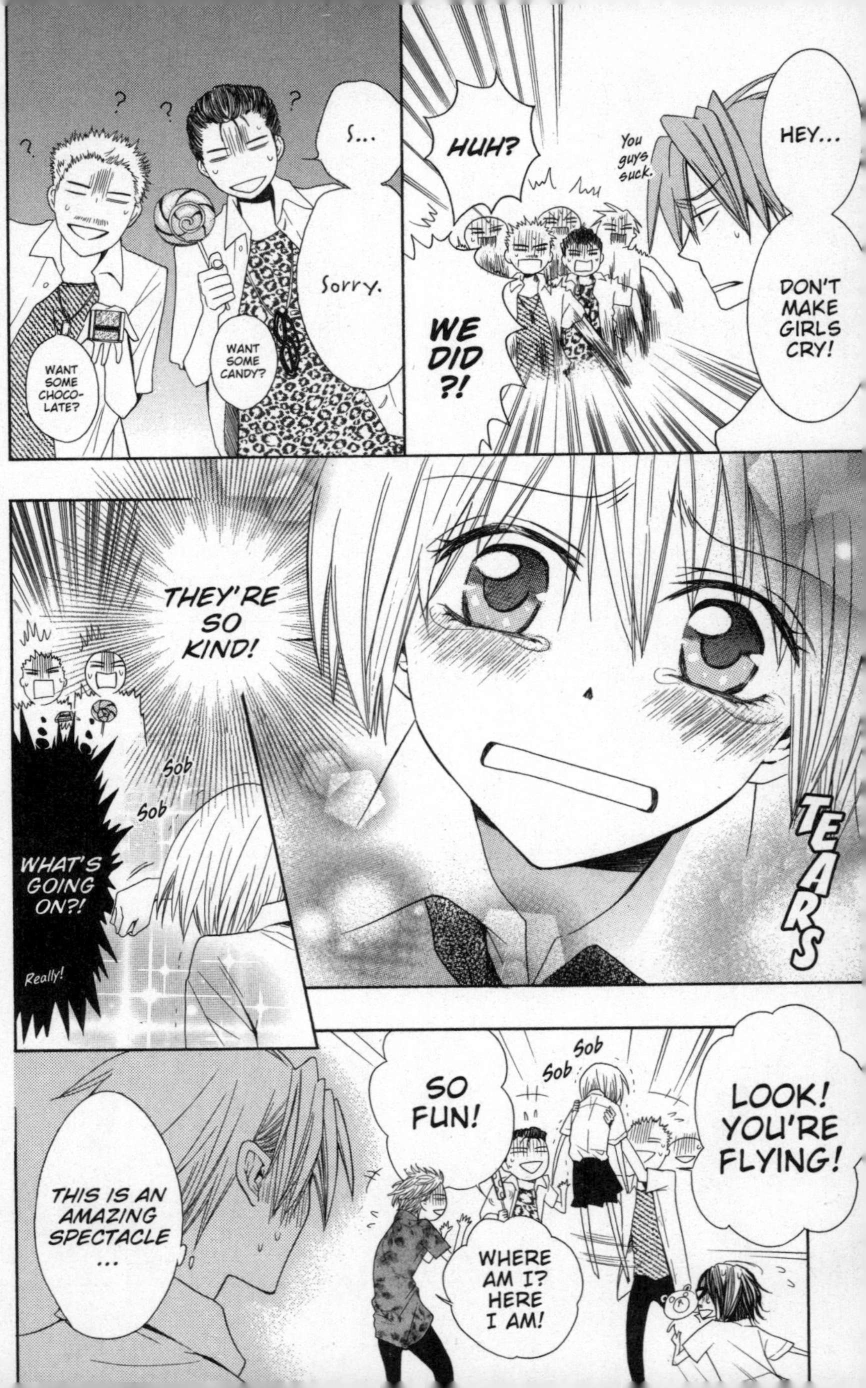
HEY...
DON'T MAKE GIRLS CRY!
You guys suck.
HUH?
WE DID?!
S...
Sorry.
WANT SOME CANDY?
WANT SOME CHOCOLATE?
TEARS
THEY'RE SO KIND!
Sob
Sob
WHAT'S GOING ON?!
Really!
LOOK! YOU'RE FLYING!
Sob
Sob
SO FUN!
WHERE AM I? HERE I AM!
THIS IS AN AMAZING SPECTACLE ...

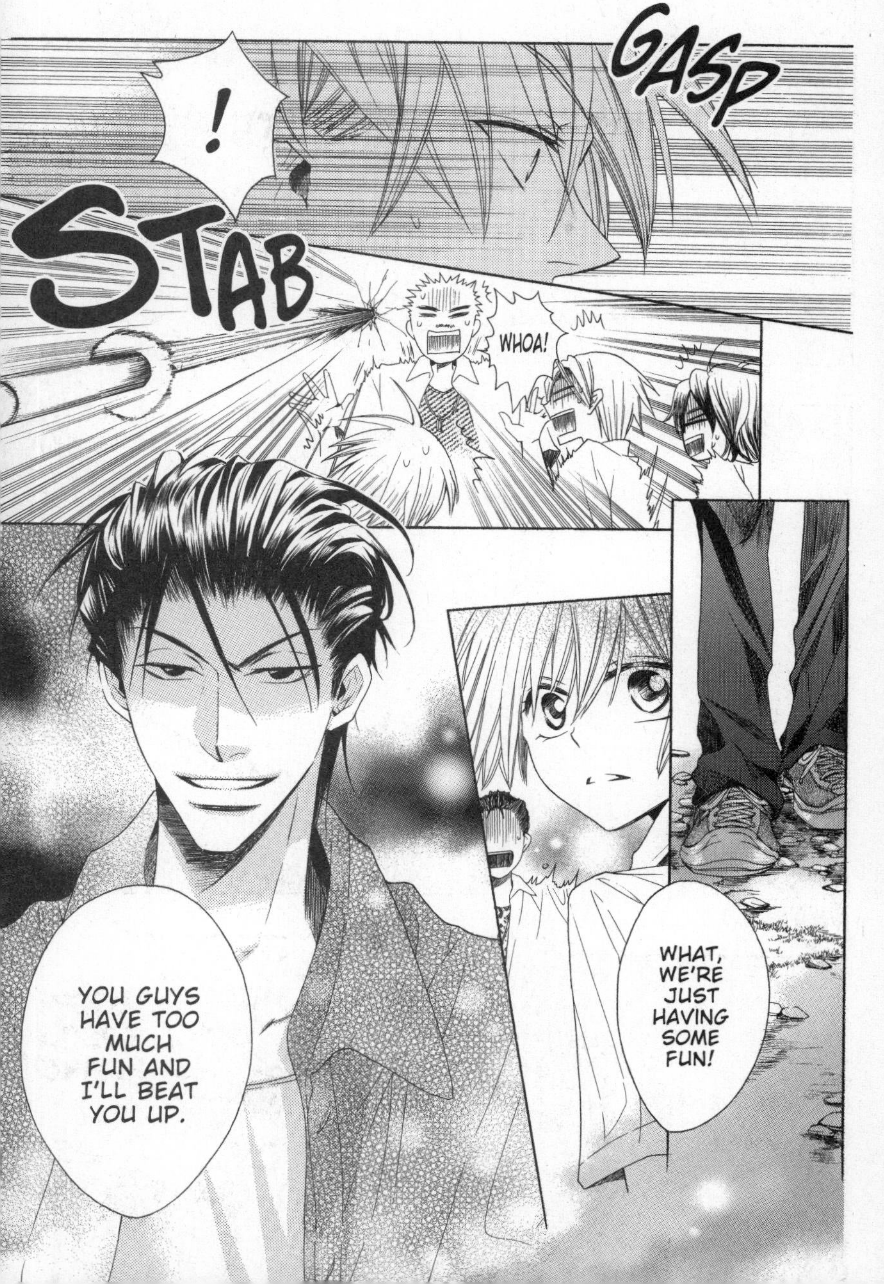
GASP
!
STAB
WHOA!
WHAT, WE'RE JUST HAVING SOME FUN!
YOU GUYS HAVE TOO MUCH FUN AND I'LL BEAT YOU UP.

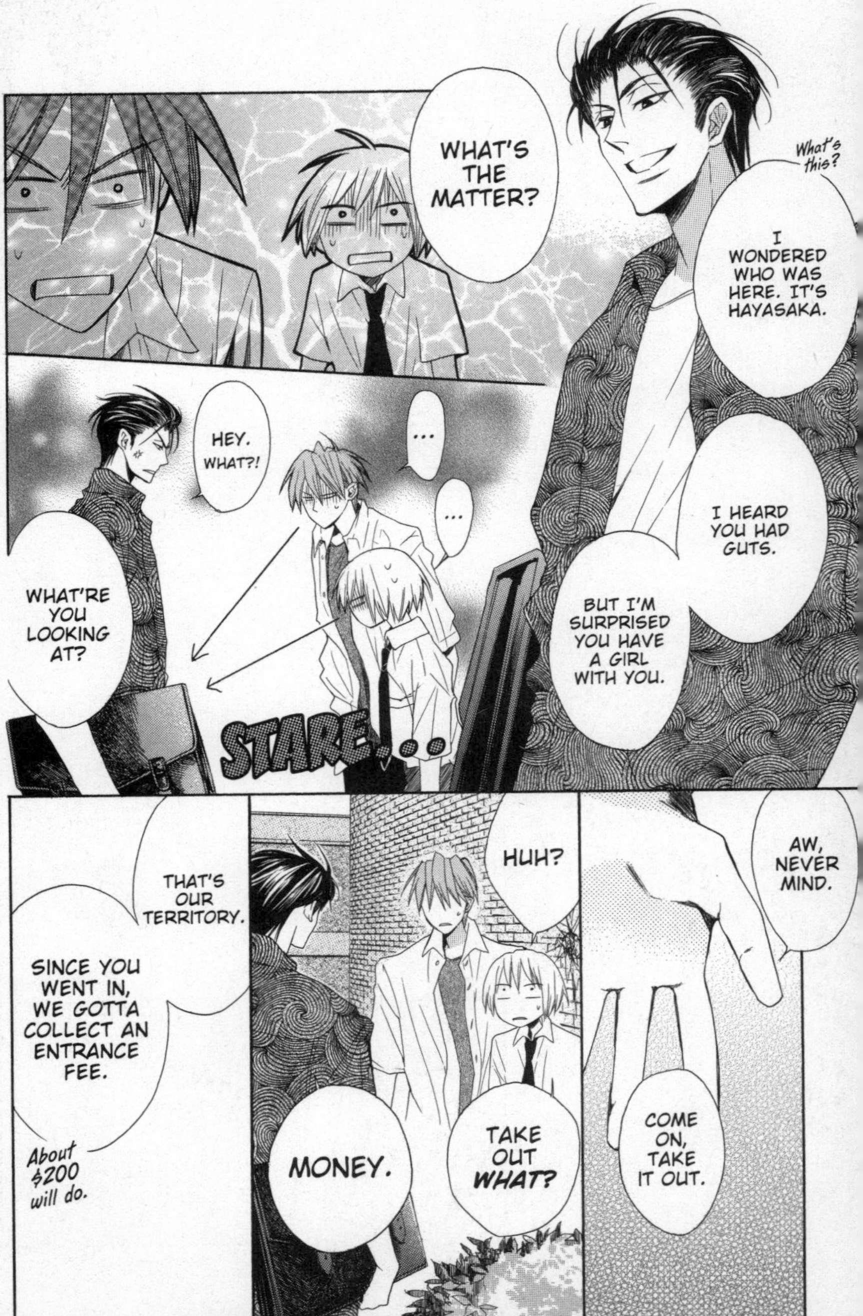
WHAT'S THE MATTER?
What's this?
I WONDERED WHO WAS HERE. IT'S HAYASAKA.
I HEARD YOU HAD GUTS.
BUT I'M SURPRISED YOU HAVE A GIRL WITH YOU.
HEY. WHAT?!
...
...
WHAT'RE YOU LOOKING AT?
STARE...
AW, NEVER MIND.
COME ON, TAKE IT OUT.
HUH?
TAKE OUT WHAT?
MONEY.
THAT'S OUR TERRITORY.
SINCE YOU WENT IN, WE GOTTA COLLECT AN ENTRANCE FEE.
About $200 will do.

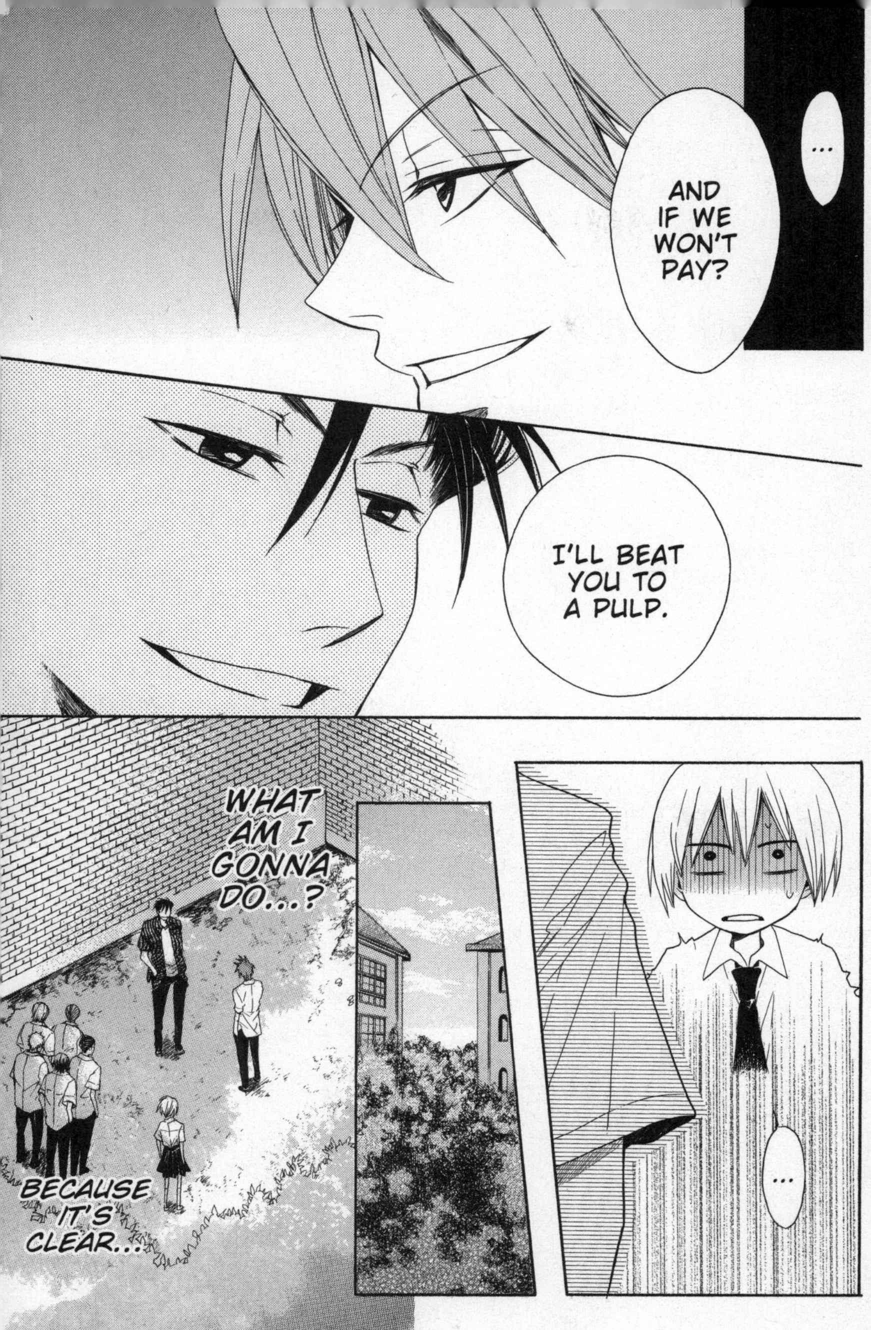
...
AND IF WE WON'T PAY?
I'LL BEAT YOU TO A PULP.
...
WHAT AM I GONNA DO...?
BECAUSE IT'S CLEAR...

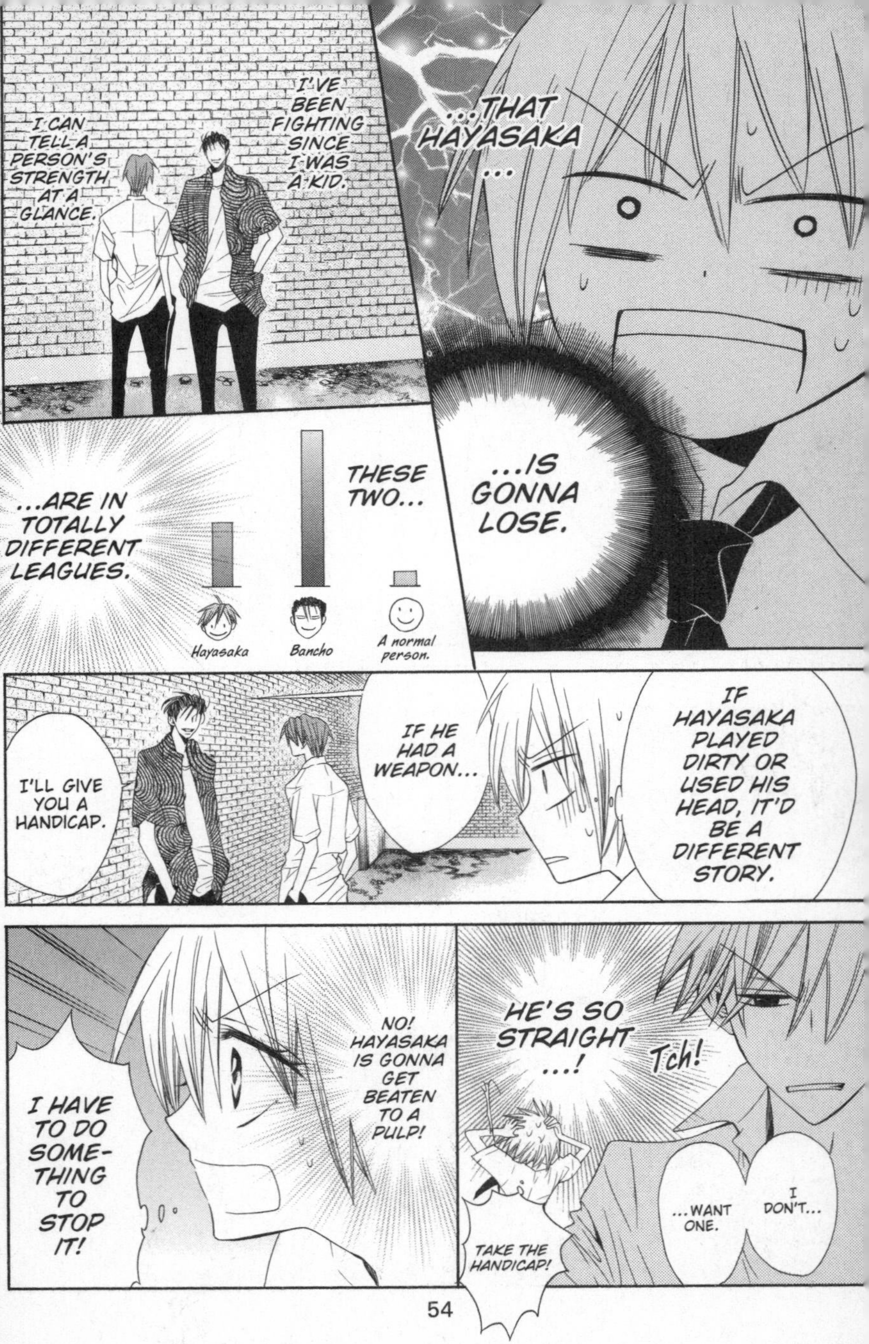
...THAT HAYASAKA ...
...IS GONNA LOSE.
I'VE BEEN FIGHTING SINCE I WAS A KID.
I CAN TELL A PERSON'S STRENGTH AT A GLANCE.
THESE TWO...
...ARE IN TOTALLY DIFFERENT LEAGUES.
Hayasaka
Bancho
A normal person.
IF HAYASAKA PLAYED DIRTY OR USED HIS HEAD, IT'D BE A DIFFERENT STORY.
IF HE HAD A WEAPON...
I'LL GIVE YOU A HANDICAP.
I DON'T...
...WANT ONE.
Tch!
HE'S SO STRAIGHT ...!
TAKE THE HANDICAP!
NO! HAYASAKA IS GONNA GET BEATEN TO A PULP!
I HAVE TO DO SOMETHING TO STOP IT!

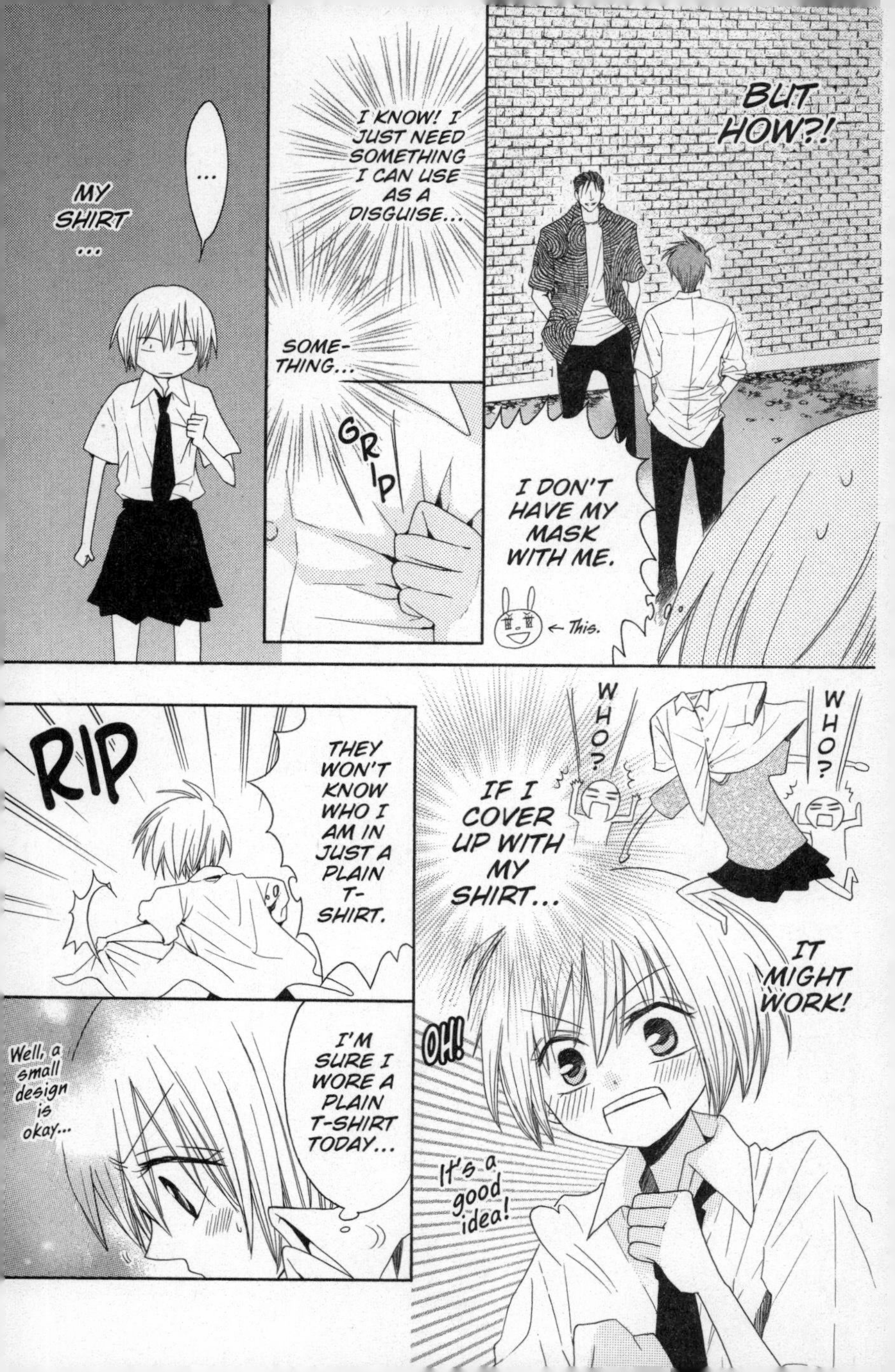
BUT HOW?!
I DON'T HAVE MY MASK WITH ME.
← This.
I KNOW! I JUST NEED SOMETHING I CAN USE AS A DISGUISE...
SOME-THING...
GRIP
...
MY SHIRT ...
WHO?
WHO?
IF I COVER UP WITH MY SHIRT...
IT MIGHT WORK!
OH!
It's a good idea!
RIP
THEY WON'T KNOW WHO I AM IN JUST A PLAIN T-SHIRT.
I'M SURE I WORE A PLAIN T-SHIRT TODAY...
Well, a small design is okay...

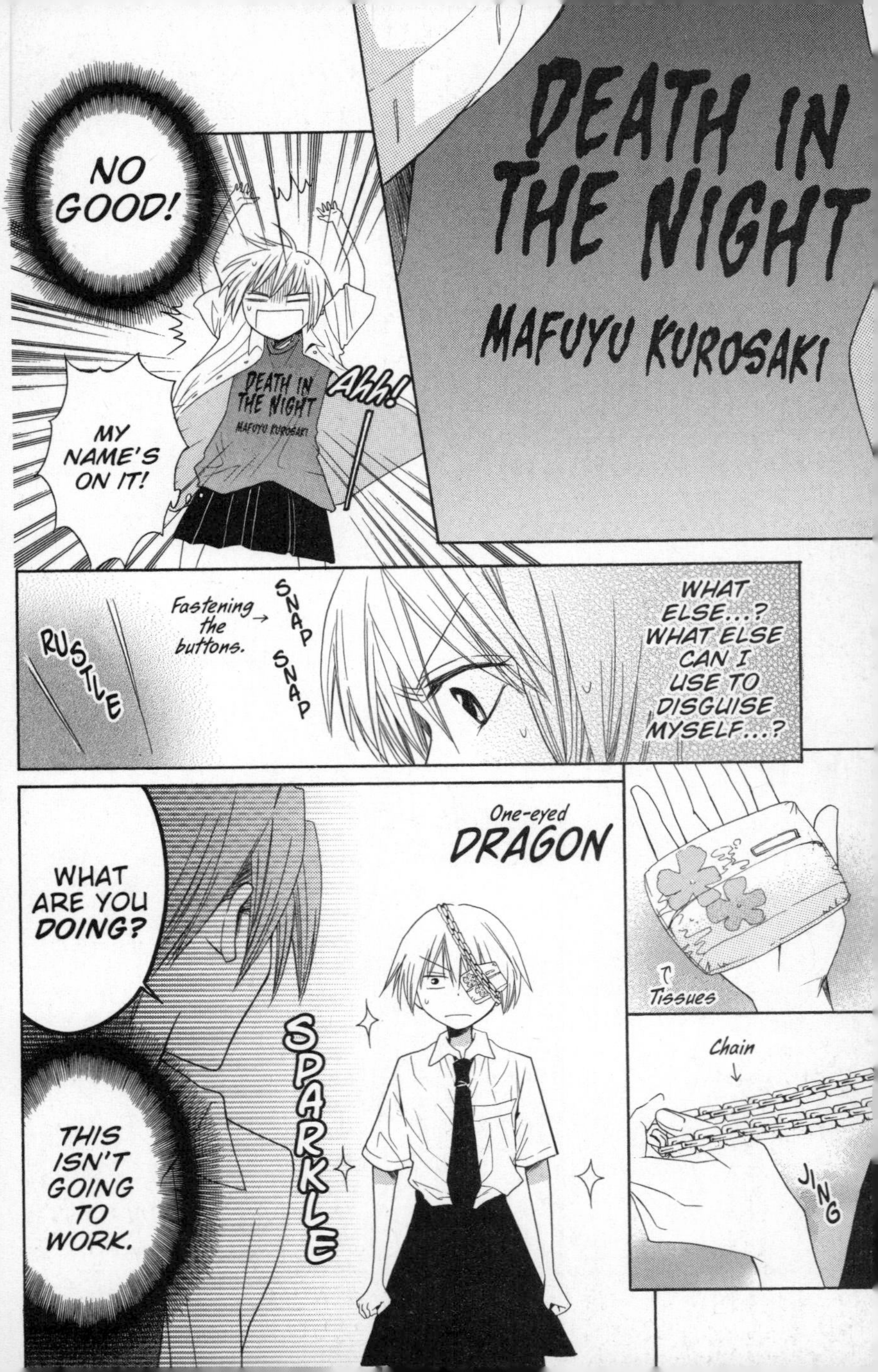
DEATH IN THE NIGHT
MAFUYU KUROSAKI
NO GOOD!
Ahh!
DEATH IN THE NIGHT
MAFUYU KUROSAKI
MY NAME'S ON IT!
WHAT ELSE...? WHAT ELSE CAN I USE TO DISGUISE MYSELF...?
SNAP
SNAP
Fastening the buttons.
RUSTLE
Tissues
Chain
JING
One-eyed
DRAGON
SPARKLE
WHAT ARE YOU DOING?
THIS ISN'T GOING TO WORK.

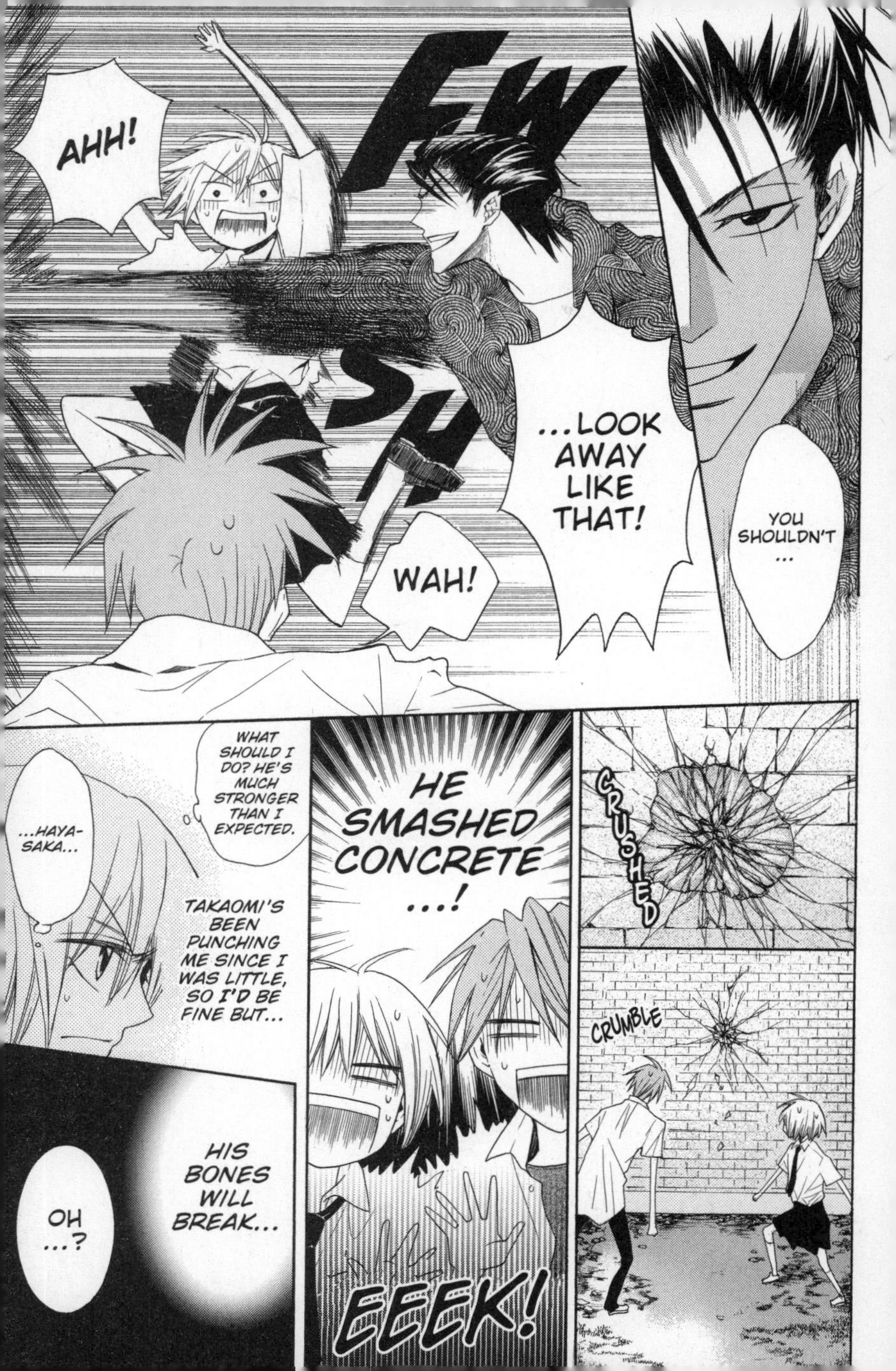
YOU SHOULDN'T ...
...LOOK AWAY LIKE THAT!
FW SH
WAH!
AHH!
CRUSHED
CRUMBLE
HE SMASHED CONCRETE ...!
EEEK!
WHAT SHOULD I DO? HE'S MUCH STRONGER THAN I EXPECTED.
...HAYA-SAKA...
TAKAOMI'S BEEN PUNCHING ME SINCE I WAS LITTLE, SO I'D BE FINE BUT...
HIS BONES WILL BREAK...
OH ...?

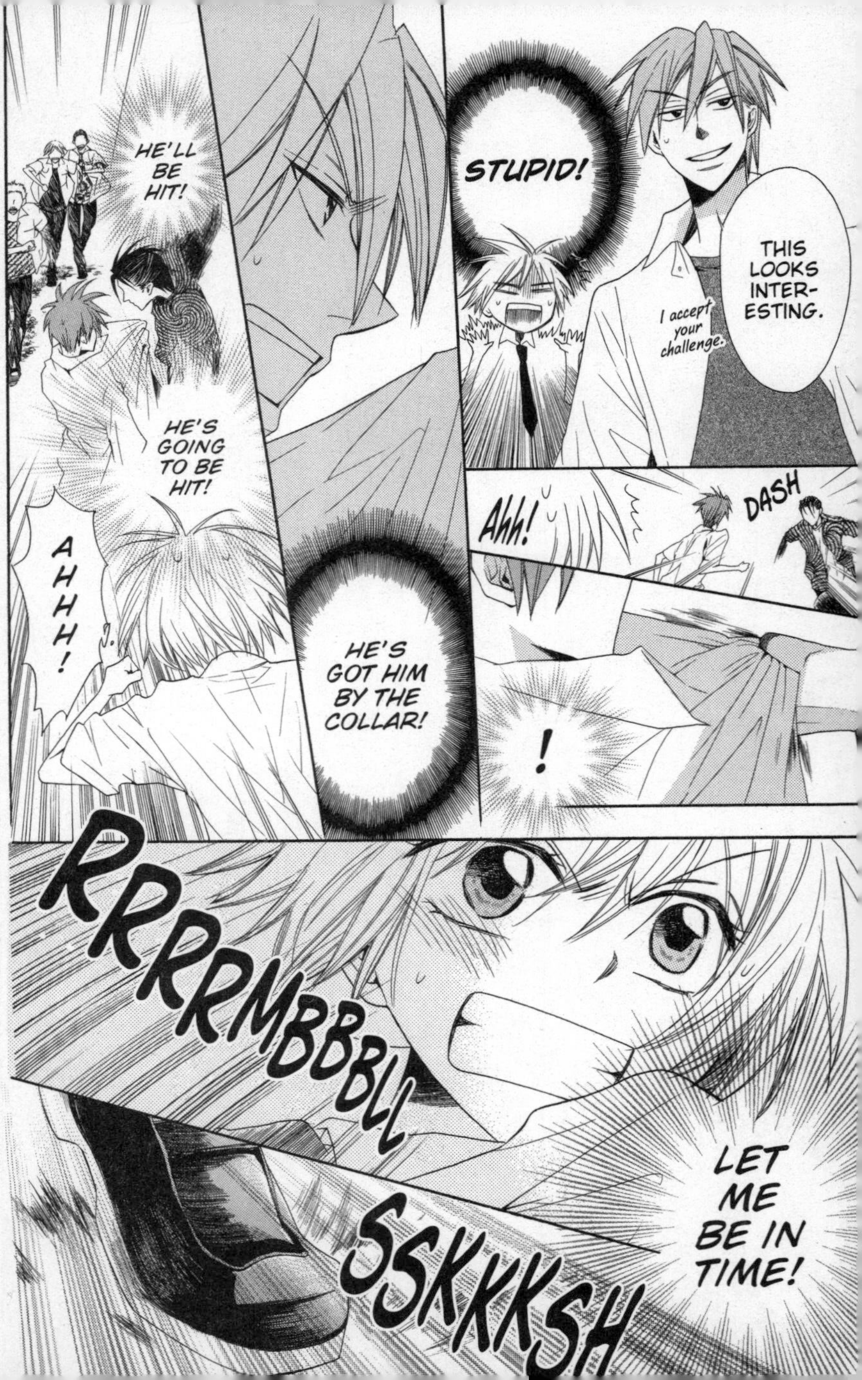

THIS LOOKS INTER-ESTING.
I accept your challenge.
STUPID!
DASH
Ahh!
!
HE'S GOT HIM BY THE COLLAR!
HE'LL BE HIT!
HE'S GOING TO BE HIT!
AHHHH!
LET ME BE IN TIME!
RRRRMBBBLL
SSKKKSH

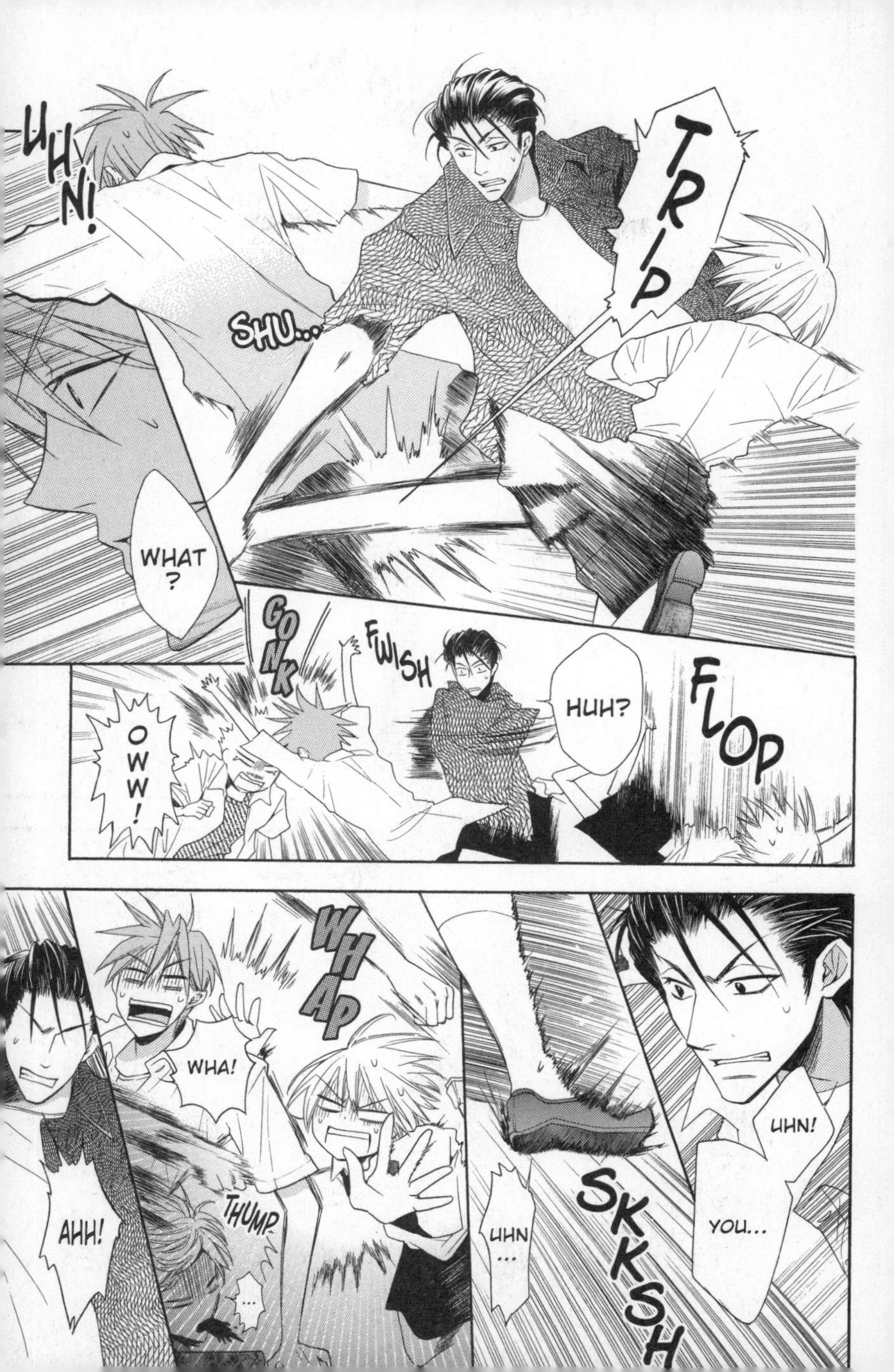
TRIP
SHU...
UHN!
WHAT?
FLOP
HUH?
FWISH
GONK
OWW!
UHN!
YOU...
SKKSH
UHN...
WHAP
WHA!
THUMP
AHH!
...

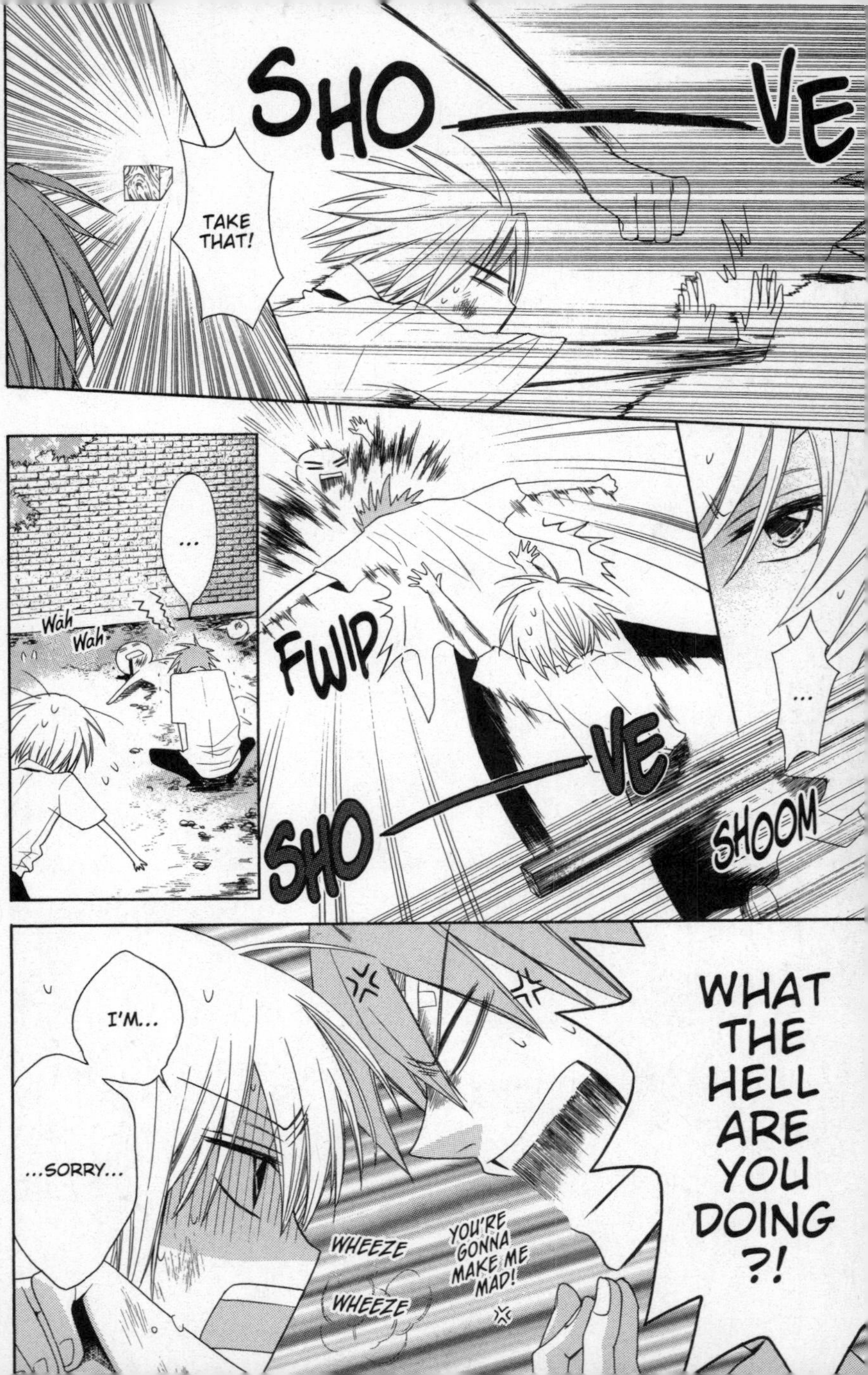
SHO——VE
TAKE THAT!
...
SHOOM
FWIP
SHO——VE
...
Wah Wah
WHAT THE HELL ARE YOU DOING?!
YOU'RE GONNA MAKE ME MAD!
WHEEZE
WHEEZE
I'M...
...SORRY...

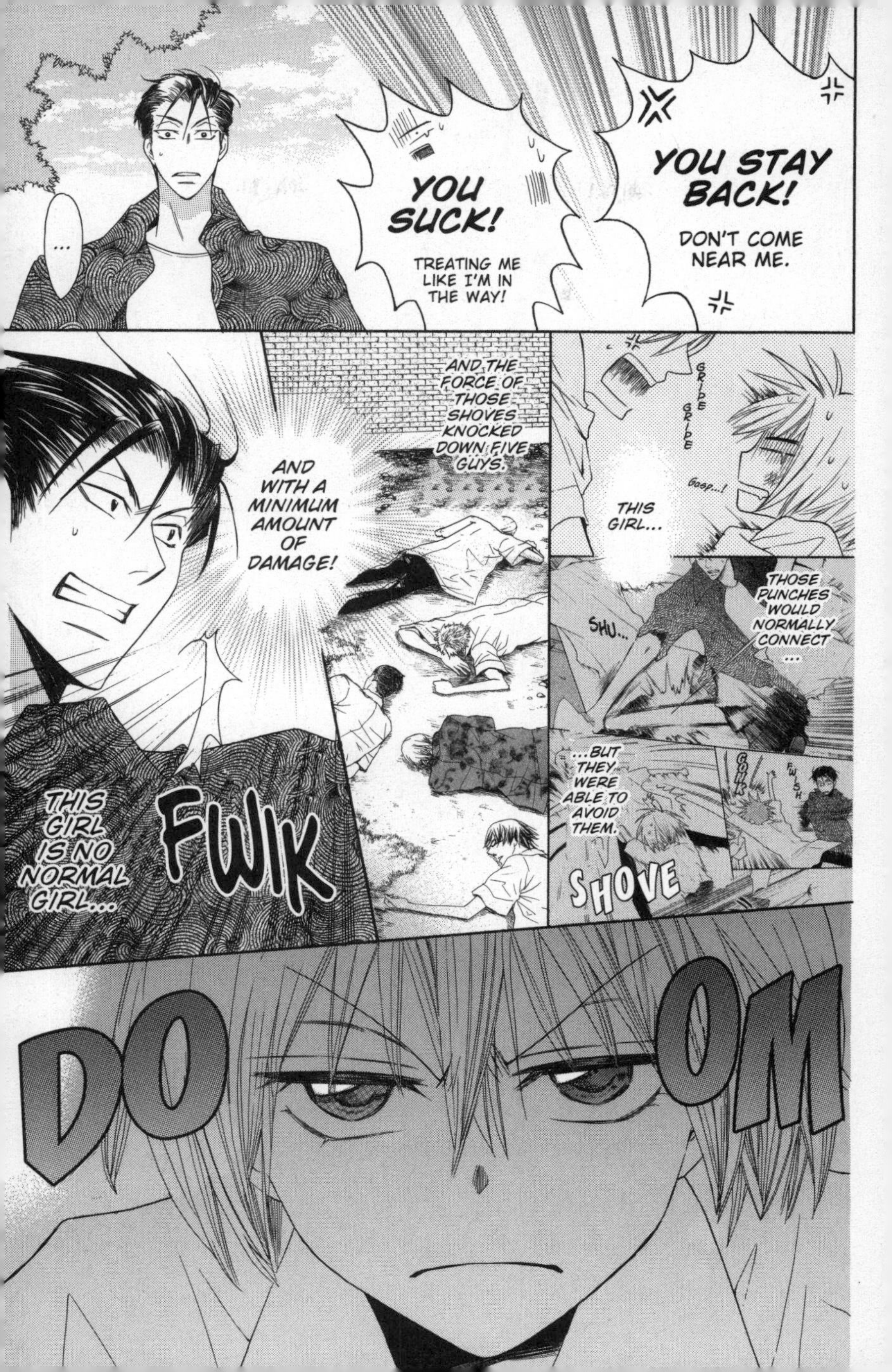
YOU STAY BACK!
DON'T COME NEAR ME.
YOU SUCK!
TREATING ME LIKE I'M IN THE WAY!
...
GRIPE GRIPE
Gasp...!
THIS GIRL...
THOSE PUNCHES WOULD NORMALLY CONNECT...
SHU...
...BUT THEY WERE ABLE TO AVOID THEM.
FWISH
SHOVE
AND THE FORCE OF THOSE SHOVES KNOCKED DOWN FIVE GUYS.
AND WITH A MINIMUM AMOUNT OF DAMAGE!
THIS GIRL IS NO NORMAL GIRL...
FWIK
DO OM

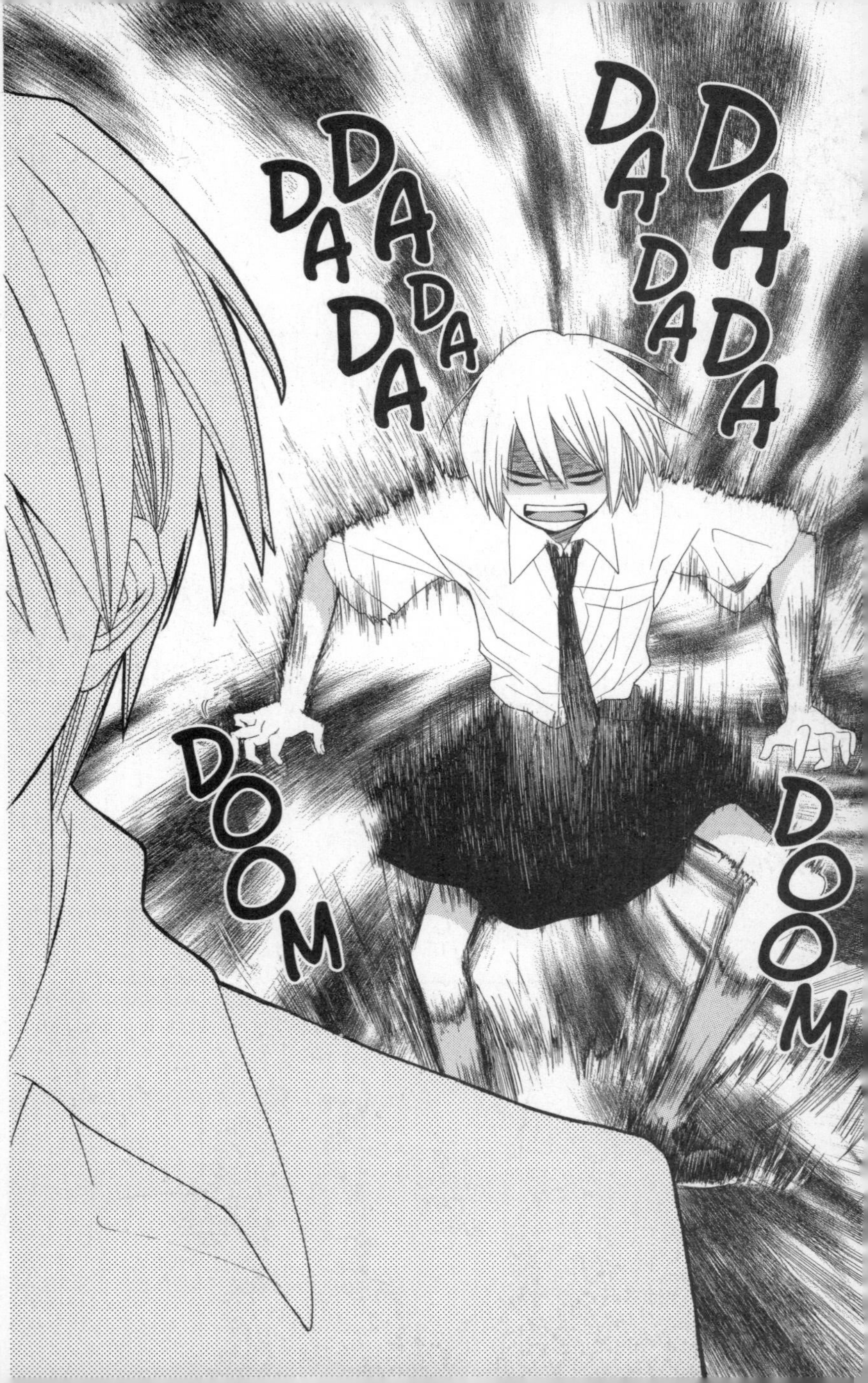
DADADADA
DADADADA
DOOOM
DOOOM

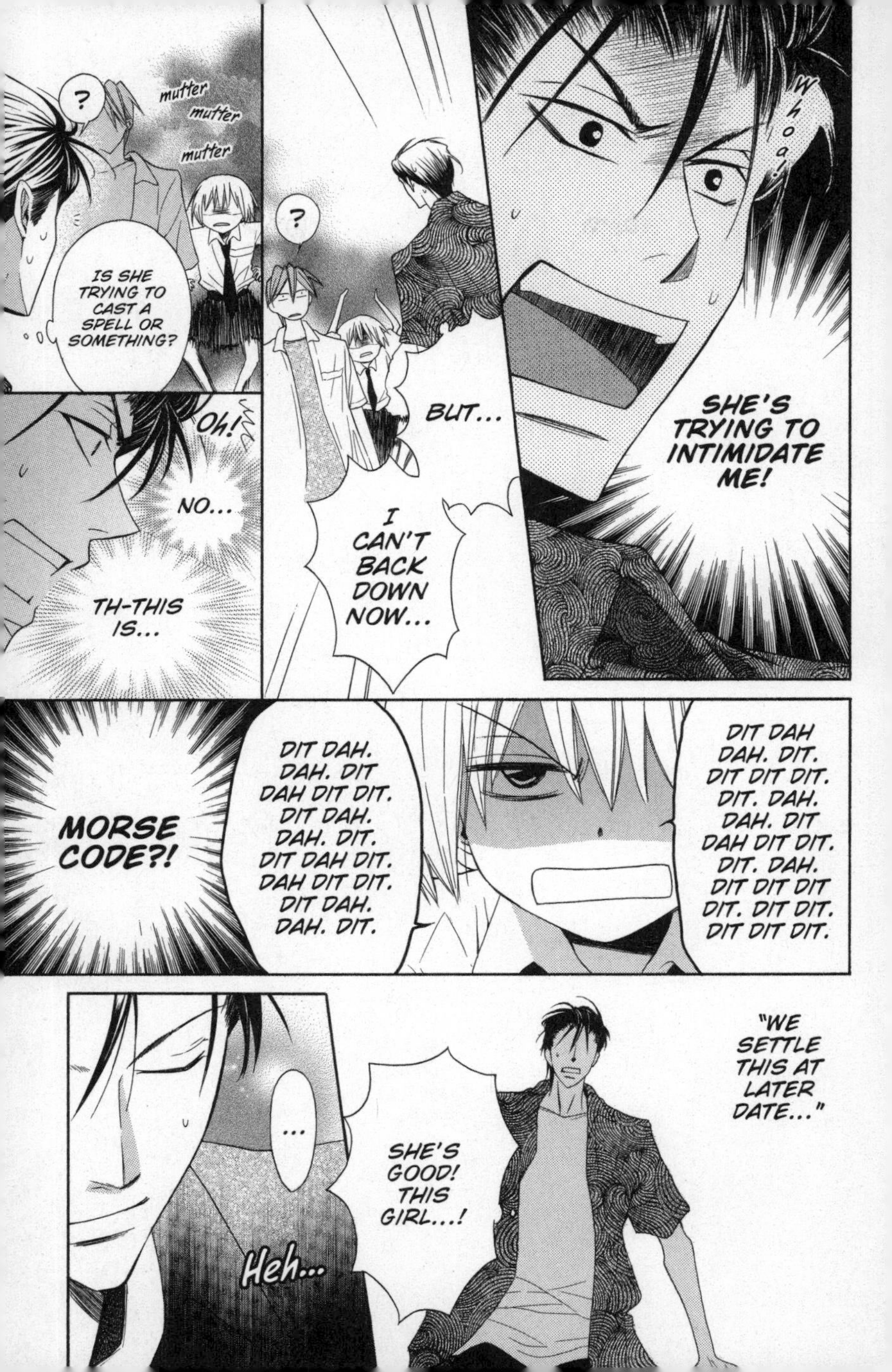
Whoa!
SHE'S TRYING TO INTIMIDATE ME!
?
BUT...
I CAN'T BACK DOWN NOW...
?
mutter mutter mutter
IS SHE TRYING TO CAST A SPELL OR SOMETHING?
Oh!
NO...
TH-THIS IS...
DIT DAH DAH. DIT. DIT DIT DIT. DIT. DAH. DAH. DIT DAH DIT DIT. DIT. DAH. DIT DIT DIT DIT. DIT DIT. DIT DIT DIT.
DIT DAH. DAH. DIT DAH DIT DIT. DIT DAH. DAH. DIT. DIT DAH DIT. DAH DIT DIT. DIT DAH. DAH. DIT.
MORSE CODE?!
"WE SETTLE THIS AT LATER DATE..."
SHE'S GOOD! THIS GIRL...!
...
Heh...

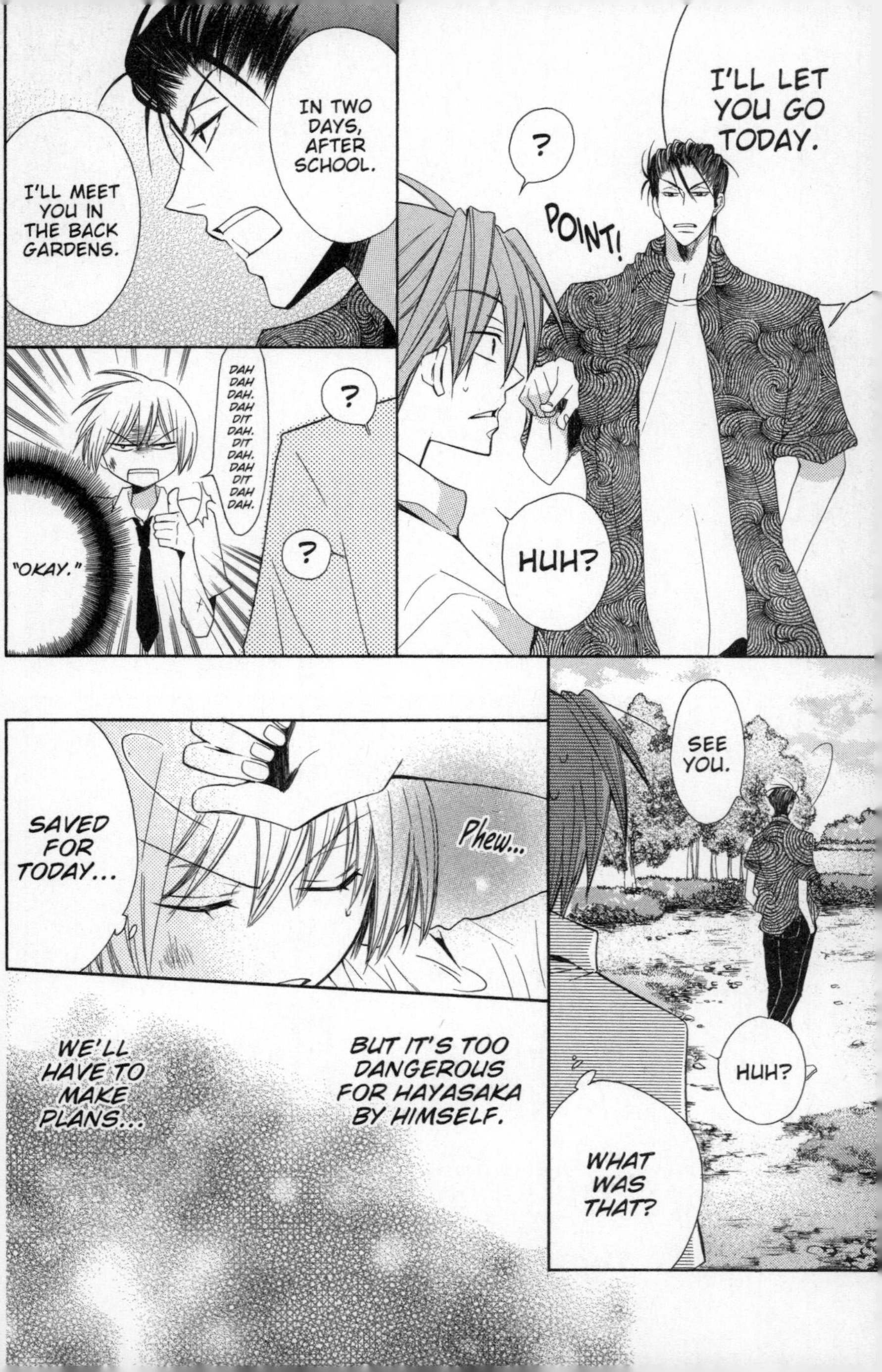

I'LL LET YOU GO TODAY.
?
POINT!
HUH?
IN TWO DAYS, AFTER SCHOOL.
I'LL MEET YOU IN THE BACK GARDENS.
?
DAH DAH DAH. DAH DIT DAH. DIT DAH. DAH DIT DAH DAH.
?
"OKAY."
SEE YOU.
HUH?
WHAT WAS THAT?
SAVED FOR TODAY...
Phew...
BUT IT'S TOO DANGEROUS FOR HAYASAKA BY HIMSELF.
WE'LL HAVE TO MAKE PLANS...

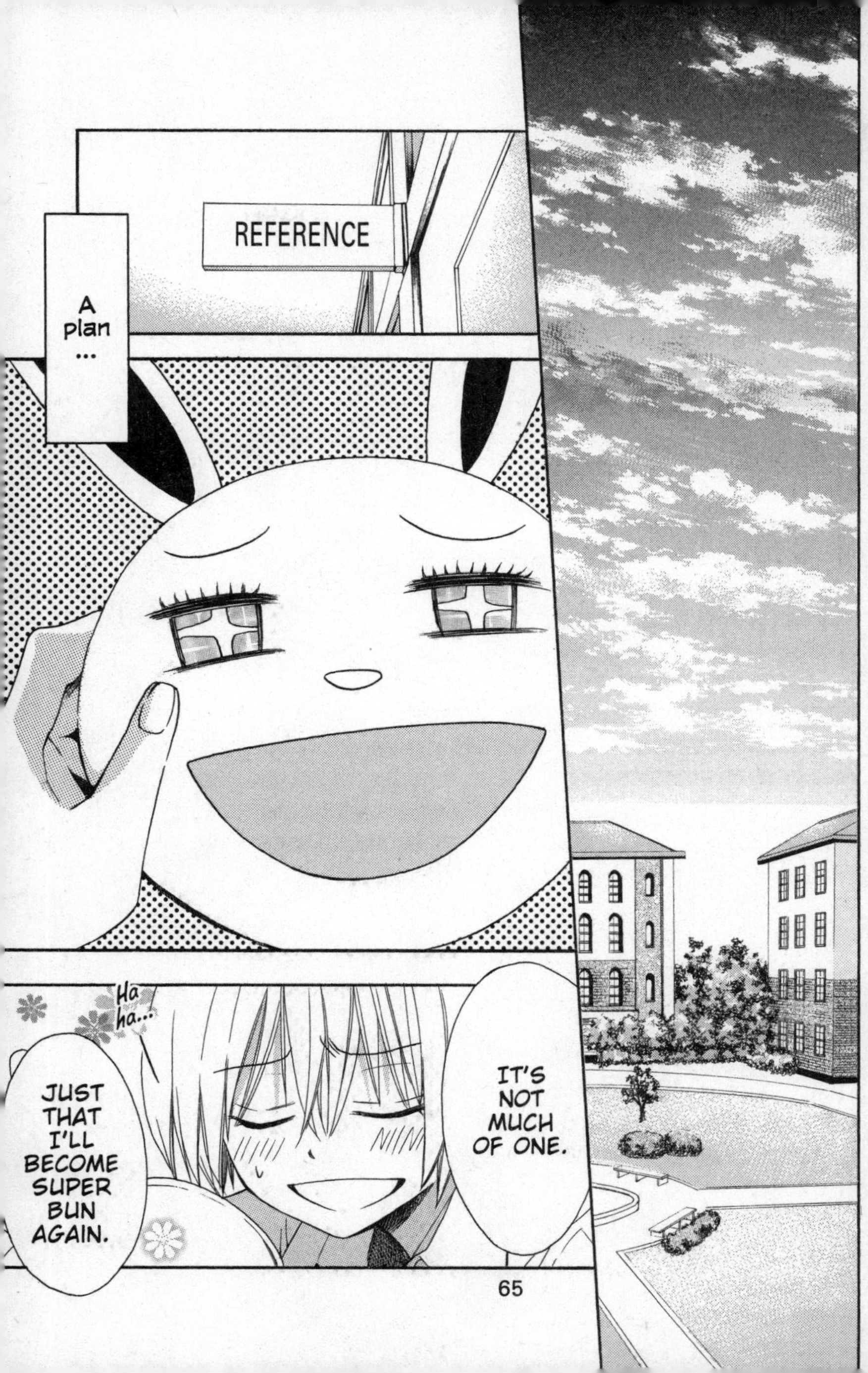
REFERENCE
A plan ...
IT'S NOT MUCH OF ONE.
Ha ha...
JUST THAT I'LL BECOME SUPER BUN AGAIN.

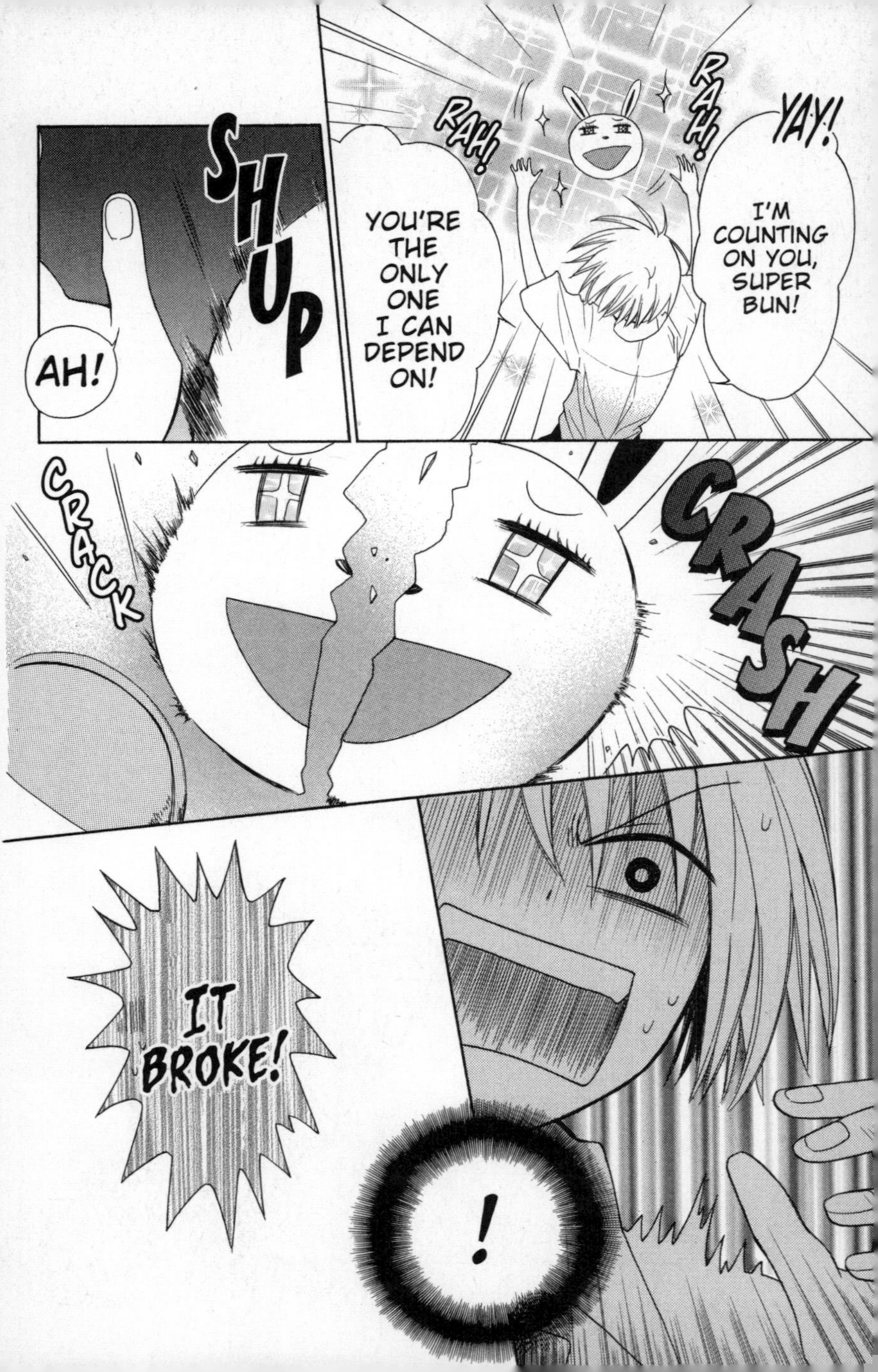

YAY!
I'M COUNTING ON YOU, SUPER BUN!
RAH!
RAH!
YOU'RE THE ONLY ONE I CAN DEPEND ON!
SHUP
AH!
CRASH
CRACK
!
IT BROKE!

Chapter 8

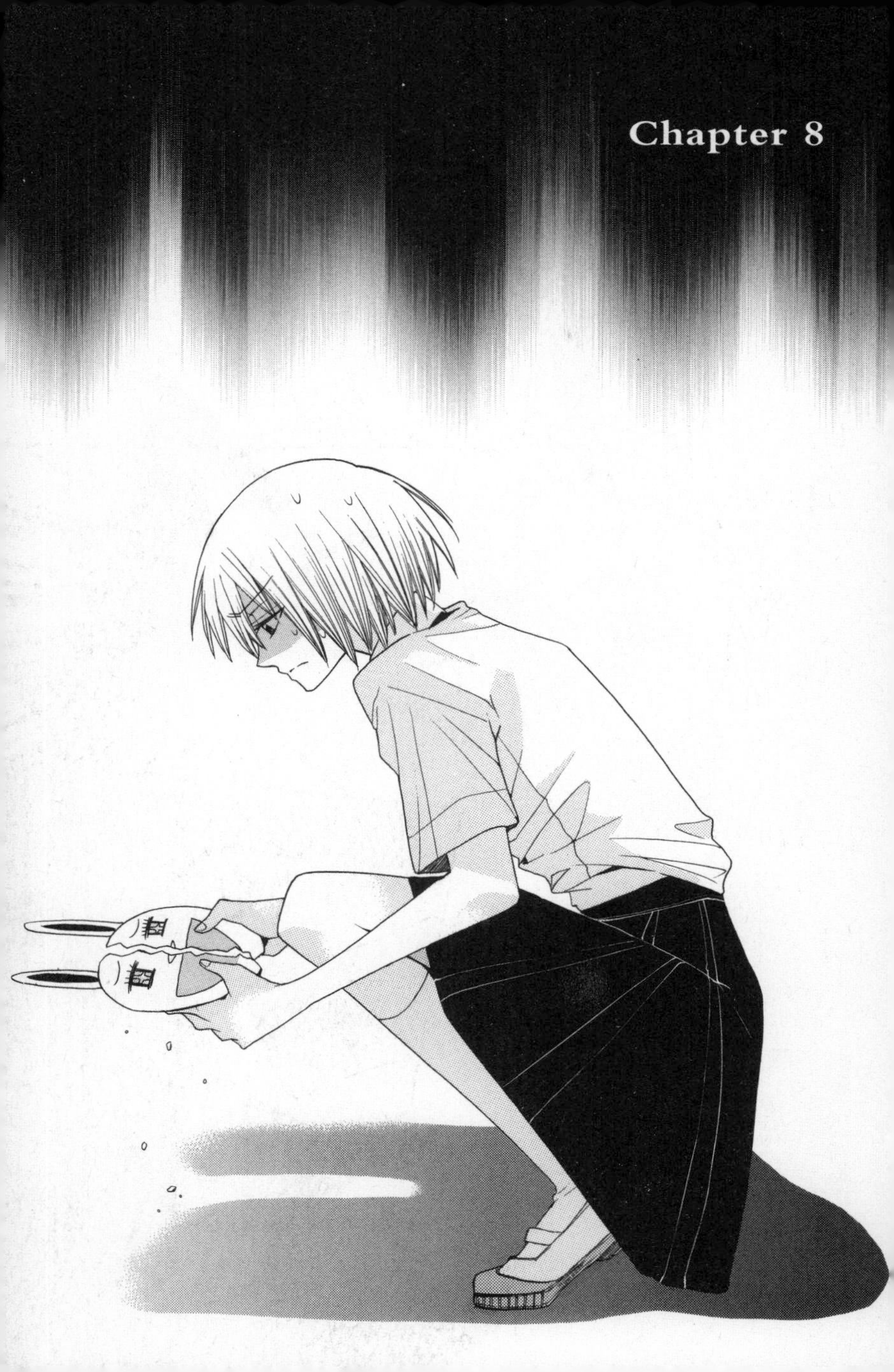

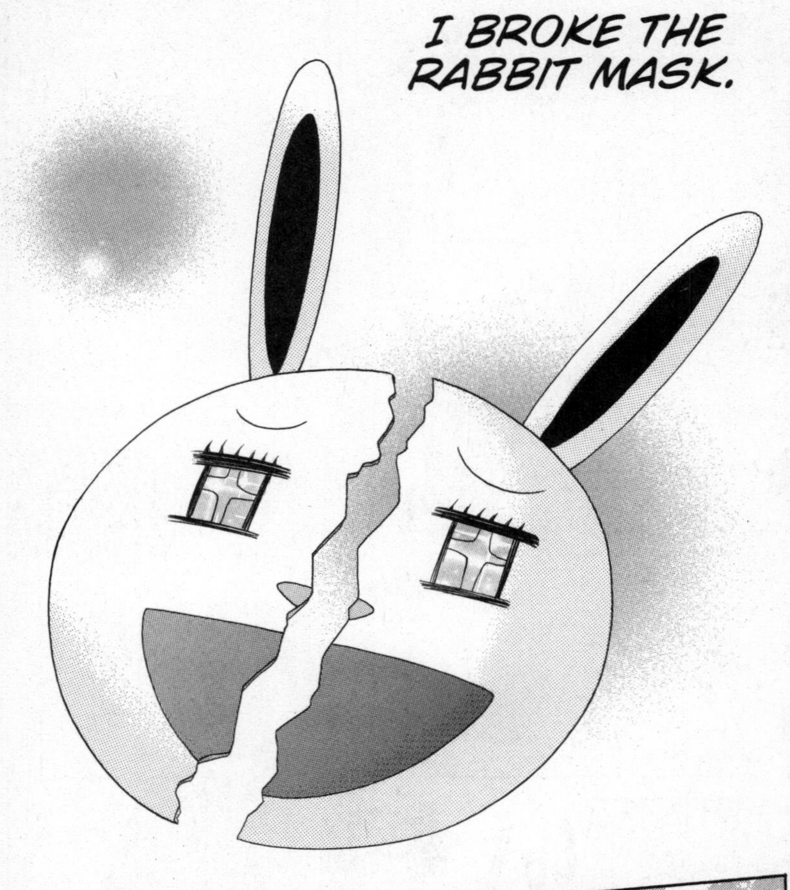
I BROKE THE RABBIT MASK.
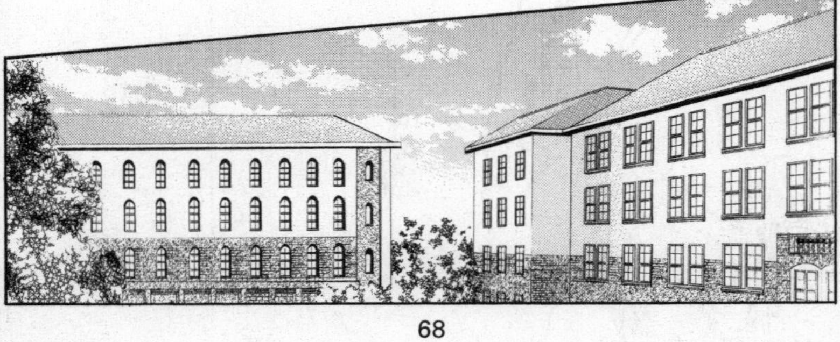

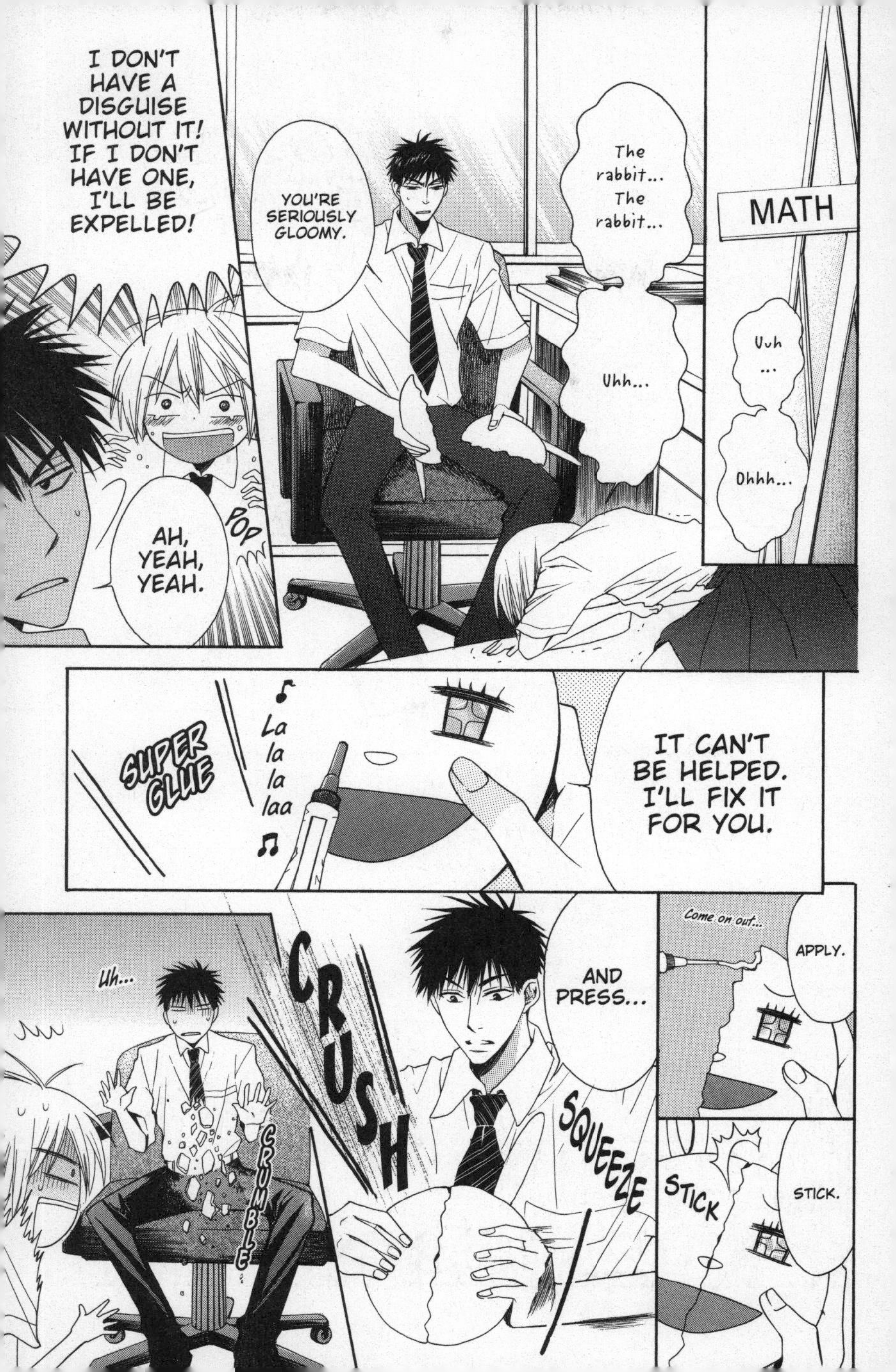
MATH
Uuh ...
Ohhh...
The rabbit... The rabbit...
Uhh...
YOU'RE SERIOUSLY GLOOMY.
I DON'T HAVE A DISGUISE WITHOUT IT! IF I DON'T HAVE ONE, I'LL BE EXPELLED!
POP
AH, YEAH, YEAH.
IT CAN'T BE HELPED. I'LL FIX IT FOR YOU.
La la la laa
SUPER GLUE
Come on out...
APPLY.
STICK.
STICK
AND PRESS...
SQUEEZE
CRUSH
Uh...
CRUMBLE

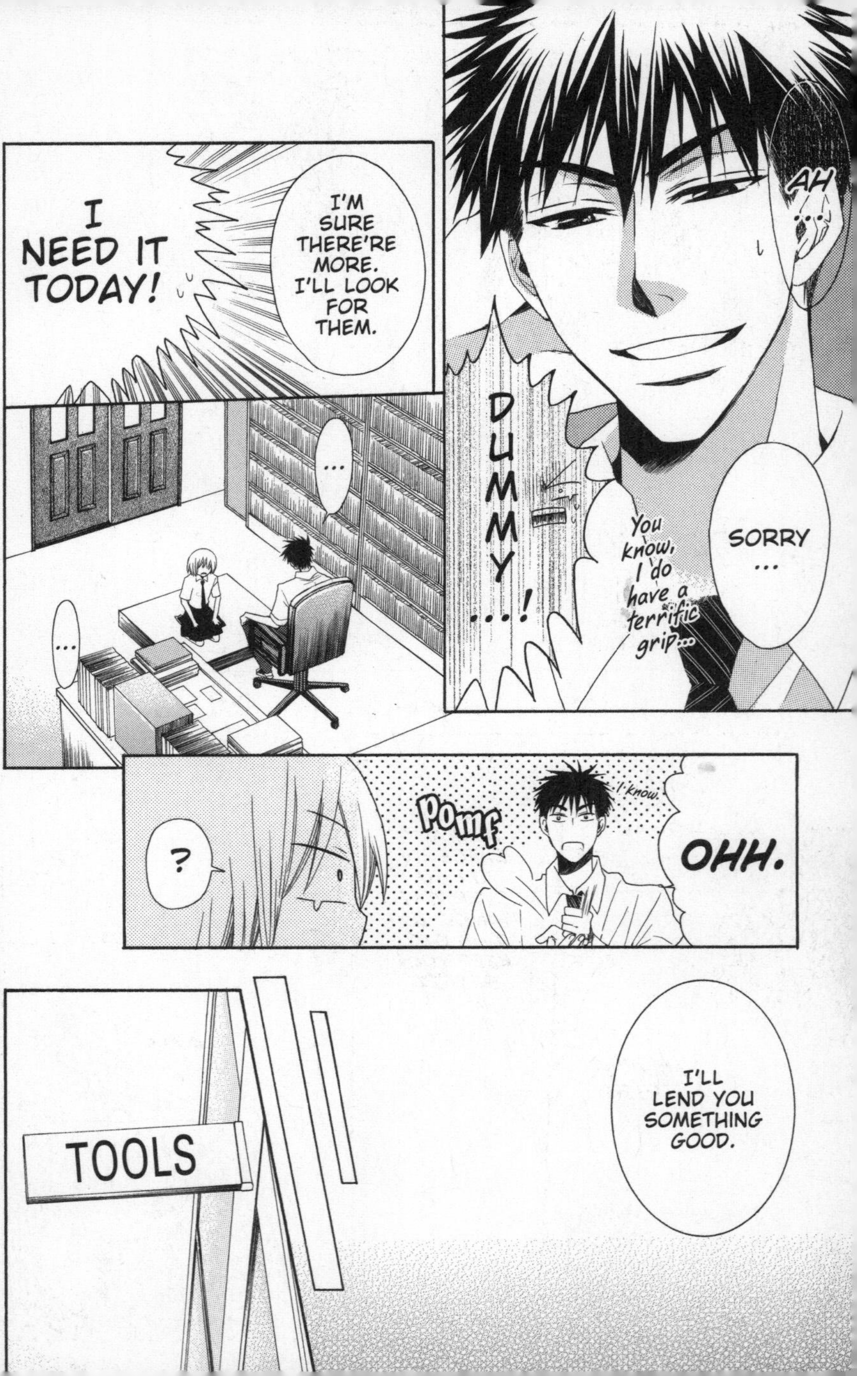

AH...
SORRY...
You know, I do have a terrific grip...
DUMMY...!
I'M SURE THERE'RE MORE. I'LL LOOK FOR THEM.
I NEED IT TODAY!
...
...
OHH.
I know.
pomf
?
I'LL LEND YOU SOMETHING GOOD.
TOOLS

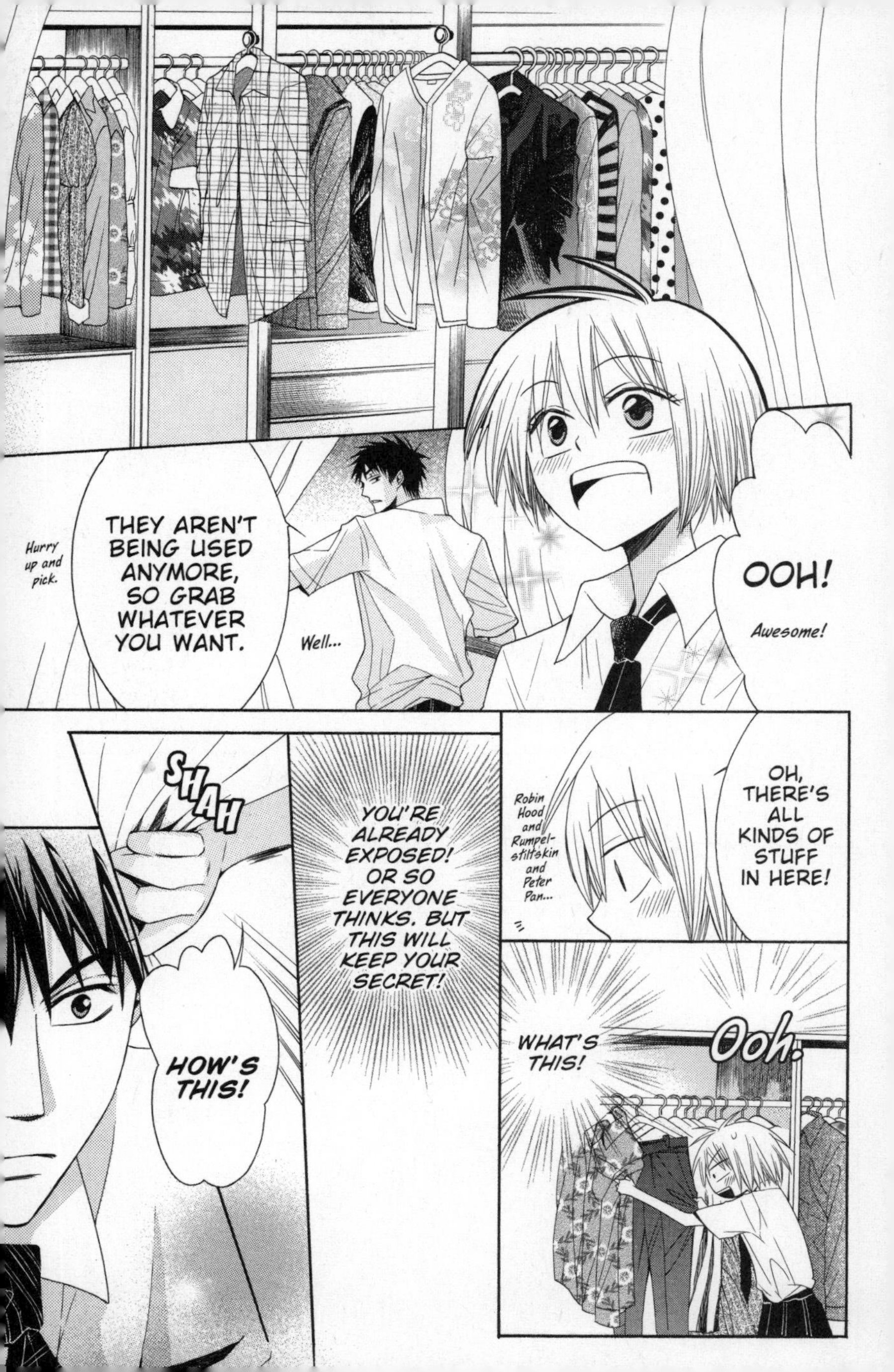
OOH!
Awesome!
Well...
THEY AREN'T BEING USED ANYMORE, SO GRAB WHATEVER YOU WANT.
Hurry up and pick.
OH, THERE'S ALL KINDS OF STUFF IN HERE!
Robin Hood and Rumpel-stiltskin and Peter Pan...
Ooh.
WHAT'S THIS!
YOU'RE ALREADY EXPOSED! OR SO EVERYONE THINKS. BUT THIS WILL KEEP YOUR SECRET!
SHAH
HOW'S THIS!

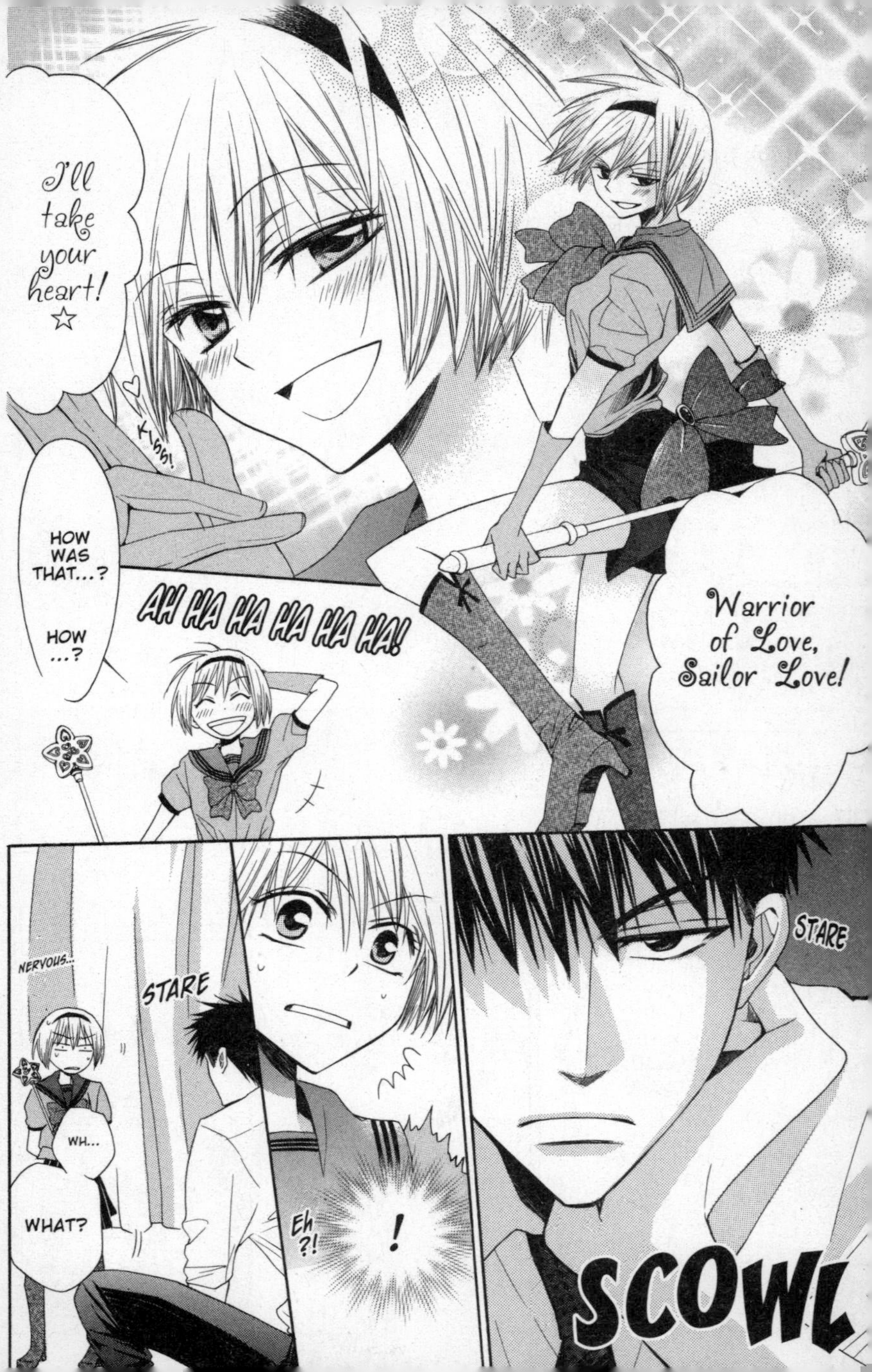
Warrior of Love, Sailor Love!
I'll take your heart! ☆
KISS!
AH HA HA HA HA HA HA!
HOW WAS THAT...?
HOW ...?
STARE
SCOWL
!
Eh ?!
NERVOUS...
STARE
WH...
WHAT?

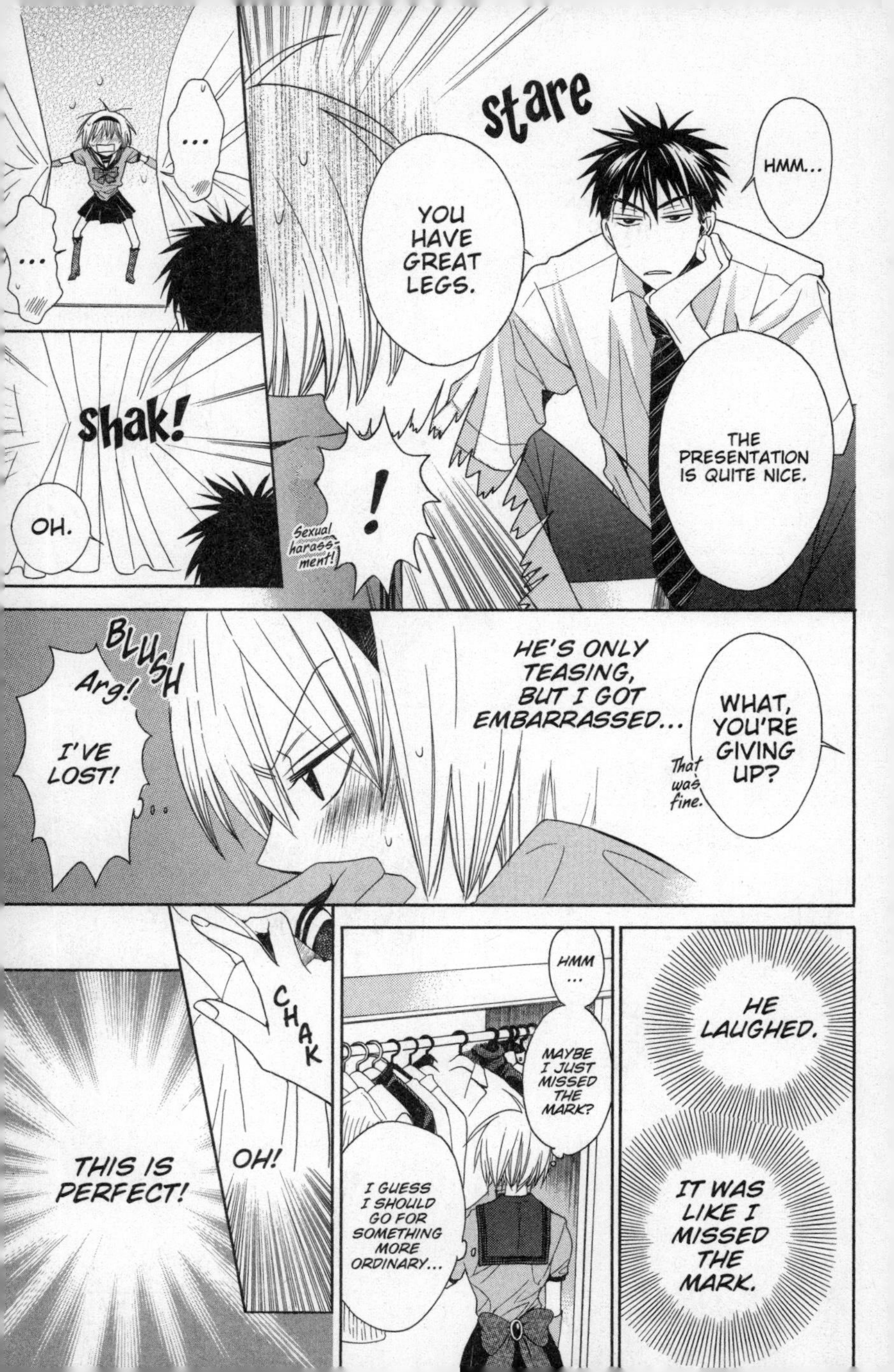
stare
HMM...
YOU HAVE GREAT LEGS.
THE PRESENTATION IS QUITE NICE.
!
Sexual harassment!
...
...
Shak!
OH.
WHAT, YOU'RE GIVING UP?
That was fine.
HE'S ONLY TEASING, BUT I GOT EMBARRASSED...
BLUSH
Arg!
I'VE LOST!
HE LAUGHED.
IT WAS LIKE I MISSED THE MARK.
HMM...
MAYBE I JUST MISSED THE MARK?
I GUESS I SHOULD GO FOR SOMETHING MORE ORDINARY...
CHAK
OH!
THIS IS PERFECT!

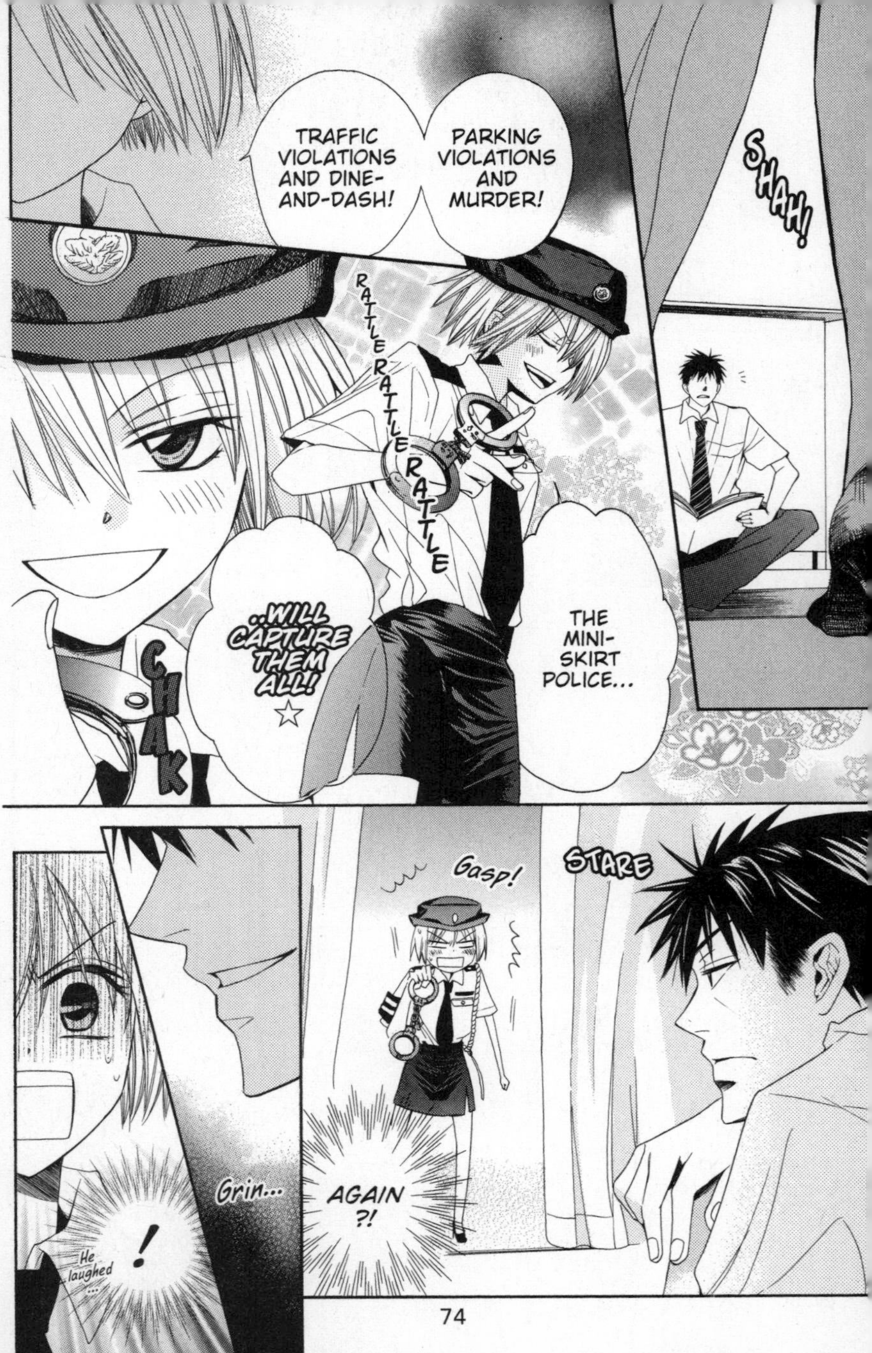
SHAH!
PARKING VIOLATIONS AND MURDER!
TRAFFIC VIOLATIONS AND DINE-AND-DASH!
RATTLE RATTLE RATTLE RATTLE
THE MINI-SKIRT POLICE...
..WILL CAPTURE THEM ALL! ☆
CHAK
STARE
Gasp!
AGAIN ?!
Grin...
!
He laughed...

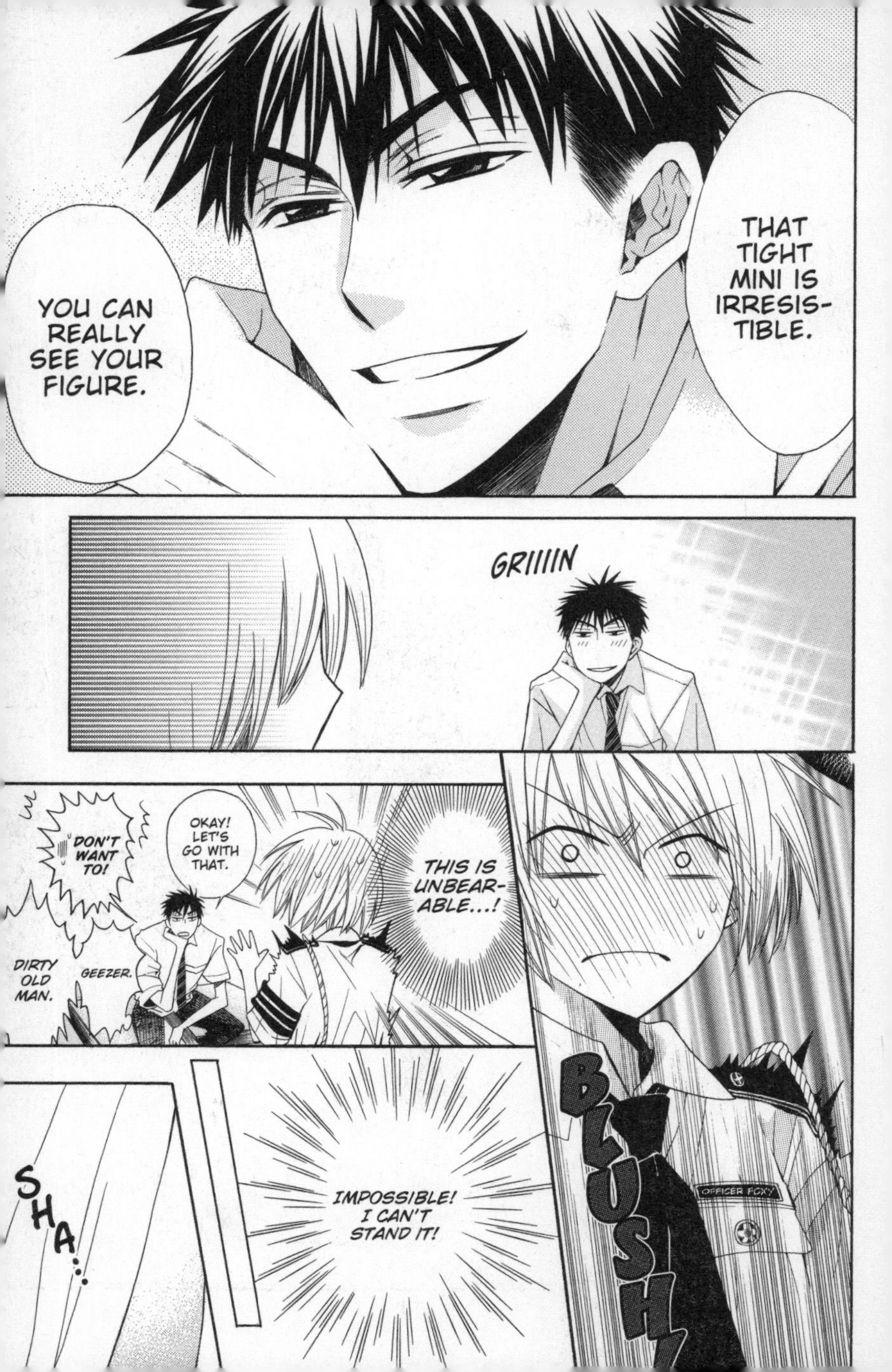
THAT TIGHT MINI IS IRRESIS-TIBLE.
YOU CAN REALLY SEE YOUR FIGURE.
GRIIIIN
BLUSH
OFFICER FOXY
THIS IS UNBEARABLE...!
OKAY! LET'S GO WITH THAT.
DON'T WANT TO!
GEEZER.
DIRTY OLD MAN.
IMPOSSIBLE! I CAN'T STAND IT!
SHA...

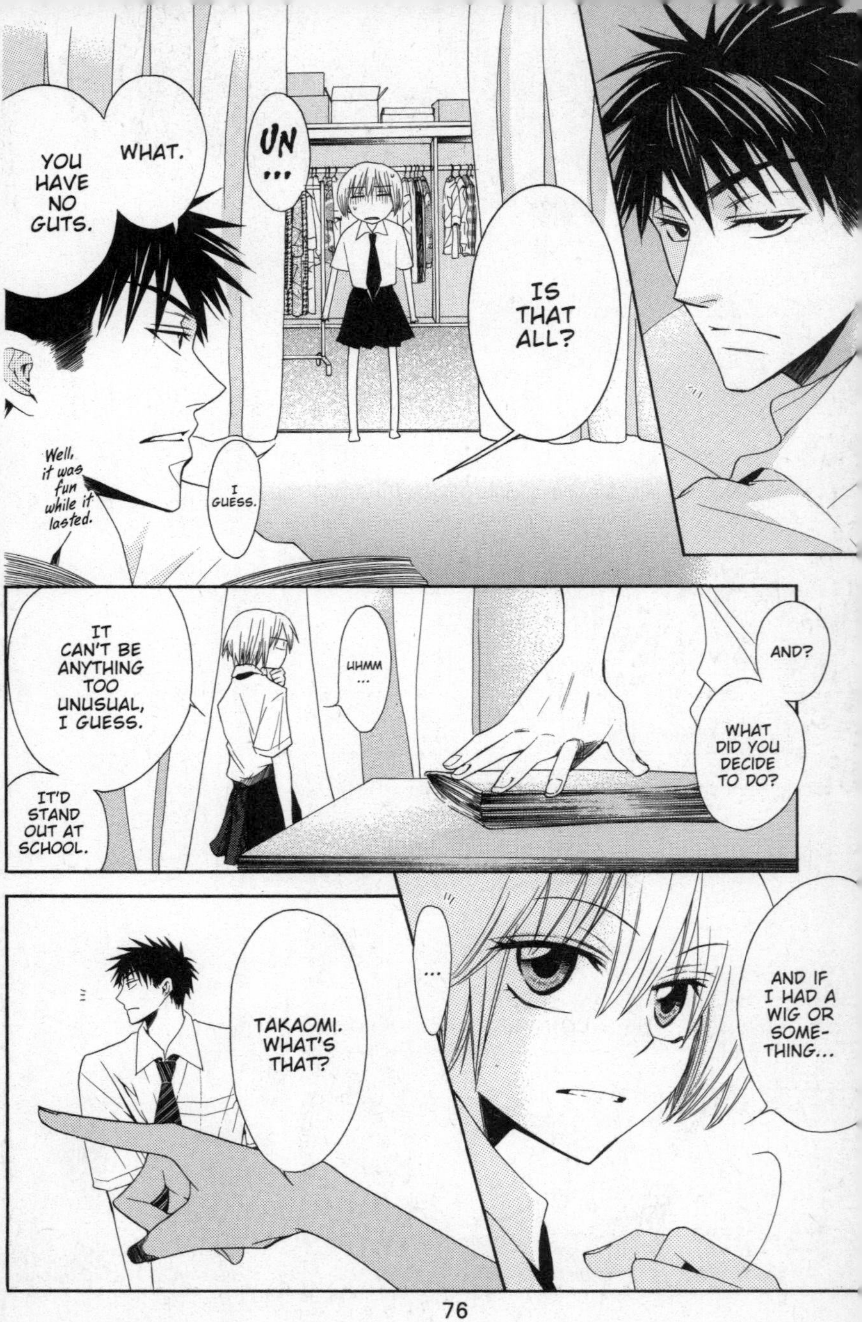
IS THAT ALL?
UN...
WHAT.
YOU HAVE NO GUTS.
I GUESS.
Well, it was fun while it lasted.
AND?
WHAT DID YOU DECIDE TO DO?
UHMM...
IT CAN'T BE ANYTHING TOO UNUSUAL, I GUESS.
IT'D STAND OUT AT SCHOOL.
AND IF I HAD A WIG OR SOME-THING...
...
TAKAOMI. WHAT'S THAT?

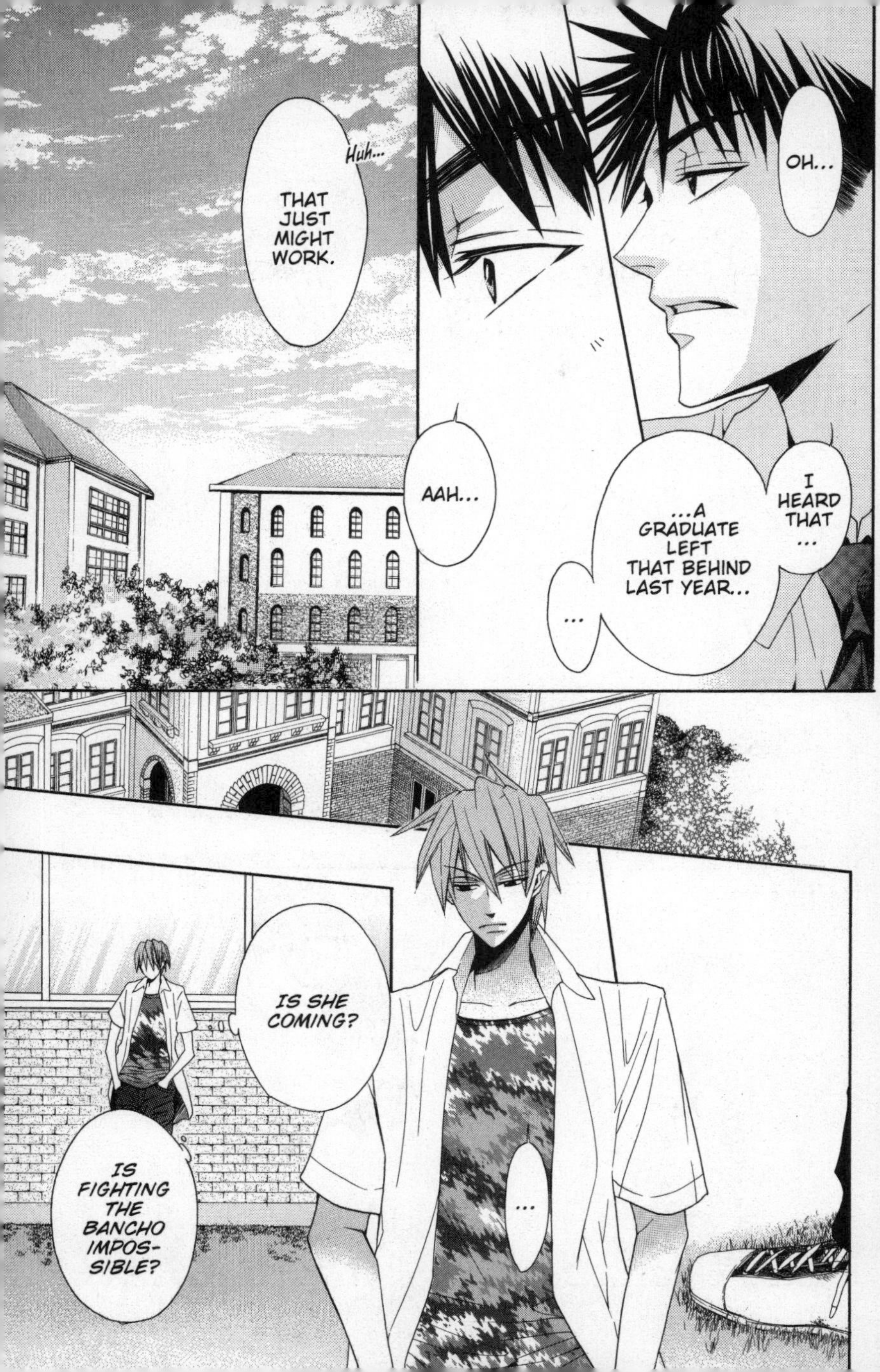
OH...
I HEARD THAT ...
...A GRADUATE LEFT THAT BEHIND LAST YEAR...
...
AAH...
Huh...
THAT JUST MIGHT WORK.
...
IS SHE COMING?
IS FIGHTING THE BANCHO IMPOSSIBLE?

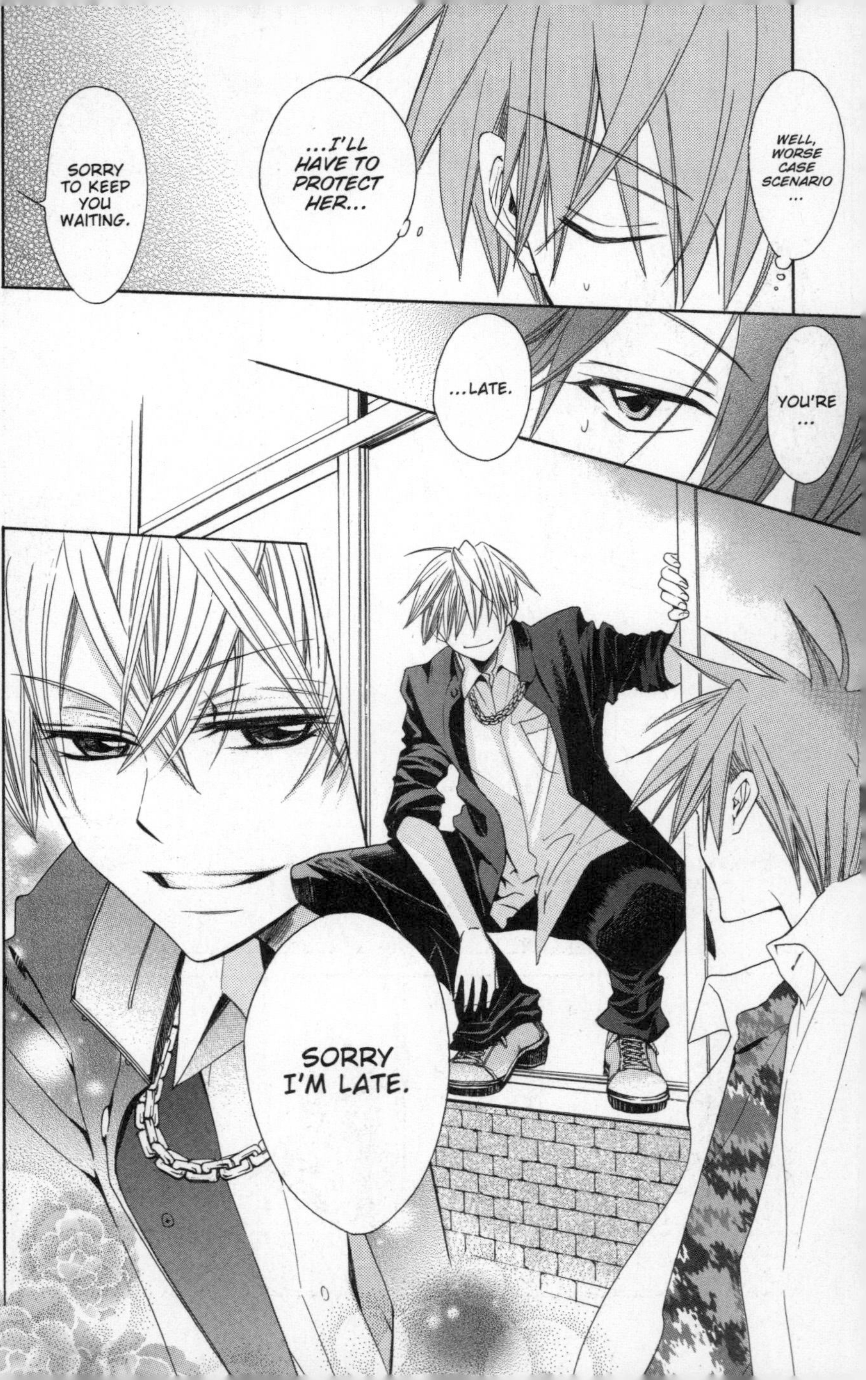
WELL, WORSE CASE SCENARIO ...
...I'LL HAVE TO PROTECT HER...
SORRY TO KEEP YOU WAITING.
YOU'RE ...
...LATE.
SORRY I'M LATE.

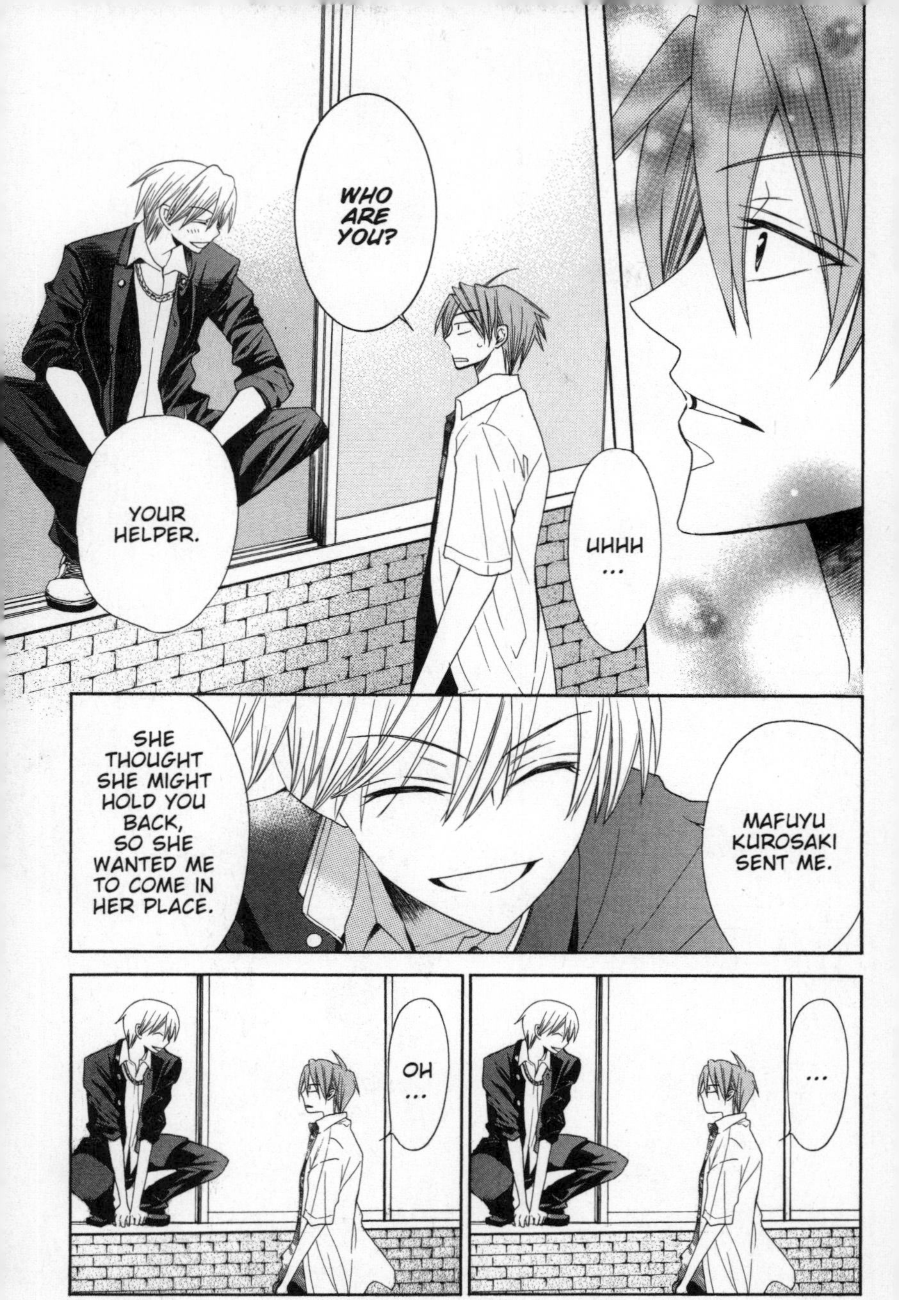
UHHH ...
WHO ARE YOU?
YOUR HELPER.
MAFUYU KUROSAKI SENT ME.
SHE THOUGHT SHE MIGHT HOLD YOU BACK, SO SHE WANTED ME TO COME IN HER PLACE.
...
OH ...

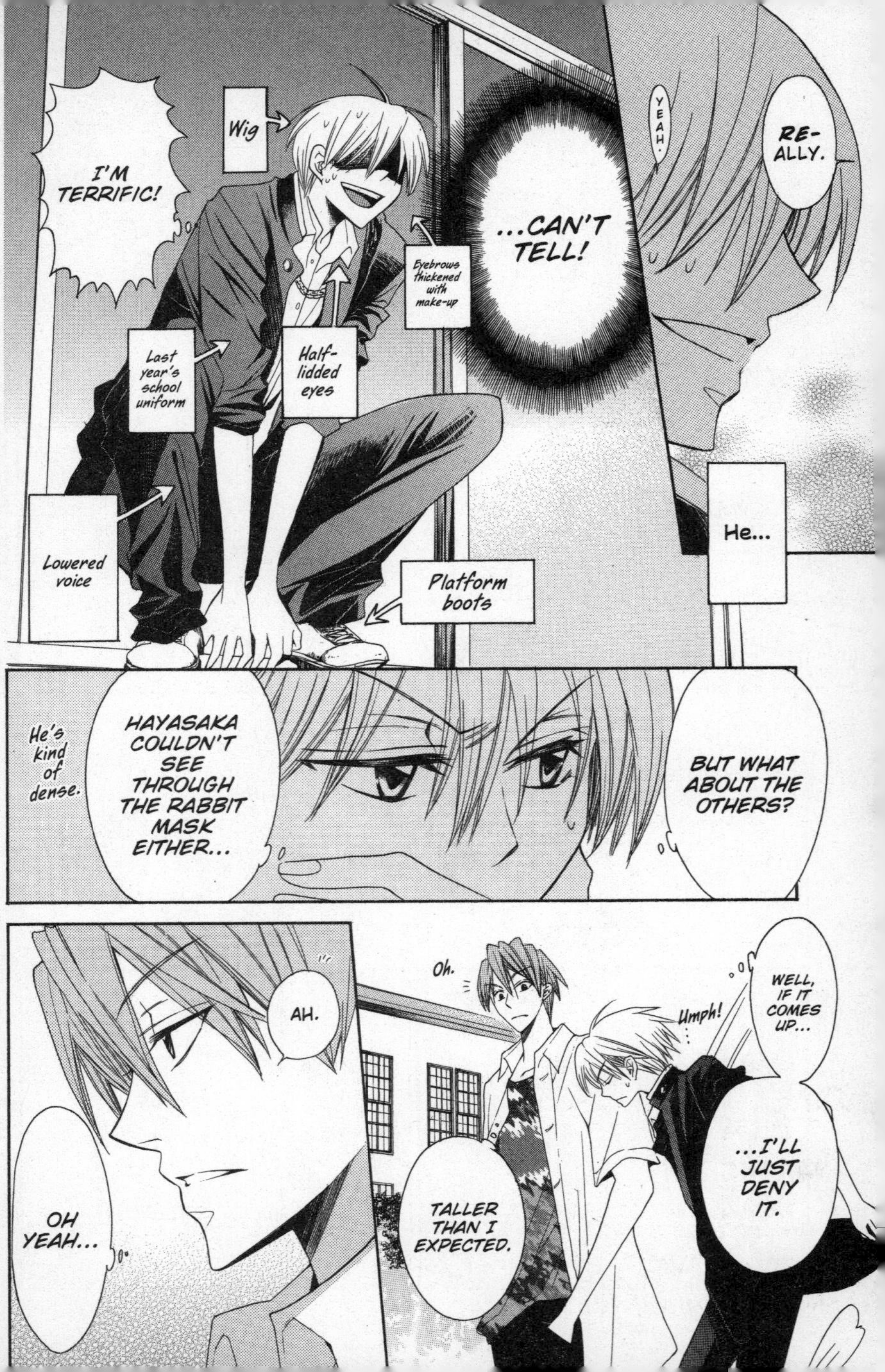

RE-ALLY.
YEAH.
He...
...CAN'T TELL!
I'M TERRIFIC!
Wig
Eyebrows thickened with make-up
Half-lidded eyes
Last year's school uniform
Lowered voice
Platform boots
BUT WHAT ABOUT THE OTHERS?
HAYASAKA COULDN'T SEE THROUGH THE RABBIT MASK EITHER...
He's kind of dense.
WELL, IF IT COMES UP...
...I'LL JUST DENY IT.
Umph!
Oh.
TALLER THAN I EXPECTED.
AH.
OH YEAH...

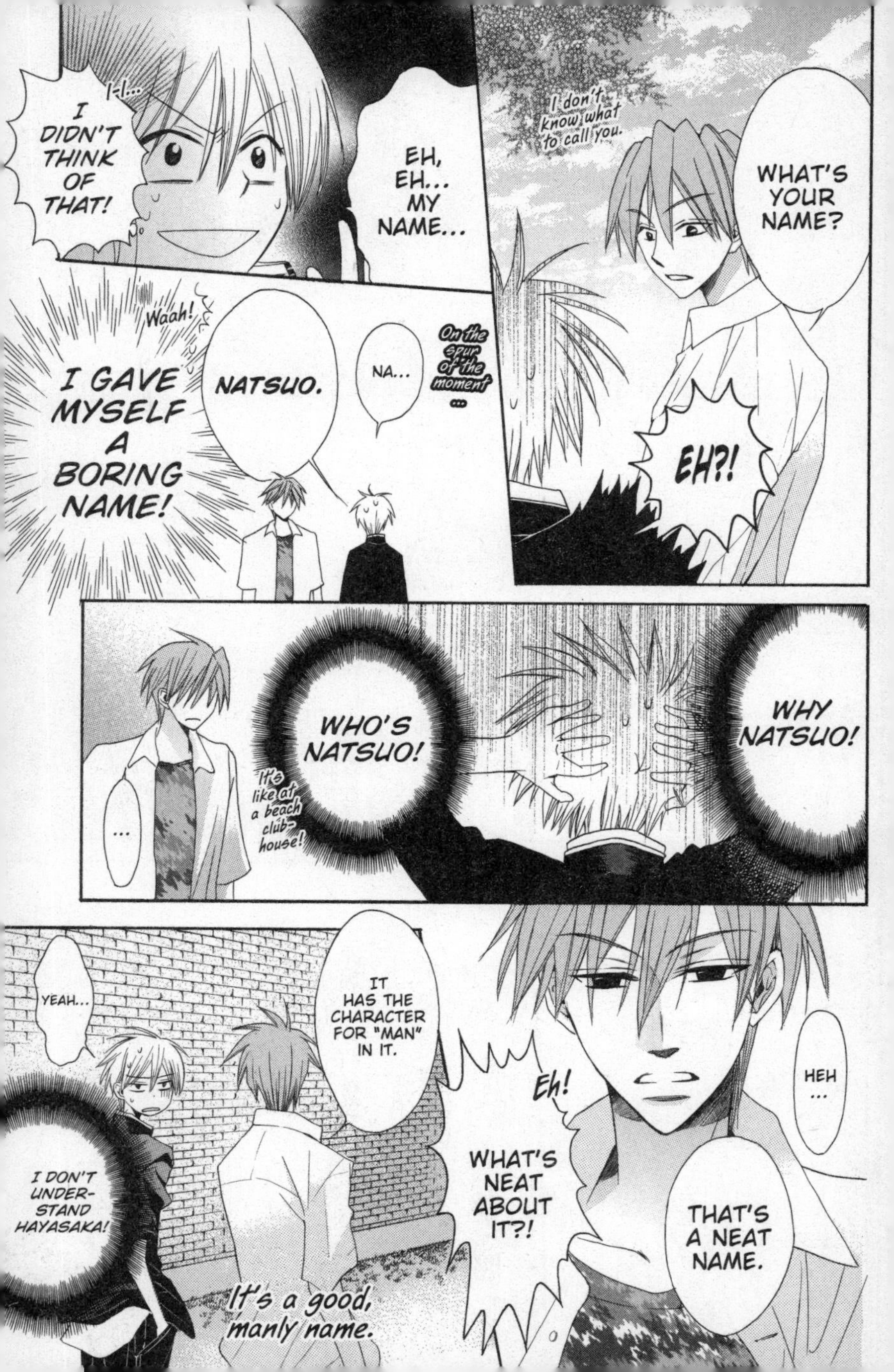
WHAT'S YOUR NAME?
I don't know what to call you.
EH?!
EH, EH... MY NAME...
I-I...
I DIDN'T THINK OF THAT!
On the spur of the moment...
NA...
NATSUO.
Waah!
I GAVE MYSELF A BORING NAME!
WHY NATSUO!
WHO'S NATSUO!
It's like at a beach club-house!
...
HEH...
THAT'S A NEAT NAME.
WHAT'S NEAT ABOUT IT?!
Eh!
IT HAS THE CHARACTER FOR "MAN" IN IT.
YEAH...
I DON'T UNDER-STAND HAYASAKA!
It's a good, manly name.

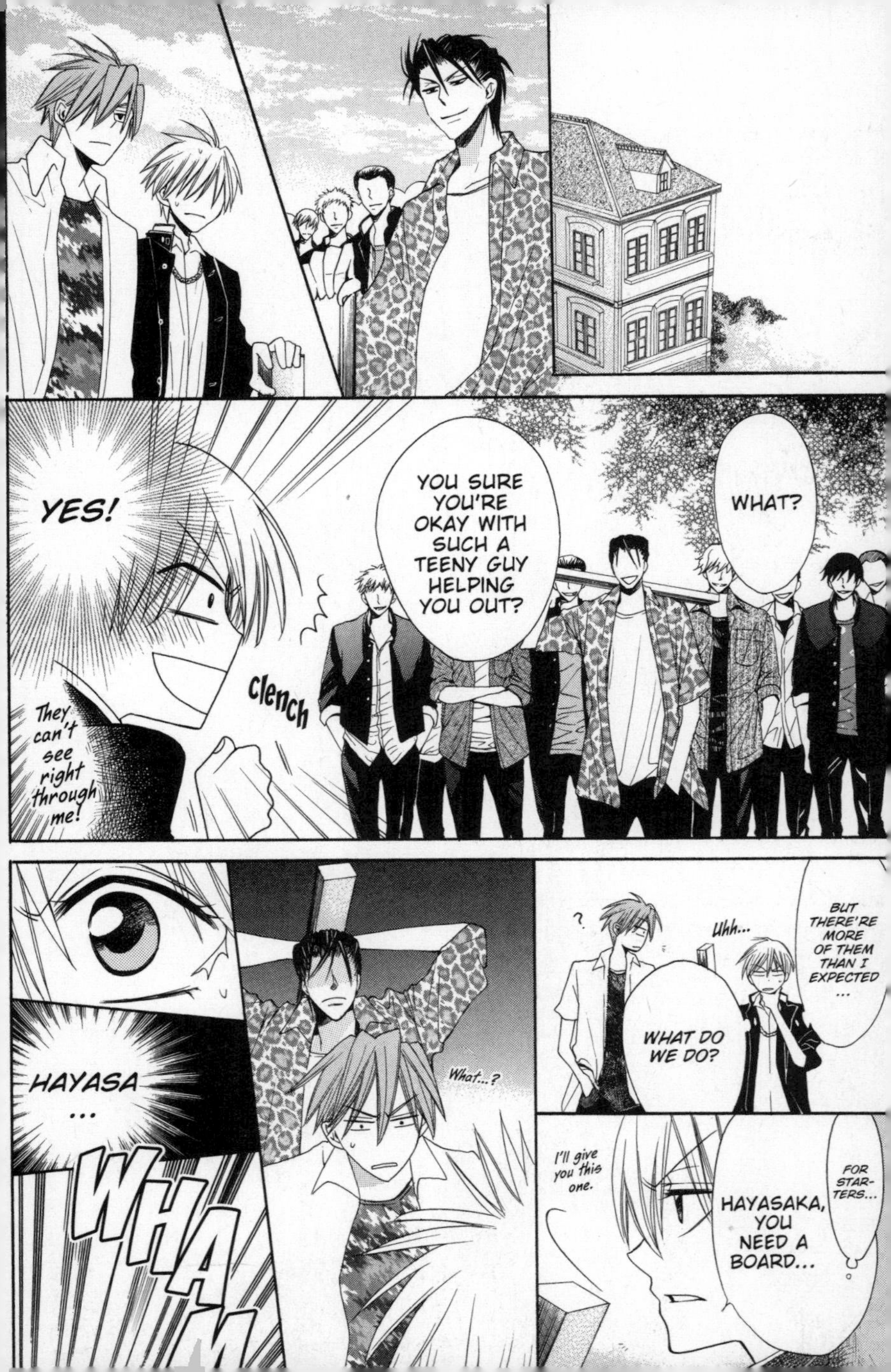
WHAT?
YOU SURE YOU'RE OKAY WITH SUCH A TEENY GUY HELPING YOU OUT?
YES!
clench
They can't see right through me!
BUT THERE'RE MORE OF THEM THAN I EXPECTED ...
Uhh...
WHAT DO WE DO?
FOR STARTERS...
HAYASAKA, YOU NEED A BOARD...
I'll give you this one.
What...?
HAYASA ...
WHAM

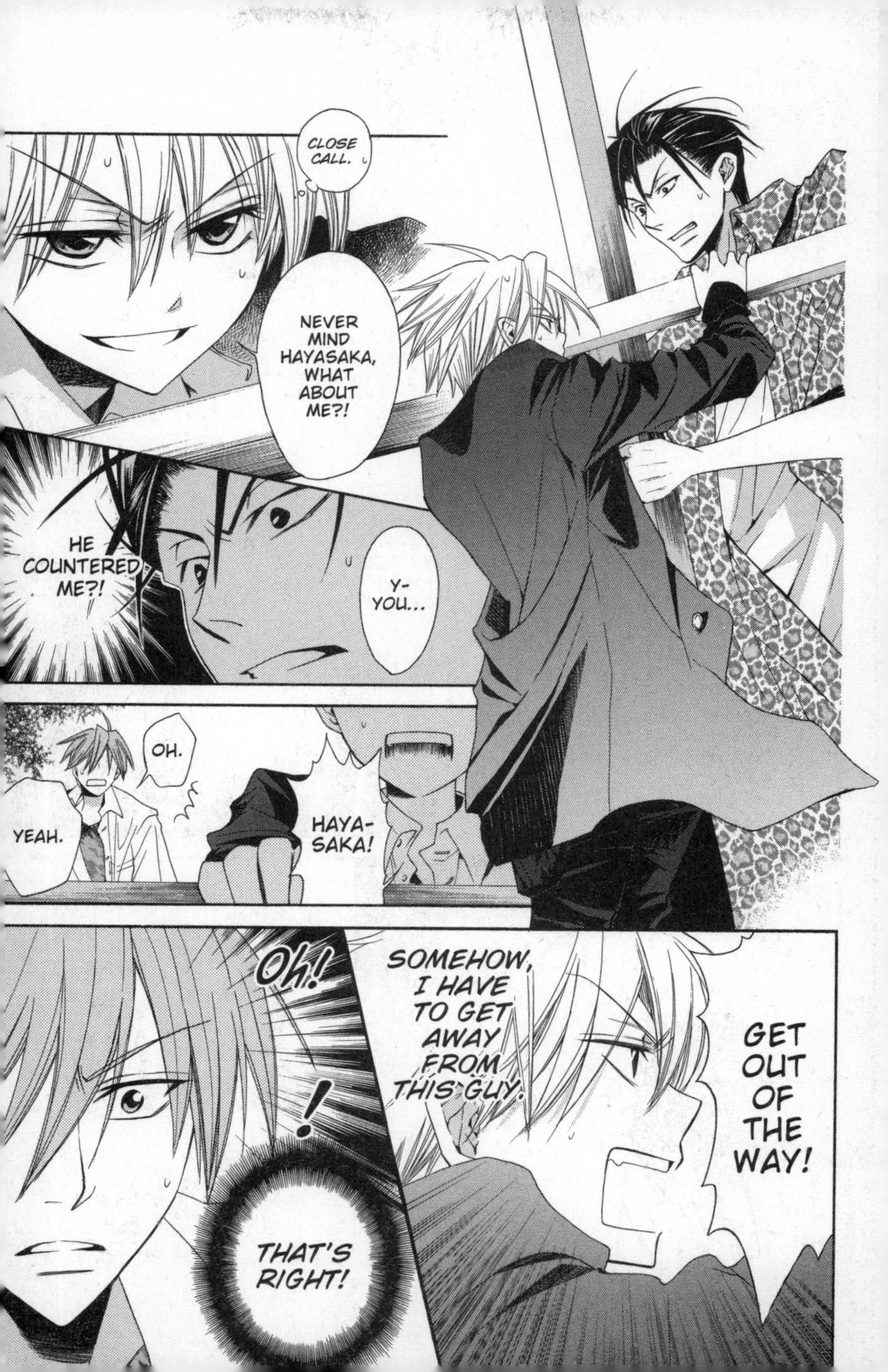
NEVER MIND HAYASAKA, WHAT ABOUT ME?!
CLOSE CALL.
Y- YOU...
HE COUNTERED ME?!
HAYA- SAKA!
OH.
YEAH.
GET OUT OF THE WAY!
SOMEHOW, I HAVE TO GET AWAY FROM THIS GUY.
Oh!
!
THAT'S RIGHT!

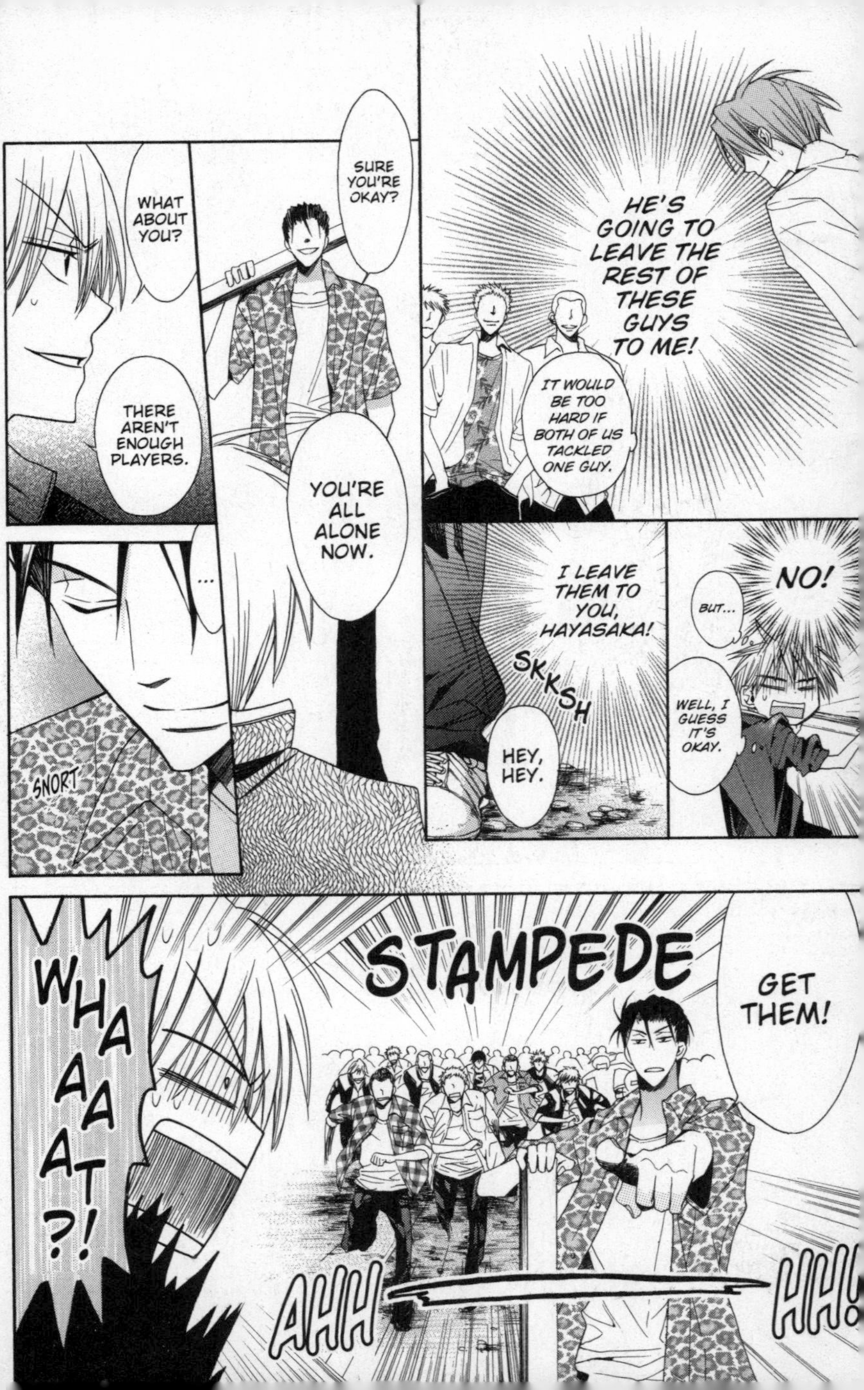
HE'S GOING TO LEAVE THE REST OF THESE GUYS TO ME!
IT WOULD BE TOO HARD IF BOTH OF US TACKLED ONE GUY.
SURE YOU'RE OKAY?
WHAT ABOUT YOU?
THERE AREN'T ENOUGH PLAYERS.
NO!
BUT...
WELL, I GUESS IT'S OKAY.
I LEAVE THEM TO YOU, HAYASAKA!
SKKSH
HEY, HEY.
YOU'RE ALL ALONE NOW.
...
SNORT
GET THEM!
STAMPEDE
AHH HH!
WHAAAAT?!

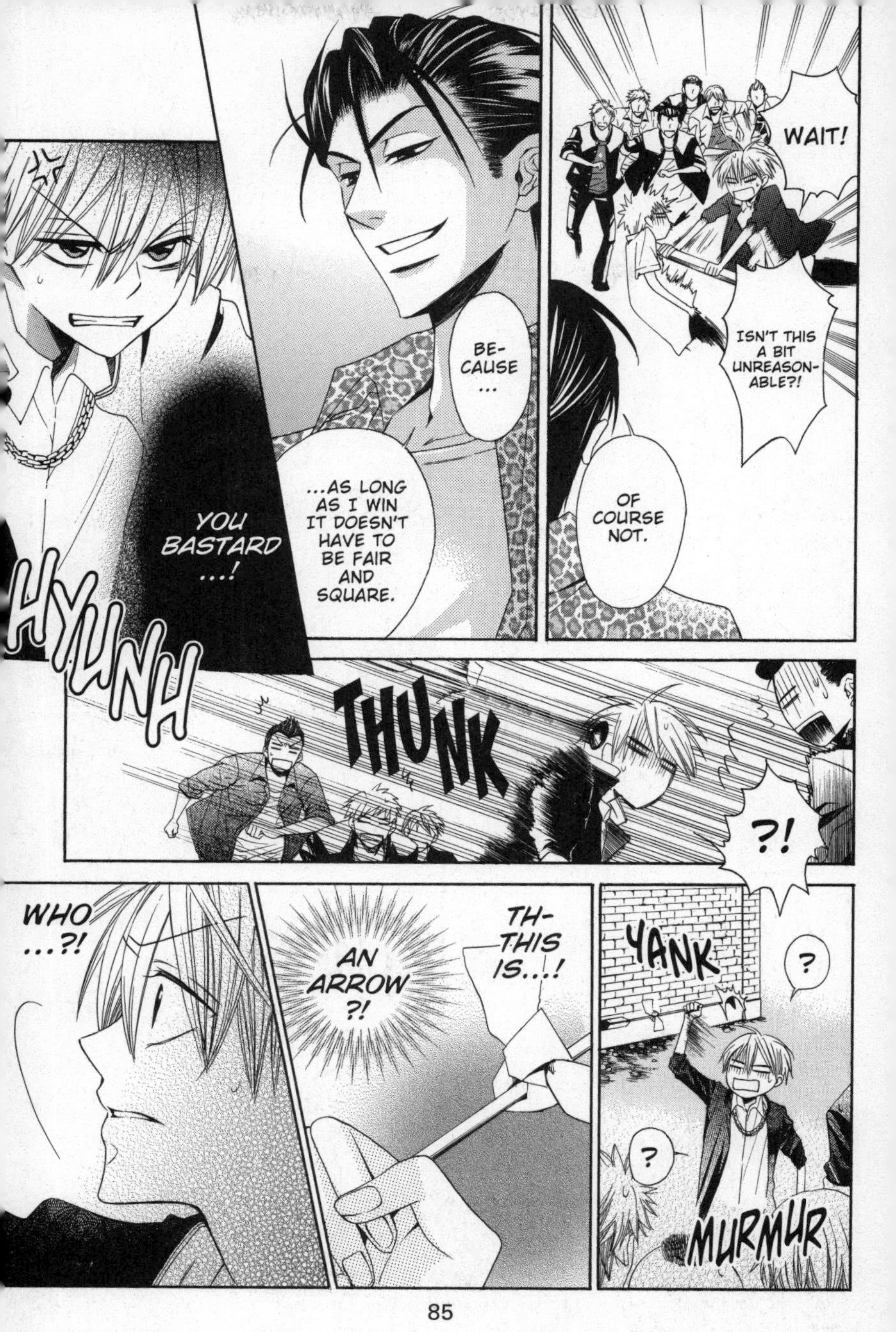
WAIT!
ISN'T THIS A BIT UNREASONABLE?!
OF COURSE NOT.
BE-CAUSE...
...AS LONG AS I WIN IT DOESN'T HAVE TO BE FAIR AND SQUARE.
YOU BASTARD...!
HYUNH
THUNK
?!
YANK
?
?
MURMUR
TH-THIS IS...!
AN ARROW?!
WHO...?!

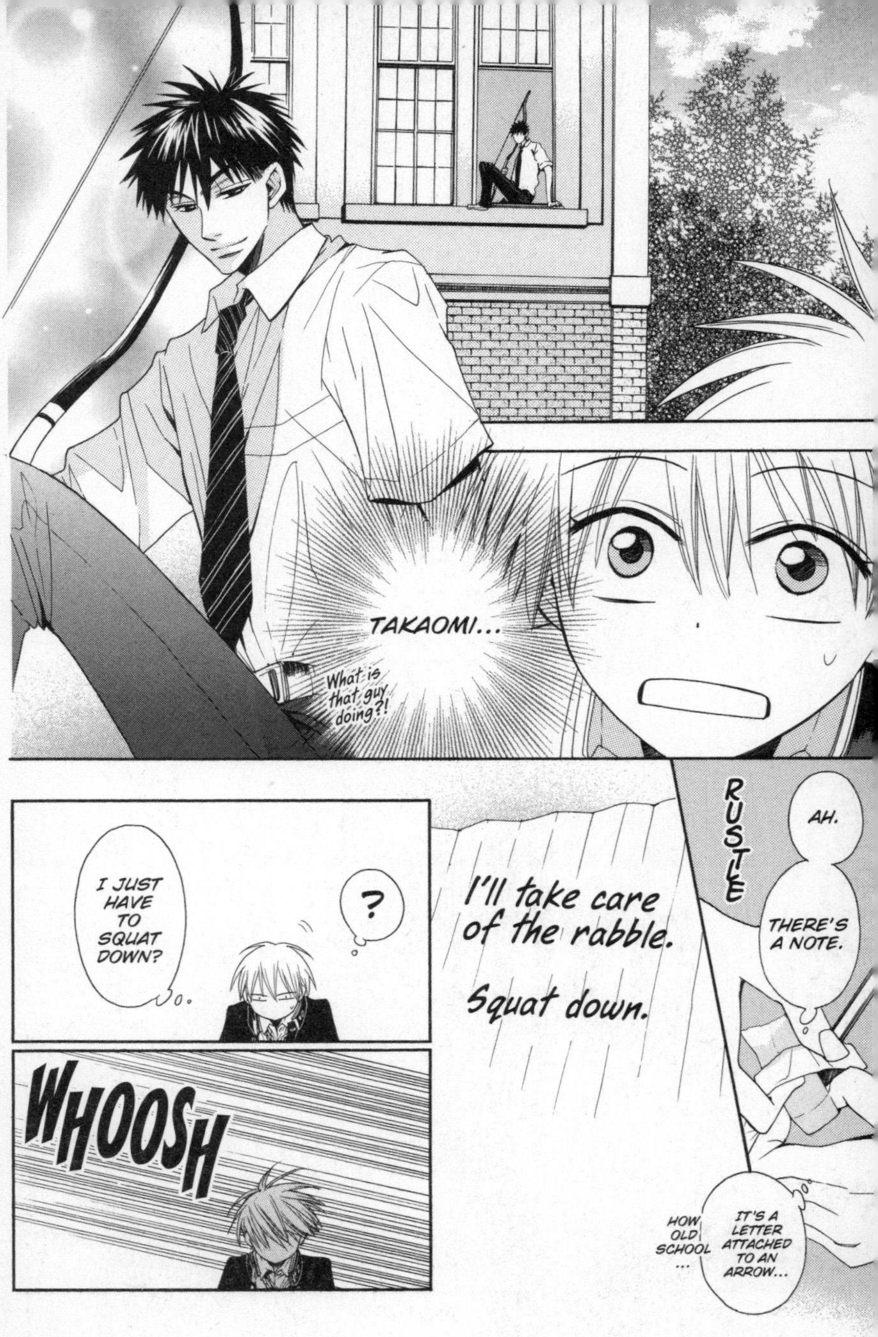
TAKAOMI...
What is that guy doing?!
RUSTLE
AH.
THERE'S A NOTE.
I'll take care of the rabble.
Squat down.
IT'S A LETTER ATTACHED TO AN ARROW...
HOW OLD SCHOOL...
I JUST HAVE TO SQUAT DOWN?
?
WHOOSH

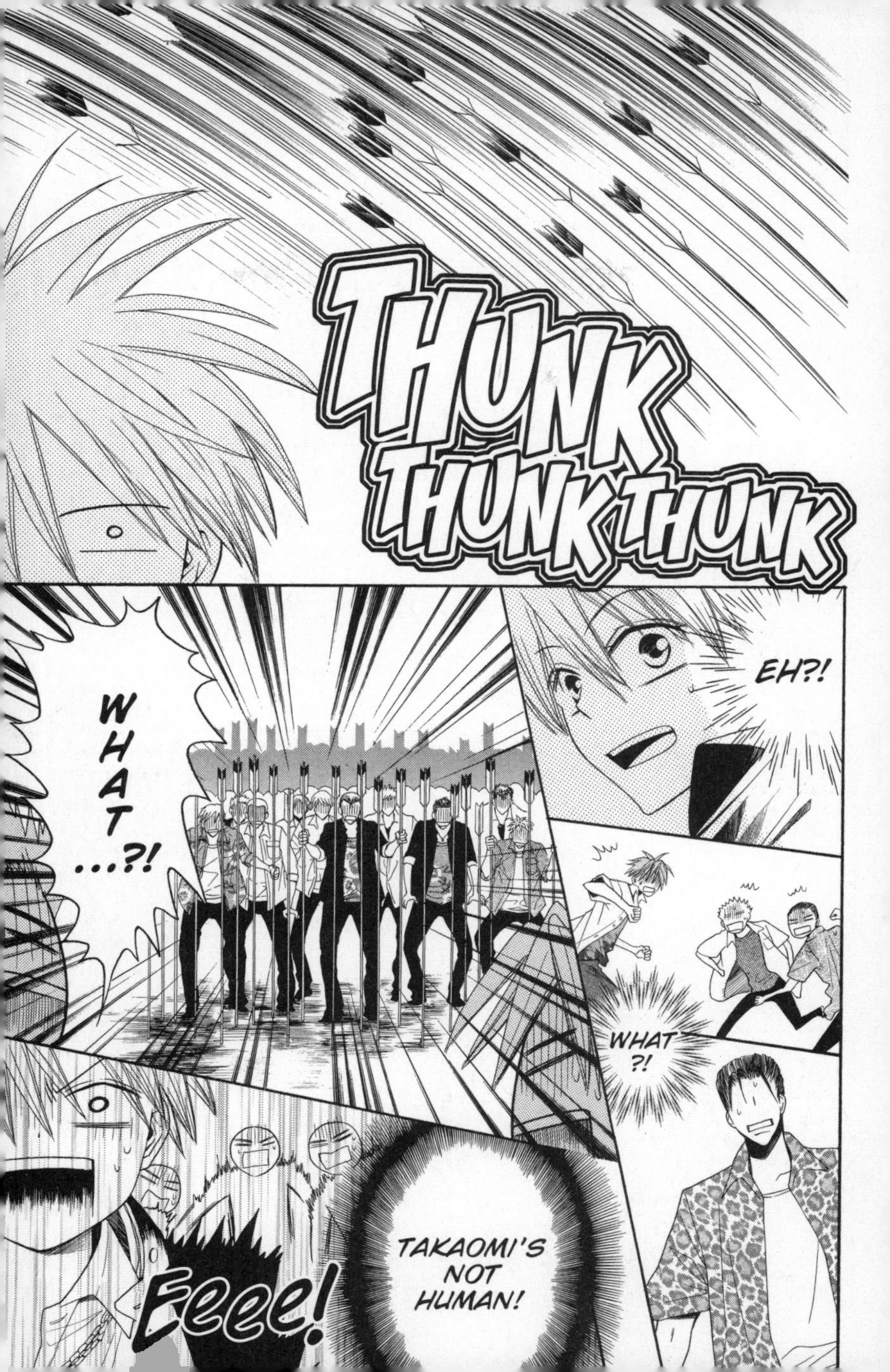
THUNK
THUNK THUNK
EH?!
WHAT...?!
WHAT?!
TAKAOMI'S NOT HUMAN!
Feee!

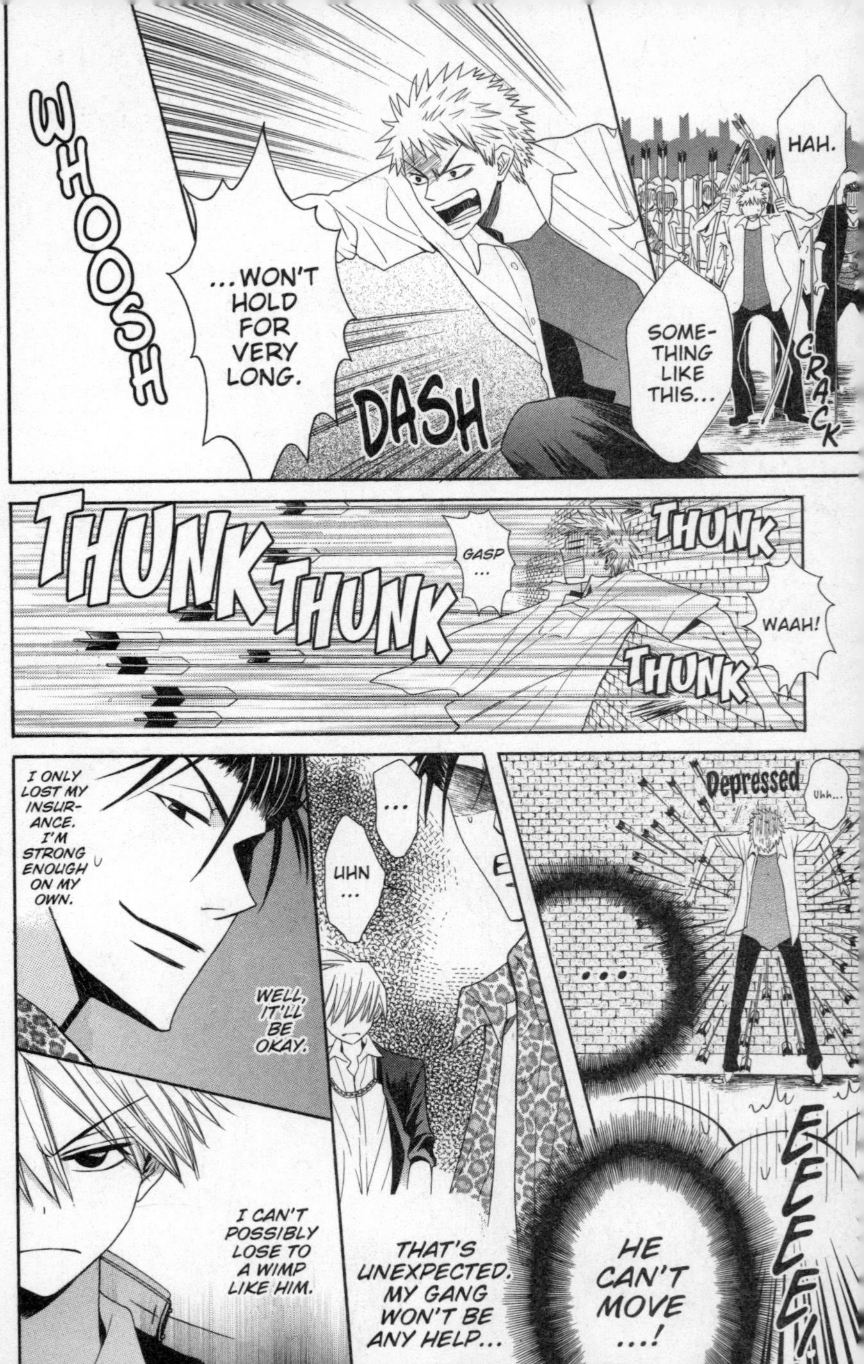
HAH.
SOME-THING LIKE THIS...
CRACK
...WON'T HOLD FOR VERY LONG.
DASH
WHOOSH
THUNK
WAAH!
THUNK
GASP...
THUNK THUNK
Depressed
Uhh...
...
HE CAN'T MOVE...!
EEEE!
...
UHN...
THAT'S UNEXPECTED. MY GANG WON'T BE ANY HELP...
I ONLY LOST MY INSUR-ANCE. I'M STRONG ENOUGH ON MY OWN.
WELL, IT'LL BE OKAY.
I CAN'T POSSIBLY LOSE TO A WIMP LIKE HIM.

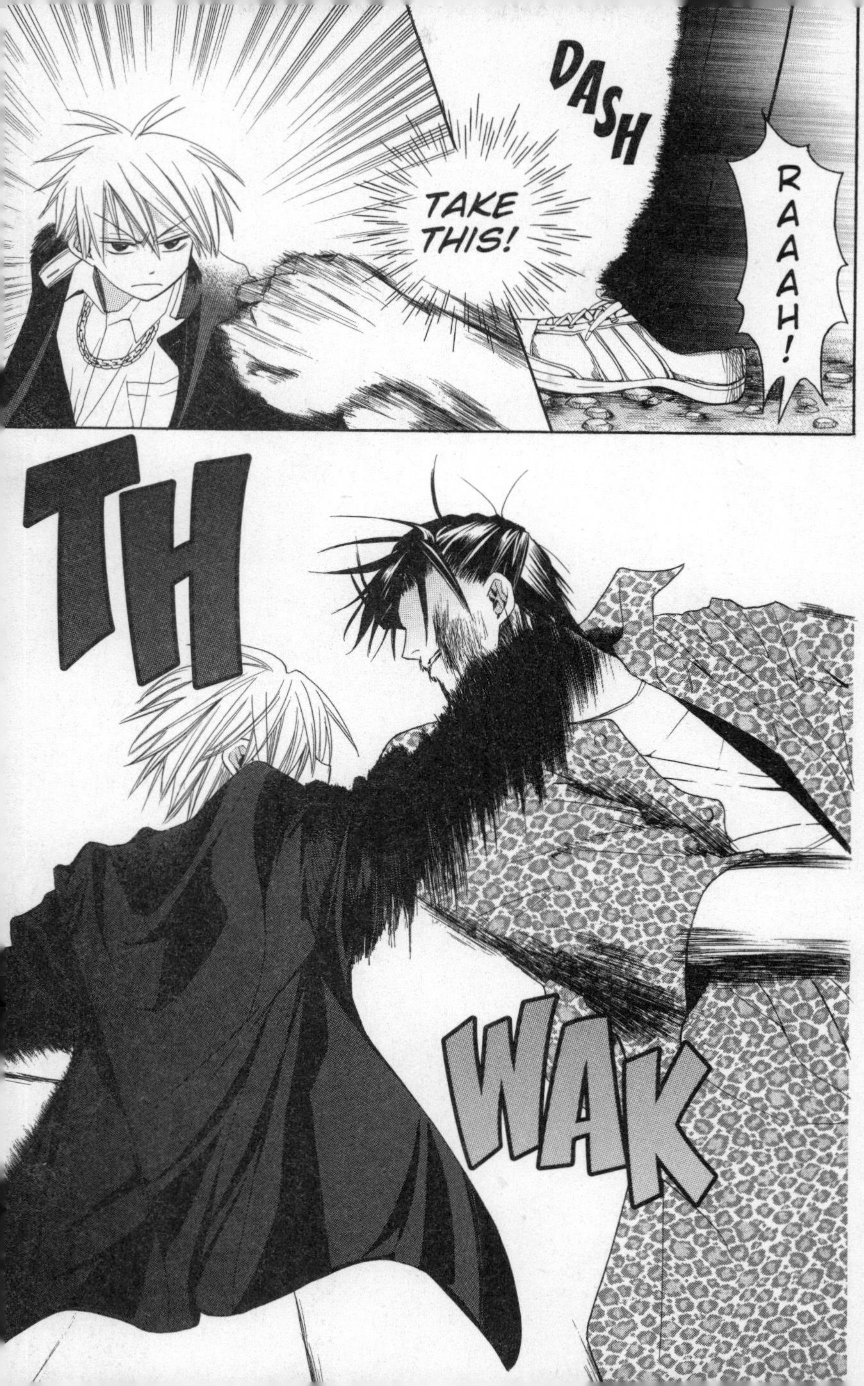
RAAAAH!
DASH
TAKE THIS!
TH
WAK

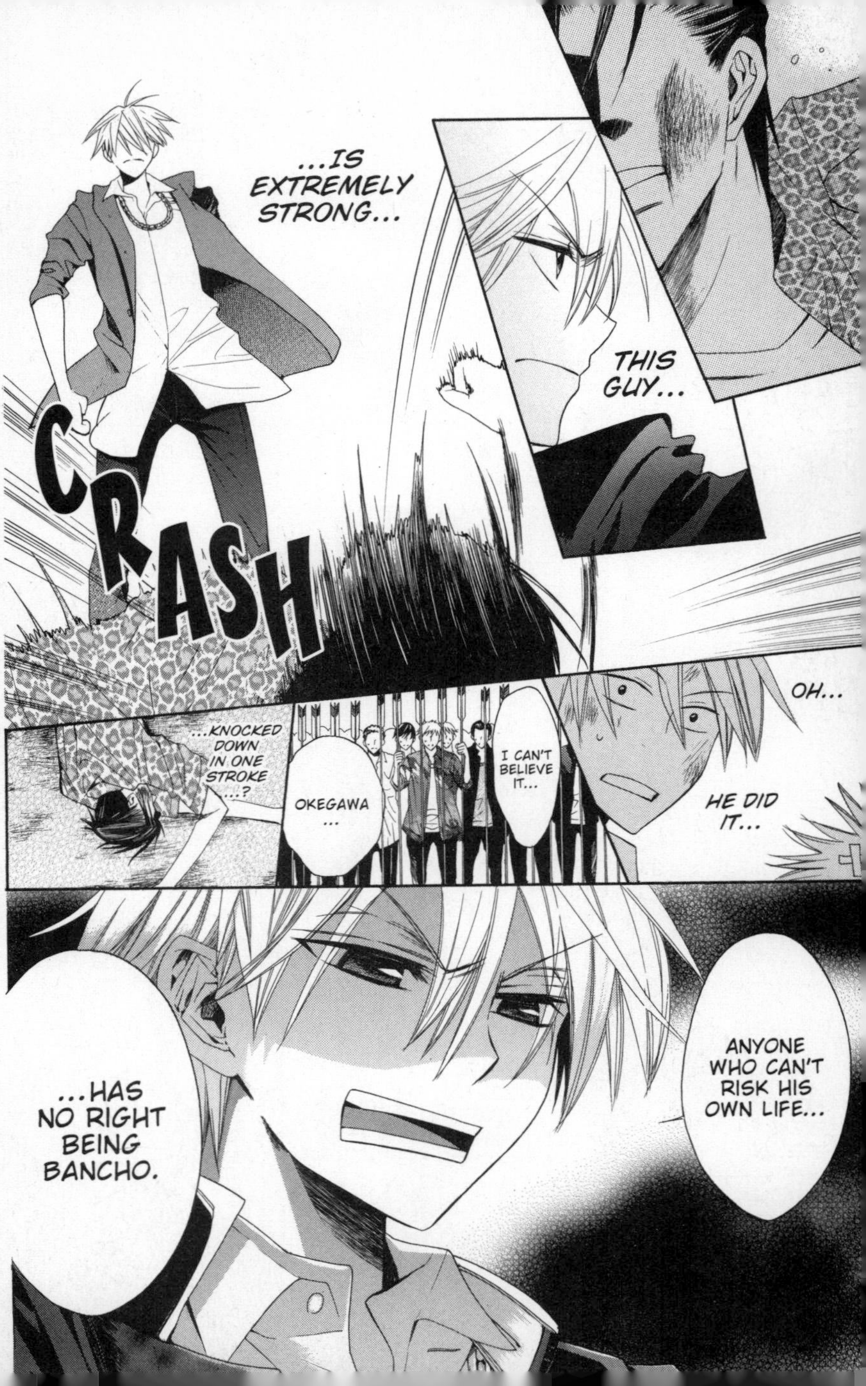
THIS GUY...
...IS EXTREMELY STRONG...
CRASH
OH...
HE DID IT...
I CAN'T BELIEVE IT...
OKEGAWA...
...KNOCKED DOWN IN ONE STROKE ...?
ANYONE WHO CAN'T RISK HIS OWN LIFE...
...HAS NO RIGHT BEING BANCHO.

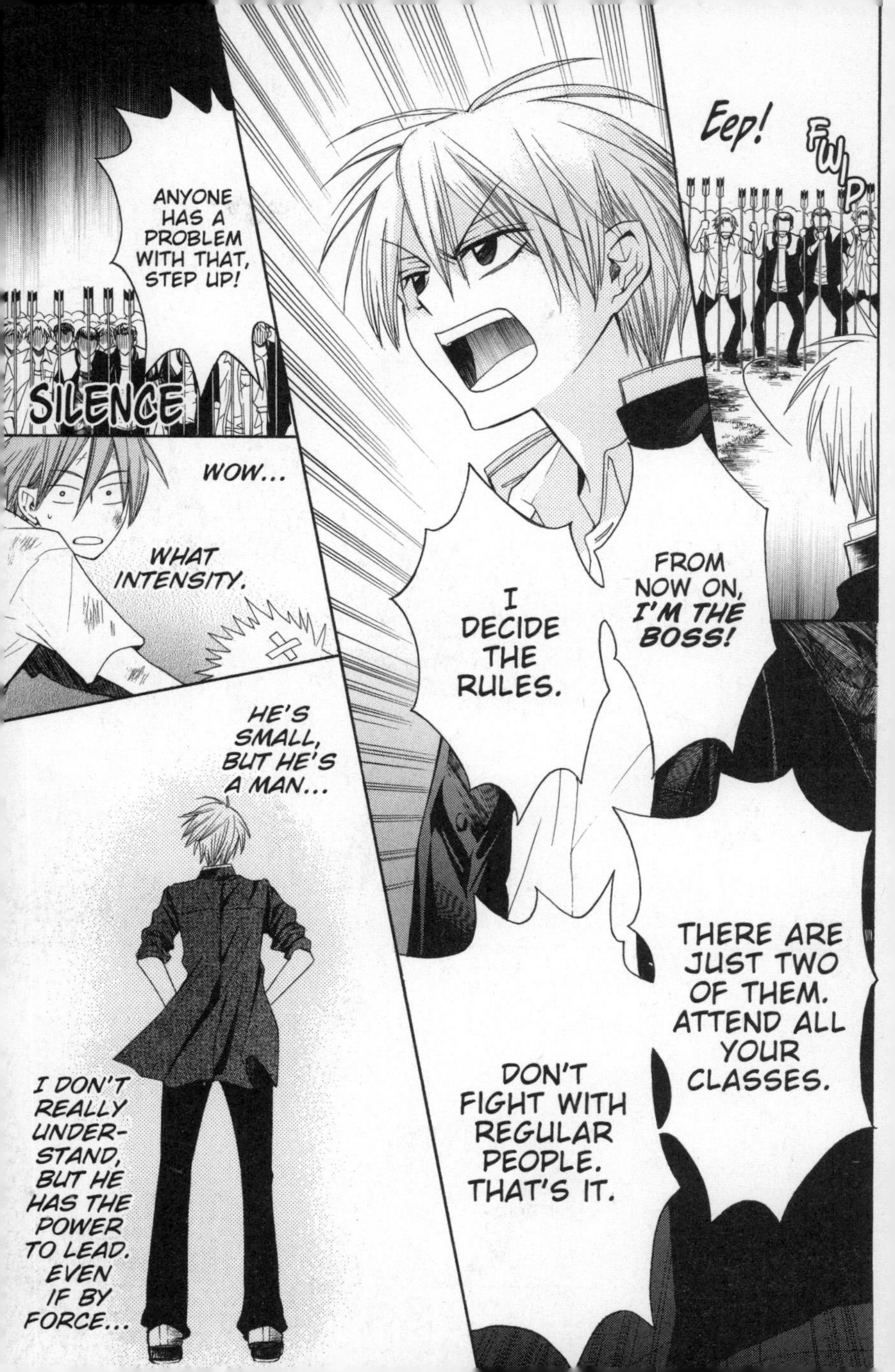
Eep!
FWIP
FROM NOW ON, I'M THE BOSS!
I DECIDE THE RULES.
THERE ARE JUST TWO OF THEM. ATTEND ALL YOUR CLASSES.
DON'T FIGHT WITH REGULAR PEOPLE. THAT'S IT.
ANYONE HAS A PROBLEM WITH THAT, STEP UP!
SILENCE
WOW...
WHAT INTENSITY.
HE'S SMALL, BUT HE'S A MAN...
I DON'T REALLY UNDER-STAND, BUT HE HAS THE POWER TO LEAD. EVEN IF BY FORCE...

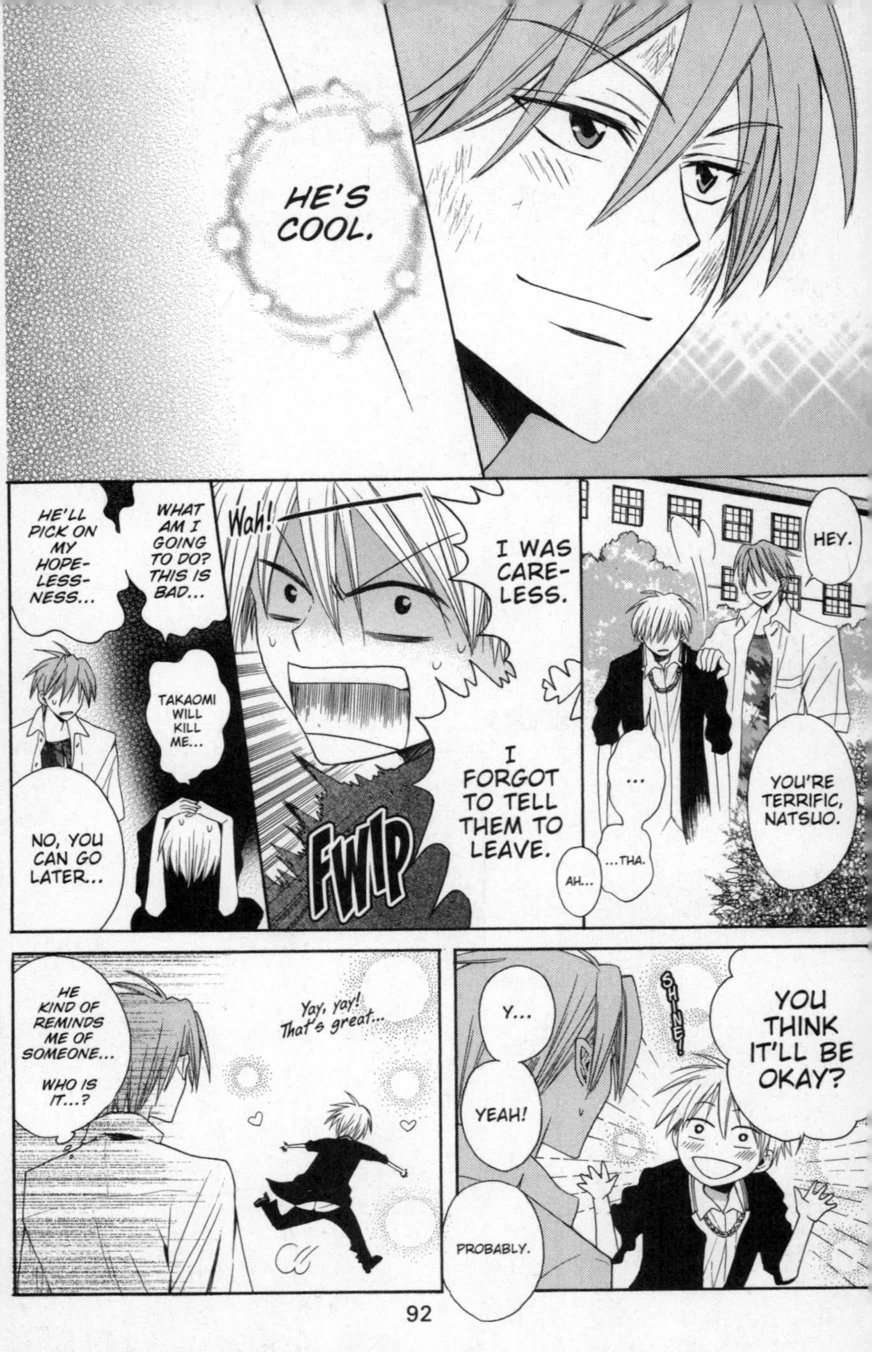
HE'S COOL.
HEY.
YOU'RE TERRIFIC, NATSUO.
...
...THA.
AH...
Wah!
I WAS CARELESS.
I FORGOT TO TELL THEM TO LEAVE.
FWIP
WHAT AM I GOING TO DO? THIS IS BAD...
HE'LL PICK ON MY HOPELESSNESS...
TAKAOMI WILL KILL ME...
NO, YOU CAN GO LATER...
YOU THINK IT'LL BE OKAY?
SHINE!
Y...
YEAH!
PROBABLY.
Yay, yay! That's great...
HE KIND OF REMINDS ME OF SOMEONE...
WHO IS IT...?

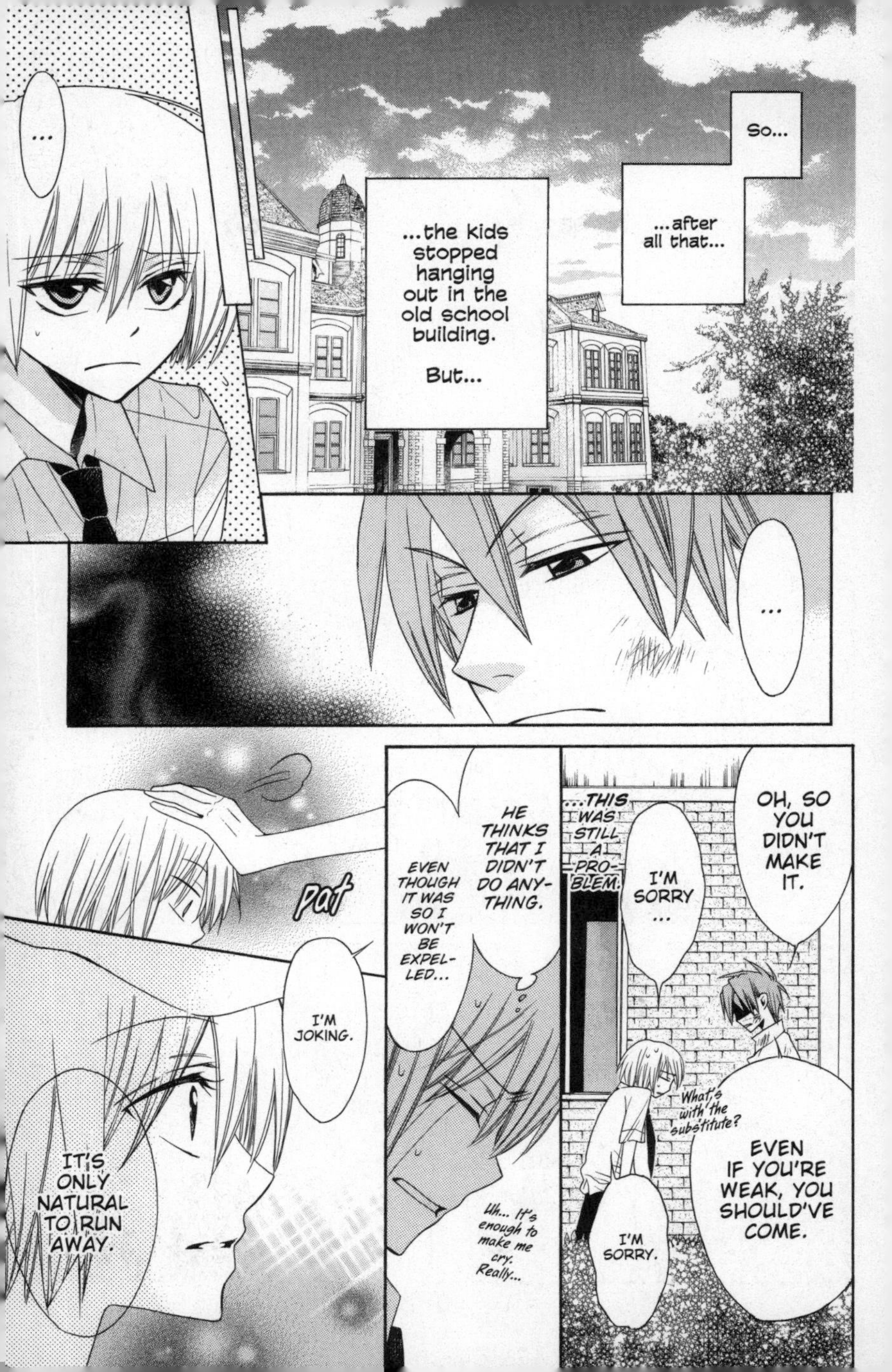
So...
...after all that...
...the kids stopped hanging out in the old school building.
But...
...
...
OH, SO YOU DIDN'T MAKE IT.
I'M SORRY...
...THIS WAS STILL A PROBLEM.
What's with the substitute?
EVEN IF YOU'RE WEAK, YOU SHOULD'VE COME.
I'M SORRY.
HE THINKS THAT I DIDN'T DO ANYTHING.
EVEN THOUGH IT WAS SO I WON'T BE EXPELLED...
Uh... It's enough to make me cry. Really...
pat
I'M JOKING.
IT'S ONLY NATURAL TO RUN AWAY.

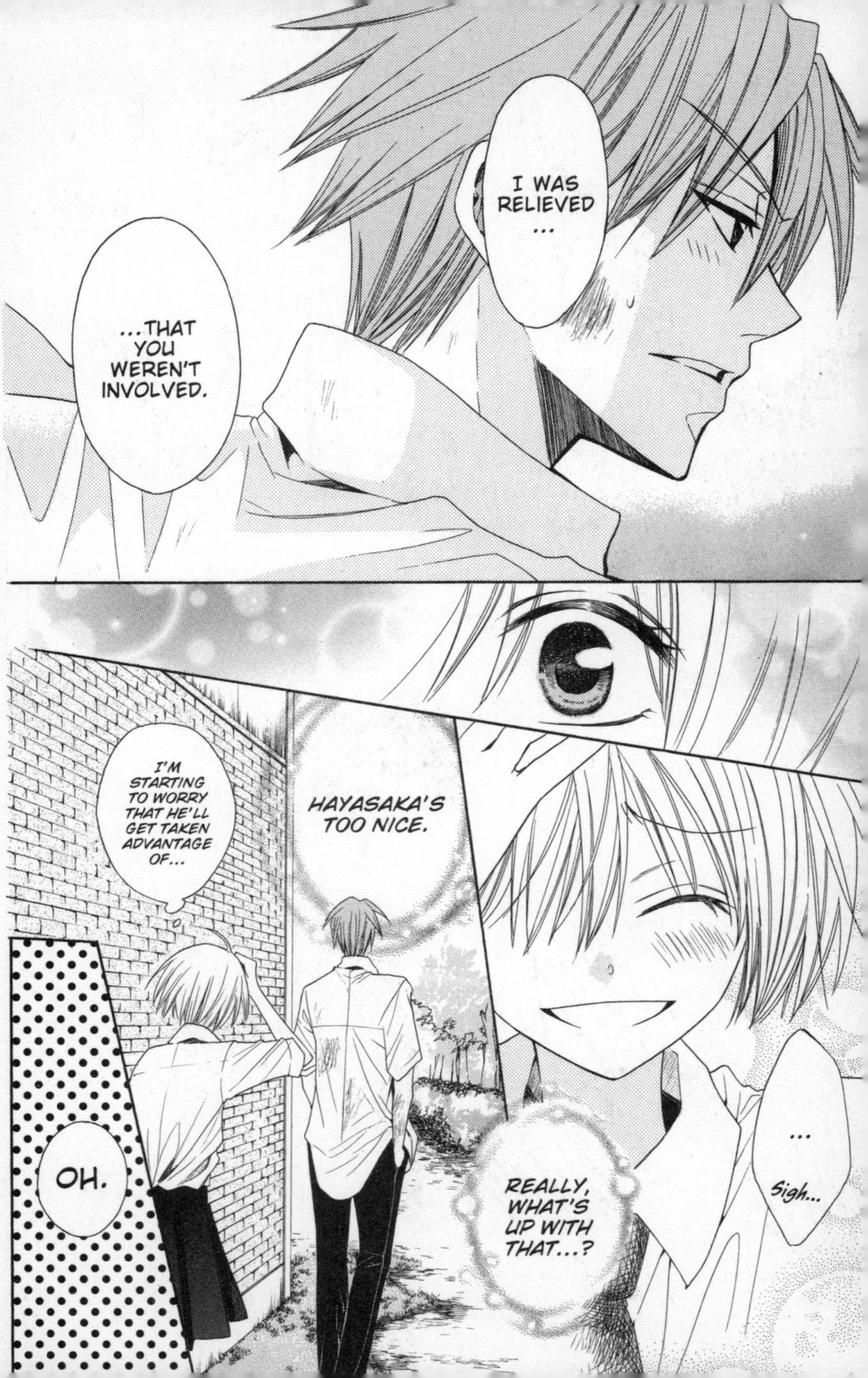
I WAS RELIEVED ...
...THAT YOU WEREN'T INVOLVED.
...
Sigh...
REALLY, WHAT'S UP WITH THAT...?
HAYASAKA'S TOO NICE.
I'M STARTING TO WORRY THAT HE'LL GET TAKEN ADVANTAGE OF...
OH.

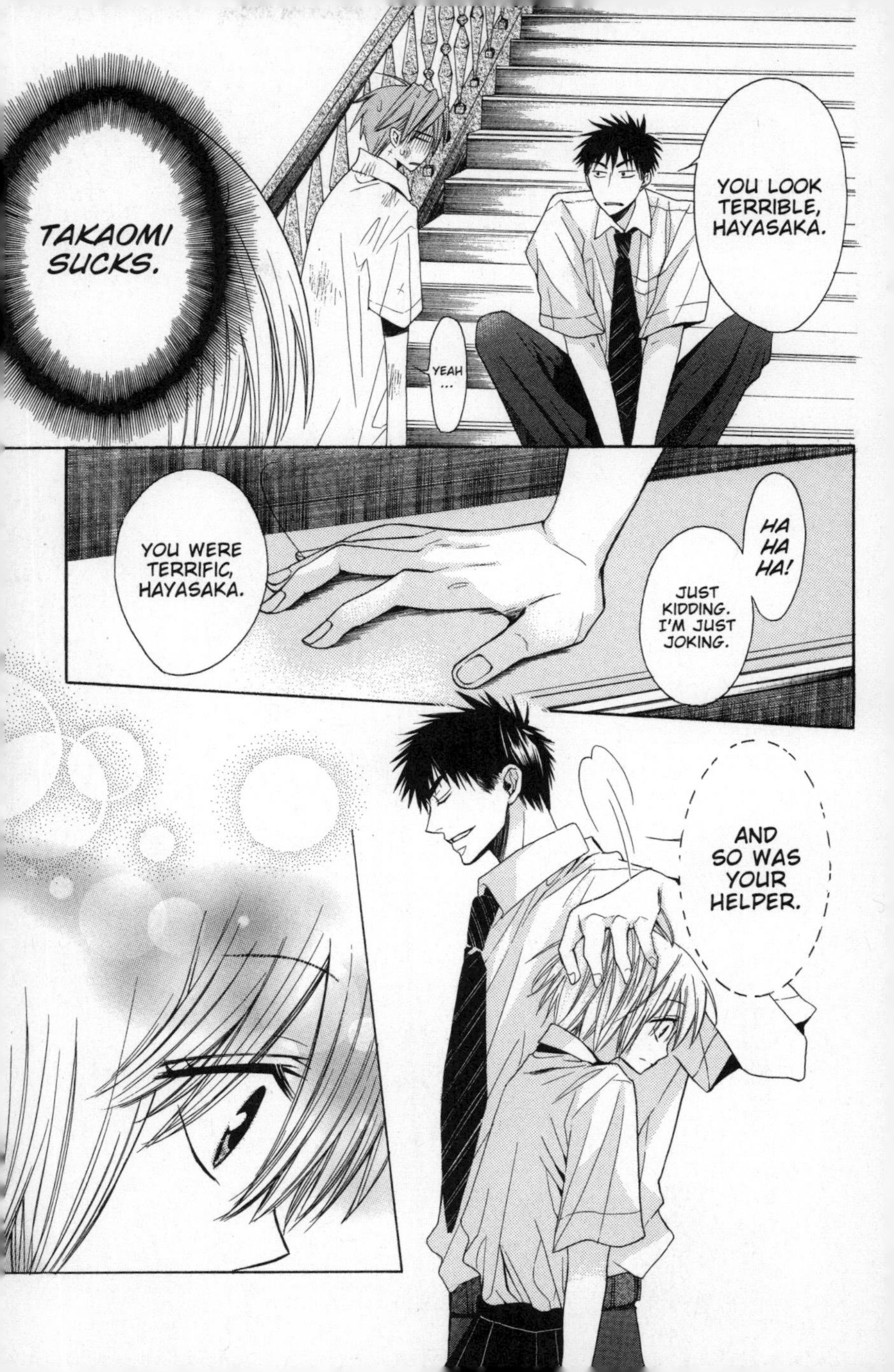
YOU LOOK TERRIBLE, HAYASAKA.
YEAH ...
TAKAOMI SUCKS.
HA HA HA!
JUST KIDDING. I'M JUST JOKING.
YOU WERE TERRIFIC, HAYASAKA.
AND SO WAS YOUR HELPER.

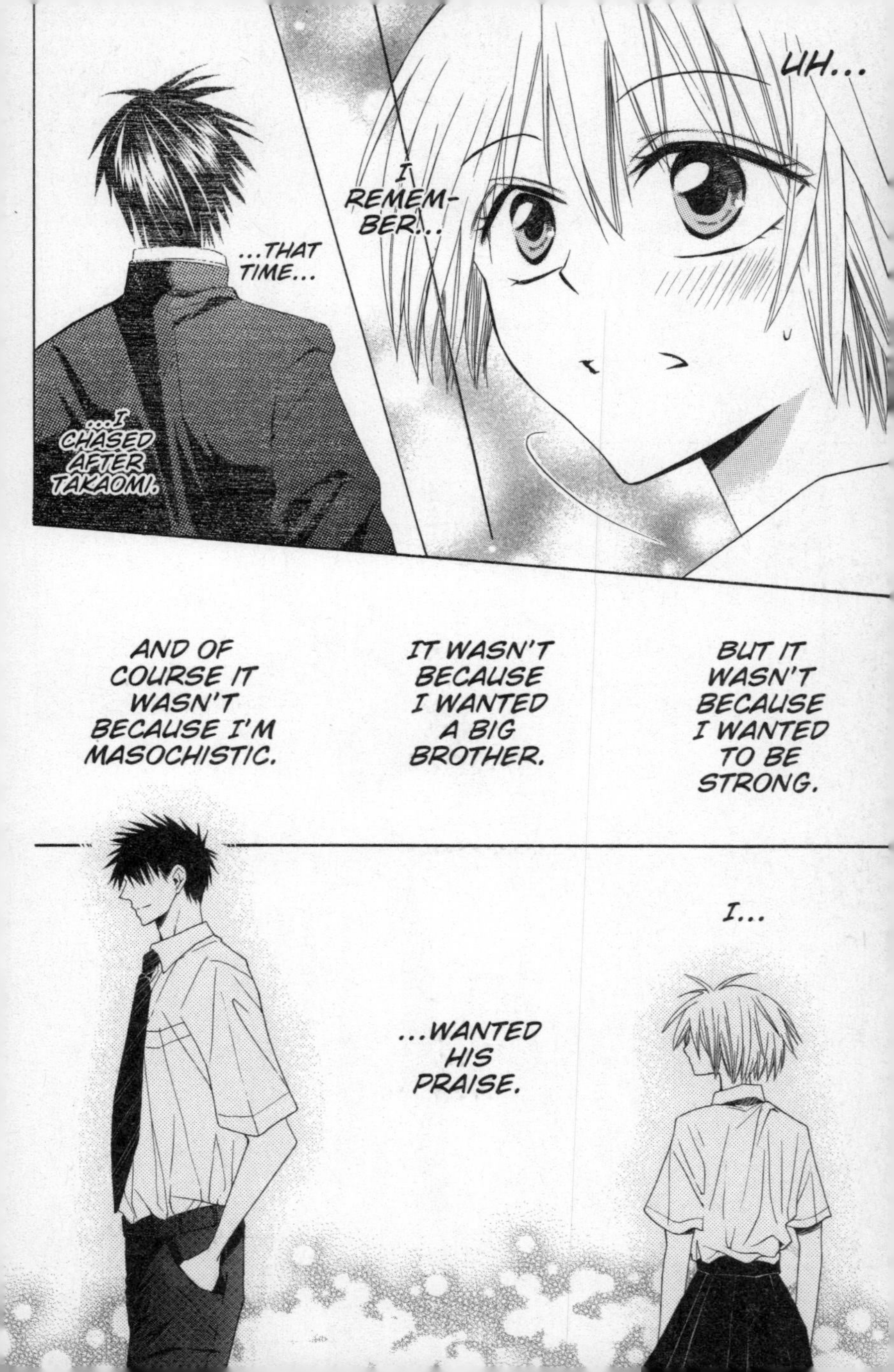
UH...
I REMEMBER...
...THAT TIME...
...I CHASED AFTER TAKAOMI.
BUT IT WASN'T BECAUSE I WANTED TO BE STRONG.
IT WASN'T BECAUSE I WANTED A BIG BROTHER.
AND OF COURSE IT WASN'T BECAUSE I'M MASOCHISTIC.
I...
...WANTED HIS PRAISE.

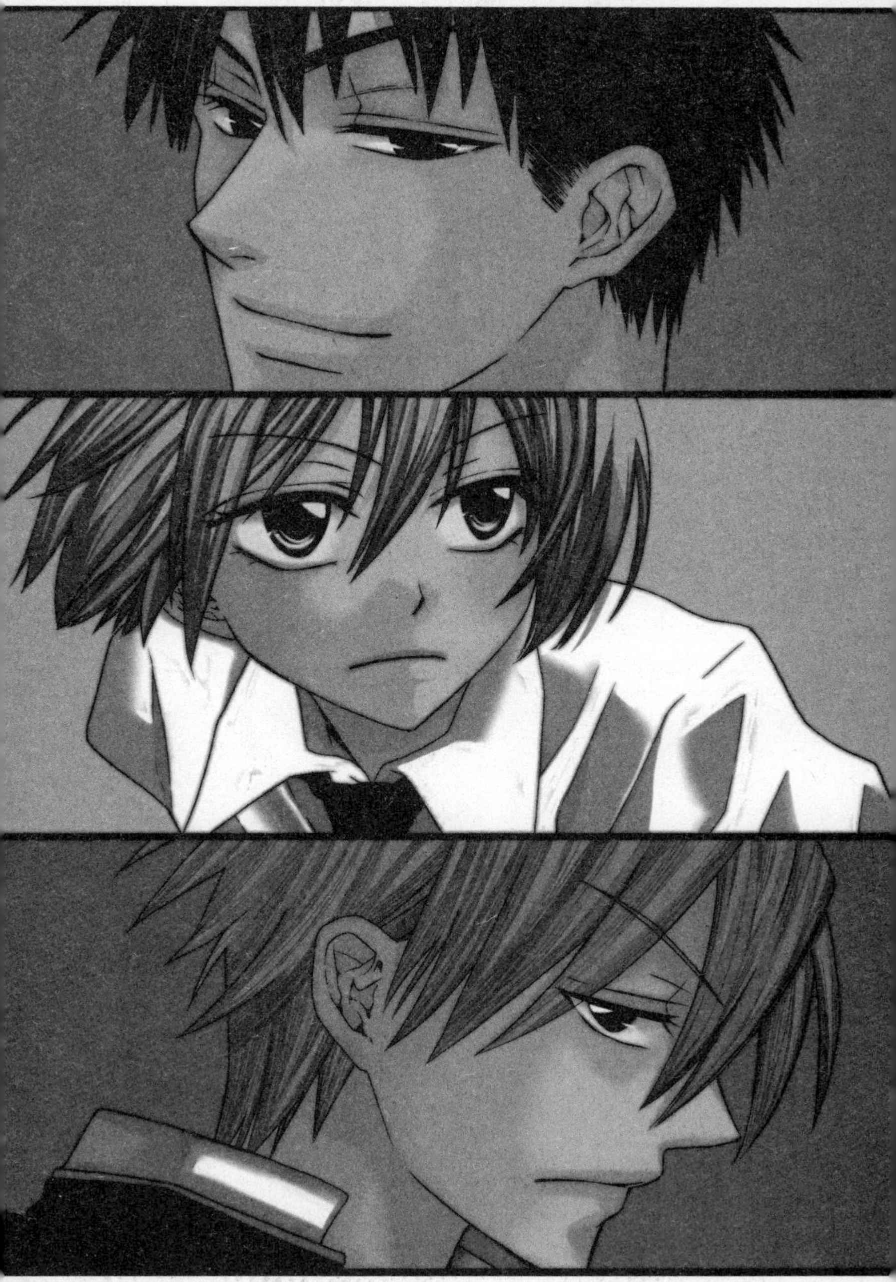

Chapter 9

HAYASAKA AND THE LETTER OF CHALLENGE

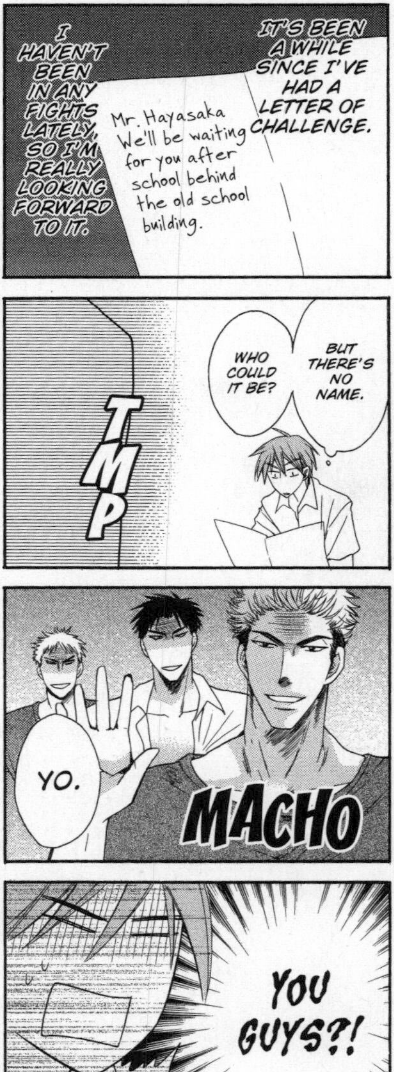
IT'S BEEN A WHILE SINCE I'VE HAD A LETTER OF CHALLENGE.
Mr. Hayasaka We'll be waiting for you after school behind the old school building.
I HAVEN'T BEEN IN ANY FIGHTS LATELY, SO I'M REALLY LOOKING FORWARD TO IT.
BUT THERE'S NO NAME.
WHO COULD IT BE?
TMP
YO.
MACHO
YOU GUYS?!

HAYASAKA AND THE CRAFTS CLUB

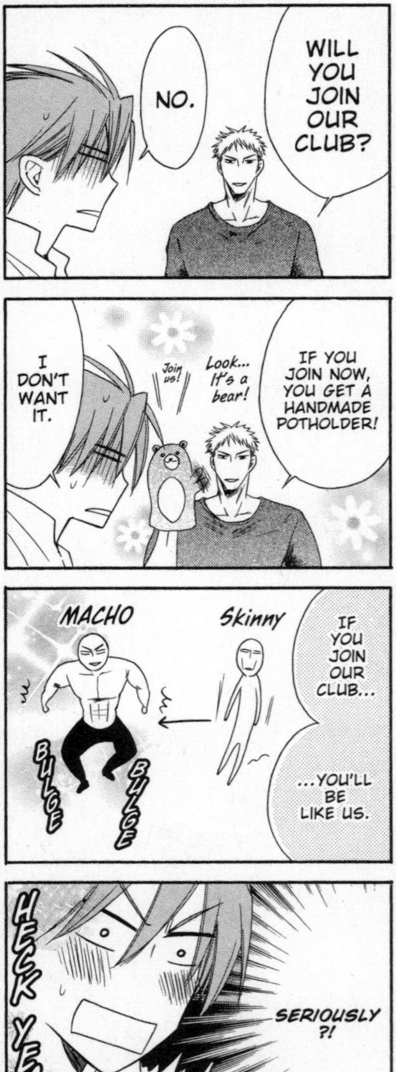
WILL YOU JOIN OUR CLUB?
NO.
IF YOU JOIN NOW, YOU GET A HANDMADE POTHOLDER!
Look... It's a bear!
Join us!
I DON'T WANT IT.
IF YOU JOIN OUR CLUB...
Skinny
MACHO
BULGE
BULGE
...YOU'LL BE LIKE US.
SERIOUSLY ?!
HECK YEAH!☆

It's a secret that he wavered.

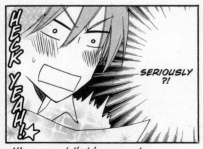

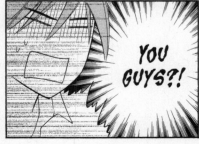

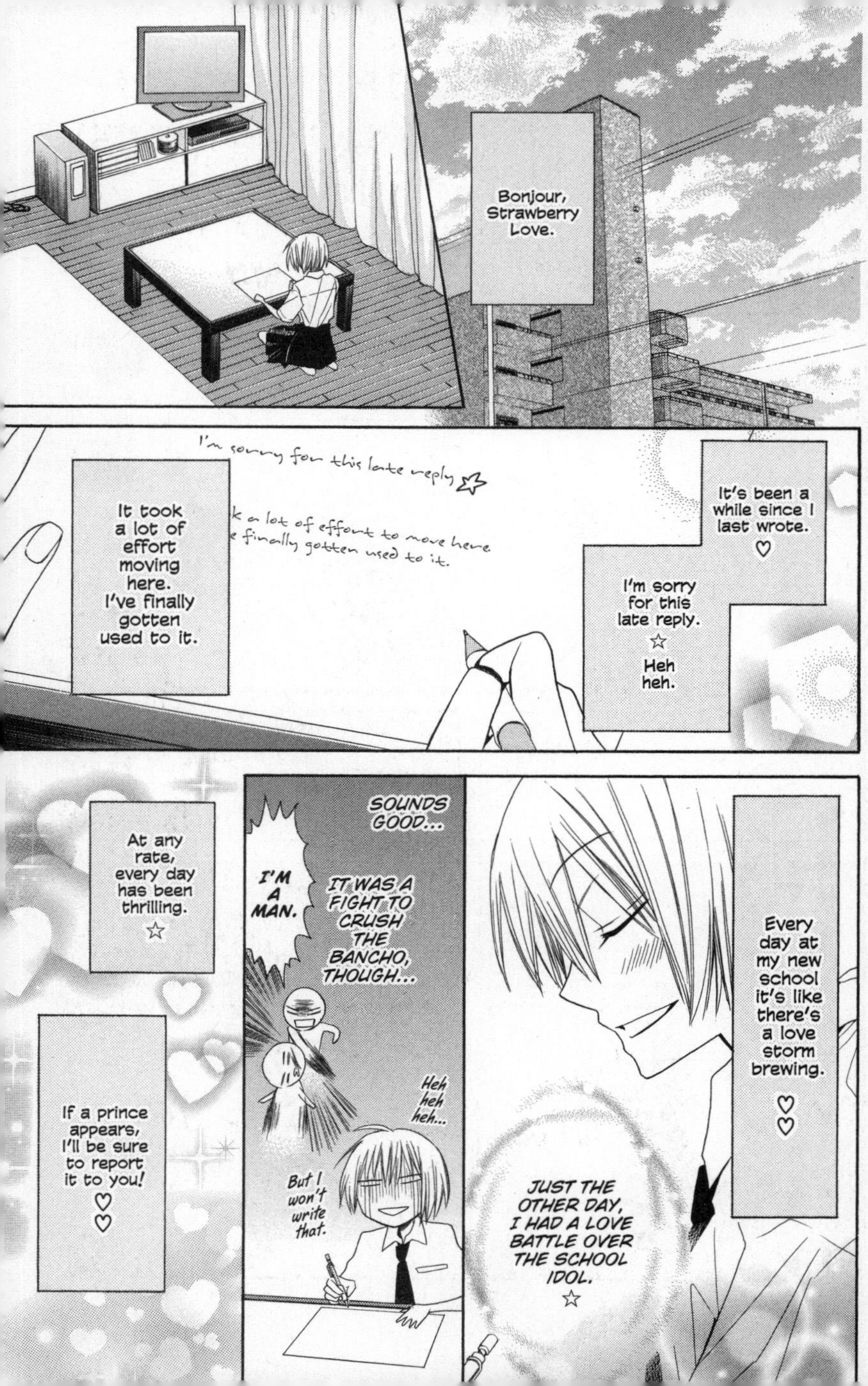

Bonjour, Strawberry Love.
It's been a while since I last wrote. ♡
I'm sorry for this late reply. ☆
Heh heh.
I'm sorry for this late reply ☆
It took a lot of effort moving here. I've finally gotten used to it.
Every day at my new school it's like there's a love storm brewing. ♡ ♡
JUST THE OTHER DAY, I HAD A LOVE BATTLE OVER THE SCHOOL IDOL. ☆
SOUNDS GOOD...
I'M A MAN.
IT WAS A FIGHT TO CRUSH THE BANCHO, THOUGH...
Heh heh heh...
But I won't write that.
At any rate, every day has been thrilling. ☆
If a prince appears, I'll be sure to report it to you! ♡ ♡

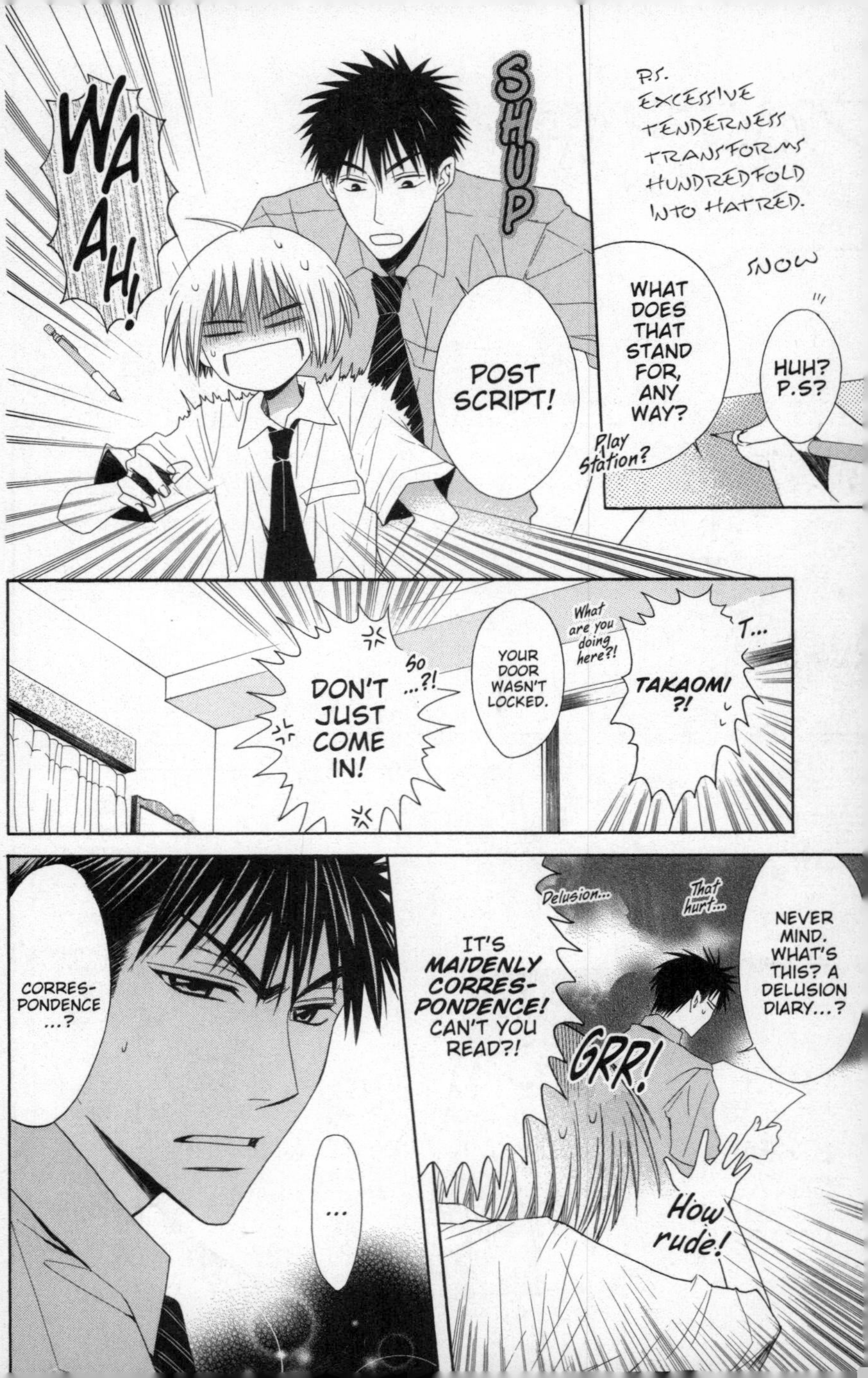
P.S.
EXCESSIVE TENDERNESS TRANSFORMS HUNDREDFOLD INTO HATRED.
SNOW
HUH? P.S?
WHAT DOES THAT STAND FOR, ANY WAY?
Play Station?
SHUP
POST SCRIPT!
WAAH!
T...
TAKAOMI ?!
What are you doing here?!
YOUR DOOR WASN'T LOCKED.
So ...?!
DON'T JUST COME IN!
NEVER MIND. WHAT'S THIS? A DELUSION DIARY...?
That hurt...
Delusion...
IT'S MAIDENLY CORRES-PONDENCE! CAN'T YOU READ?!
GRR!
How rude!
CORRES-PONDENCE ...?
...

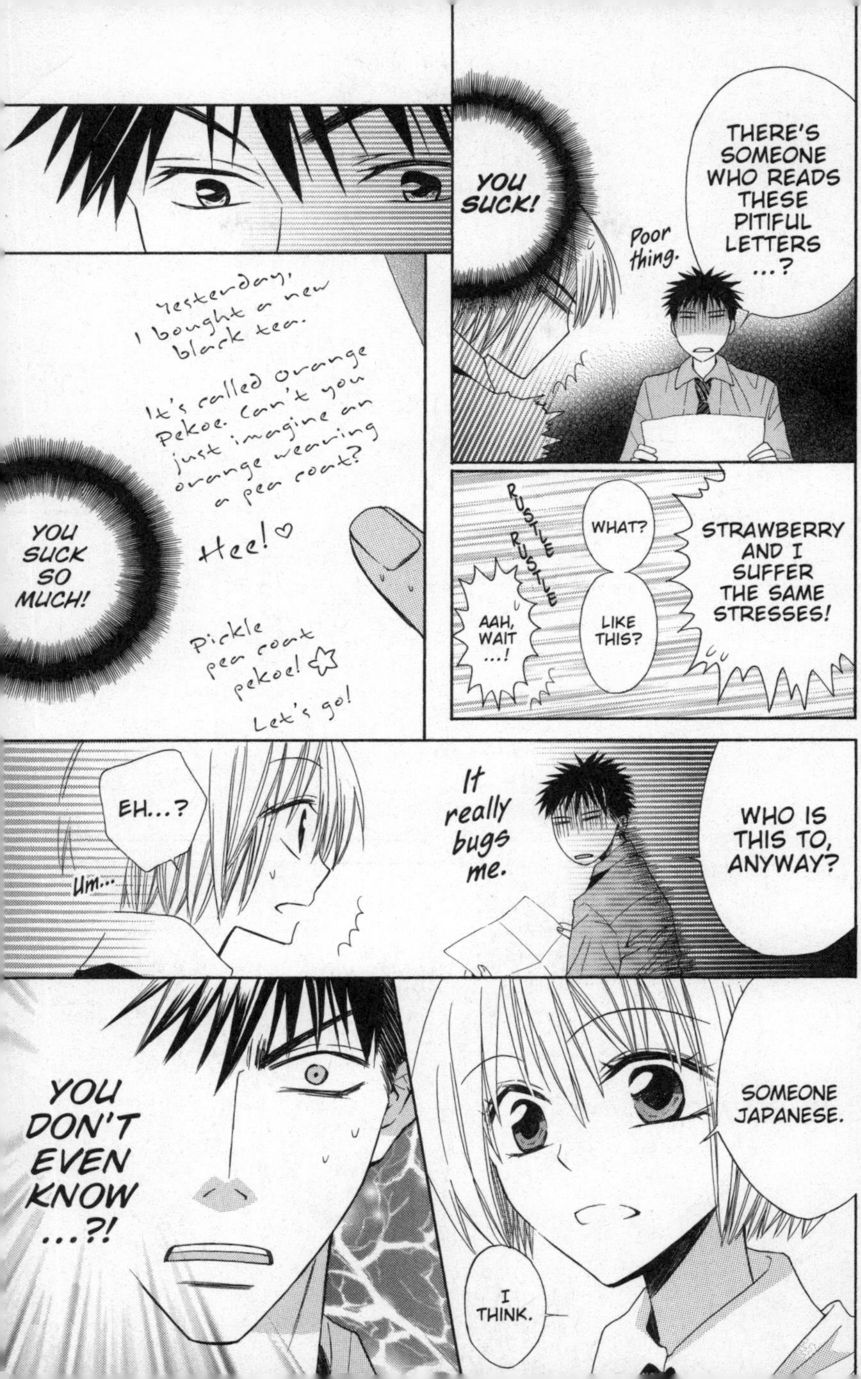
THERE'S SOMEONE WHO READS THESE PITIFUL LETTERS ...?
Poor thing.
YOU SUCK!
STRAWBERRY AND I SUFFER THE SAME STRESSES!
WHAT?
LIKE THIS?
RUSTLE RUSTLE
AAH, WAIT ...!
Yesterday, I bought a new black tea.
It's called Orange Pekoe. Can't you just imagine an orange wearing a pea coat?
Hee! ♡
Pickle pea coat pekoe! ☆
Let's go!
YOU SUCK SO MUCH!
WHO IS THIS TO, ANYWAY?
It really bugs me.
EH...?
Um...
SOMEONE JAPANESE.
I THINK.
YOU DON'T EVEN KNOW ...?!

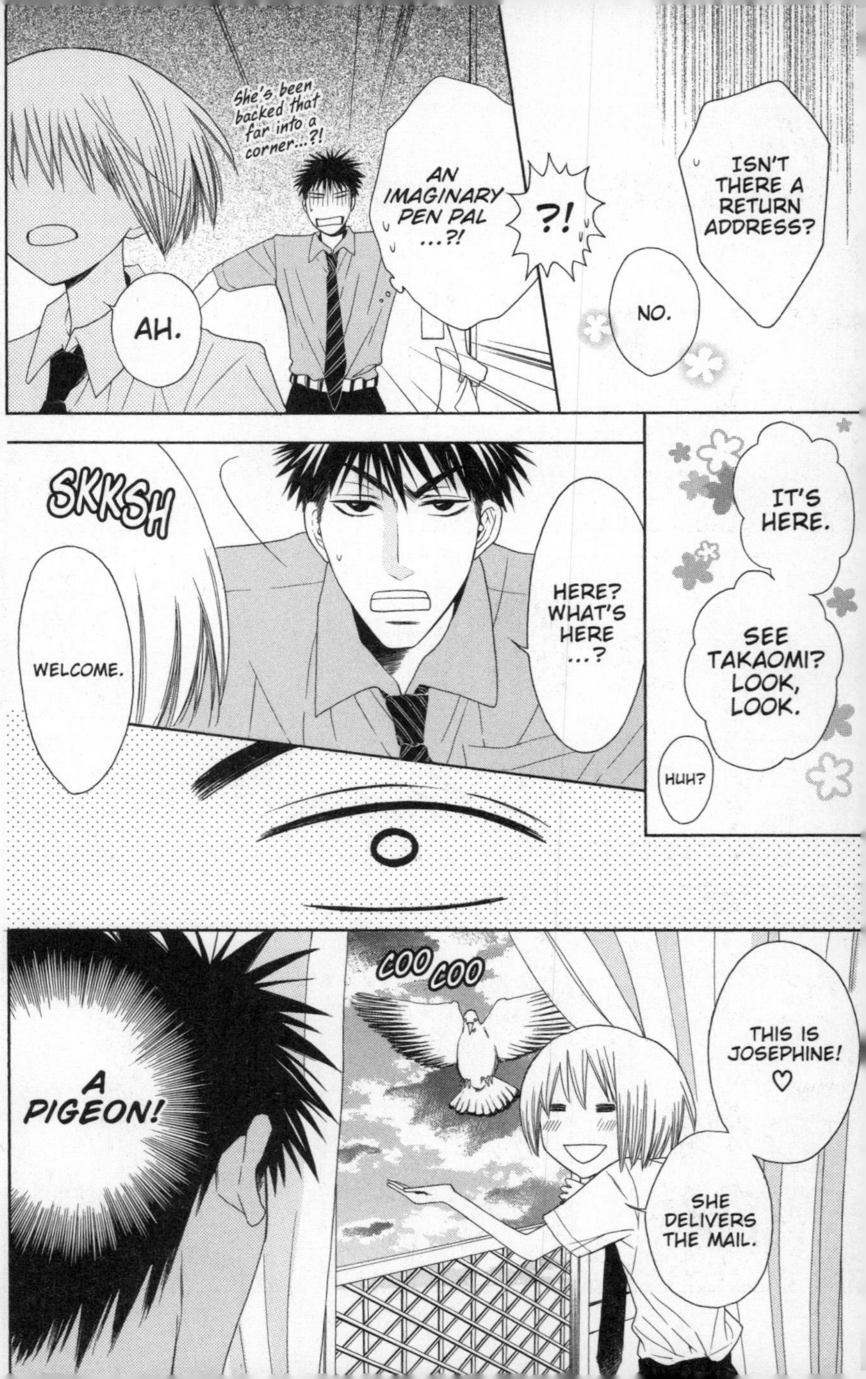
ISN'T THERE A RETURN ADDRESS?
NO.
?!
AN IMAGINARY PEN PAL ...?!
She's been backed that far into a corner...?!
AH.
IT'S HERE.
SEE TAKAOMI? LOOK, LOOK.
HUH?
HERE? WHAT'S HERE ...?
SKKSH
WELCOME.
THIS IS JOSEPHINE! ♡
SHE DELIVERS THE MAIL.
COO COO
A PIGEON!

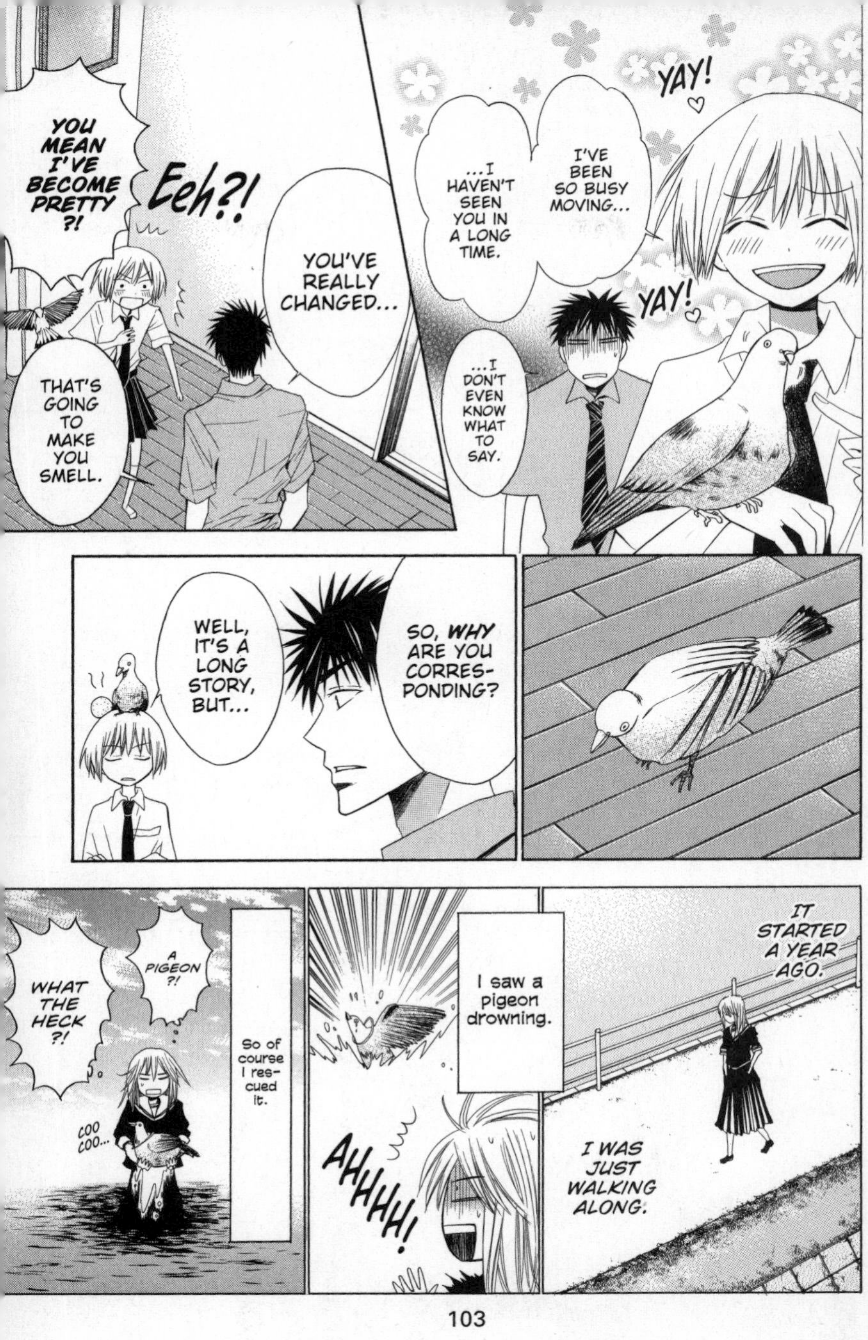
YAY!
I'VE BEEN SO BUSY MOVING...
...I HAVEN'T SEEN YOU IN A LONG TIME.
YAY!
...I DON'T EVEN KNOW WHAT TO SAY.
YOU'VE REALLY CHANGED...
Eeh?!
YOU MEAN I'VE BECOME PRETTY?!
THAT'S GOING TO MAKE YOU SMELL.
SO, WHY ARE YOU CORRES-PONDING?
WELL, IT'S A LONG STORY, BUT...
IT STARTED A YEAR AGO.
I WAS JUST WALKING ALONG.
I saw a pigeon drowning.
AHHHH!
So of course I res-cued it.
A PIGEON?!
WHAT THE HECK?!
COO COO...

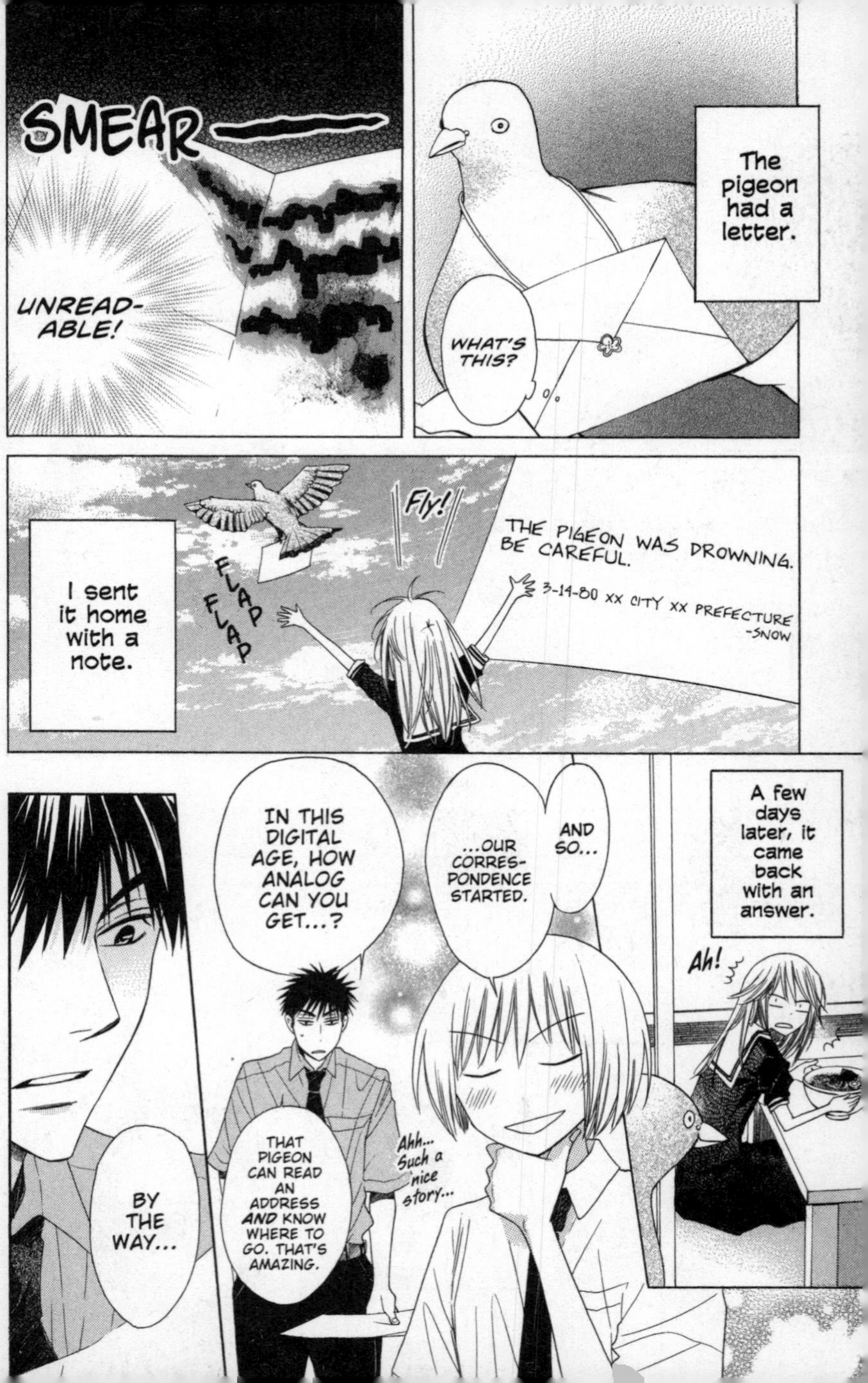
The pigeon had a letter.
WHAT'S THIS?
SMEAR
UNREAD-ABLE!
THE PIGEON WAS DROWNING. BE CAREFUL.
3-14-80 XX CITY XX PREFECTURE -SNOW
Fly!
FLAP FLAP
I sent it home with a note.
A few days later, it came back with an answer.
Ah!
AND SO...
...OUR CORRES-PONDENCE STARTED.
IN THIS DIGITAL AGE, HOW ANALOG CAN YOU GET...?
Ahh... Such a nice story...
THAT PIGEON CAN READ AN ADDRESS AND KNOW WHERE TO GO. THAT'S AMAZING.
BY THE WAY...

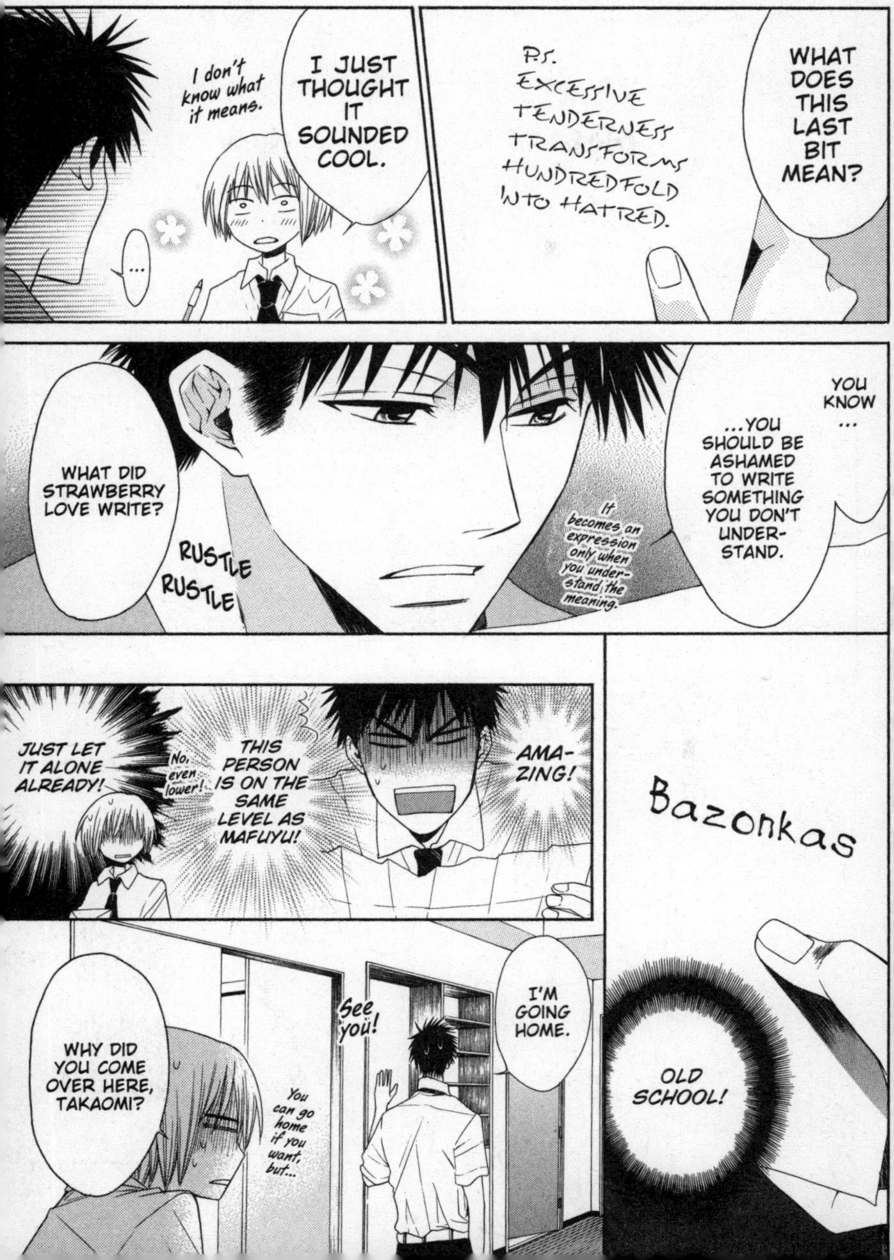
WHAT DOES THIS LAST BIT MEAN?
P.S. EXCESSIVE TENDERNESS TRANSFORMS HUNDREDFOLD INTO HATRED.
I JUST THOUGHT IT SOUNDED COOL.
I don't know what it means.
...
YOU KNOW ...
...YOU SHOULD BE ASHAMED TO WRITE SOMETHING YOU DON'T UNDER-STAND.
It becomes an expression only when you under-stand the meaning.
WHAT DID STRAWBERRY LOVE WRITE?
RUSTLE
RUSTLE
Bazonkas
OLD SCHOOL!
AMA-ZING!
THIS PERSON IS ON THE SAME LEVEL AS MAFUYU!
No, even lower!
JUST LET IT ALONE ALREADY!
I'M GOING HOME.
See you!
You can go home if you want, but...
WHY DID YOU COME OVER HERE, TAKAOMI?

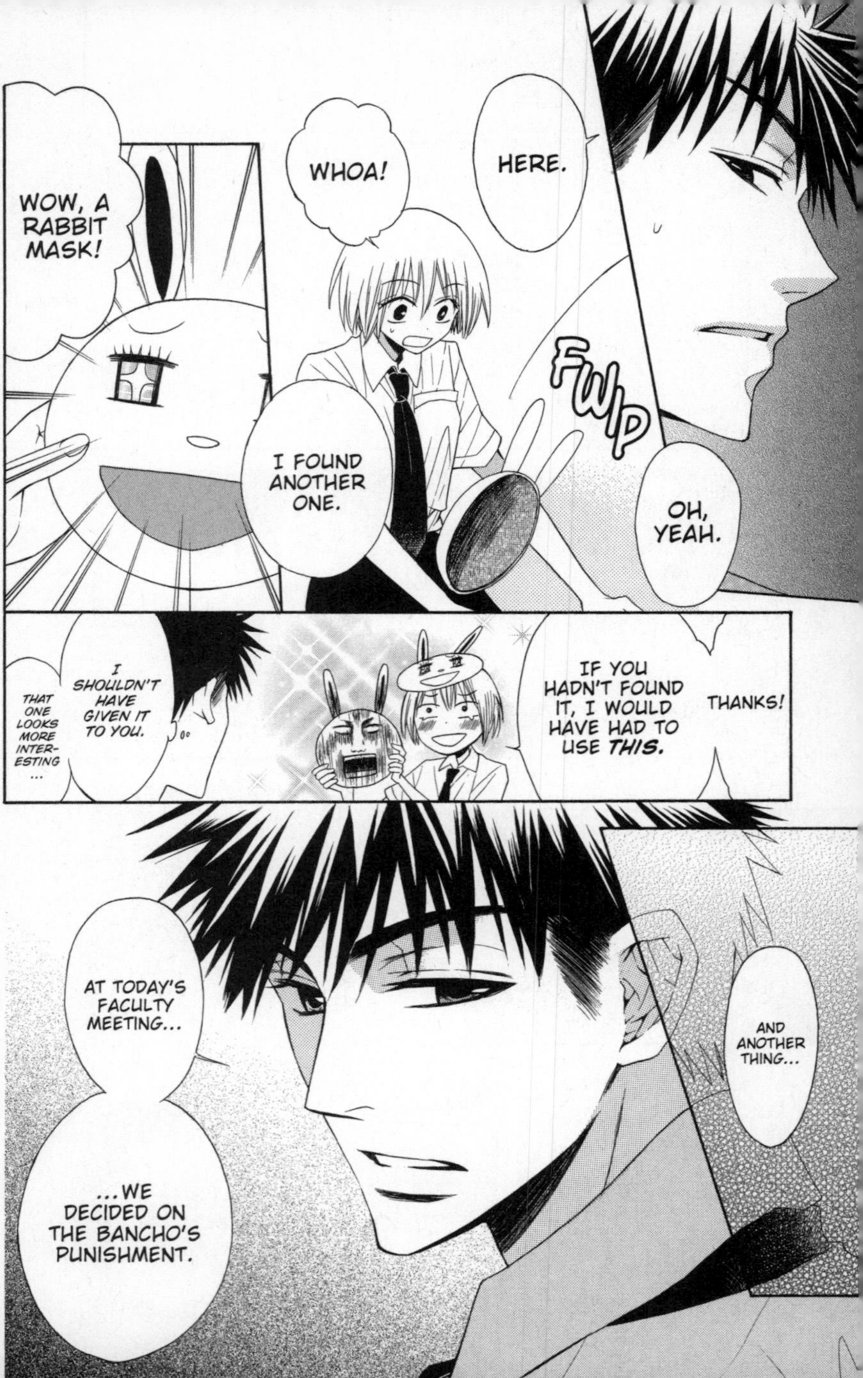
HERE.
WHOA!
FWIP
I FOUND ANOTHER ONE.
OH, YEAH.
WOW, A RABBIT MASK!
THANKS!
IF YOU HADN'T FOUND IT, I WOULD HAVE HAD TO USE *THIS.*
I SHOULDN'T HAVE GIVEN IT TO YOU.
THAT ONE LOOKS MORE INTER-ESTING...
AND ANOTHER THING...
AT TODAY'S FACULTY MEETING...
...WE DECIDED ON THE BANCHO'S PUNISHMENT.

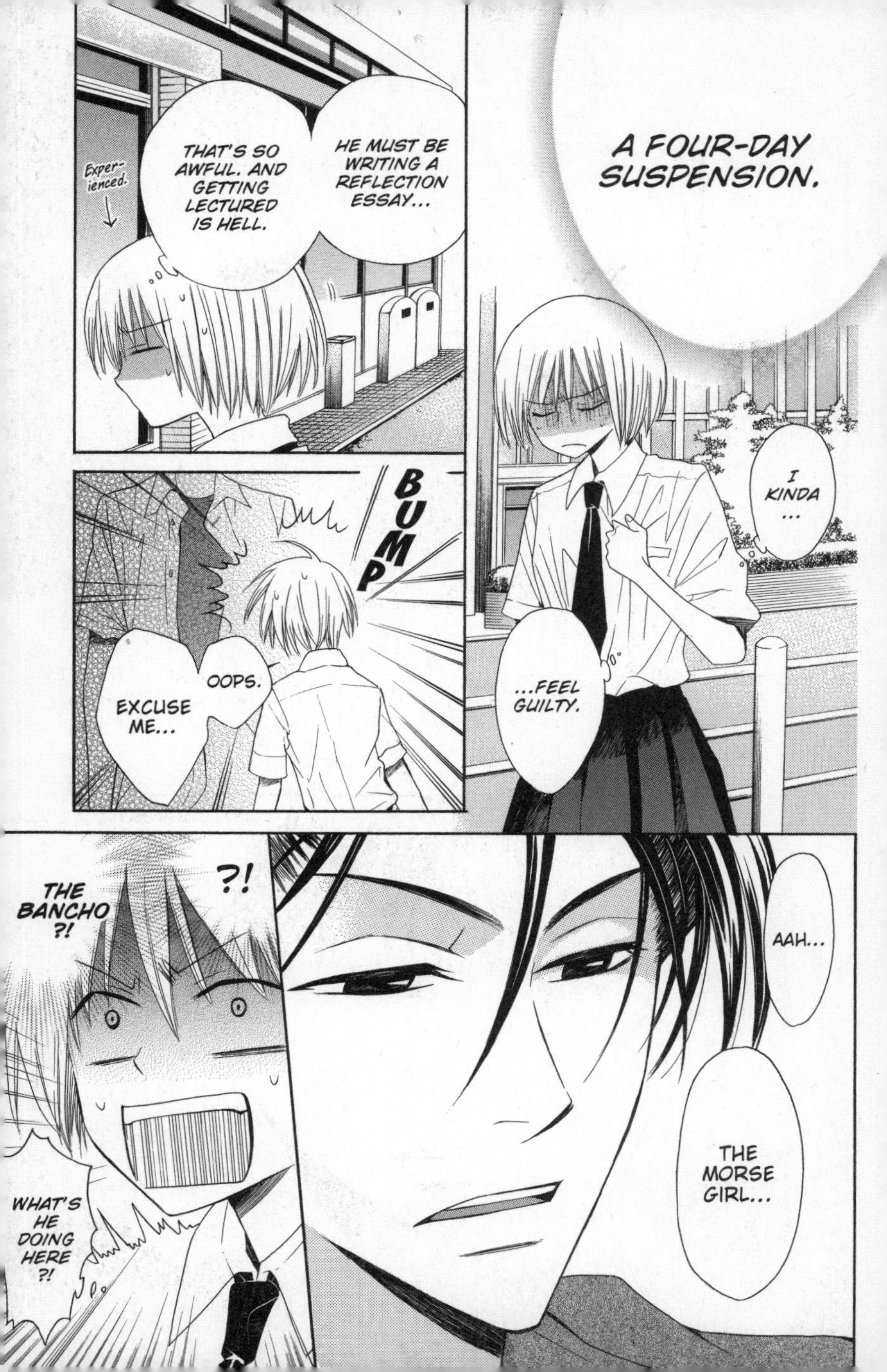
A FOUR-DAY SUSPENSION.
I KINDA ...
...FEEL GUILTY.
HE MUST BE WRITING A REFLECTION ESSAY...
THAT'S SO AWFUL. AND GETTING LECTURED IS HELL.
Experienced.
BUMP
OOPS.
EXCUSE ME...
AAH...
THE MORSE GIRL...
?!
THE BANCHO ?!
WHAT'S HE DOING HERE ?!

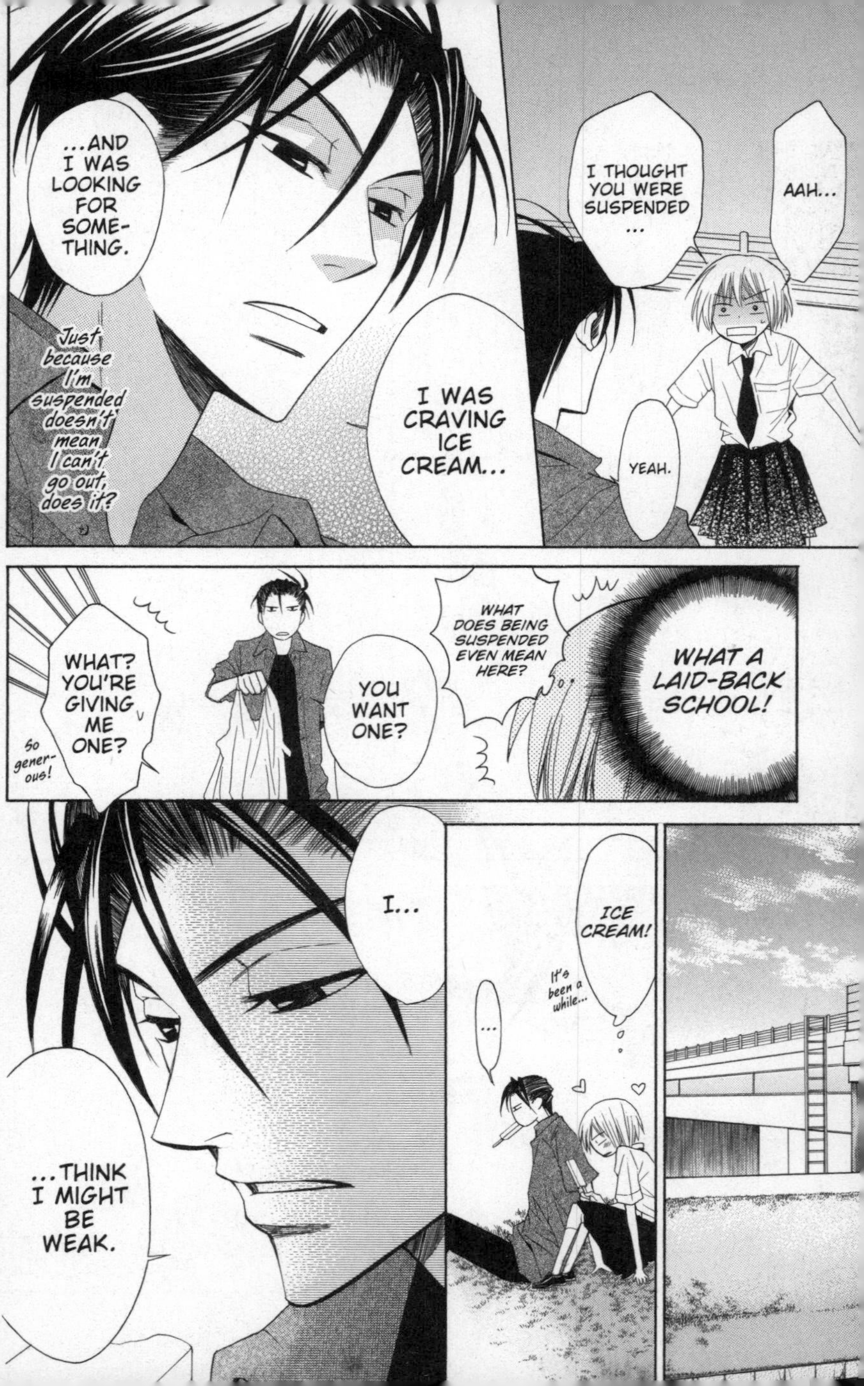
AAH...
I THOUGHT YOU WERE SUSPENDED...
YEAH.
I WAS CRAVING ICE CREAM...
...AND I WAS LOOKING FOR SOMETHING.
Just because I'm suspended doesn't mean I can't go out, does it?
WHAT A LAID-BACK SCHOOL!
WHAT DOES BEING SUSPENDED EVEN MEAN HERE?
YOU WANT ONE?
WHAT? YOU'RE GIVING ME ONE?
So generous!
ICE CREAM!
It's been a while...
...
I...
...THINK I MIGHT BE WEAK.

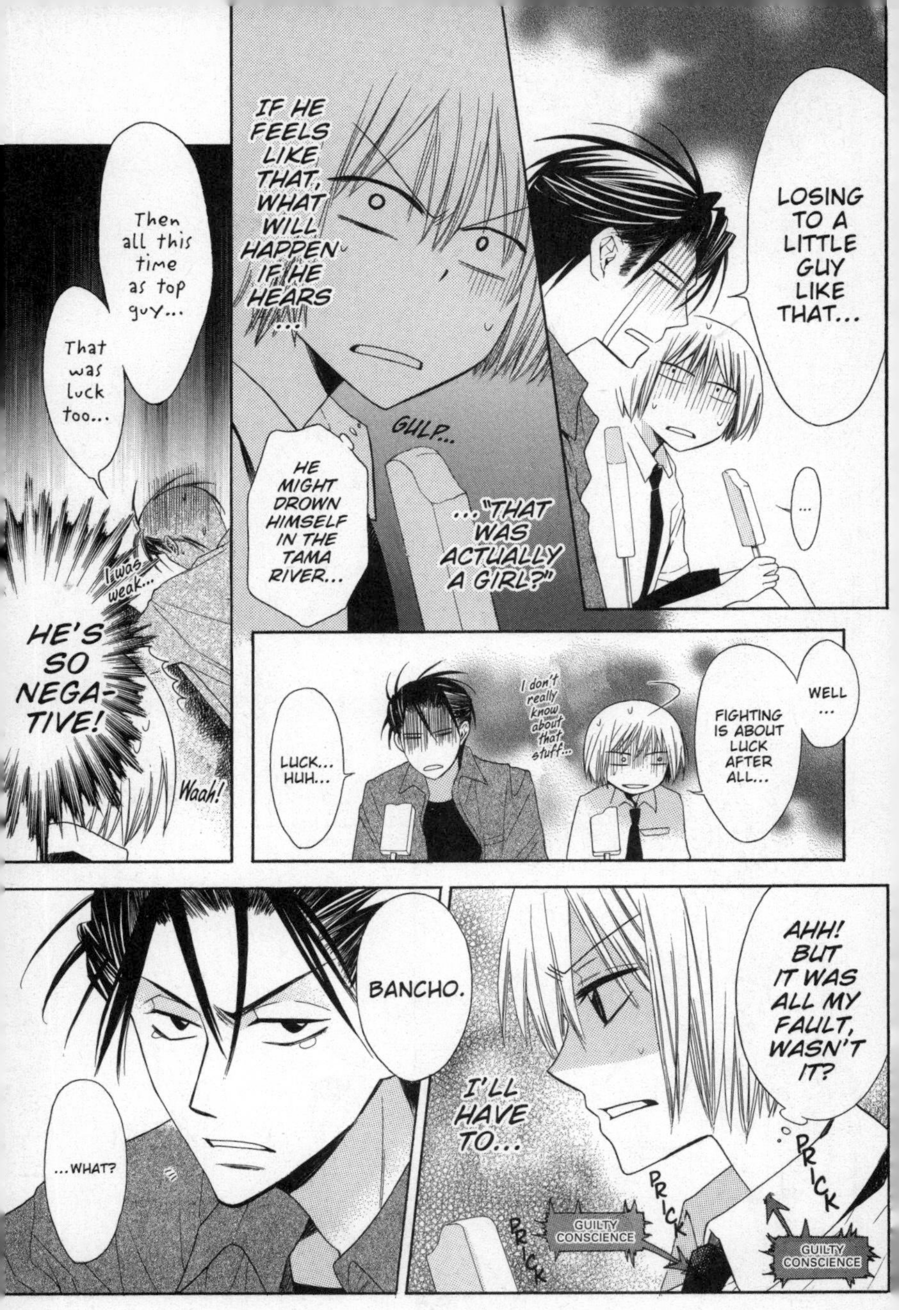
LOSING TO A LITTLE GUY LIKE THAT...
...
IF HE FEELS LIKE THAT, WHAT WILL HAPPEN IF HE HEARS...
GULP..
...."THAT WAS ACTUALLY A GIRL?"
HE MIGHT DROWN HIMSELF IN THE TAMA RIVER...
WELL...
FIGHTING IS ABOUT LUCK AFTER ALL...
I don't really know about that stuff...
LUCK... HUH...
Then all this time as top guy...
That was luck too...
I was weak...
HE'S SO NEGA-TIVE!
Waah!
AHH! BUT IT WAS ALL MY FAULT, WASN'T IT?
PRICK
GUILTY CONSCIENCE
PRICK
GUILTY CONSCIENCE
PRICK
I'LL HAVE TO...
BANCHO.
...WHAT?

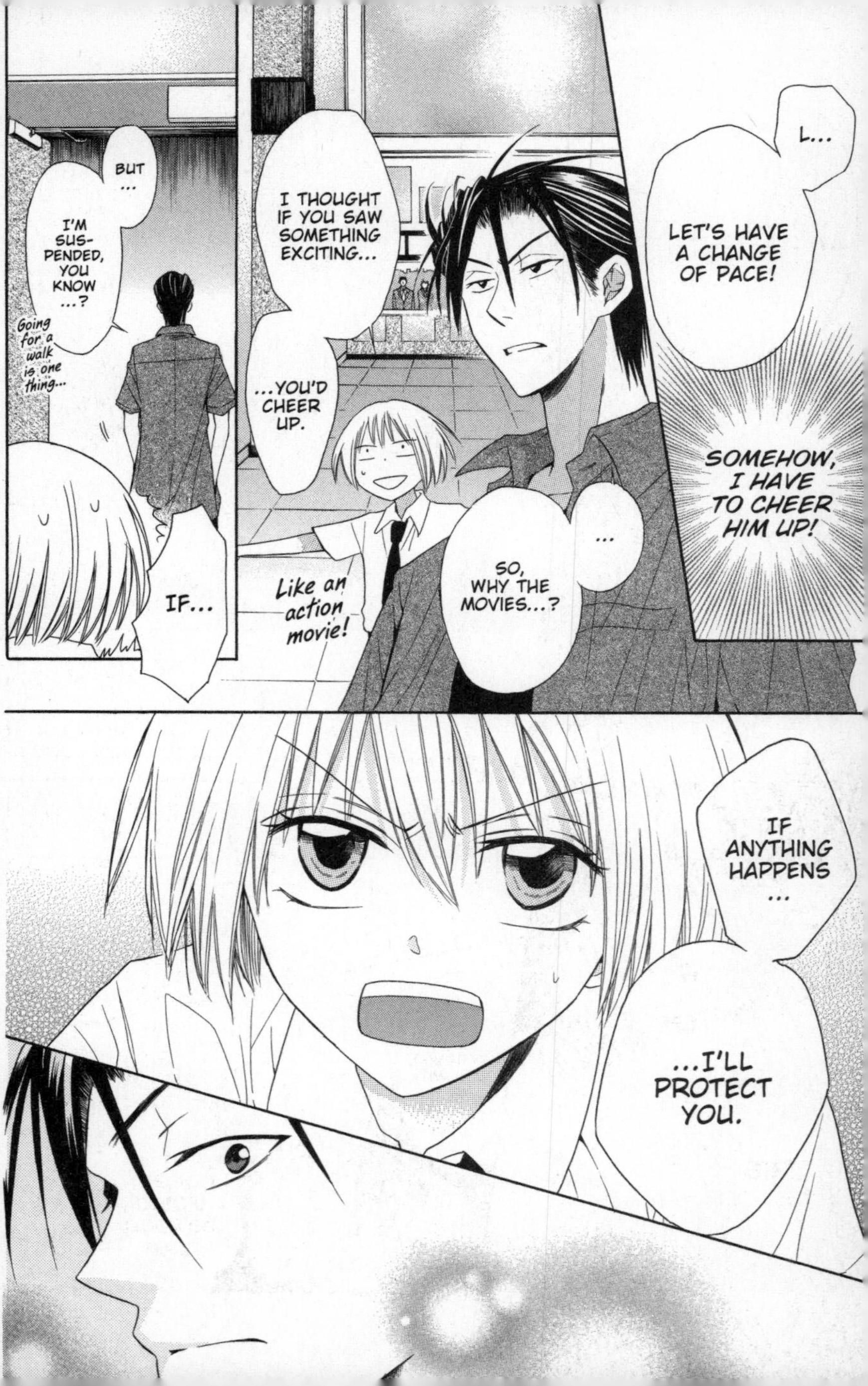
L...
LET'S HAVE A CHANGE OF PACE!
SOMEHOW, I HAVE TO CHEER HIM UP!
...
SO, WHY THE MOVIES...?
I THOUGHT IF YOU SAW SOMETHING EXCITING...
...YOU'D CHEER UP.
Like an action movie!
BUT...
I'M SUSPENDED, YOU KNOW...?
Going for a walk is one thing...
IF...
IF ANYTHING HAPPENS...
...I'LL PROTECT YOU.

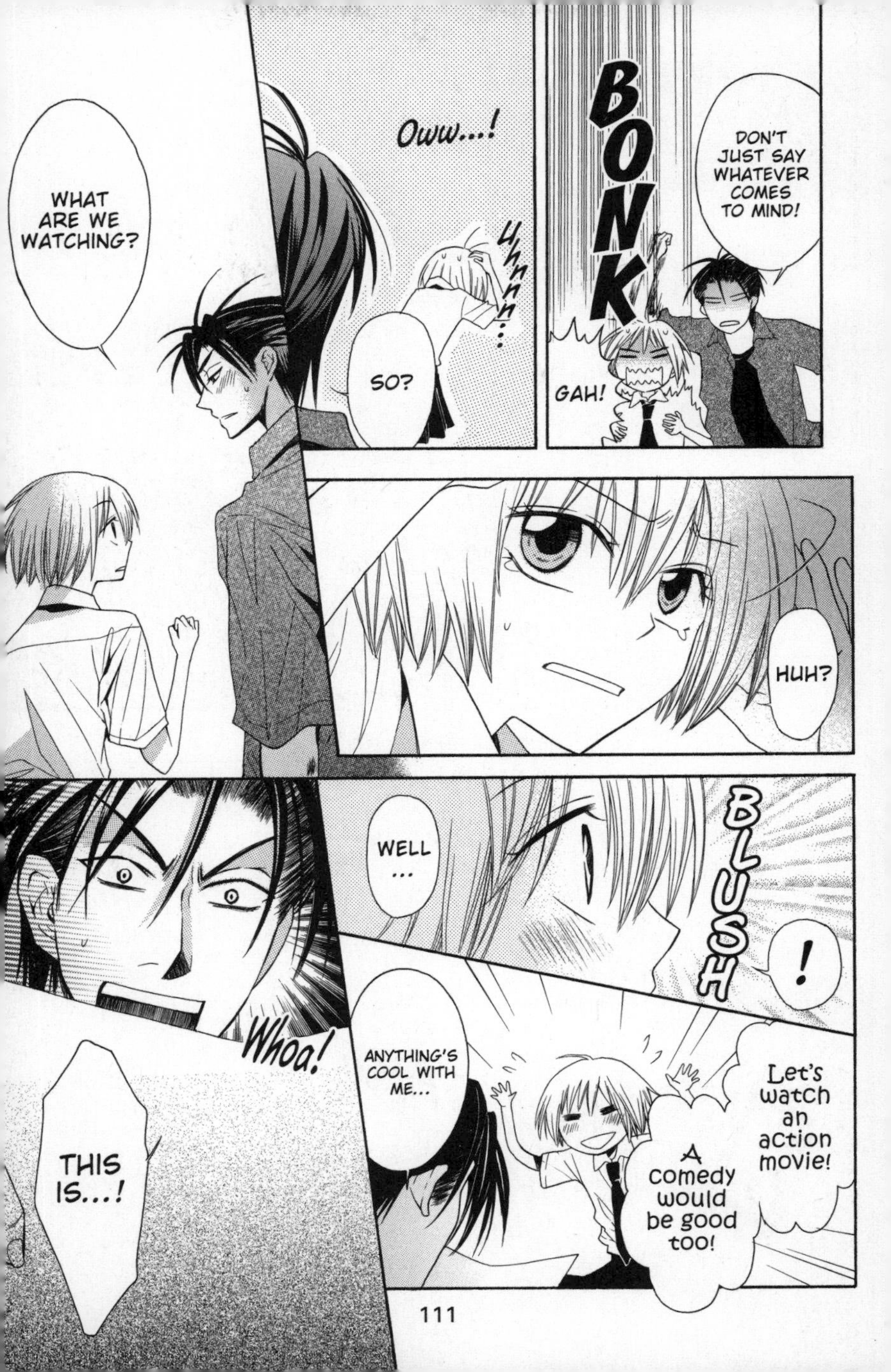
DON'T JUST SAY WHATEVER COMES TO MIND!
BONK
GAH!
Oww...!
Uhnnn...
SO?
WHAT ARE WE WATCHING?
HUH?
WELL...
BLUSH
!
Whoa!
ANYTHING'S COOL WITH ME...
Let's watch an action movie!
A comedy would be good too!
THIS IS...!

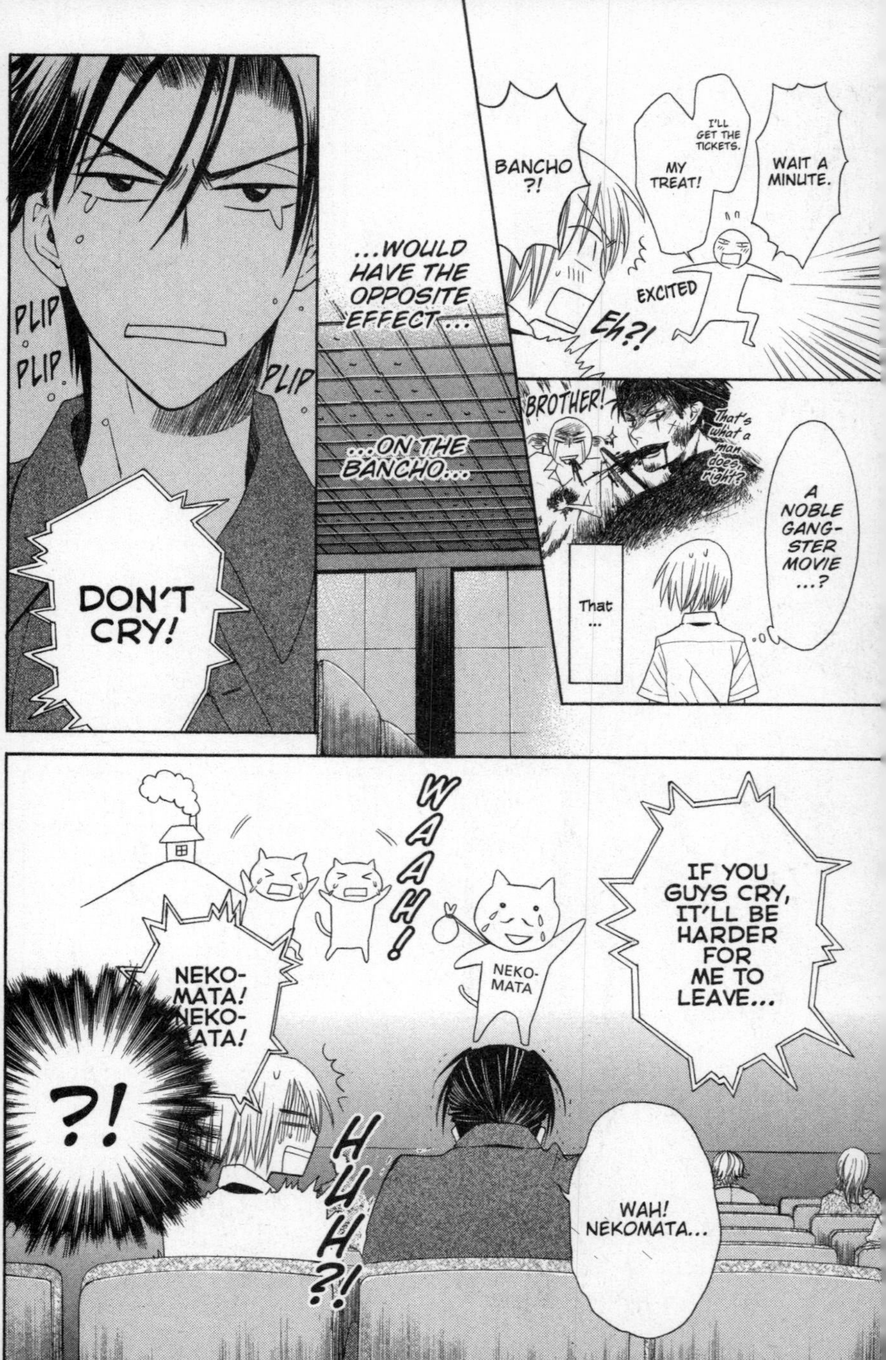

WAIT A MINUTE.
I'LL GET THE TICKETS.
MY TREAT!
EXCITED
BANCHO ?!
Eh?!
A NOBLE GANGSTER MOVIE ...?
That's what a man does, right?
BROTHER!
That ...
...WOULD HAVE THE OPPOSITE EFFECT...
...ON THE BANCHO...
PLIP
PLIP
PLIP
DON'T CRY!
IF YOU GUYS CRY, IT'LL BE HARDER FOR ME TO LEAVE...
WAAAH!
NEKOMATA
NEKO-MATA! NEKO-MATA!
WAH! NEKOMATA...
HUH?!
?!

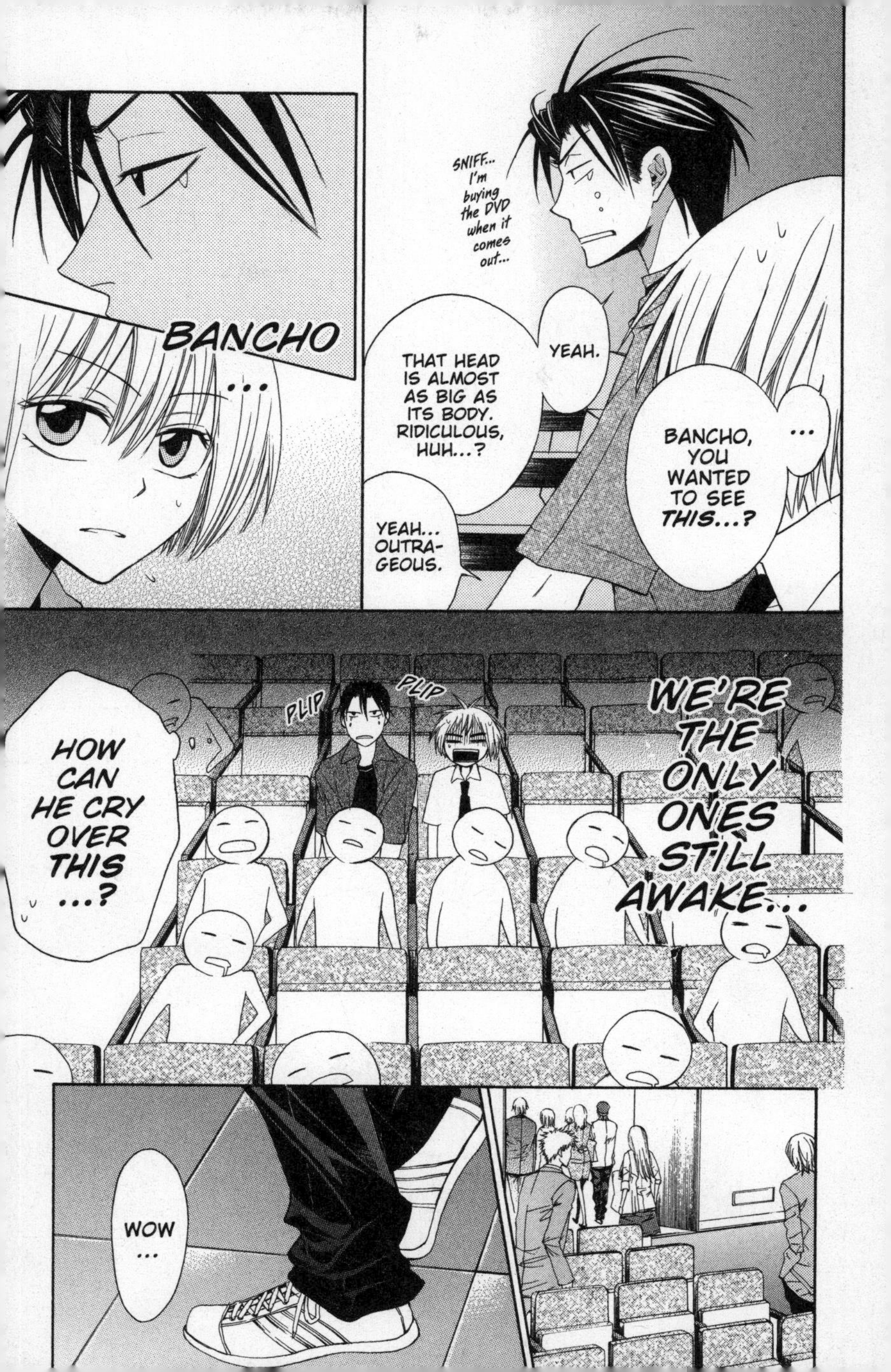

SNIFF... I'm buying the DVD when it comes out...
...
BANCHO, YOU WANTED TO SEE THIS...?
YEAH.
THAT HEAD IS ALMOST AS BIG AS ITS BODY. RIDICULOUS, HUH...?
YEAH... OUTRAGEOUS.
BANCHO
...
WE'RE THE ONLY ONES STILL AWAKE...
PLIP
PLIP
HOW CAN HE CRY OVER THIS ...?
WOW ...

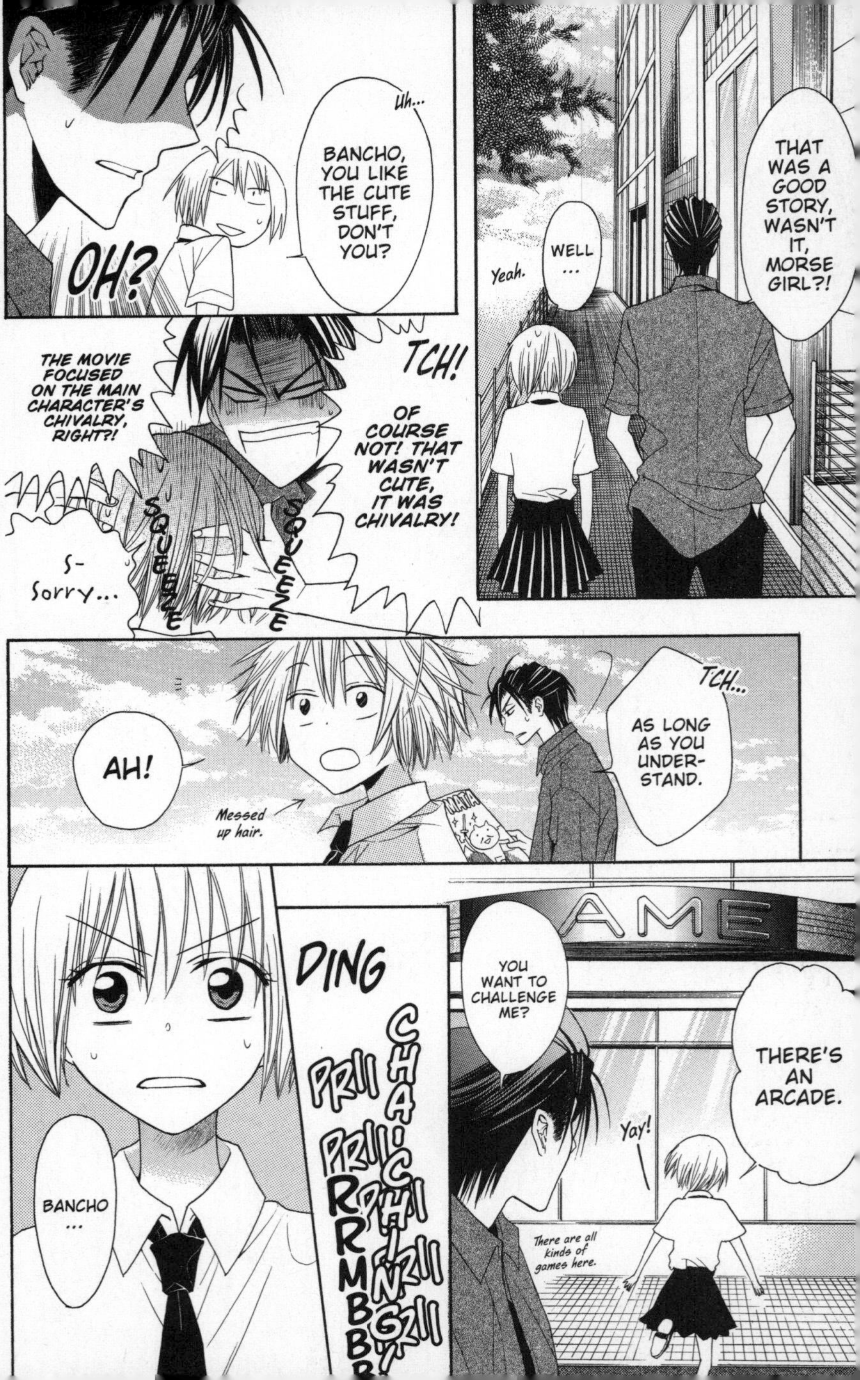
THAT WAS A GOOD STORY, WASN'T IT, MORSE GIRL?!
WELL...
Yeah.
Uh...
BANCHO, YOU LIKE THE CUTE STUFF, DON'T YOU?
OH?
TCH!
OF COURSE NOT! THAT WASN'T CUTE, IT WAS CHIVALRY!
THE MOVIE FOCUSED ON THE MAIN CHARACTER'S CHIVALRY, RIGHT?!
SQUEEZE
SQUEEZE
S-Sorry...
TCH...
AS LONG AS YOU UNDERSTAND.
AH!
Messed up hair.
THERE'S AN ARCADE.
Yay!
There are all kinds of games here.
YOU WANT TO CHALLENGE ME?
DING
BANCHO...

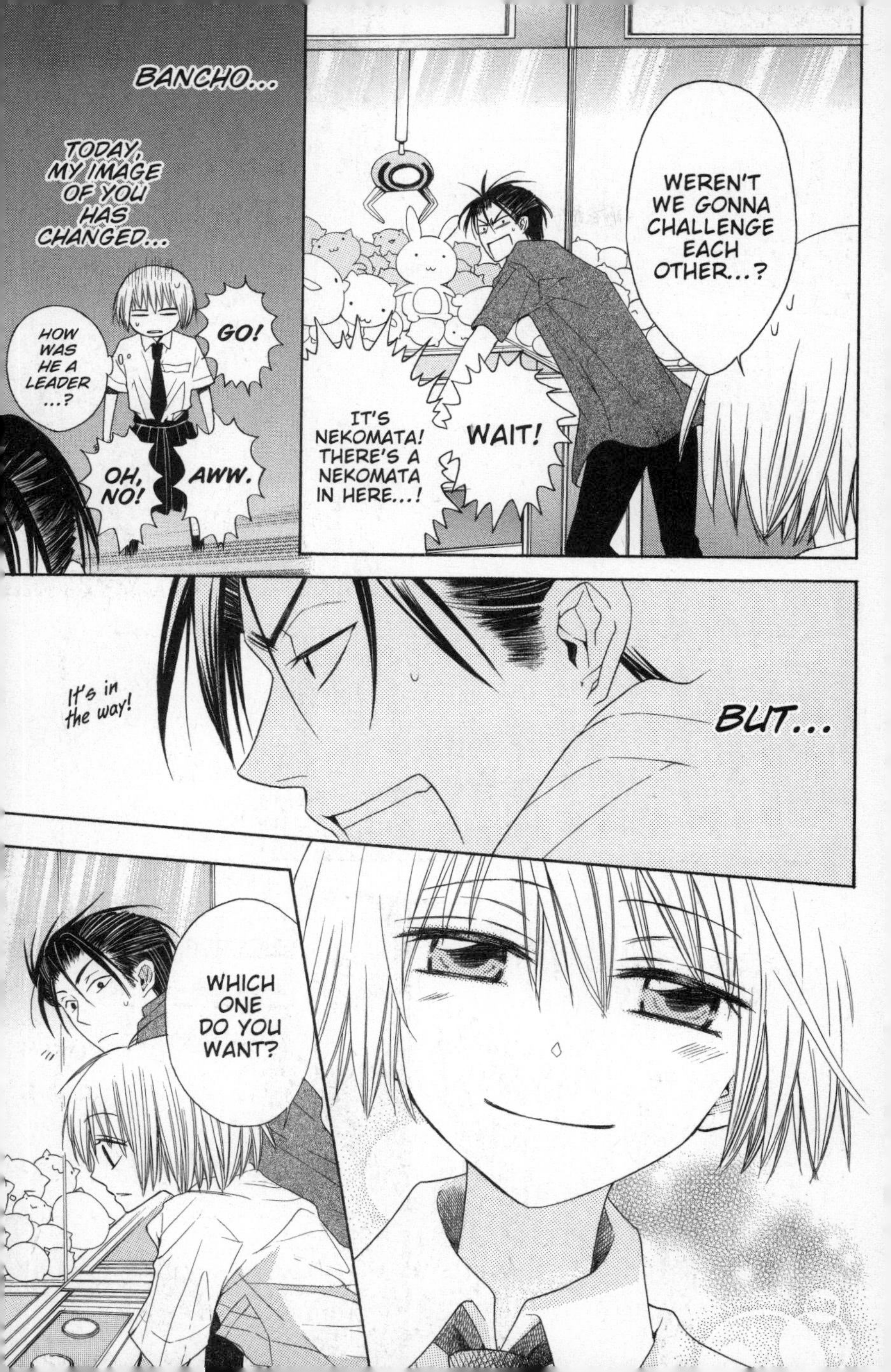
WEREN'T WE GONNA CHALLENGE EACH OTHER...?
WAIT!
IT'S NEKOMATA! THERE'S A NEKOMATA IN HERE...!
BANCHO...
TODAY, MY IMAGE OF YOU HAS CHANGED...
GO!
HOW WAS HE A LEADER ...?
AWW.
OH, NO!
BUT...
It's in the way!
WHICH ONE DO YOU WANT?

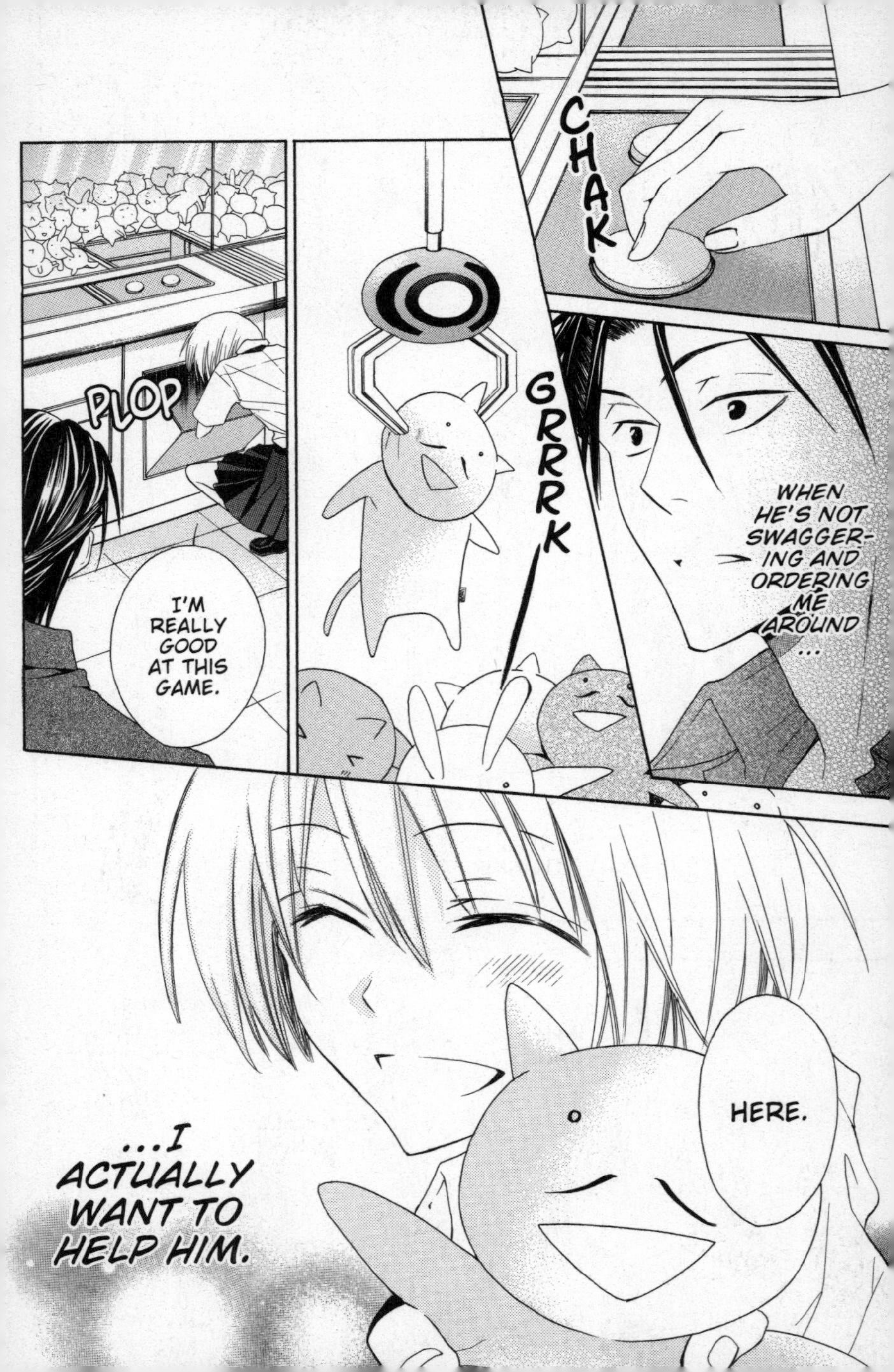
CHAK
WHEN HE'S NOT SWAGGER-ING AND ORDERING ME AROUND...
GRRRK
PLOP
I'M REALLY GOOD AT THIS GAME.
HERE.
...I ACTUALLY WANT TO HELP HIM.

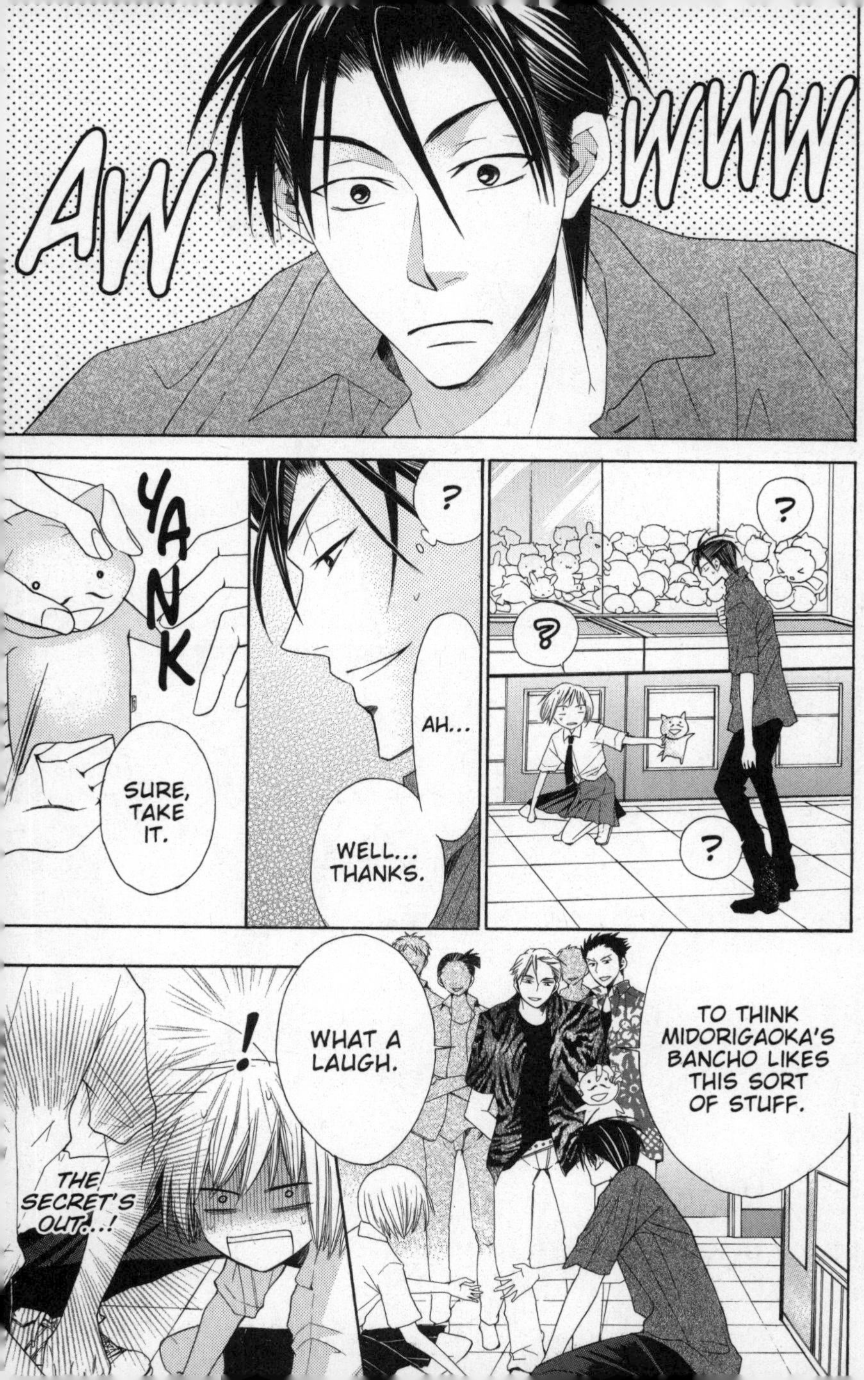
AWWWW
?
?
?
?
AH...
WELL... THANKS.
YANK
SURE, TAKE IT.
TO THINK MIDORIGAOKA'S BANCHO LIKES THIS SORT OF STUFF.
WHAT A LAUGH.
!
THE SECRET'S OUT...!

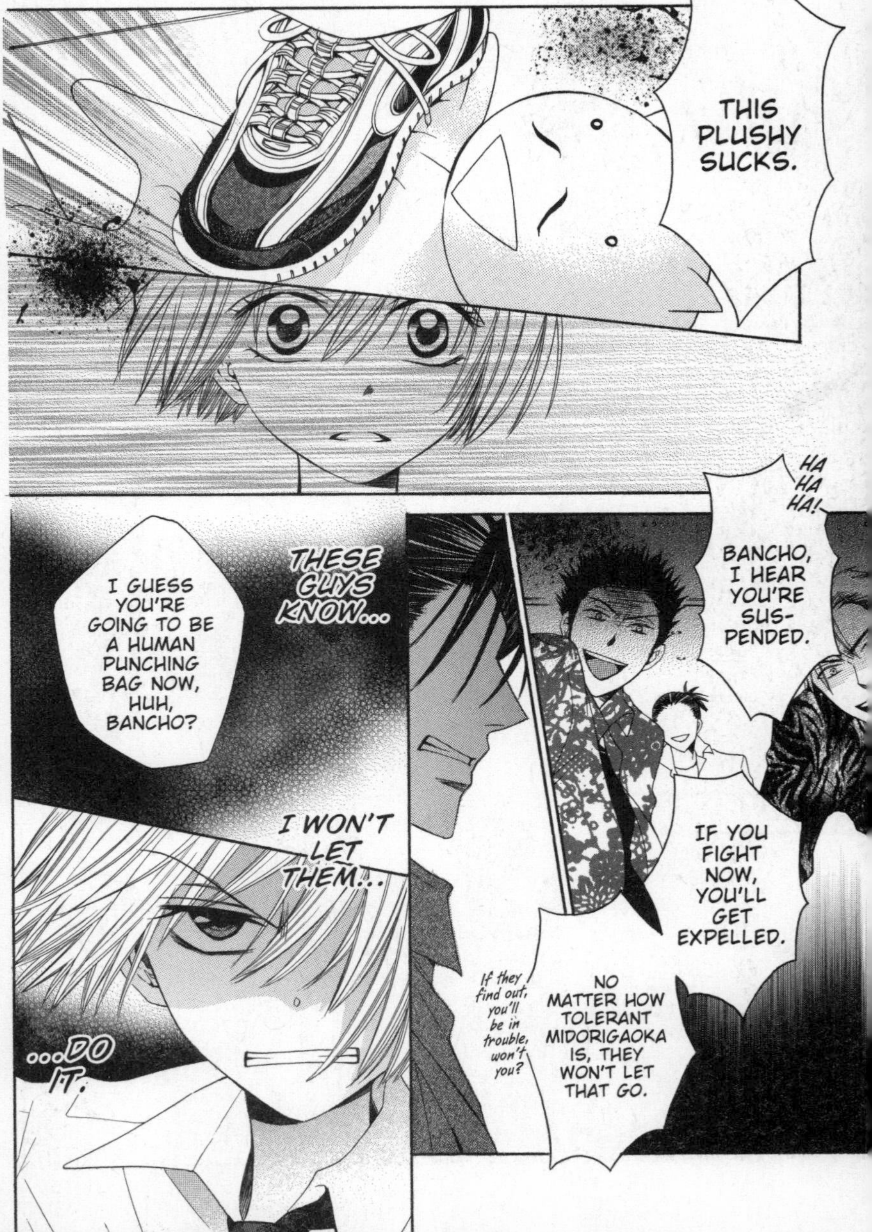
THIS PLUSHY SUCKS.
HA HA HA!
BANCHO, I HEAR YOU'RE SUS-PENDED.
IF YOU FIGHT NOW, YOU'LL GET EXPELLED.
NO MATTER HOW TOLERANT MIDORIGAOKA IS, THEY WON'T LET THAT GO.
If they find out, you'll be in trouble, won't you?
THESE GUYS KNOW...
I GUESS YOU'RE GOING TO BE A HUMAN PUNCHING BAG NOW, HUH, BANCHO?
I WON'T LET THEM...
...DO IT.

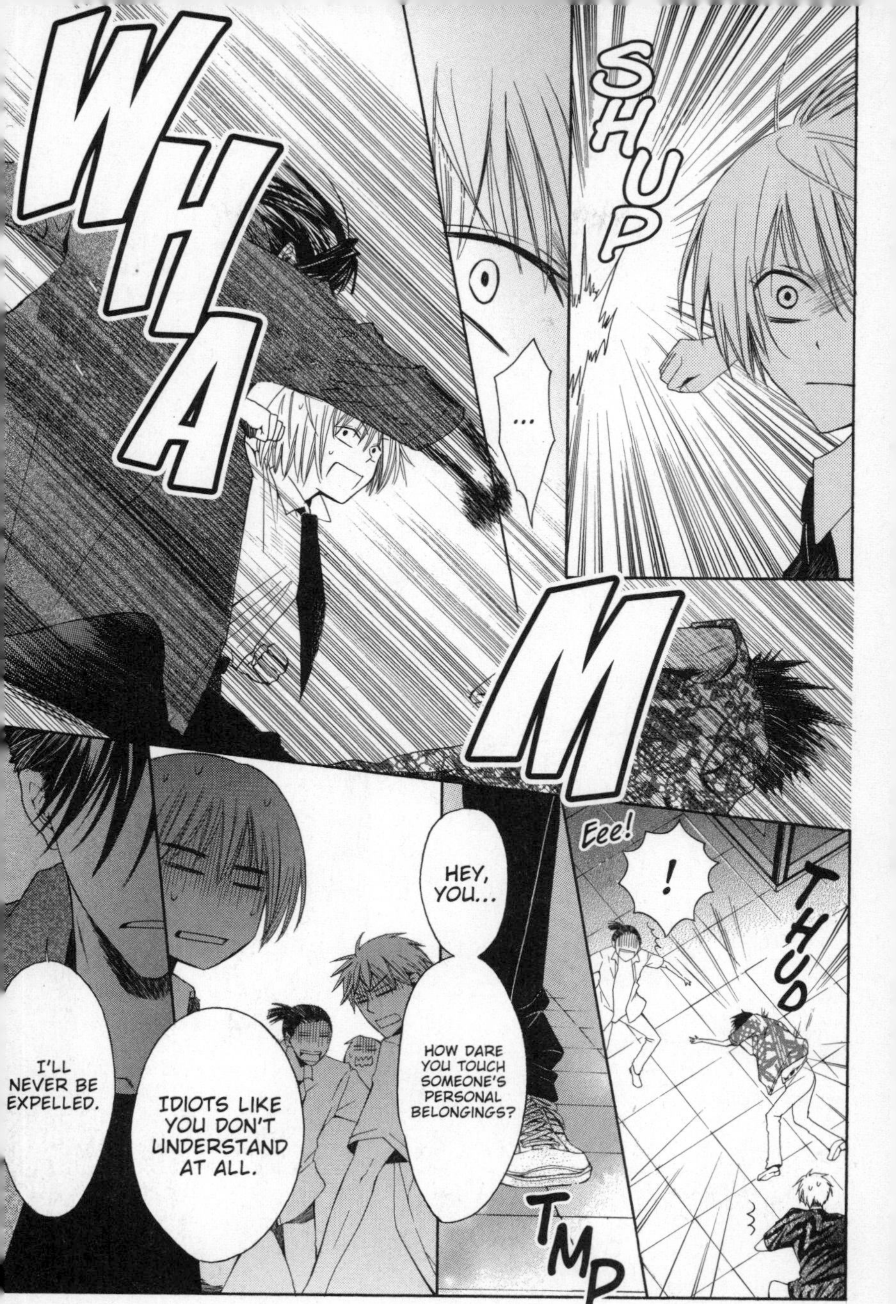
SHUP
...
WHA
M
Eee!
!
THUD
HEY, YOU...
HOW DARE YOU TOUCH SOMEONE'S PERSONAL BELONGINGS?
TMP
IDIOTS LIKE YOU DON'T UNDERSTAND AT ALL.
I'LL NEVER BE EXPELLED.

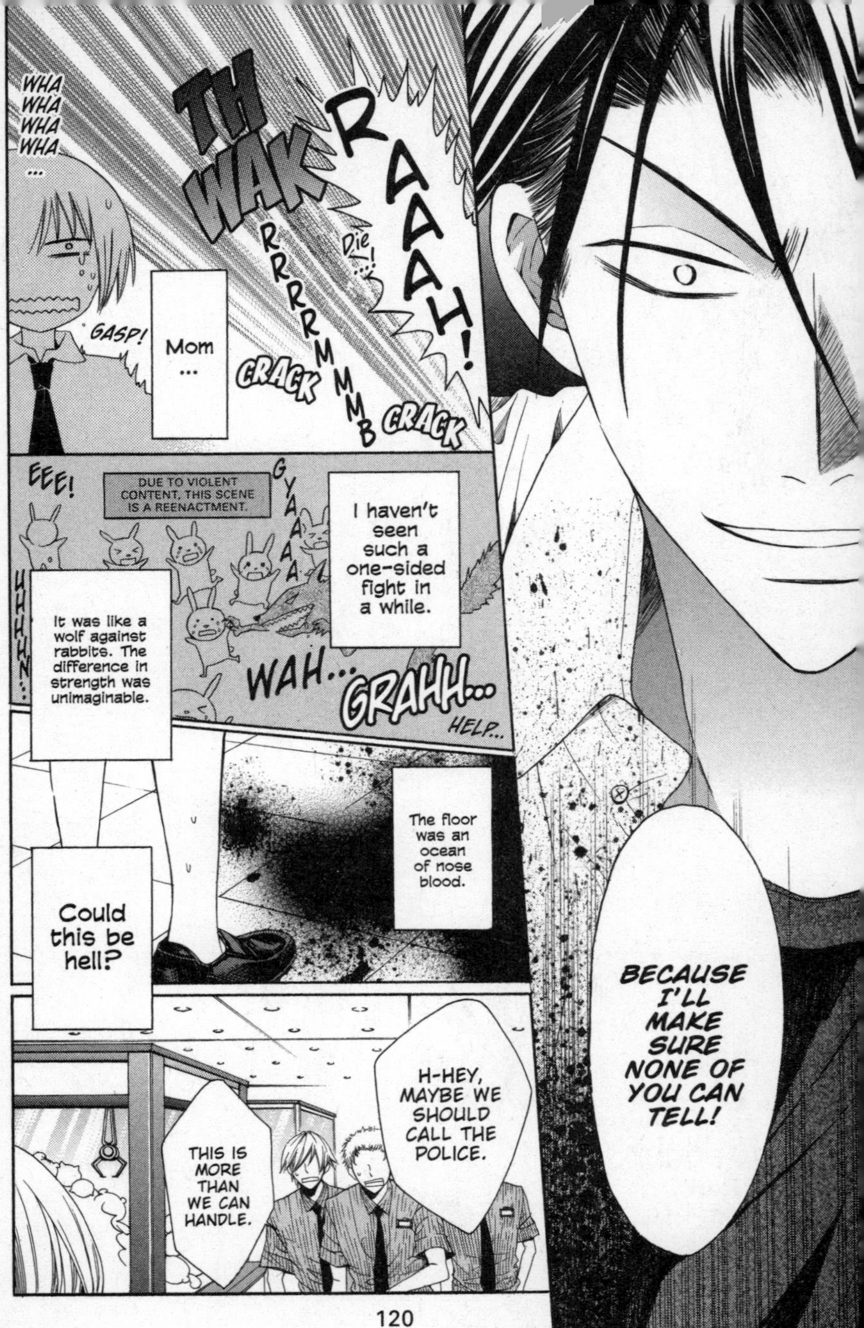
BECAUSE I'LL MAKE SURE NONE OF YOU CAN TELL!
RAAAH!
TH WAK
Die...!
RRRRRMMMB
CRACK
Mom ...
GASP!
WHA WHA WHA WHA ...
CRACK
I haven't seen such a one-sided fight in a while.
GYAAAAA
DUE TO VIOLENT CONTENT, THIS SCENE IS A REENACTMENT.
EEE!
It was like a wolf against rabbits. The difference in strength was unimaginable.
UHHHHN...
WAH...
GRAHH...
HELP...
The floor was an ocean of nose blood.
Could this be hell?
H-HEY, MAYBE WE SHOULD CALL THE POLICE.
THIS IS MORE THAN WE CAN HANDLE.

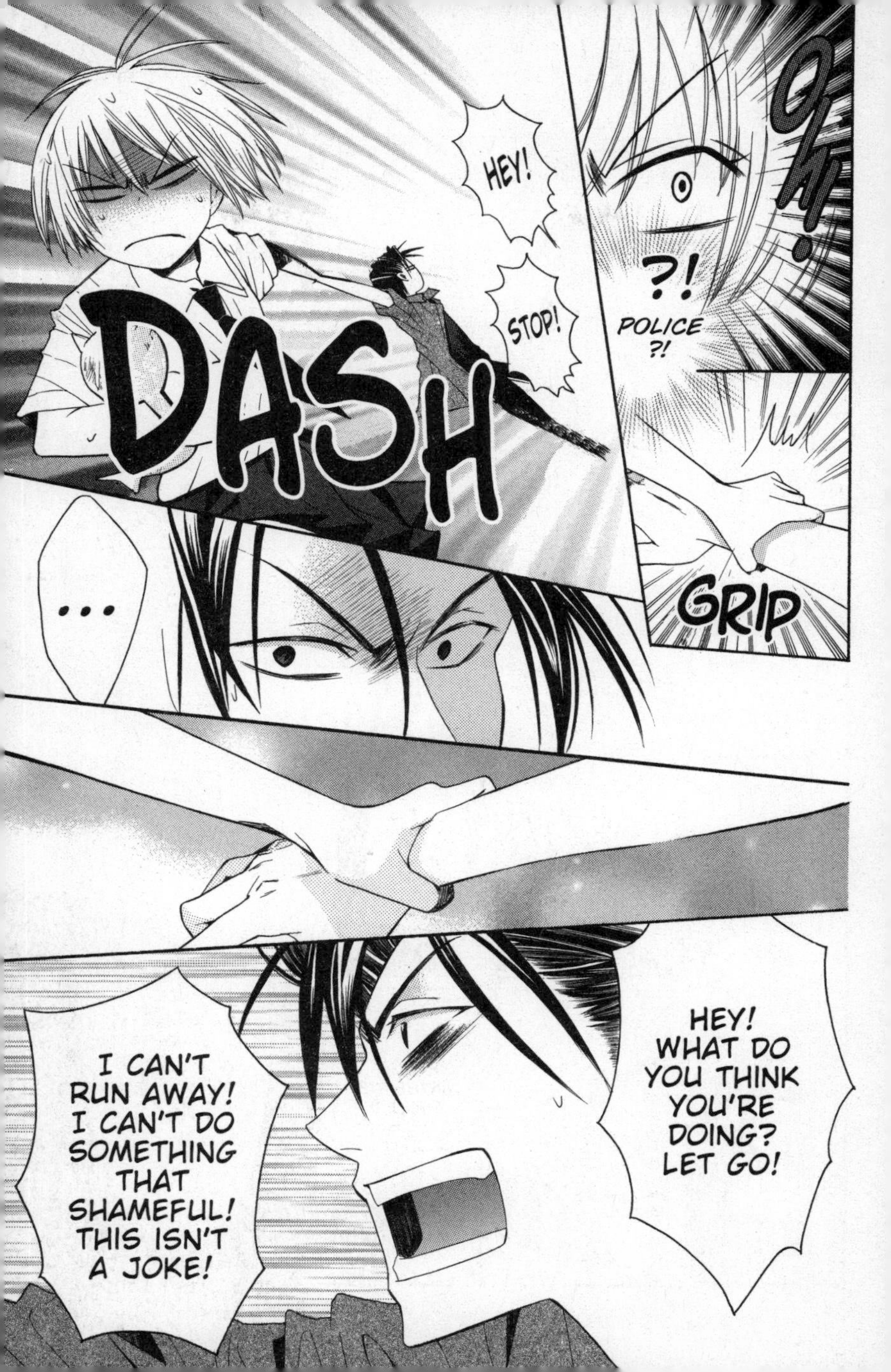
OH!
?!
POLICE ?!
GRIP
HEY!
STOP!
DASH
...
HEY! WHAT DO YOU THINK YOU'RE DOING? LET GO!
I CAN'T RUN AWAY! I CAN'T DO SOMETHING THAT SHAMEFUL! THIS ISN'T A JOKE!

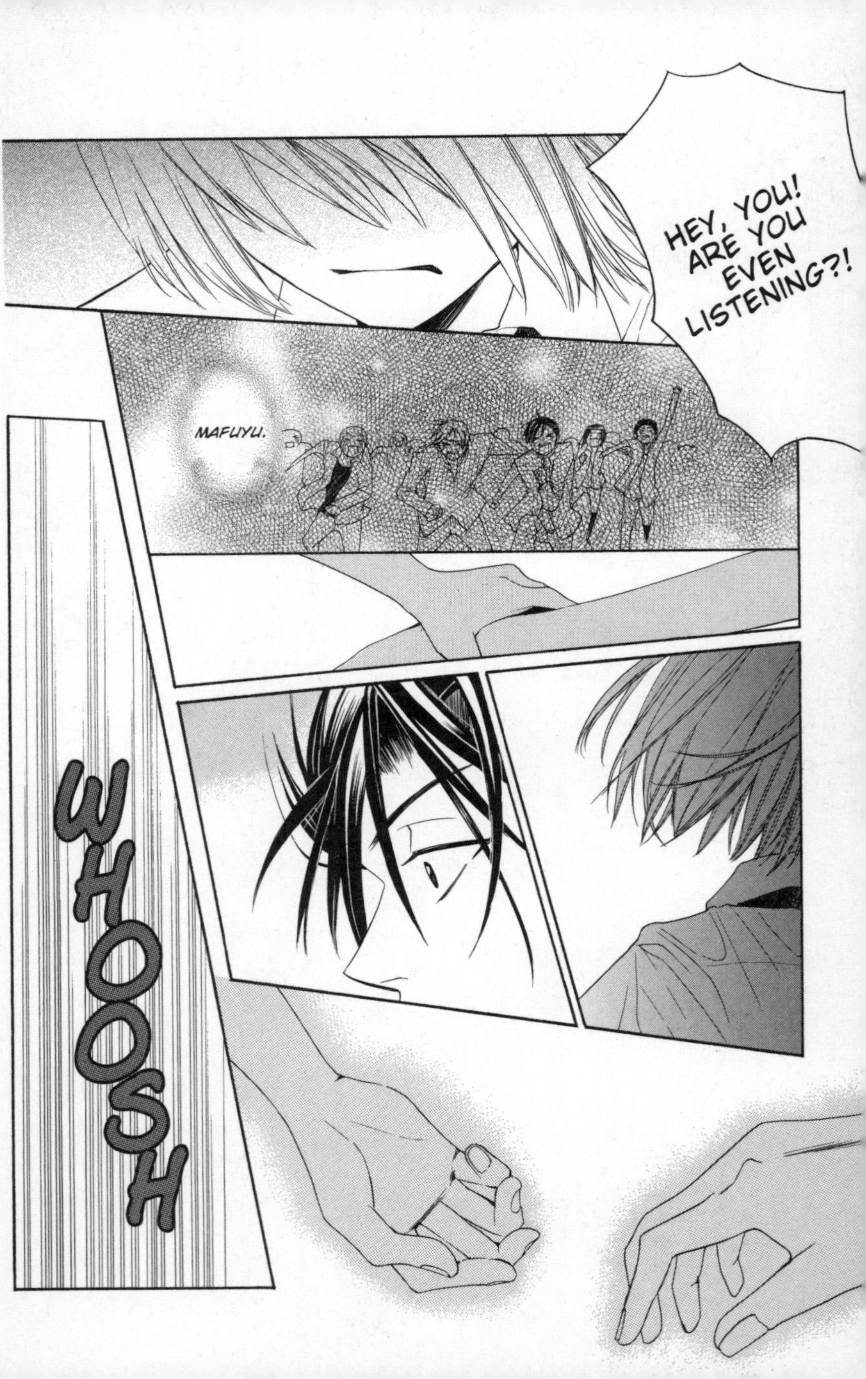
HEY, YOU! ARE YOU EVEN LISTENING?!
MAFUYU.
WHOOSH

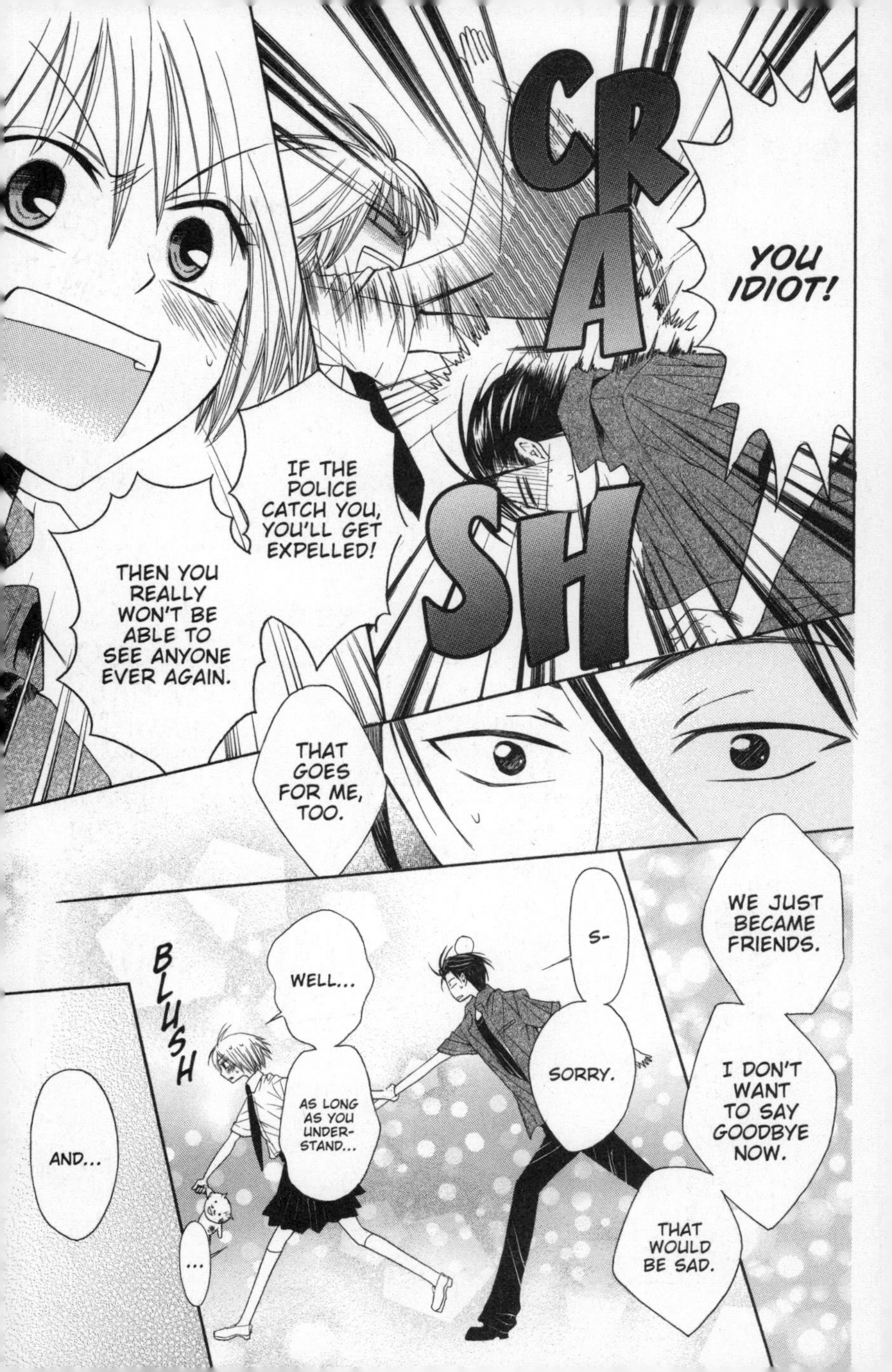
CRASH
YOU IDIOT!
IF THE POLICE CATCH YOU, YOU'LL GET EXPELLED!
THEN YOU REALLY WON'T BE ABLE TO SEE ANYONE EVER AGAIN.
THAT GOES FOR ME, TOO.
WE JUST BECAME FRIENDS.
I DON'T WANT TO SAY GOODBYE NOW.
THAT WOULD BE SAD.
S-
SORRY.
WELL...
AS LONG AS YOU UNDER-STAND...
BLUSH
AND...
...

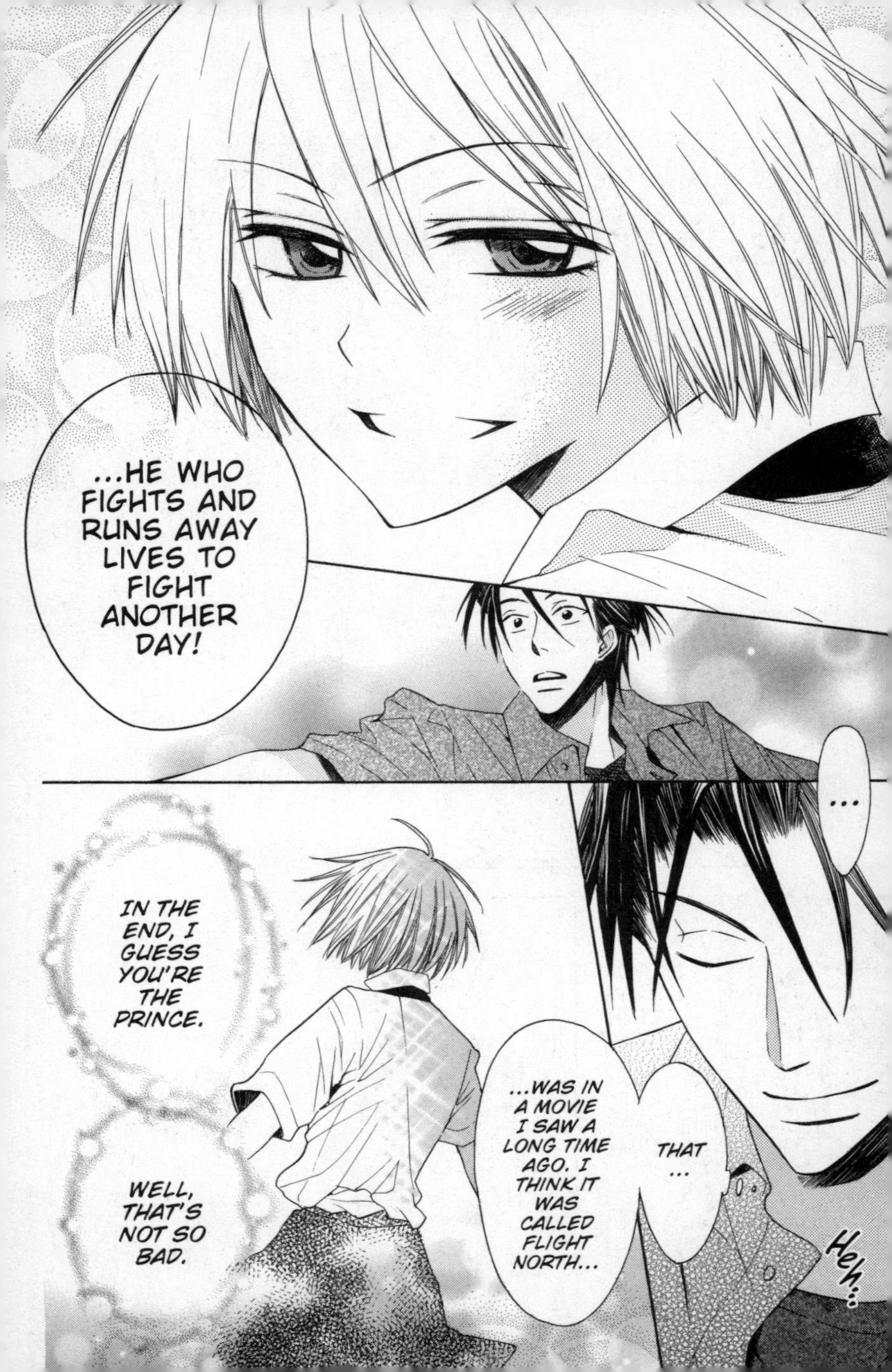
...HE WHO FIGHTS AND RUNS AWAY LIVES TO FIGHT ANOTHER DAY!
...
THAT ...
...WAS IN A MOVIE I SAW A LONG TIME AGO. I THINK IT WAS CALLED FLIGHT NORTH...
Heh..
IN THE END, I GUESS YOU'RE THE PRINCE.
WELL, THAT'S NOT SO BAD.

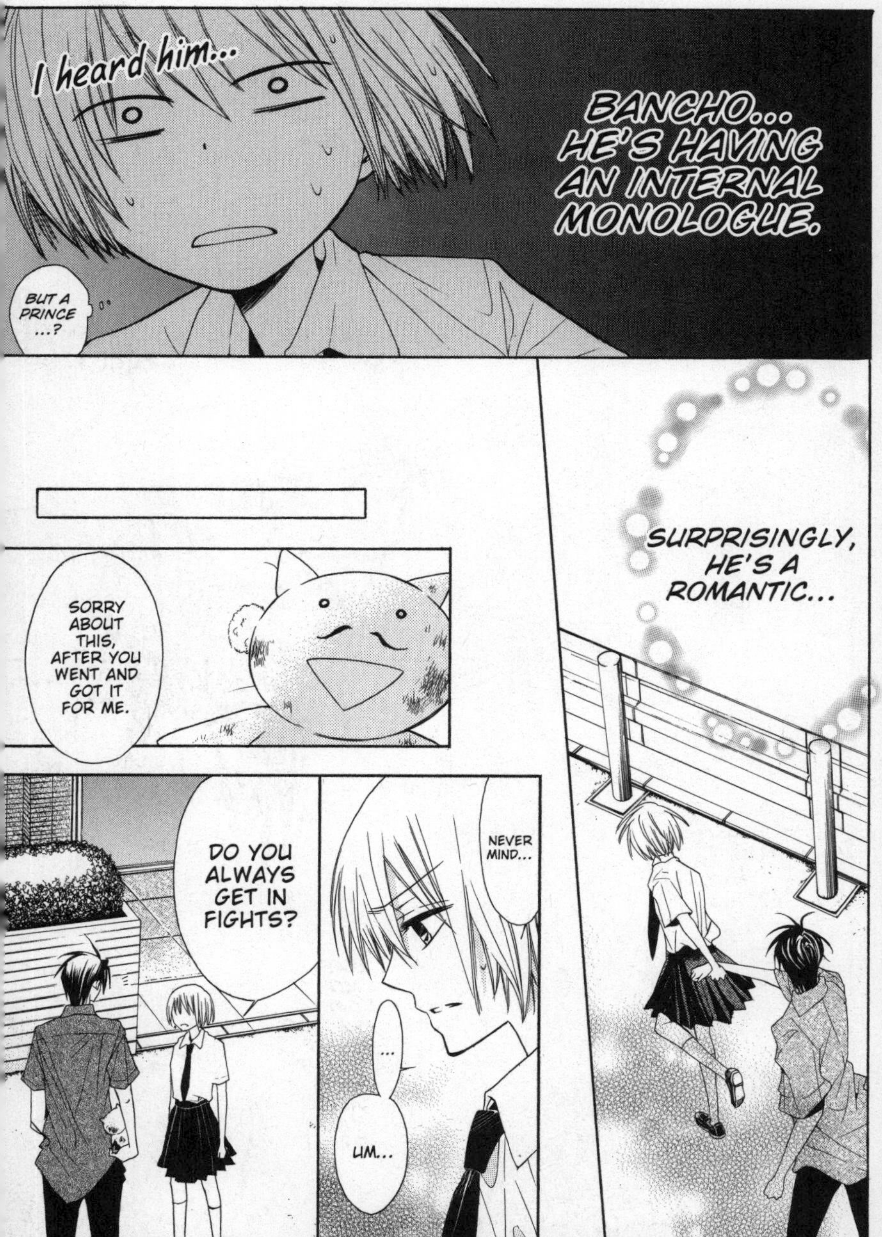

BANCHO... HE'S HAVING AN INTERNAL MONOLOGUE.
I heard him...
BUT A PRINCE ...?
SURPRISINGLY, HE'S A ROMANTIC...
SORRY ABOUT THIS, AFTER YOU WENT AND GOT IT FOR ME.
NEVER MIND...
...
UM...
DO YOU ALWAYS GET IN FIGHTS?

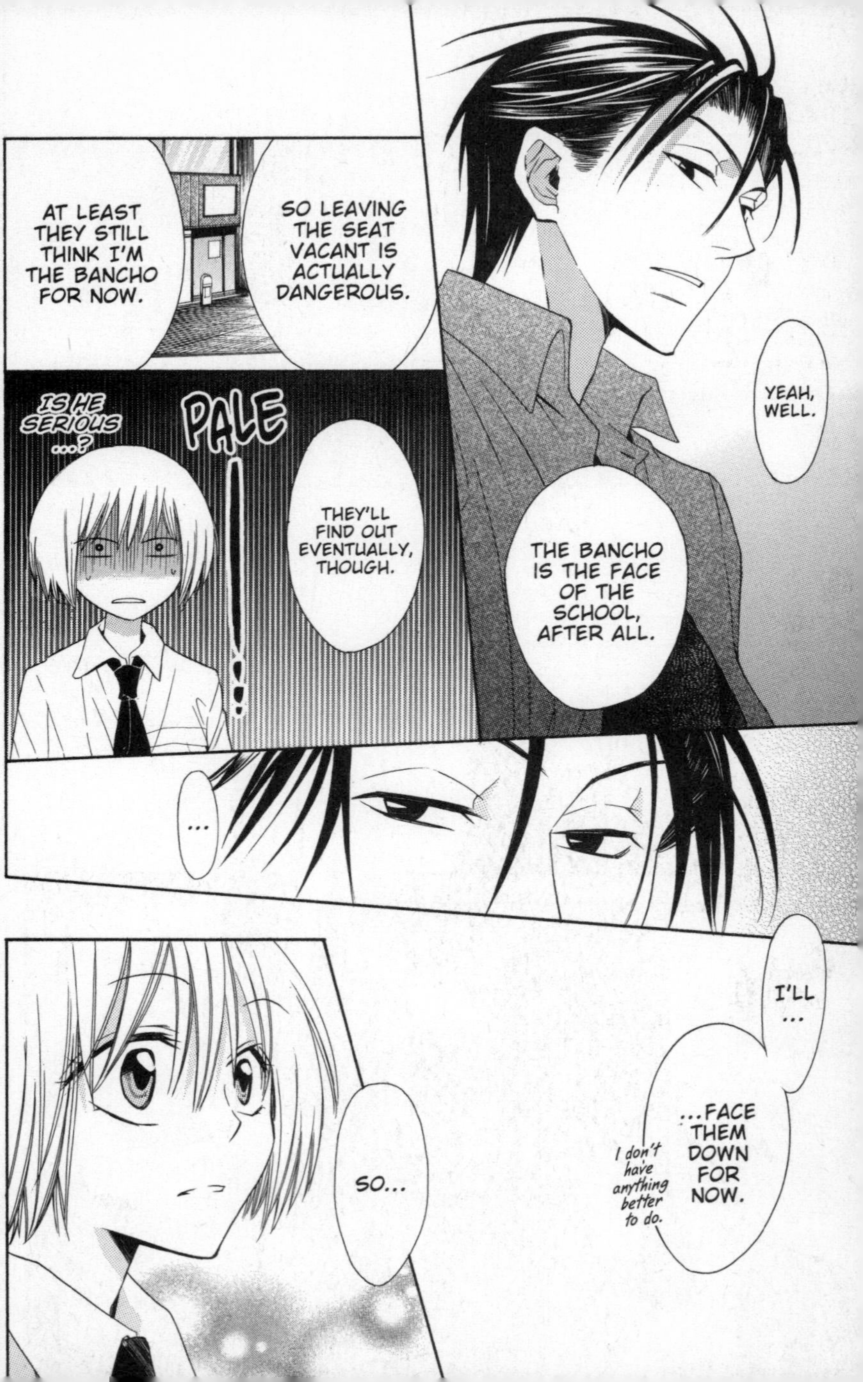
YEAH, WELL.
THE BANCHO IS THE FACE OF THE SCHOOL, AFTER ALL.
SO LEAVING THE SEAT VACANT IS ACTUALLY DANGEROUS.
AT LEAST THEY STILL THINK I'M THE BANCHO FOR NOW.
THEY'LL FIND OUT EVENTUALLY, THOUGH.
PALE
IS HE SERIOUS ...?
...
I'LL ...
...FACE THEM DOWN FOR NOW.
I don't have anything better to do.
SO...

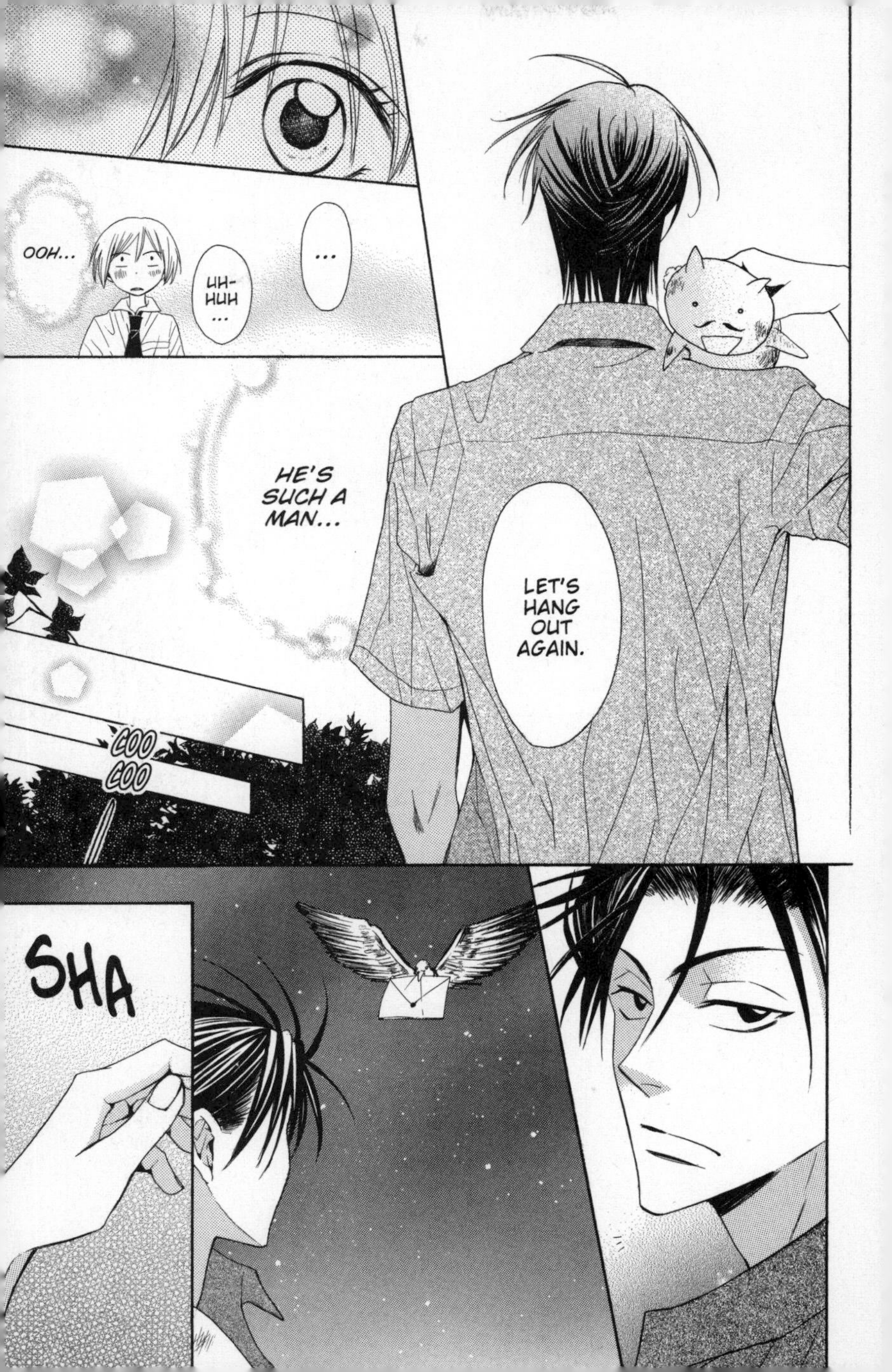
LET'S HANG OUT AGAIN.
...
UH-HUH...
OOH...
HE'S SUCH A MAN...
COO COO
SHA

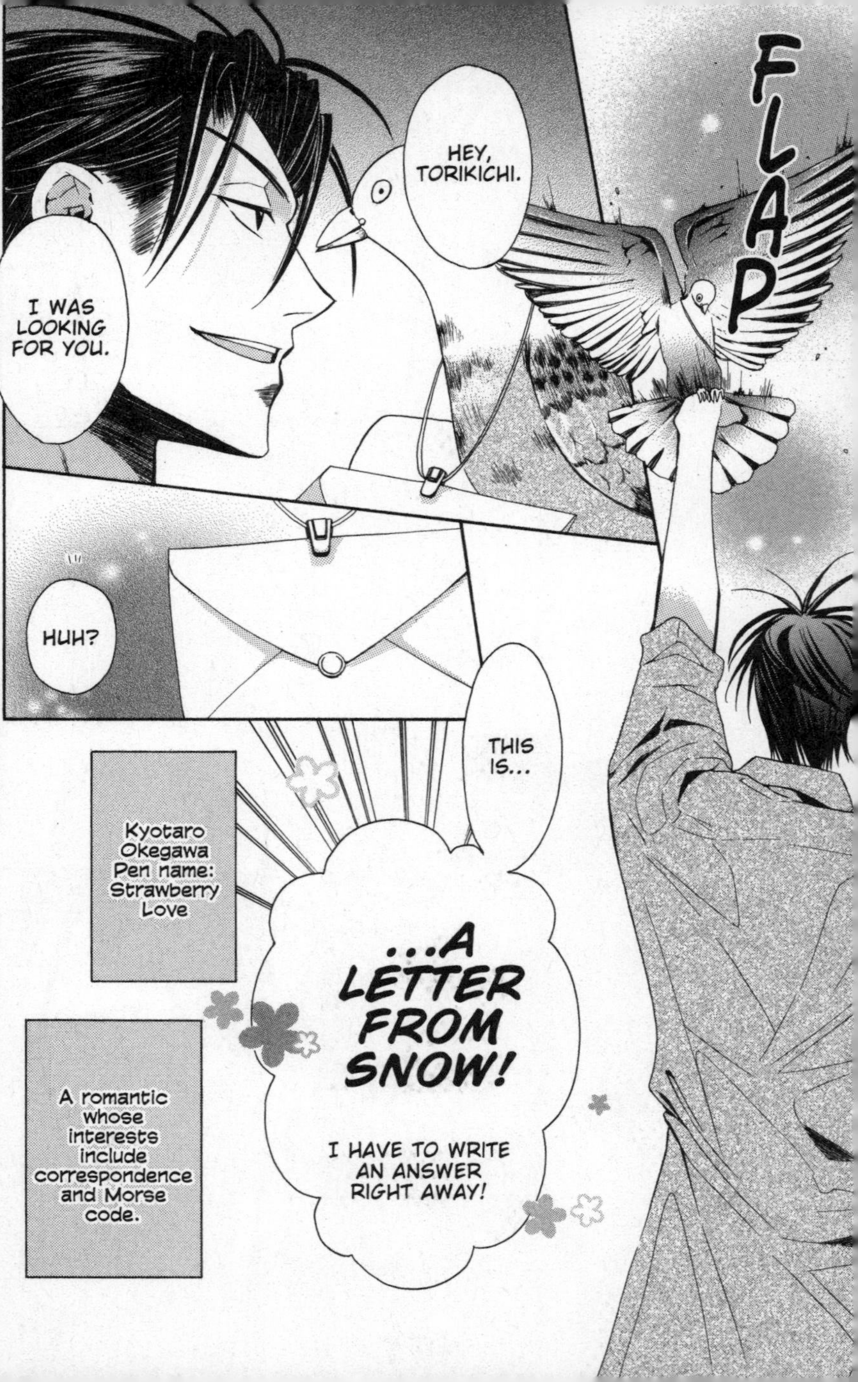
FLAP
HEY, TORIKICHI.
I WAS LOOKING FOR YOU.
HUH?
THIS IS...
...A LETTER FROM SNOW!
I HAVE TO WRITE AN ANSWER RIGHT AWAY!
Kyotaro Okegawa Pen name: Strawberry Love
A romantic whose interests include correspondence and Morse code.

Chapter 10

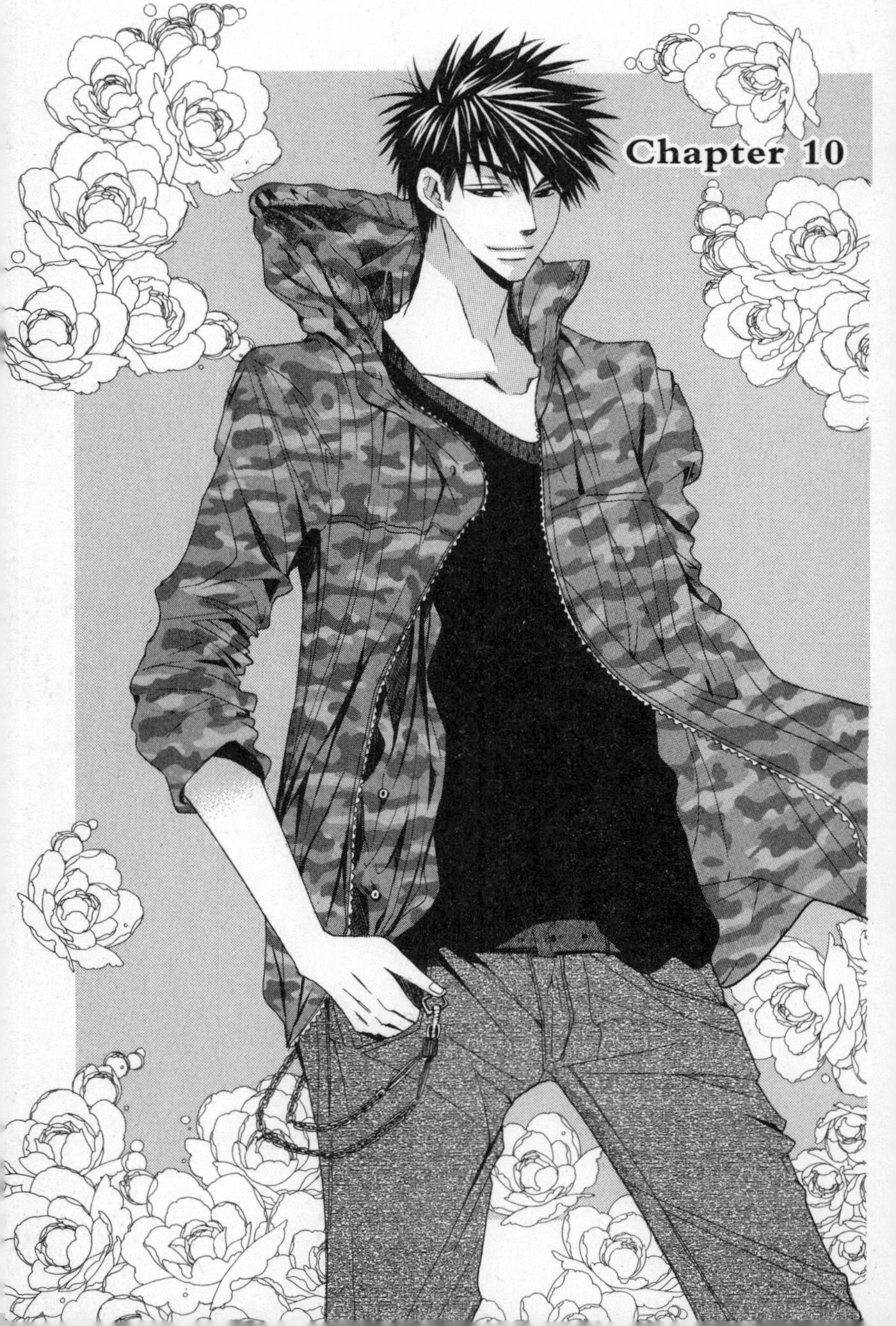

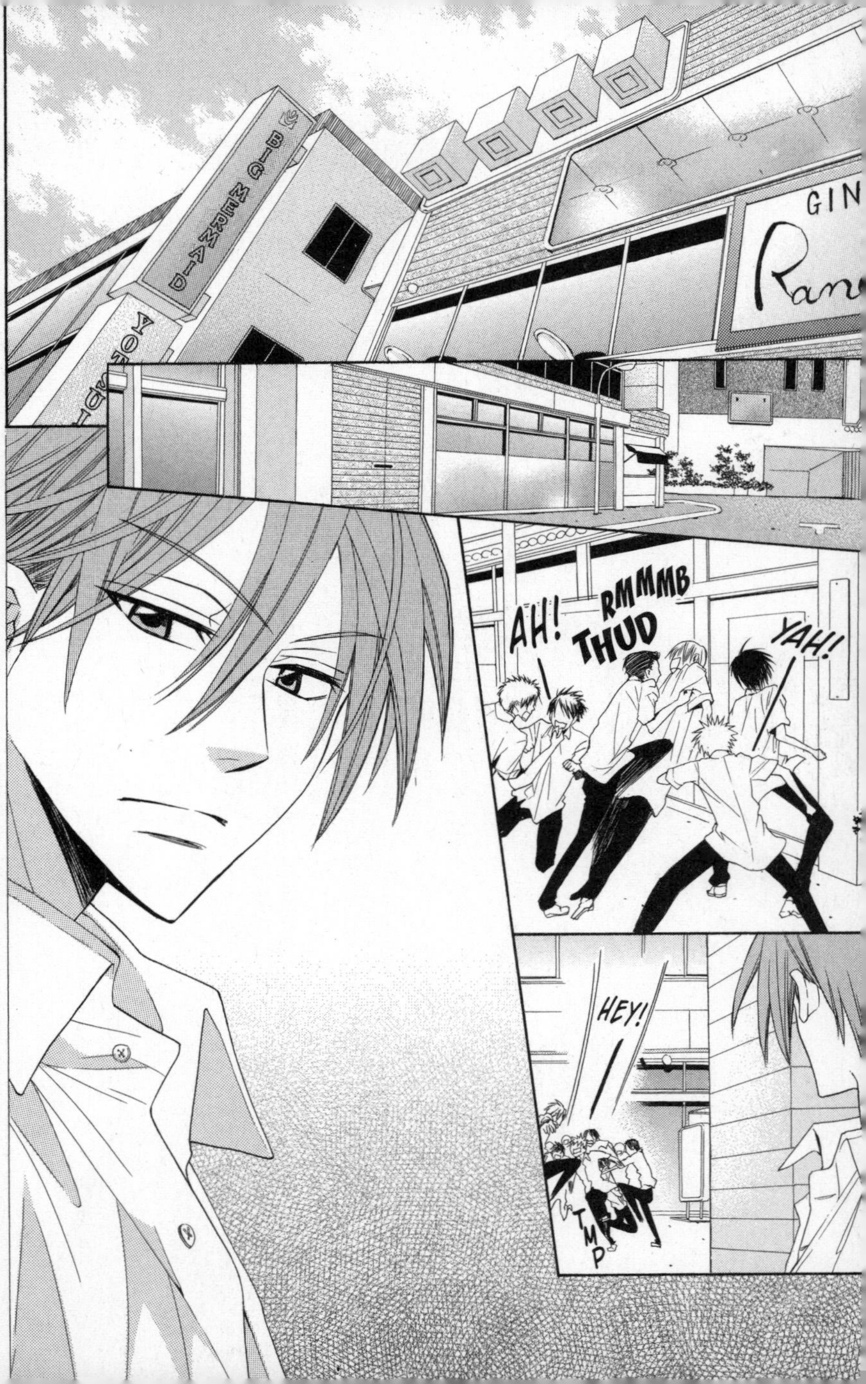
BIG MERMAID
YAH!
RMMMB
THUD
AH!
HEY!
TMP

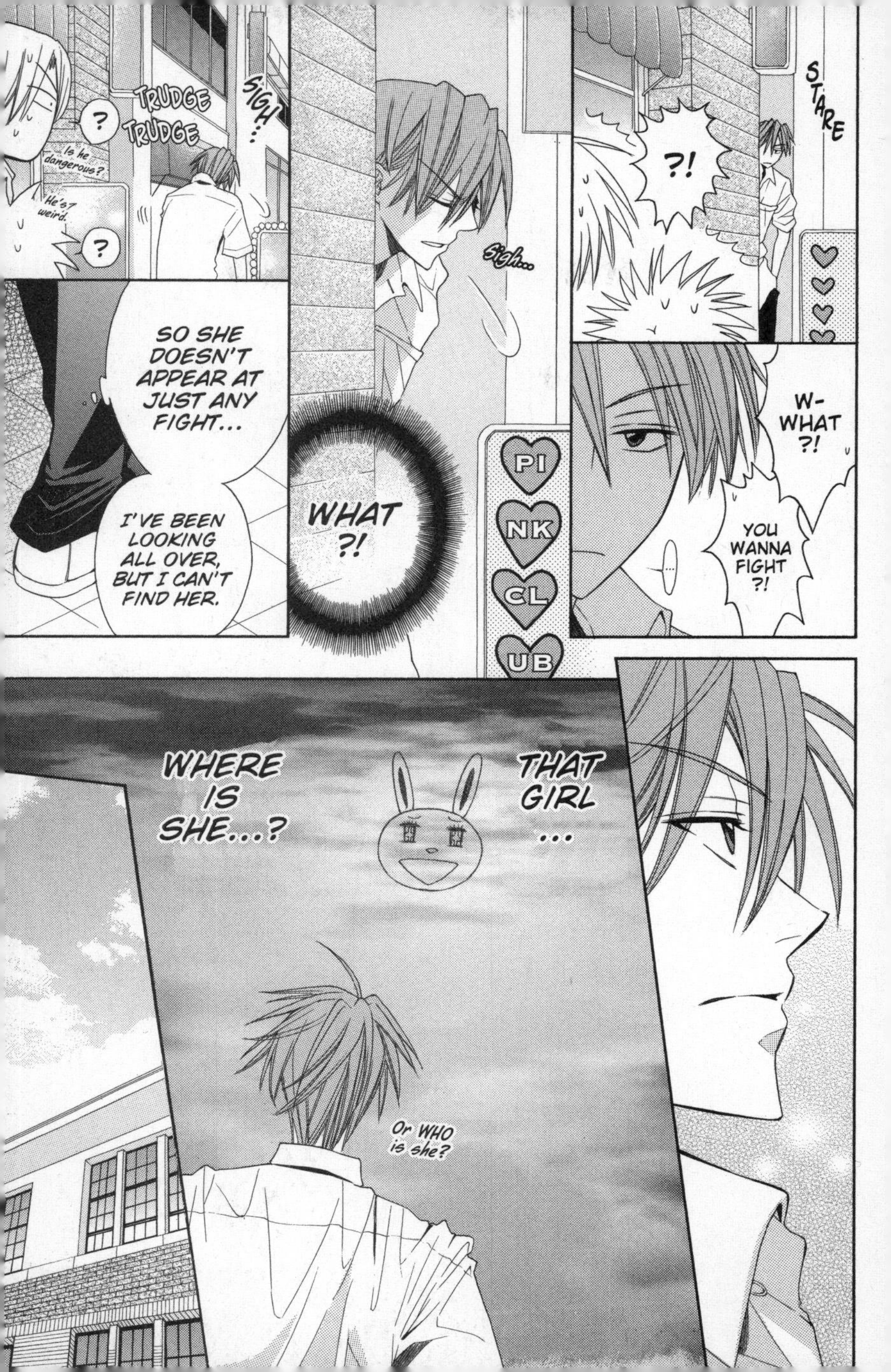
STARE
?!
W-WHAT?!
YOU WANNA FIGHT?!
...
Sigh...
WHAT?!
SIGH...
TRUDGE TRUDGE
?
Is he dangerous?
He's weird.
?
SO SHE DOESN'T APPEAR AT JUST ANY FIGHT...
I'VE BEEN LOOKING ALL OVER, BUT I CAN'T FIND HER.
PI
NK
CL
UB
THAT GIRL...
WHERE IS SHE...?
Or WHO is she?

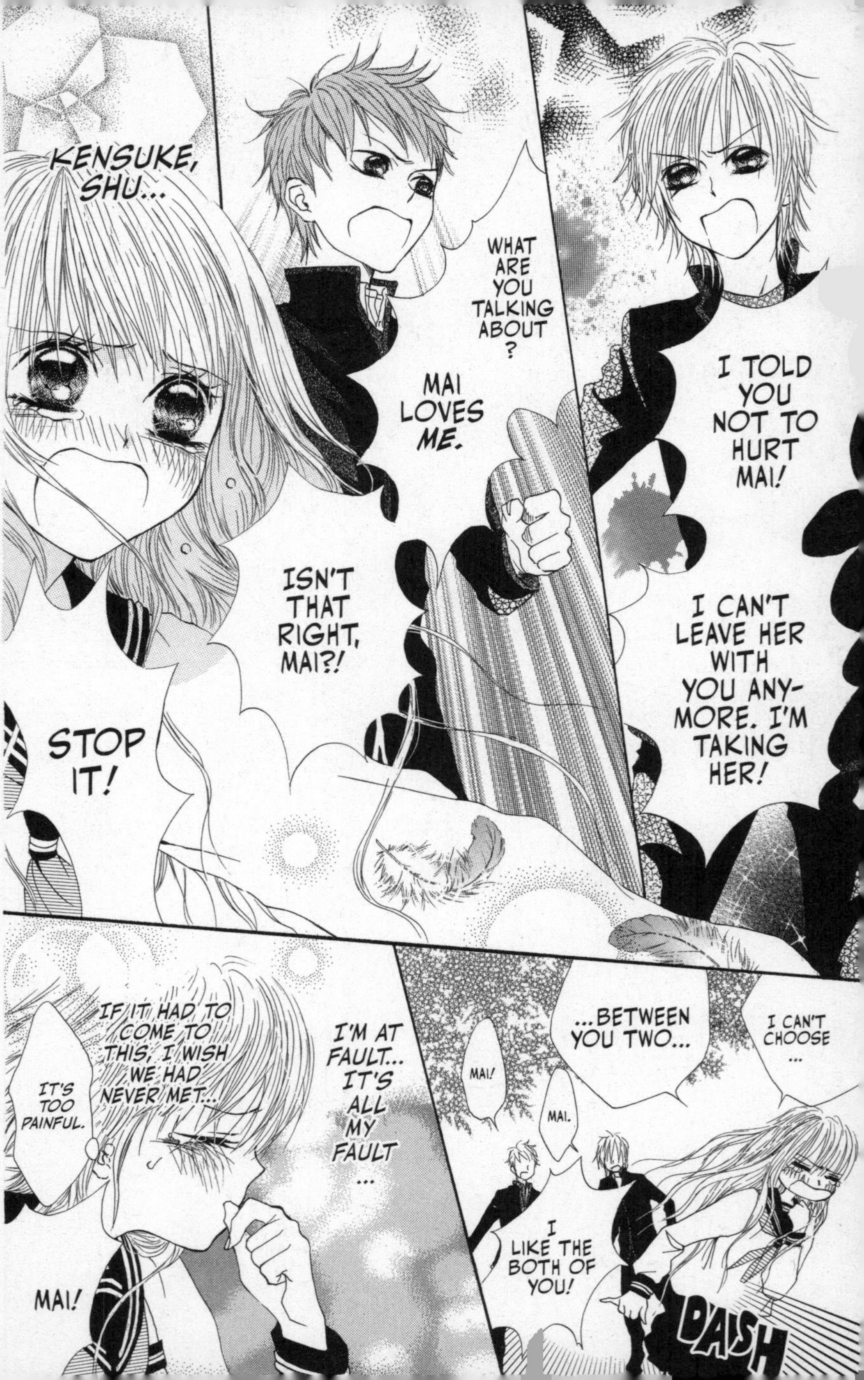
I TOLD YOU NOT TO HURT MAI!
I CAN'T LEAVE HER WITH YOU ANY-MORE. I'M TAKING HER!
WHAT ARE YOU TALKING ABOUT?
MAI LOVES ME.
ISN'T THAT RIGHT, MAI?!
KENSUKE, SHU...
STOP IT!
I CAN'T CHOOSE...
...BETWEEN YOU TWO...
MAI.
MAI!
I LIKE THE BOTH OF YOU!
DASH
I'M AT FAULT... IT'S ALL MY FAULT...
IF IT HAD TO COME TO THIS, I WISH WE HAD NEVER MET...
IT'S TOO PAINFUL.
MAI!

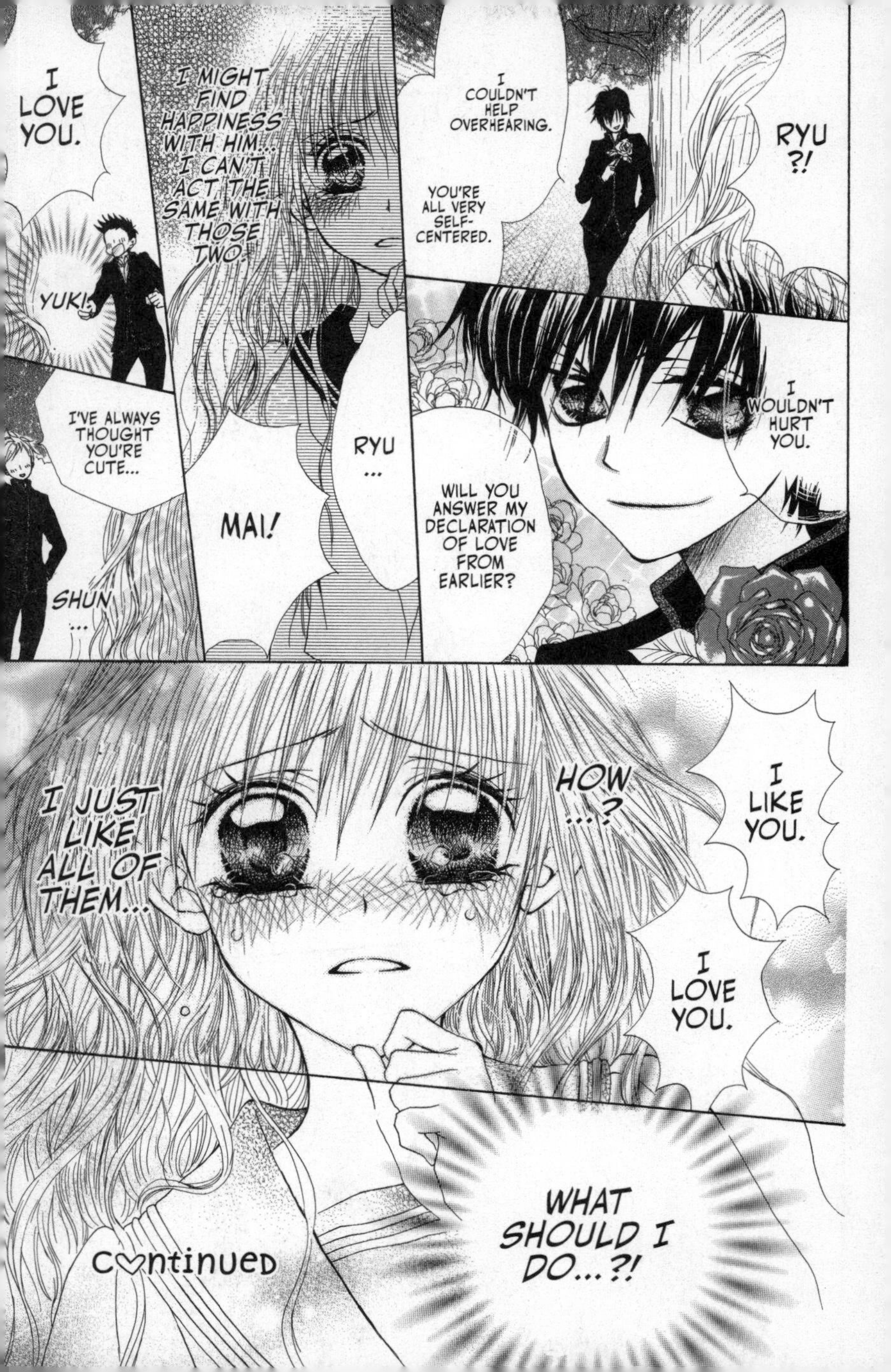
I COULDN'T HELP OVERHEARING.
YOU'RE ALL VERY SELF-CENTERED.
RYU ?!
I WOULDN'T HURT YOU.
WILL YOU ANSWER MY DECLARATION OF LOVE FROM EARLIER?
I MIGHT FIND HAPPINESS WITH HIM... I CAN'T ACT THE SAME WITH THOSE TWO.
RYU ...
MAI!
I LOVE YOU.
YUKI!
I'VE ALWAYS THOUGHT YOU'RE CUTE...
SHUN ...
I LIKE YOU.
I LOVE YOU.
HOW ...?
I JUST LIKE ALL OF THEM...
WHAT SHOULD I DO...?!
Continued

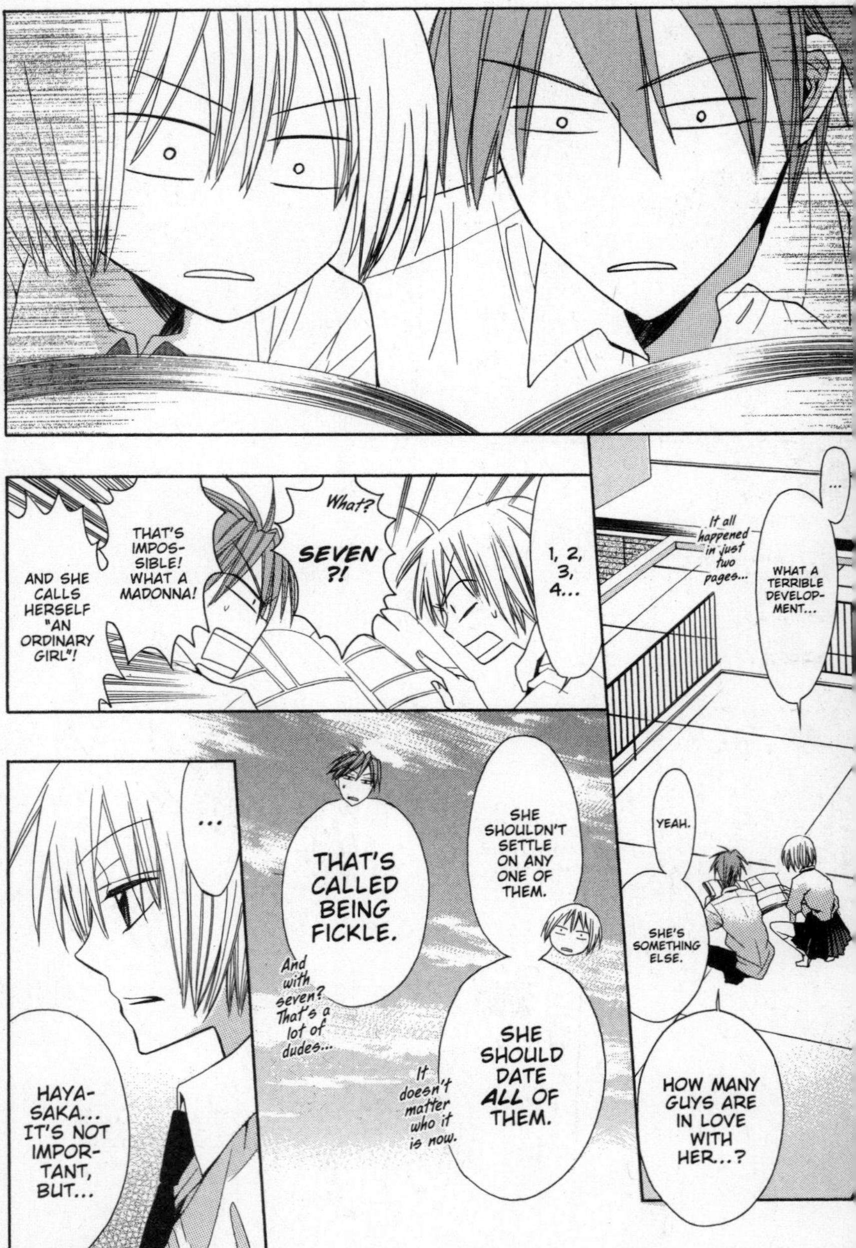
...
WHAT A TERRIBLE DEVELOPMENT...
It all happened in just two pages...
YEAH.
SHE'S SOMETHING ELSE.
HOW MANY GUYS ARE IN LOVE WITH HER...?
1, 2, 3, 4...
SEVEN ?!
What?
THAT'S IMPOSSIBLE! WHAT A MADONNA!
AND SHE CALLS HERSELF "AN ORDINARY GIRL"!
SHE SHOULDN'T SETTLE ON ANY ONE OF THEM.
SHE SHOULD DATE ALL OF THEM.
It doesn't matter who it is now.
THAT'S CALLED BEING FICKLE.
And with seven? That's a lot of dudes...
...
HAYA-SAKA... IT'S NOT IMPOR-TANT, BUT...

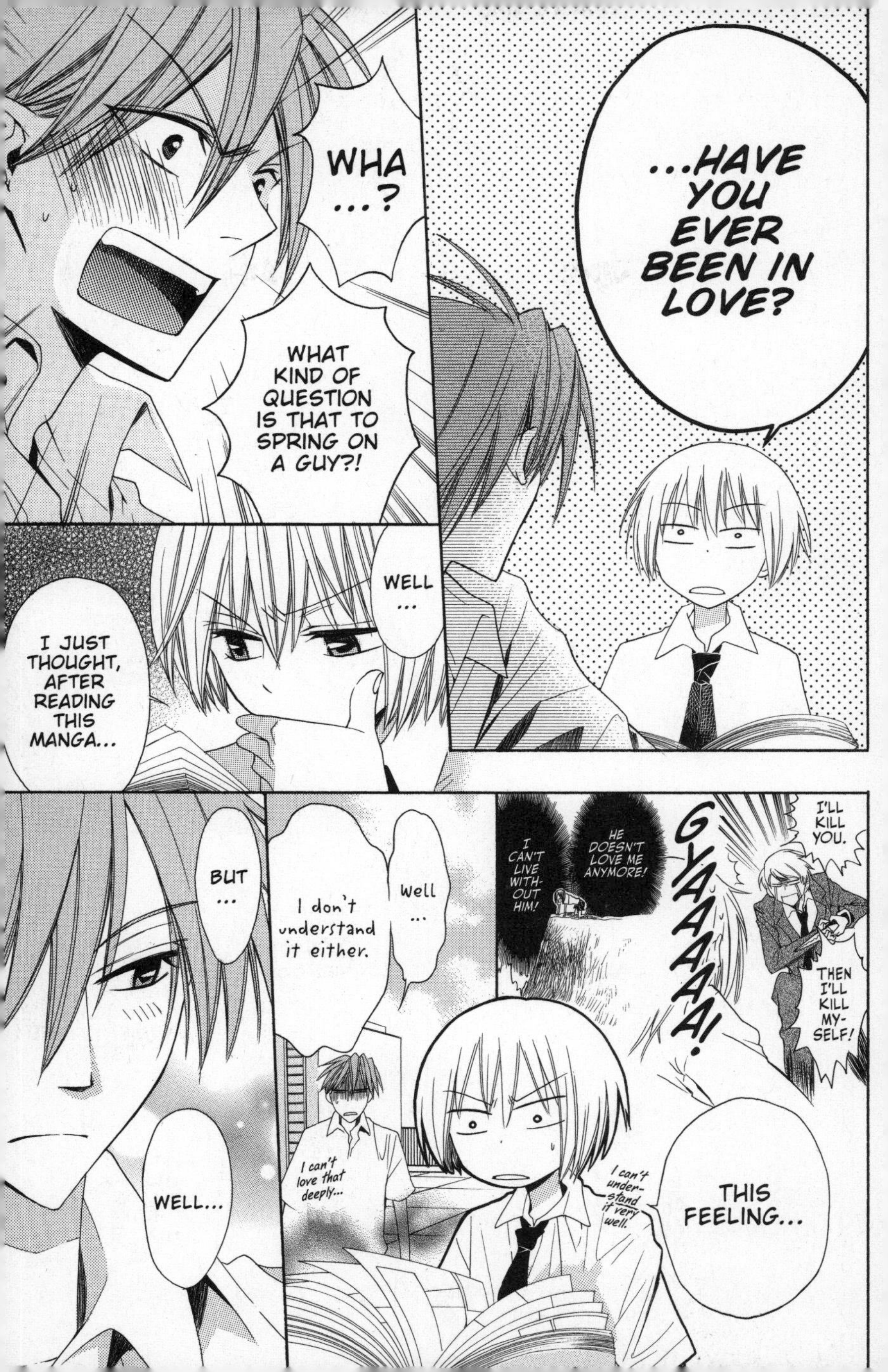
...HAVE YOU EVER BEEN IN LOVE?
WHA ...?
WHAT KIND OF QUESTION IS THAT TO SPRING ON A GUY?!
WELL ...
I JUST THOUGHT, AFTER READING THIS MANGA...
I'LL KILL YOU.
THEN I'LL KILL MY-SELF!
GYAAAAA!
HE DOESN'T LOVE ME ANYMORE!
I CAN'T LIVE WITH-OUT HIM!
THIS FEELING...
I can't under-stand it very well.
Well ...
I don't understand it either.
I can't love that deeply...
BUT ...
WELL...

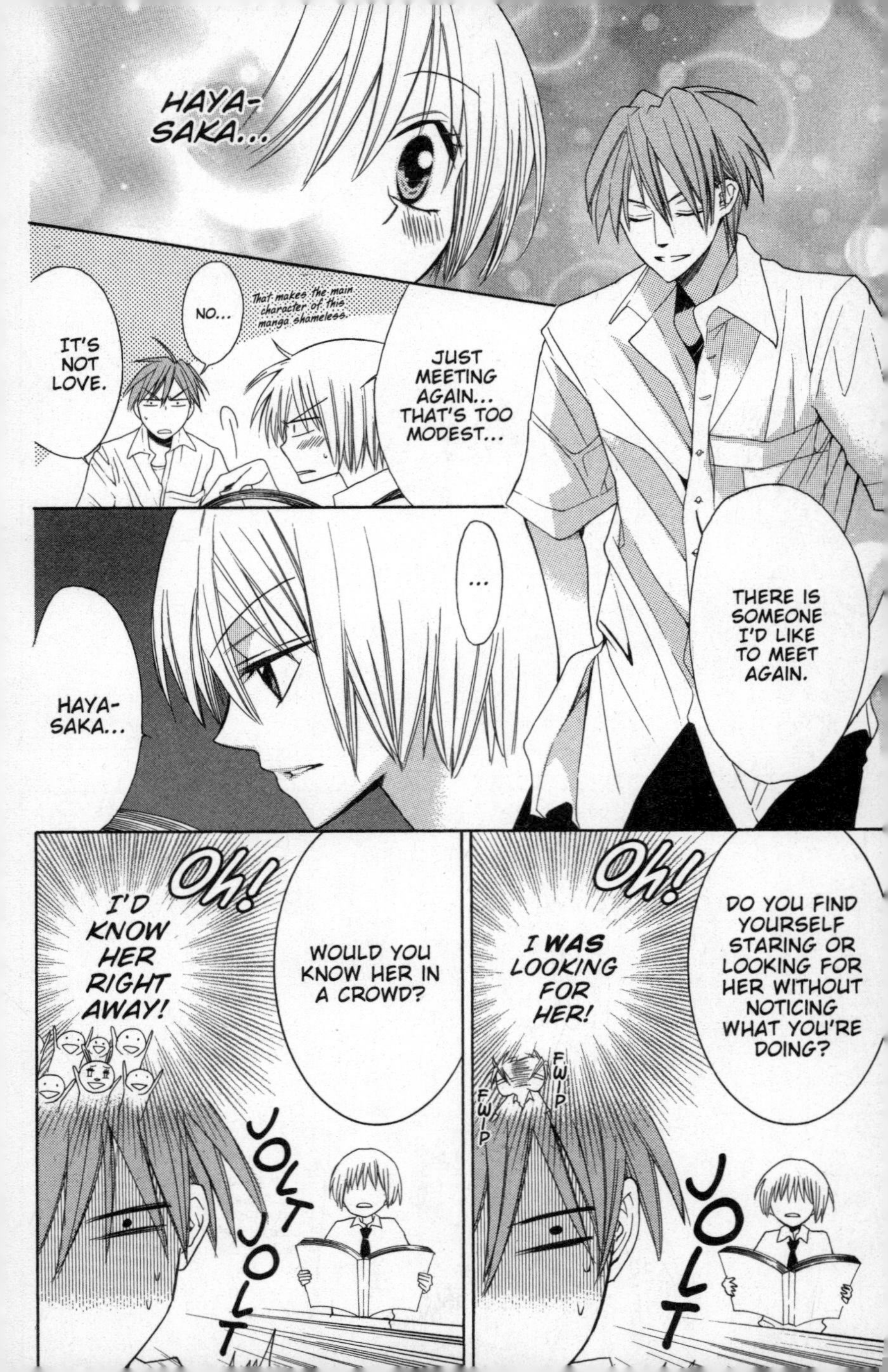

HAYA-SAKA...
THERE IS SOMEONE I'D LIKE TO MEET AGAIN.
JUST MEETING AGAIN... THAT'S TOO MODEST...
NO...
That makes the main character of this manga shameless.
IT'S NOT LOVE.
...
HAYA-SAKA...
DO YOU FIND YOURSELF STARING OR LOOKING FOR HER WITHOUT NOTICING WHAT YOU'RE DOING?
Oh!
I WAS LOOKING FOR HER!
FWIP
FWIP
JOLT
WOULD YOU KNOW HER IN A CROWD?
Oh!
I'D KNOW HER RIGHT AWAY!
JOLT
JOLT

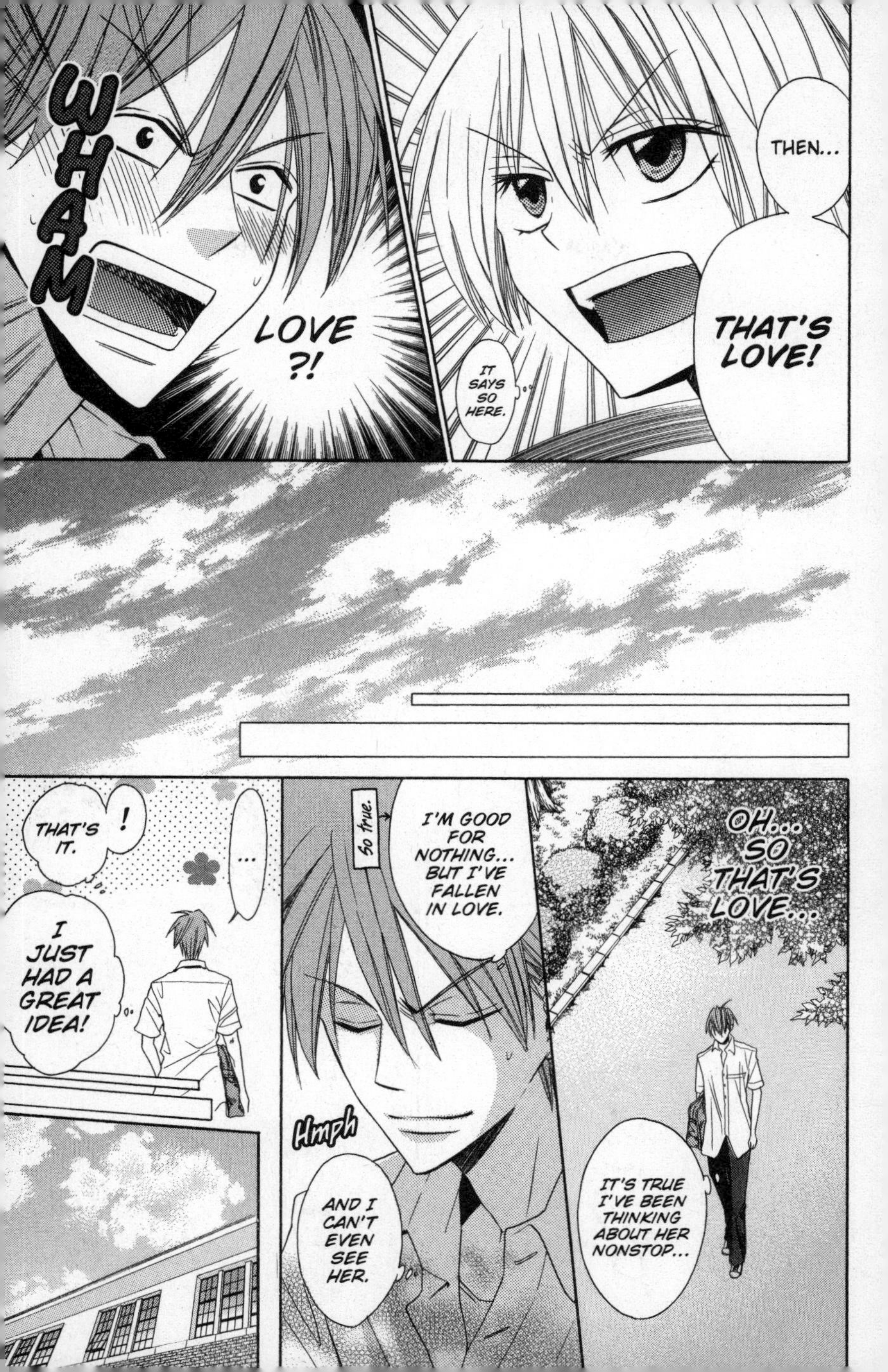
THEN...
THAT'S LOVE!
IT SAYS SO HERE.
WHAM
LOVE ?!
OH... SO THAT'S LOVE...
IT'S TRUE I'VE BEEN THINKING ABOUT HER NONSTOP...
So true.
I'M GOOD FOR NOTHING... BUT I'VE FALLEN IN LOVE.
Hmph
AND I CAN'T EVEN SEE HER.
...
!
THAT'S IT.
I JUST HAD A GREAT IDEA!

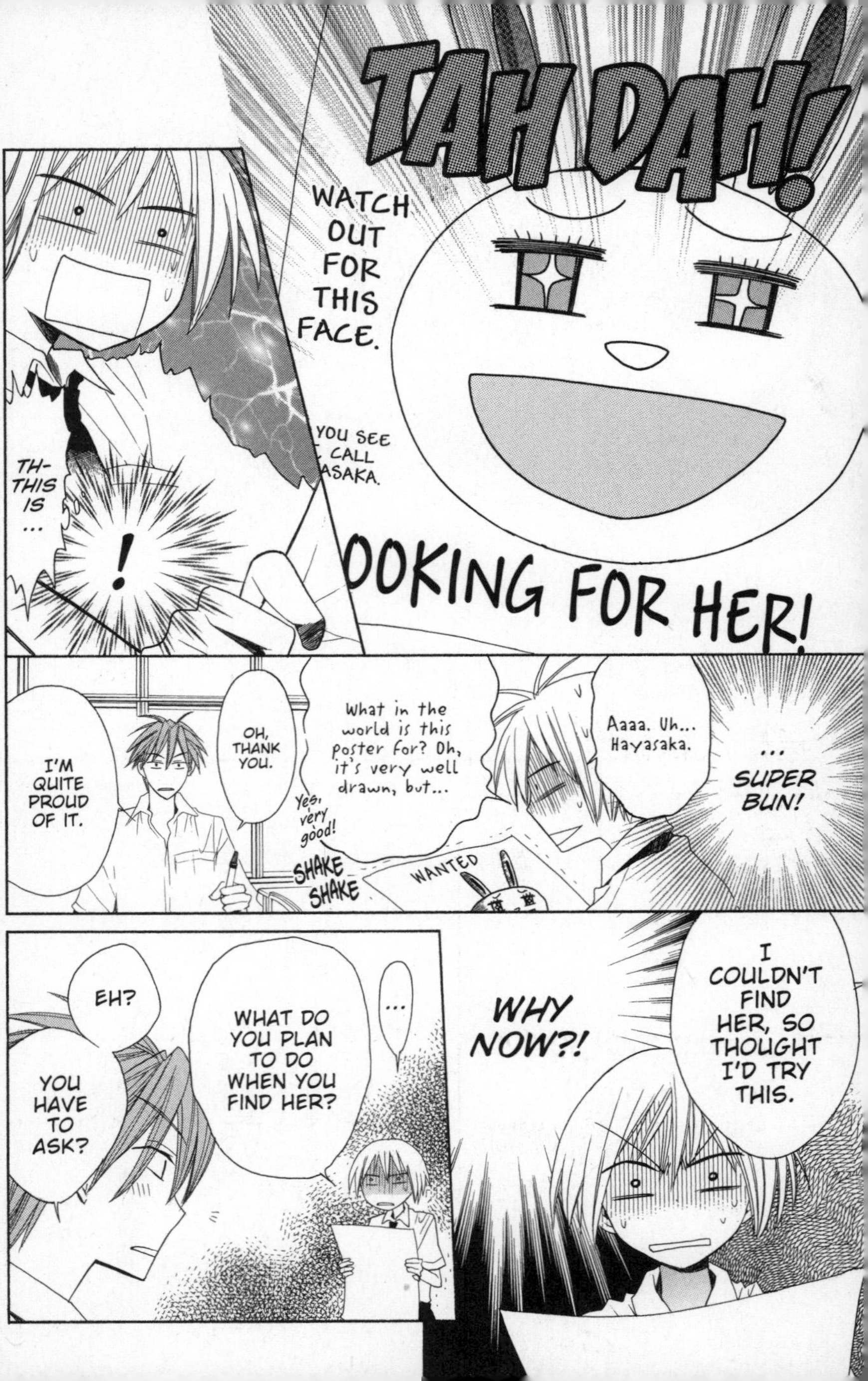
TAH DAH!
WATCH OUT FOR THIS FACE.
YOU SEE CALL ASAKA.
OOKING FOR HER!
TH-THIS IS ...
!
... SUPER BUN!
Aaaa. Uh... Hayasaka.
What in the world is this poster for? Oh, it's very well drawn, but...
Yes, very good!
WANTED
SHAKE SHAKE
OH, THANK YOU.
I'M QUITE PROUD OF IT.
I COULDN'T FIND HER, SO THOUGHT I'D TRY THIS.
WHY NOW?!
...
WHAT DO YOU PLAN TO DO WHEN YOU FIND HER?
EH?
YOU HAVE TO ASK?

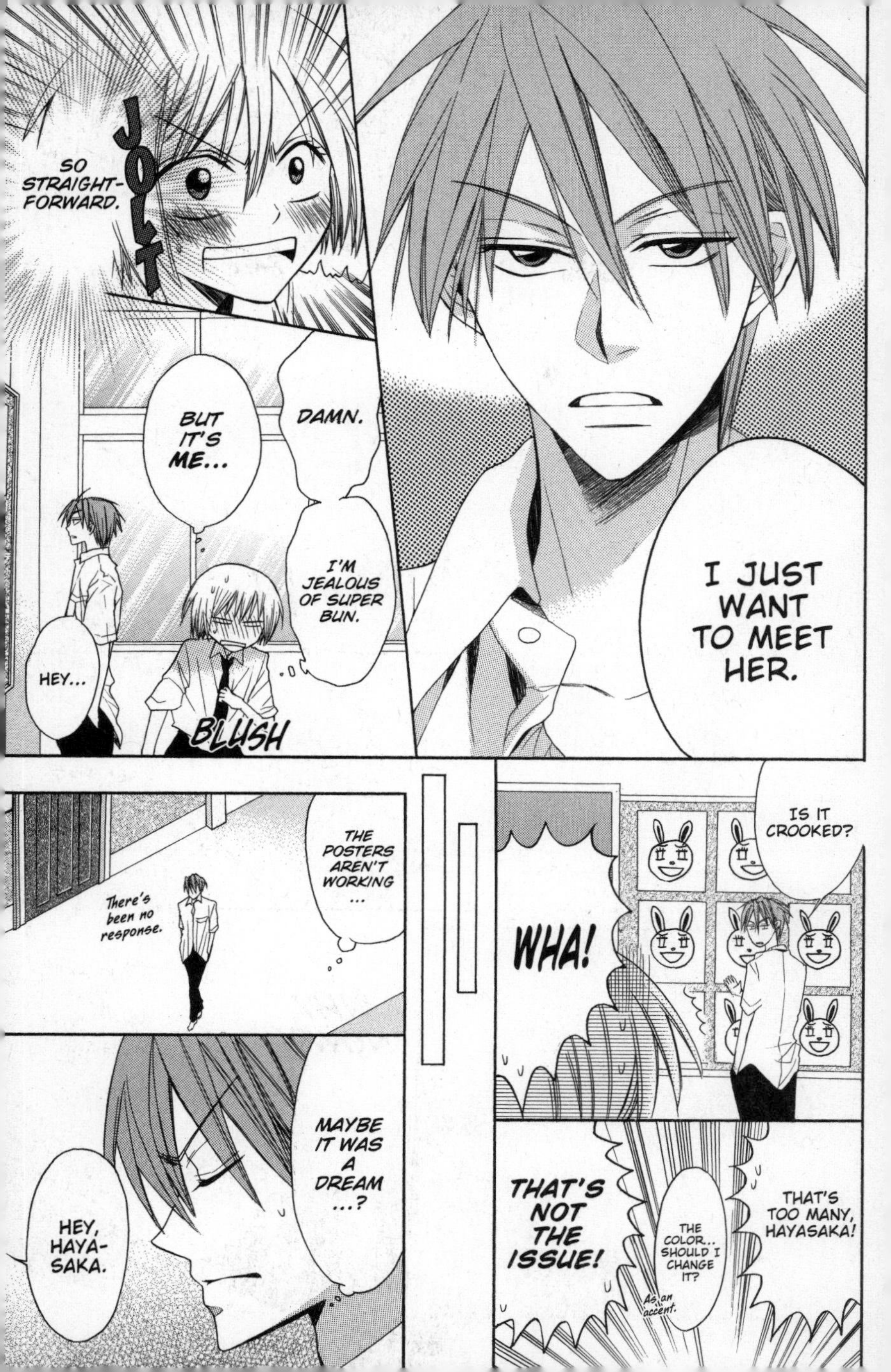
I JUST WANT TO MEET HER.
JOLT
SO STRAIGHT-FORWARD.
DAMN.
BUT IT'S ME...
I'M JEALOUS OF SUPER BUN.
BLUSH
HEY...
THE POSTERS AREN'T WORKING...
There's been no response.
MAYBE IT WAS A DREAM...?
HEY, HAYASAKA.
IS IT CROOKED?
WHA!
THAT'S TOO MANY, HAYASAKA!
THE COLOR... SHOULD I CHANGE IT?
As an accent.
THAT'S NOT THE ISSUE!

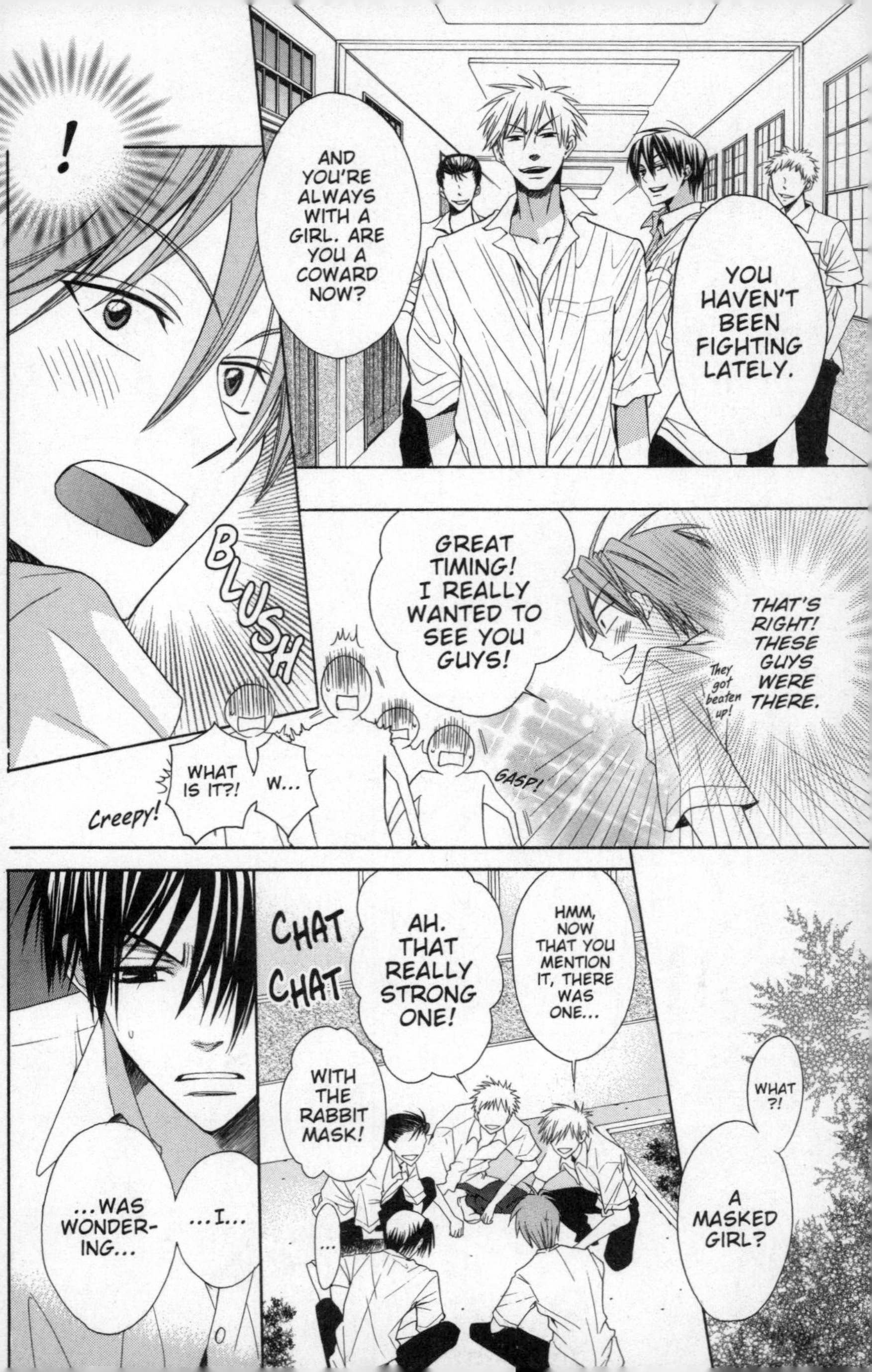
YOU HAVEN'T BEEN FIGHTING LATELY.
AND YOU'RE ALWAYS WITH A GIRL. ARE YOU A COWARD NOW?
THAT'S RIGHT! THESE GUYS WERE THERE.
They got beaten up!
GREAT TIMING! I REALLY WANTED TO SEE YOU GUYS!
GASP!
W...
WHAT IS IT?!
Creepy!
!
BLUSH
WHAT?!
A MASKED GIRL?
HMM, NOW THAT YOU MENTION IT, THERE WAS ONE...
AH. THAT REALLY STRONG ONE!
CHAT CHAT
WITH THE RABBIT MASK!
...
...I...
...WAS WONDERING...

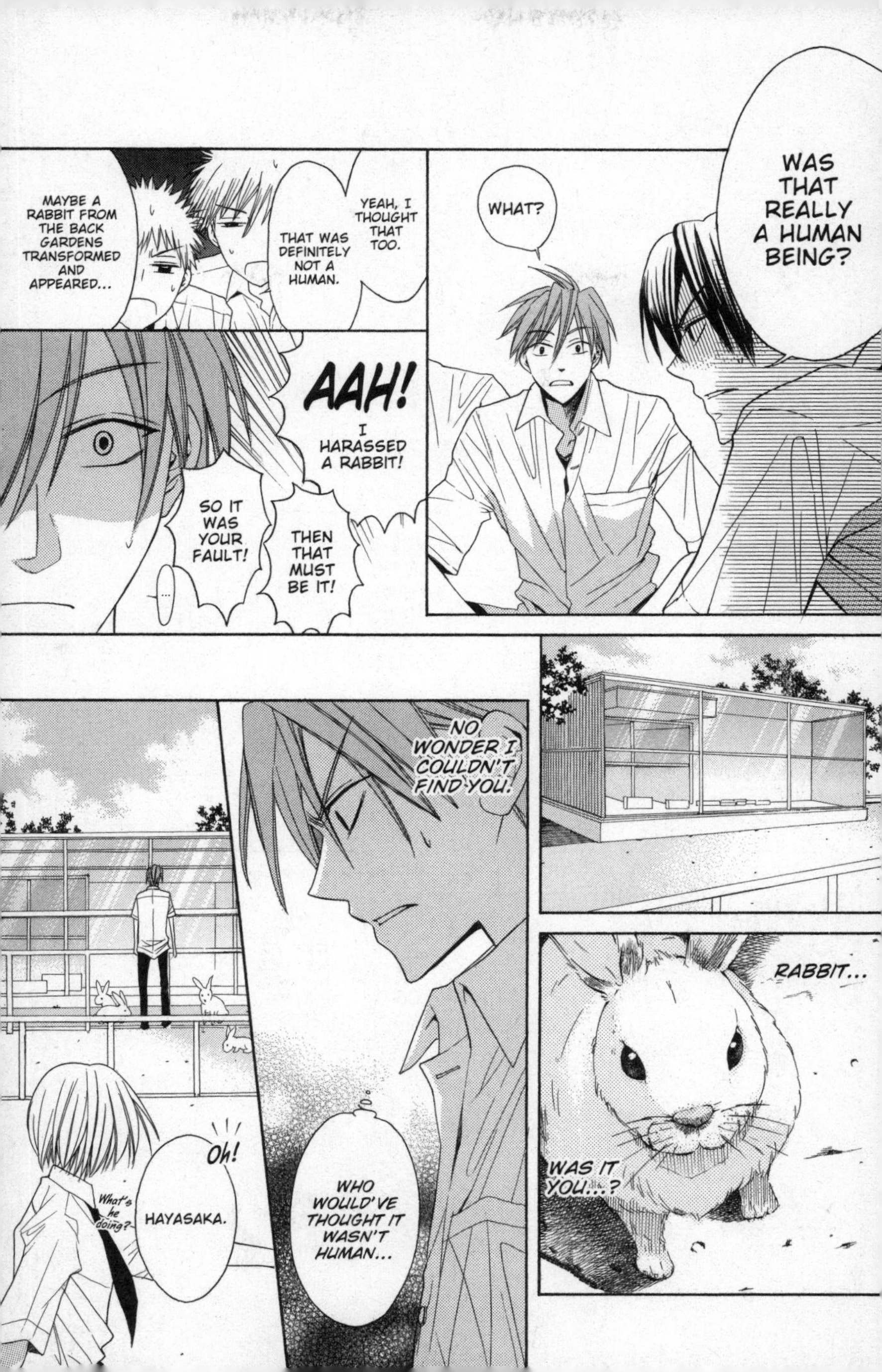

WAS THAT REALLY A HUMAN BEING?
WHAT?
YEAH, I THOUGHT THAT TOO.
THAT WAS DEFINITELY NOT A HUMAN.
MAYBE A RABBIT FROM THE BACK GARDENS TRANSFORMED AND APPEARED...
AAH! I HARASSED A RABBIT!
THEN THAT MUST BE IT!
SO IT WAS YOUR FAULT!
...
RABBIT...
WAS IT YOU...?
NO WONDER I COULDN'T FIND YOU.
WHO WOULD'VE THOUGHT IT WASN'T HUMAN...
Oh!
HAYASAKA.
What's he doing?

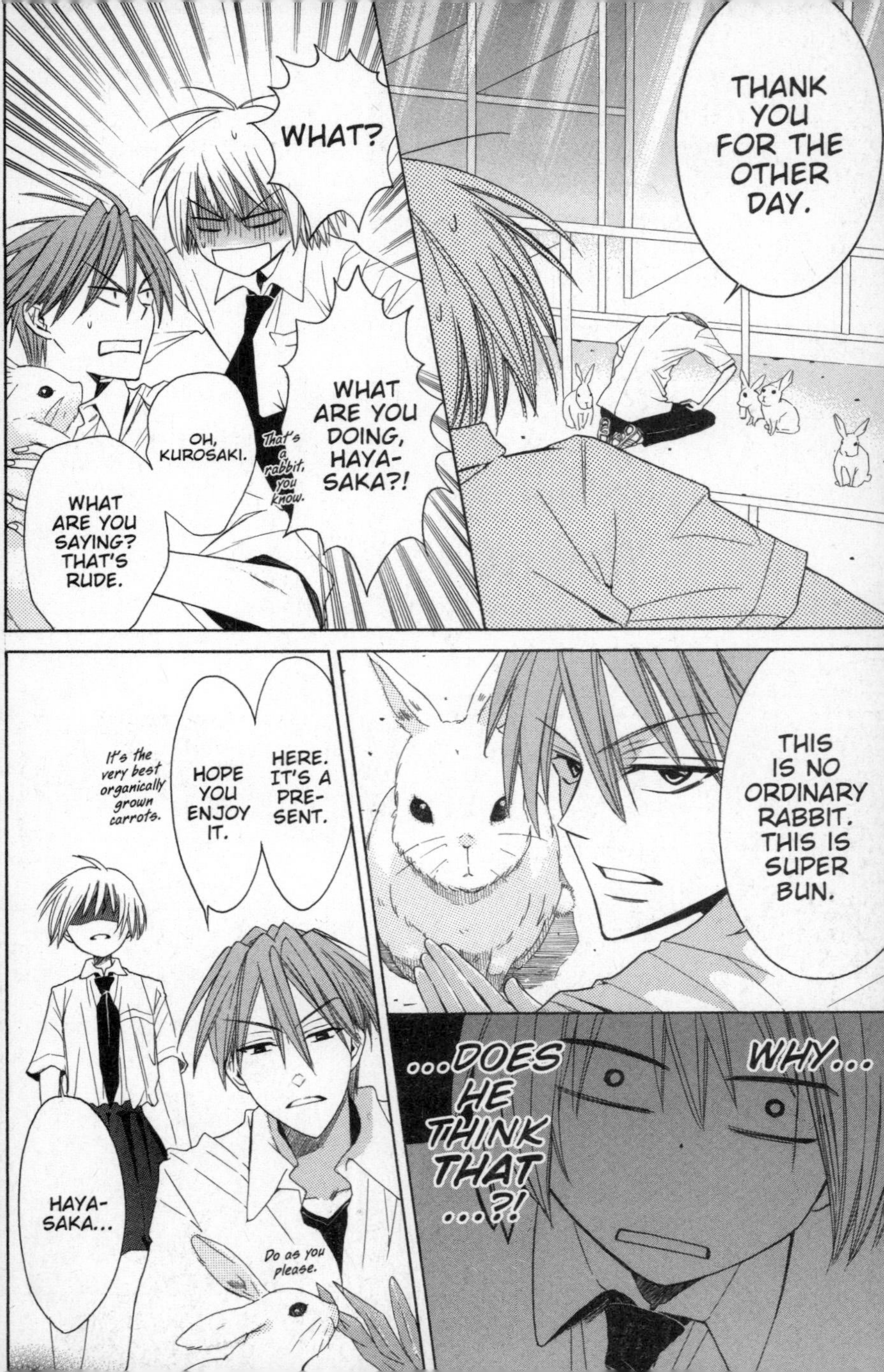
THANK YOU FOR THE OTHER DAY.
WHAT?
WHAT ARE YOU DOING, HAYA-SAKA?!
That's a rabbit, you know.
OH, KUROSAKI.
WHAT ARE YOU SAYING? THAT'S RUDE.
THIS IS NO ORDINARY RABBIT. THIS IS SUPER BUN.
WHY...
...DOES HE THINK THAT...?!
HERE. IT'S A PRE-SENT.
HOPE YOU ENJOY IT.
It's the very best organically grown carrots.
HAYA-SAKA...
Do as you please.

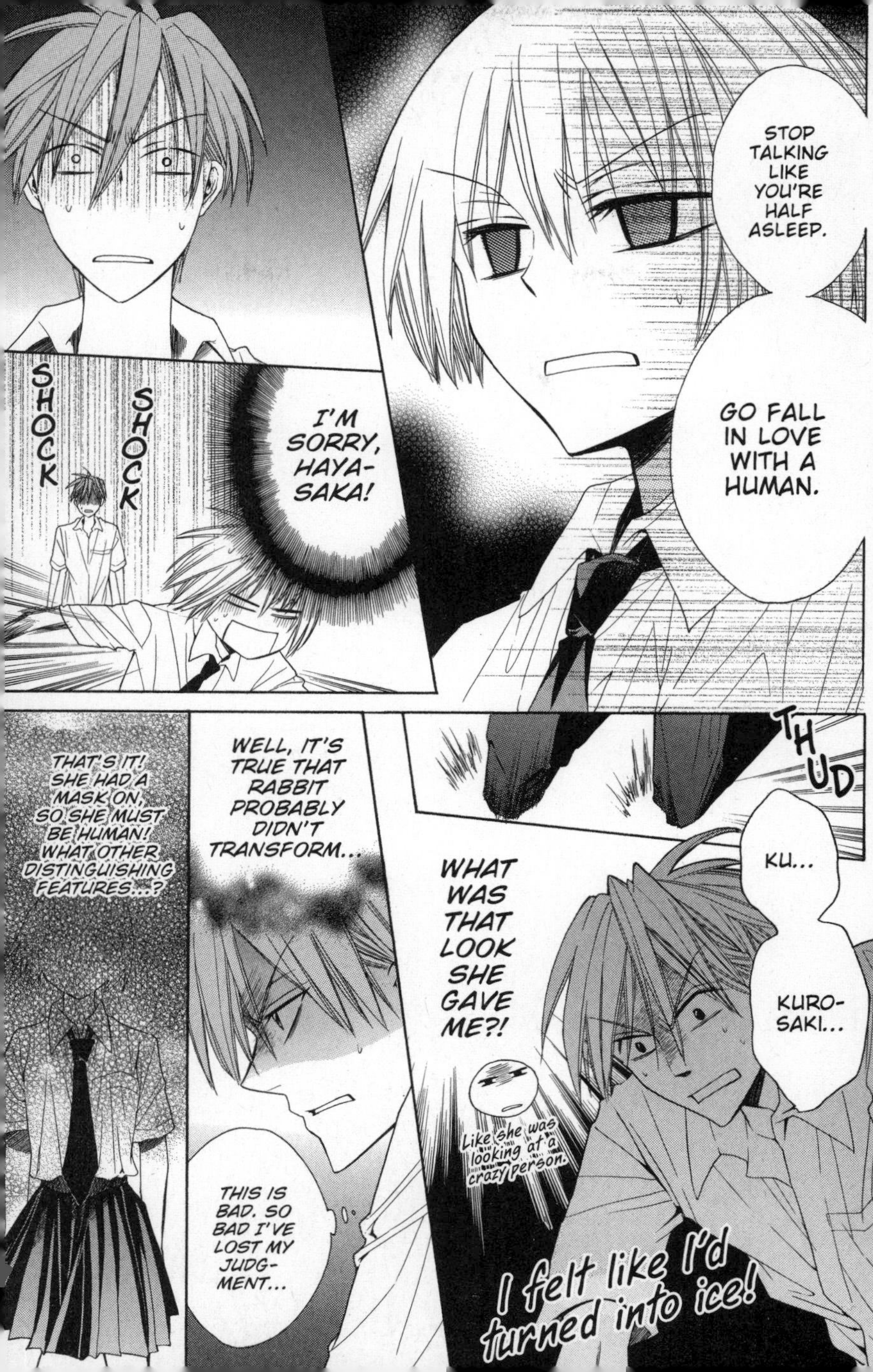
STOP TALKING LIKE YOU'RE HALF ASLEEP.
GO FALL IN LOVE WITH A HUMAN.
SHOCK SHOCK
I'M SORRY, HAYA-SAKA!
THUD
KU...
KURO-SAKI...
WHAT WAS THAT LOOK SHE GAVE ME?!
Like she was looking at a crazy person.
I felt like I'd turned into ice!
WELL, IT'S TRUE THAT RABBIT PROBABLY DIDN'T TRANSFORM...
THIS IS BAD. SO BAD I'VE LOST MY JUDG-MENT...
THAT'S IT! SHE HAD A MASK ON, SO SHE MUST BE HUMAN! WHAT OTHER DISTINGUISHING FEATURES...?

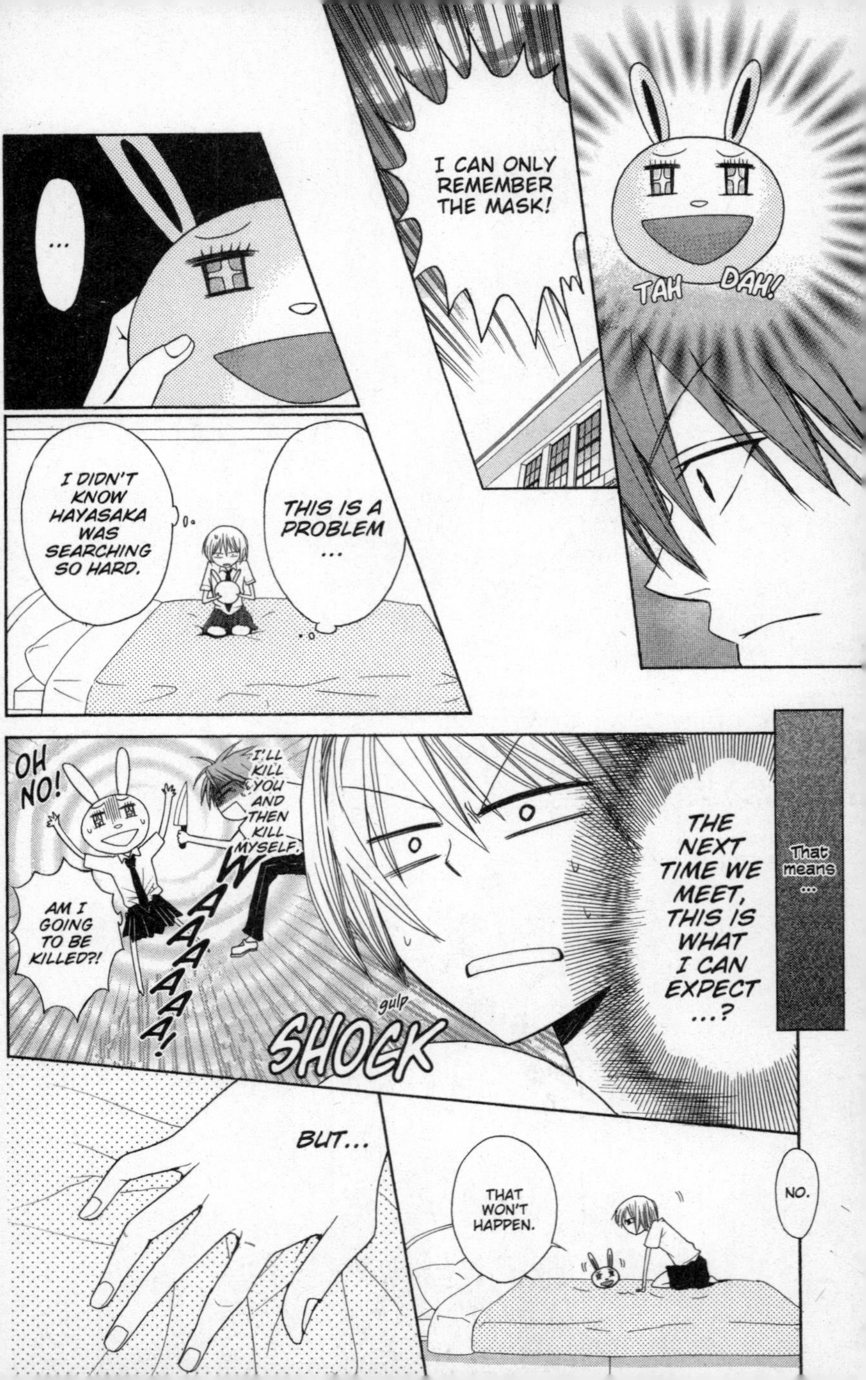
TAH DAH!
I CAN ONLY REMEMBER THE MASK!
...
THIS IS A PROBLEM ...
I DIDN'T KNOW HAYASAKA WAS SEARCHING SO HARD.
That means ...
THE NEXT TIME WE MEET, THIS IS WHAT I CAN EXPECT ...?
gulp
SHOCK
I'LL KILL YOU AND THEN KILL MYSELF.
OH NO!
WAAAAAAAA!
AM I GOING TO BE KILLED?!
NO.
THAT WON'T HAPPEN.
BUT...

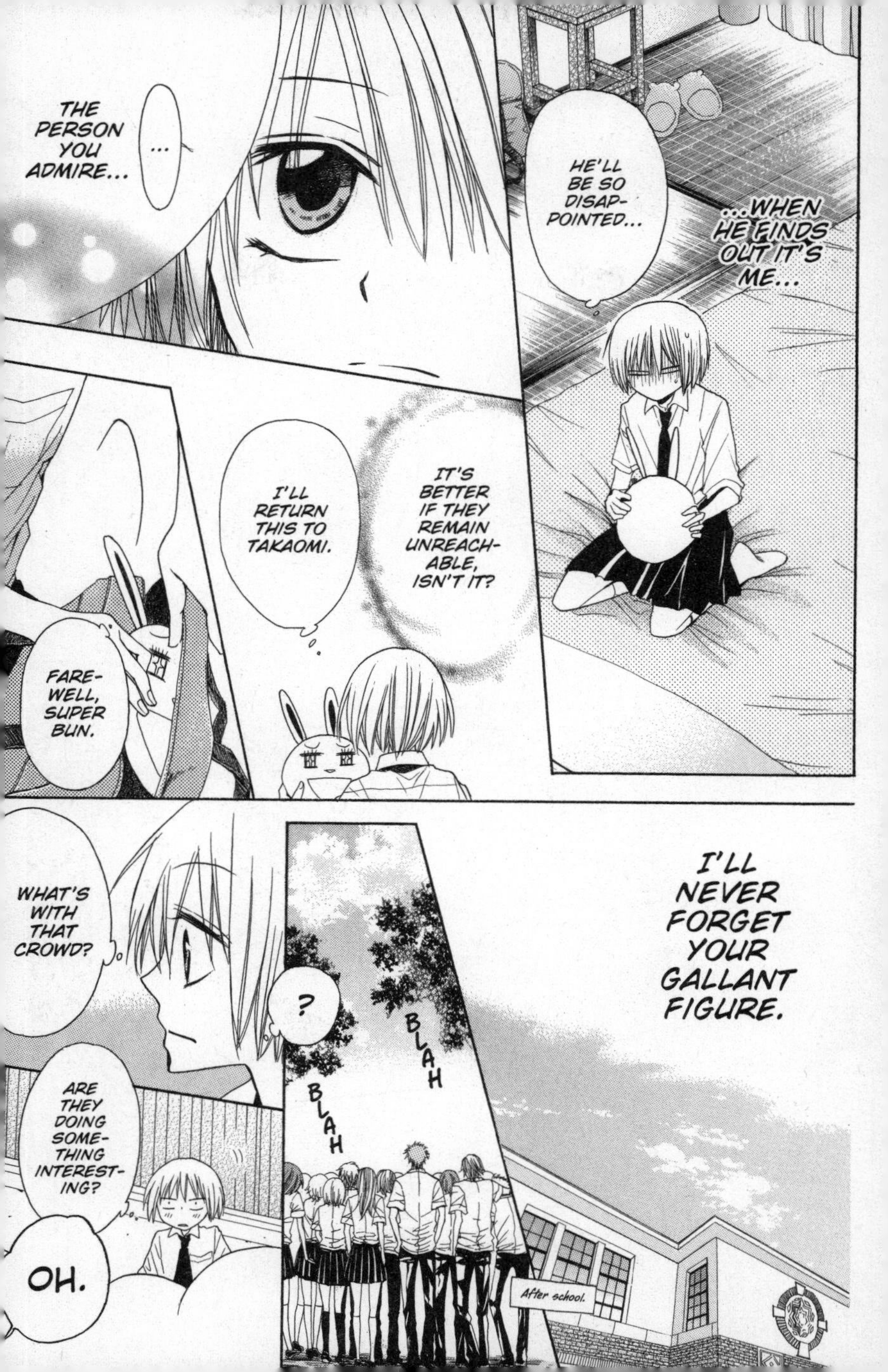
HE'LL BE SO DISAPPOINTED...
...WHEN HE FINDS OUT IT'S ME...
...
THE PERSON YOU ADMIRE...
IT'S BETTER IF THEY REMAIN UNREACHABLE, ISN'T IT?
I'LL RETURN THIS TO TAKAOMI.
FAREWELL, SUPER BUN.
I'LL NEVER FORGET YOUR GALLANT FIGURE.
BLAH
BLAH
After school.
?
WHAT'S WITH THAT CROWD?
ARE THEY DOING SOMETHING INTERESTING?
OH.

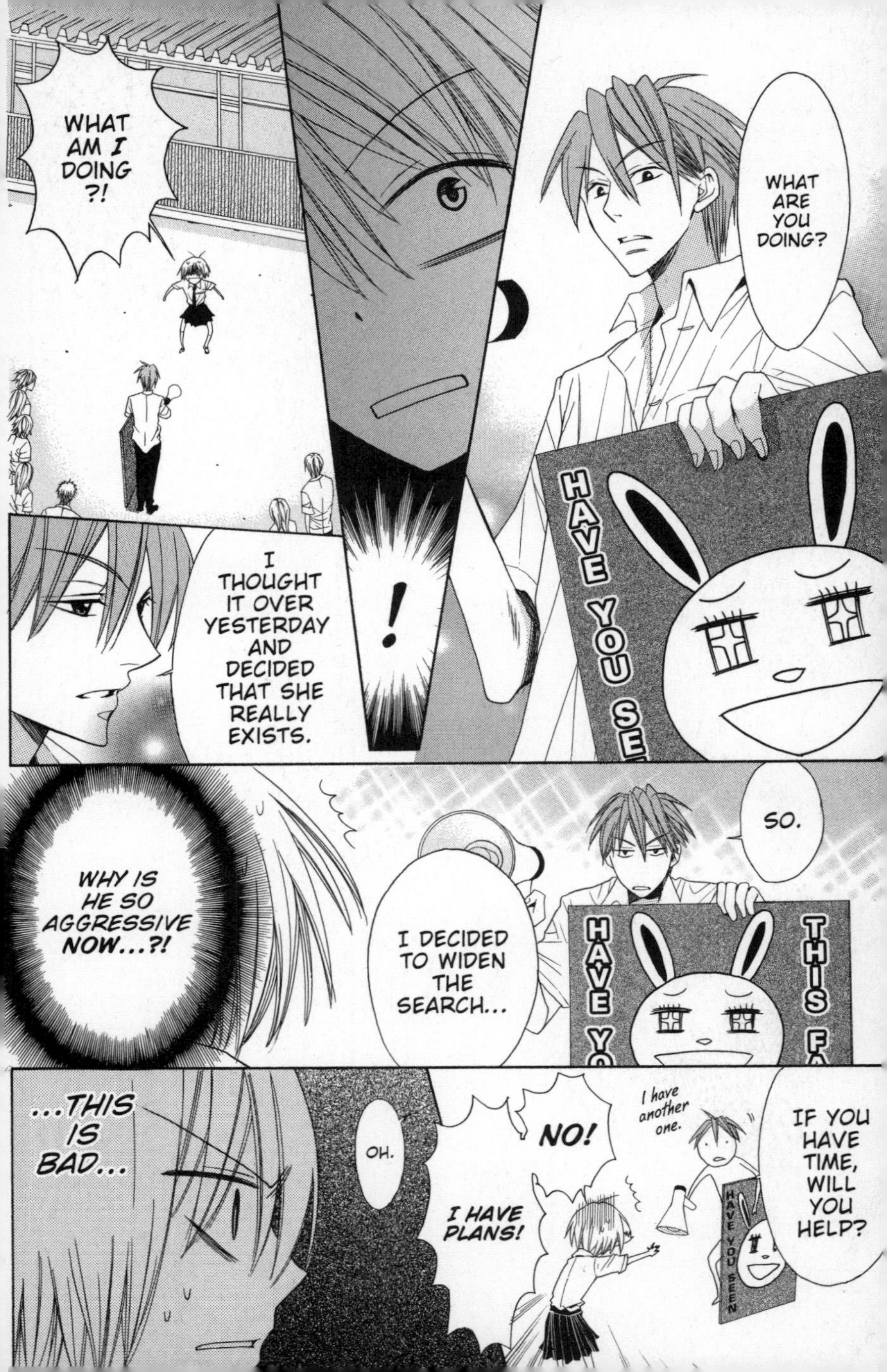
WHAT ARE YOU DOING?
!
WHAT AM I DOING?!
I THOUGHT IT OVER YESTERDAY AND DECIDED THAT SHE REALLY EXISTS.
SO.
I DECIDED TO WIDEN THE SEARCH...
WHY IS HE SO AGGRESSIVE NOW...?!
IF YOU HAVE TIME, WILL YOU HELP?
HAVE YOU SEEN
I have another one.
NO!
I HAVE PLANS!
OH.
...THIS IS BAD...

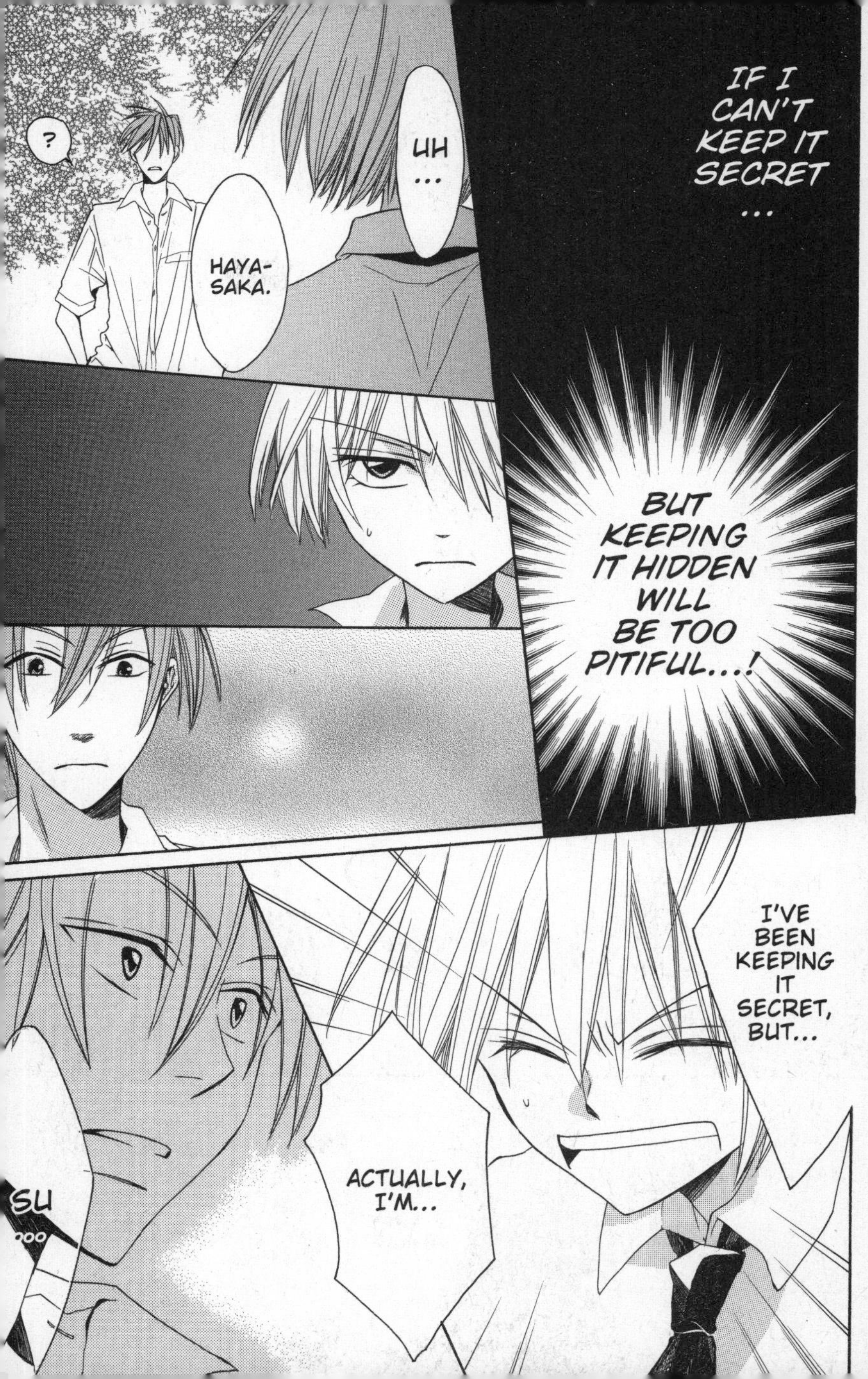

IF I CAN'T KEEP IT SECRET ...
BUT KEEPING IT HIDDEN WILL BE TOO PITIFUL...!
UH ...
HAYA-SAKA.
?
I'VE BEEN KEEPING IT SECRET, BUT...
ACTUALLY, I'M...
SU

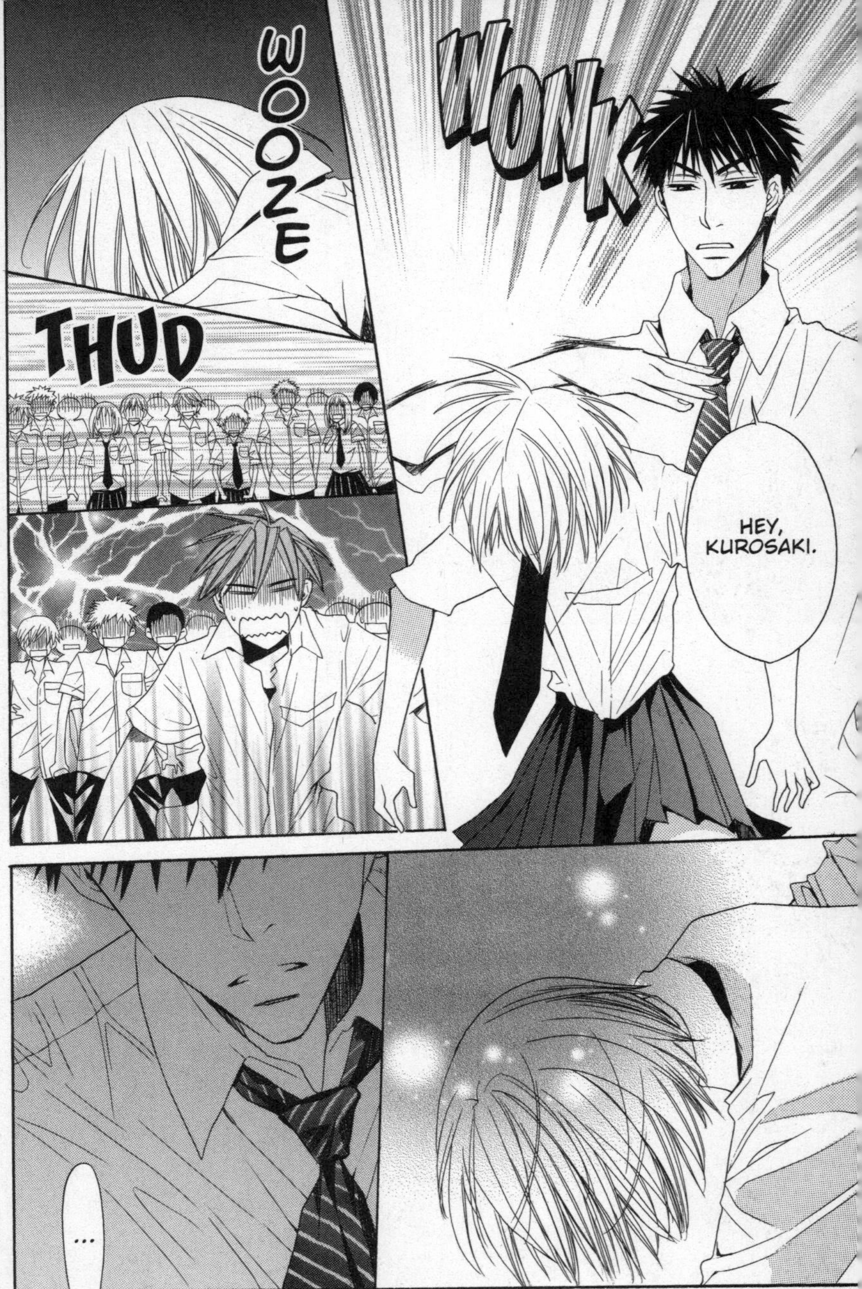
WONK
HEY, KUROSAKI.
WOOZE
THUD
...

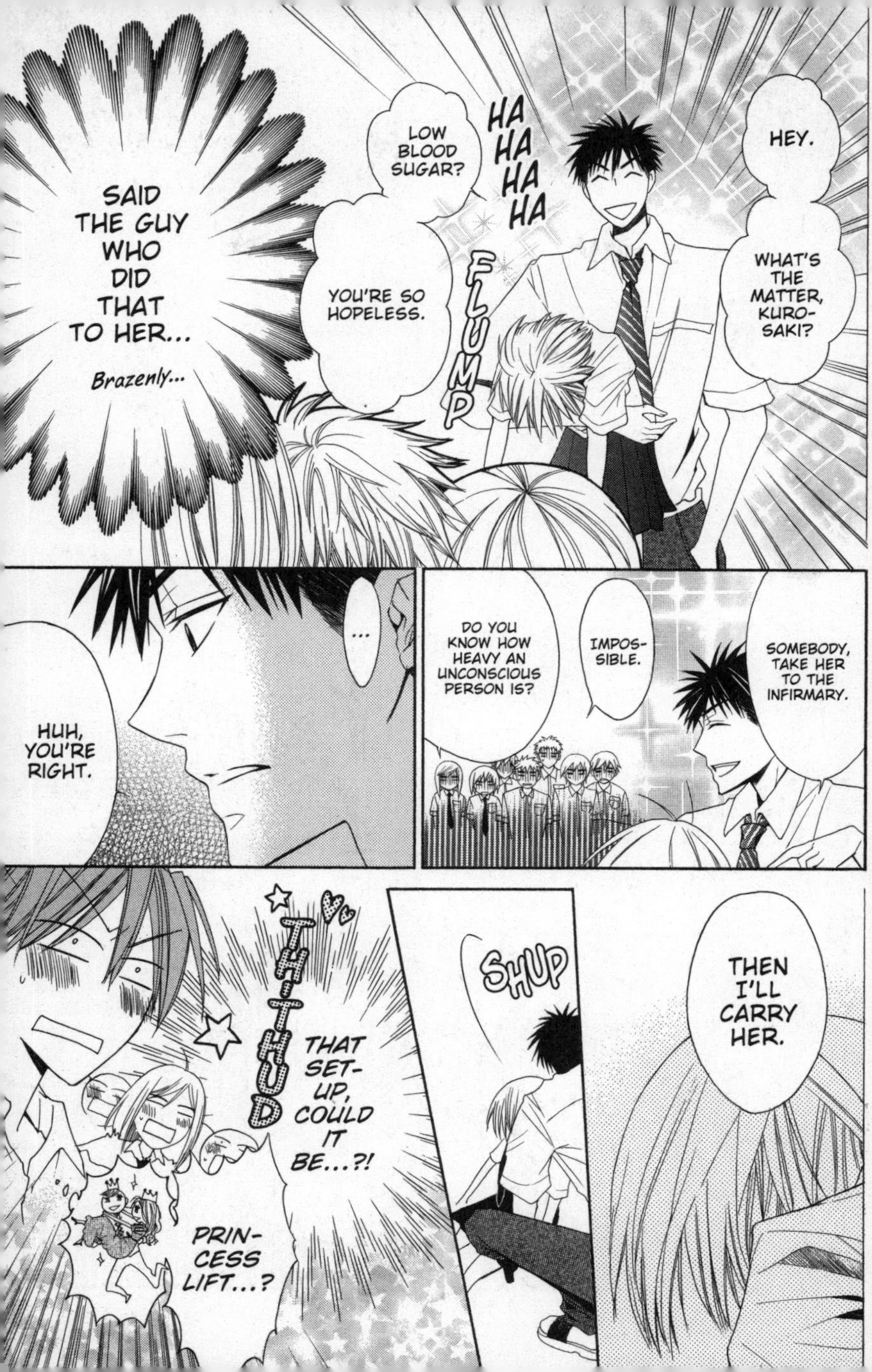
HEY.
WHAT'S THE MATTER, KURO-SAKI?
HA HA HA HA
LOW BLOOD SUGAR?
YOU'RE SO HOPELESS.
FLUMP
SAID THE GUY WHO DID THAT TO HER...
Brazenly...
SOMEBODY, TAKE HER TO THE INFIRMARY.
IMPOS-SIBLE.
DO YOU KNOW HOW HEAVY AN UNCONSCIOUS PERSON IS?
...
HUH, YOU'RE RIGHT.
THEN I'LL CARRY HER.
SHUP
THUD
THAT SET-UP, COULD IT BE...?!
PRIN-CESS LIFT...?

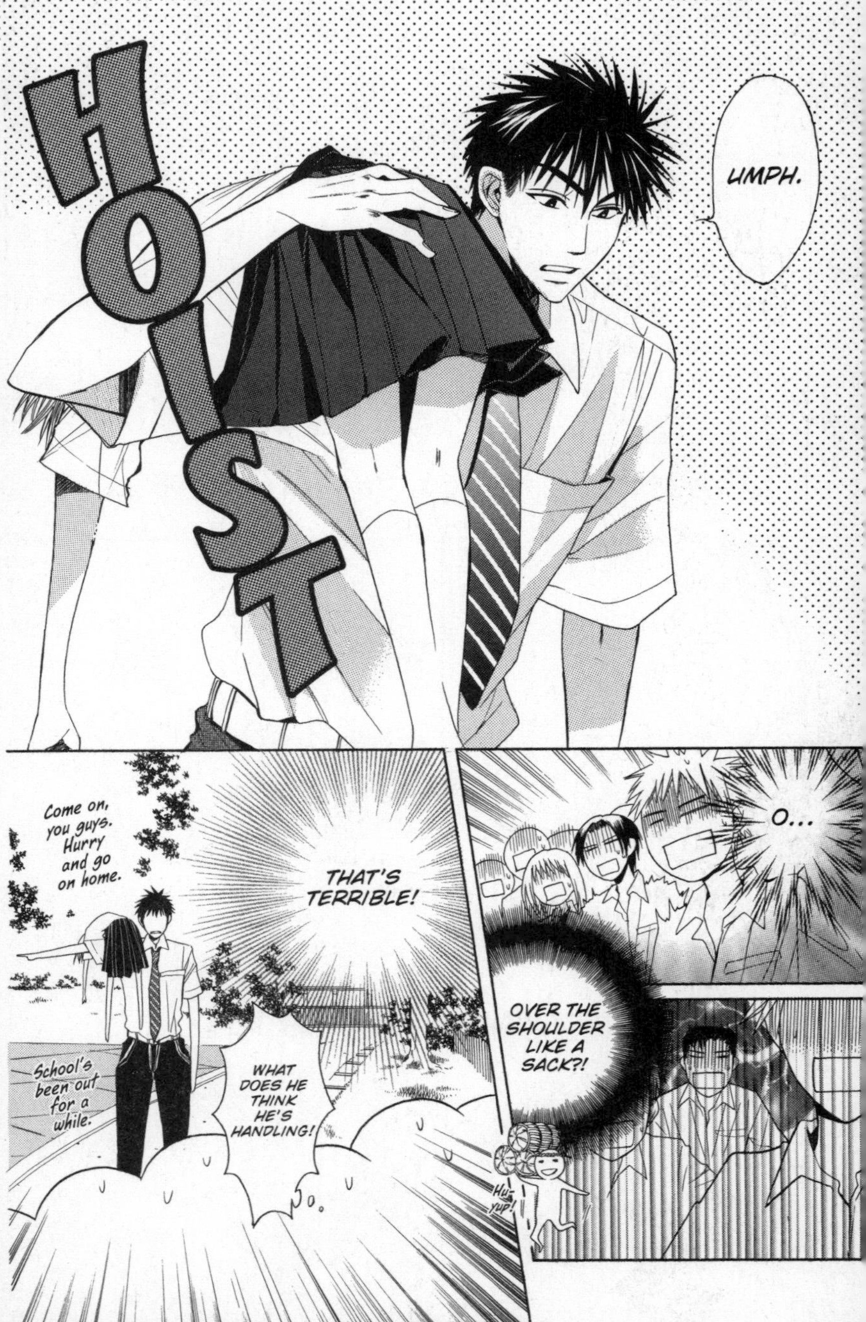

UMPH.
HOIST
O...
OVER THE SHOULDER LIKE A SACK?!
Hu-yup!
THAT'S TERRIBLE!
Come on, you guys. Hurry and go on home.
WHAT DOES HE THINK HE'S HANDLING!
School's been out for a while.

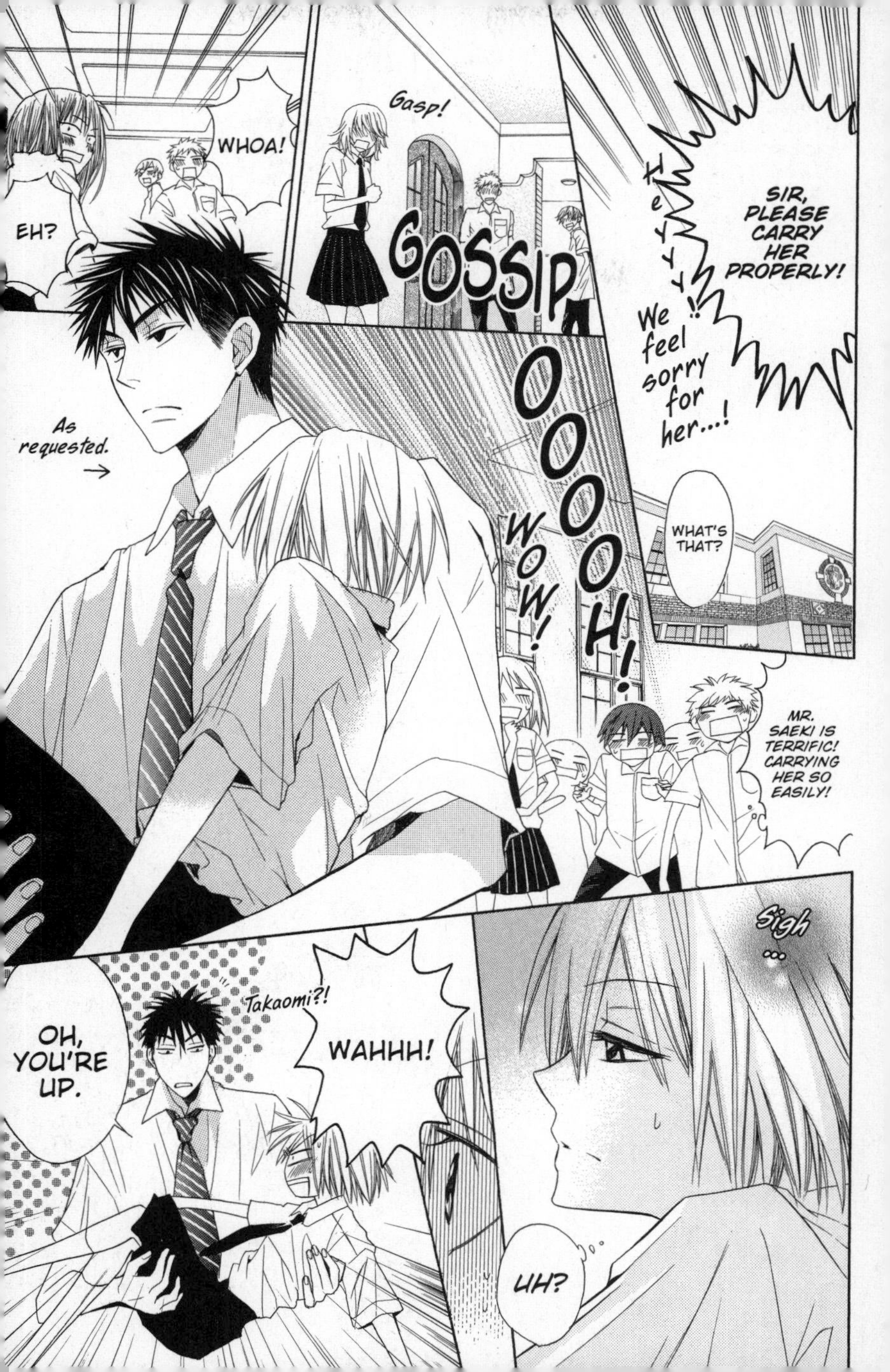

SIR, PLEASE CARRY HER PROPERLY!
We feel sorry for her...!
Gasp!
GOSSIP
WHOA!
EH?
WHAT'S THAT?
MR. SAEKI IS TERRIFIC! CARRYING HER SO EASILY!
OOOOOH!
WOW!
As requested. →
Sigh...
UH?
WAHHH!
Takaomi?!
OH, YOU'RE UP.

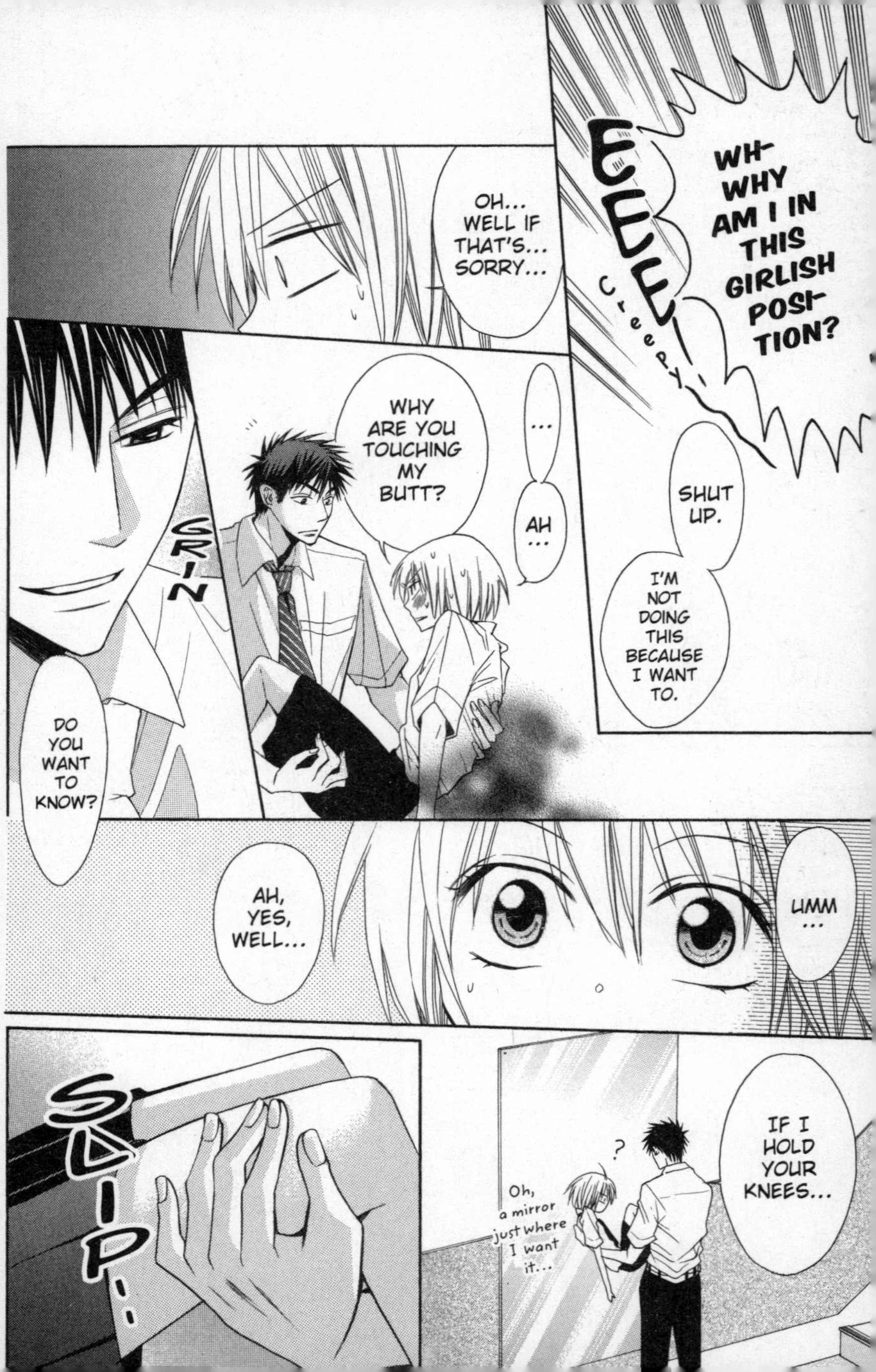
EEE!
Creepy
WH- WHY AM I IN THIS GIRLISH POSI-TION?
SHUT UP.
I'M NOT DOING THIS BECAUSE I WANT TO.
OH... WELL IF THAT'S... SORRY...
...
AH...
WHY ARE YOU TOUCHING MY BUTT?
GRIN
DO YOU WANT TO KNOW?
UMM...
AH, YES, WELL...
IF I HOLD YOUR KNEES...
?
Oh, a mirror just where I want it...
SLIP...

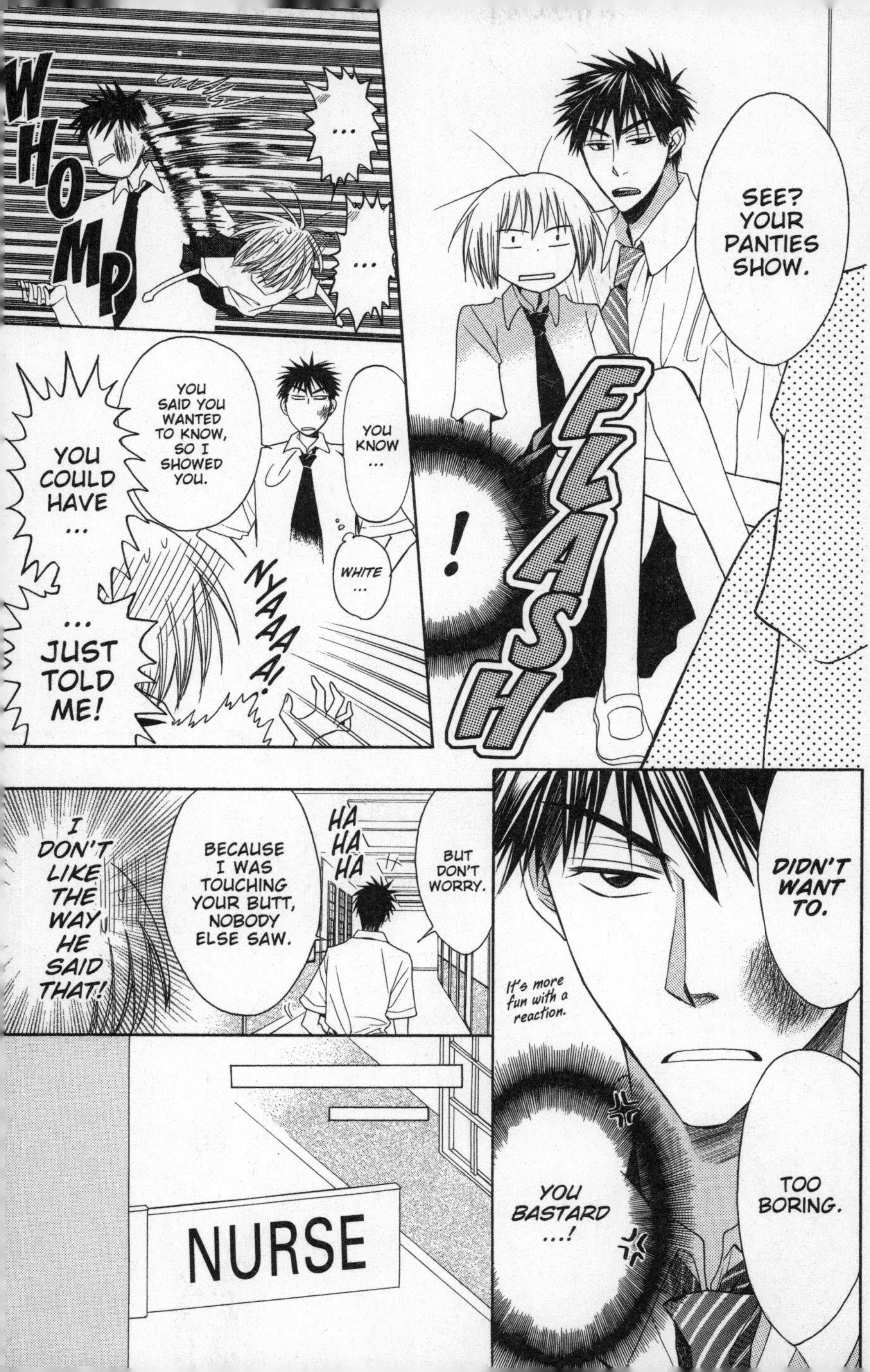
SEE? YOUR PANTIES SHOW.
FLASH
!
WHOMP
...
...
YOU KNOW...
WHITE...
YOU SAID YOU WANTED TO KNOW, SO I SHOWED YOU.
YOU COULD HAVE...
NYAAAAA!
...JUST TOLD ME!
DIDN'T WANT TO.
It's more fun with a reaction.
TOO BORING.
YOU BASTARD...!
BUT DON'T WORRY.
HA HA HA
BECAUSE I WAS TOUCHING YOUR BUTT, NOBODY ELSE SAW.
I DON'T LIKE THE WAY HE SAID THAT!
NURSE

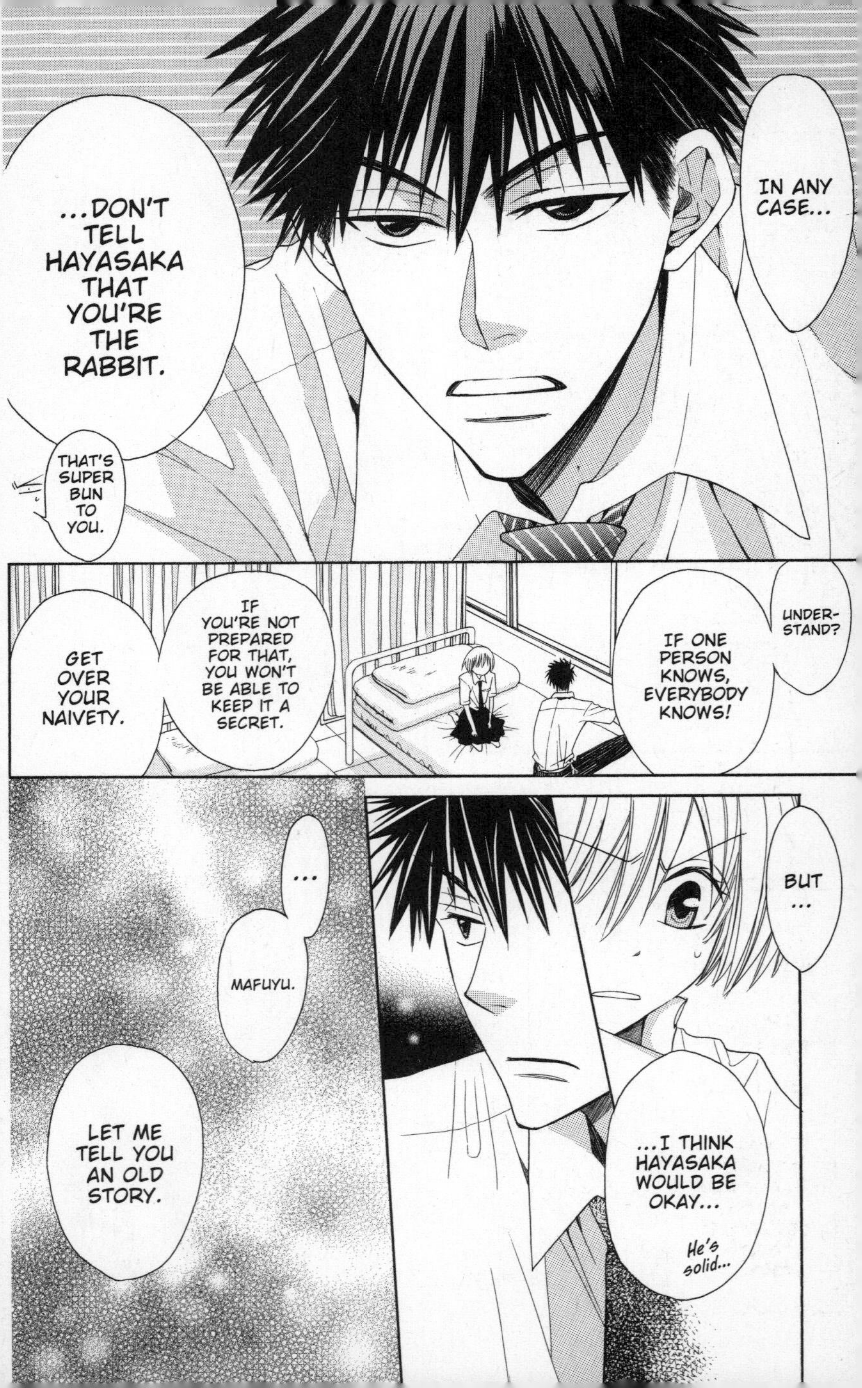
IN ANY CASE...
...DON'T TELL HAYASAKA THAT YOU'RE THE RABBIT.
THAT'S SUPER BUN TO YOU.
UNDER-STAND?
IF ONE PERSON KNOWS, EVERYBODY KNOWS!
IF YOU'RE NOT PREPARED FOR THAT, YOU WON'T BE ABLE TO KEEP IT A SECRET.
GET OVER YOUR NAIVETY.
BUT ...
...I THINK HAYASAKA WOULD BE OKAY...
He's solid...
...
MAFUYU.
LET ME TELL YOU AN OLD STORY.

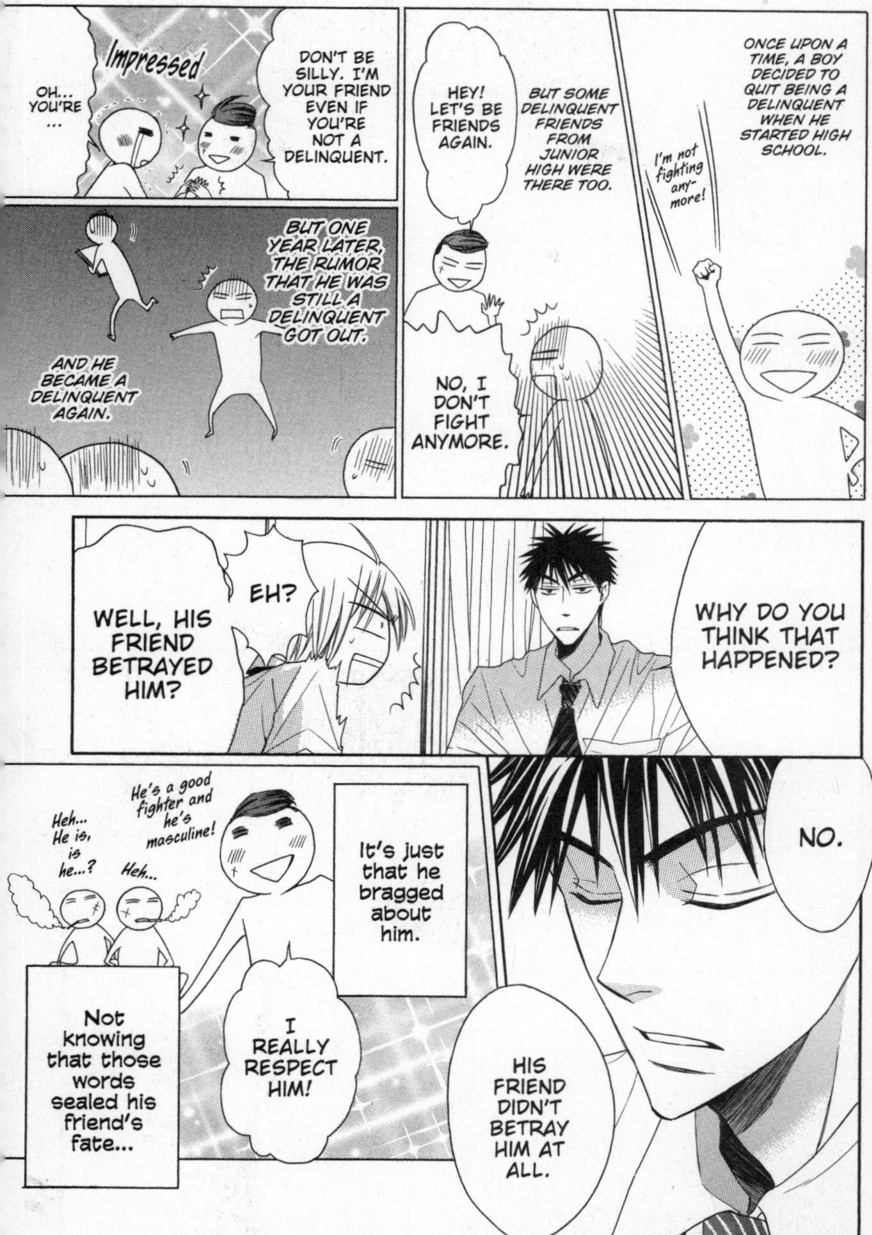
ONCE UPON A TIME, A BOY DECIDED TO QUIT BEING A DELINQUENT WHEN HE STARTED HIGH SCHOOL.
I'm not fighting any-more!
BUT SOME DELINQUENT FRIENDS FROM JUNIOR HIGH WERE THERE TOO.
HEY! LET'S BE FRIENDS AGAIN.
NO, I DON'T FIGHT ANYMORE.
DON'T BE SILLY. I'M YOUR FRIEND EVEN IF YOU'RE NOT A DELINQUENT.
Impressed
OH... YOU'RE ...
BUT ONE YEAR LATER, THE RUMOR THAT HE WAS STILL A DELINQUENT GOT OUT.
AND HE BECAME A DELINQUENT AGAIN.
WHY DO YOU THINK THAT HAPPENED?
EH?
WELL, HIS FRIEND BETRAYED HIM?
NO.
HIS FRIEND DIDN'T BETRAY HIM AT ALL.
It's just that he bragged about him.
He's a good fighter and he's masculine!
I REALLY RESPECT HIM!
Heh...
Heh... He is, is he...?
Not knowing that those words sealed his friend's fate...

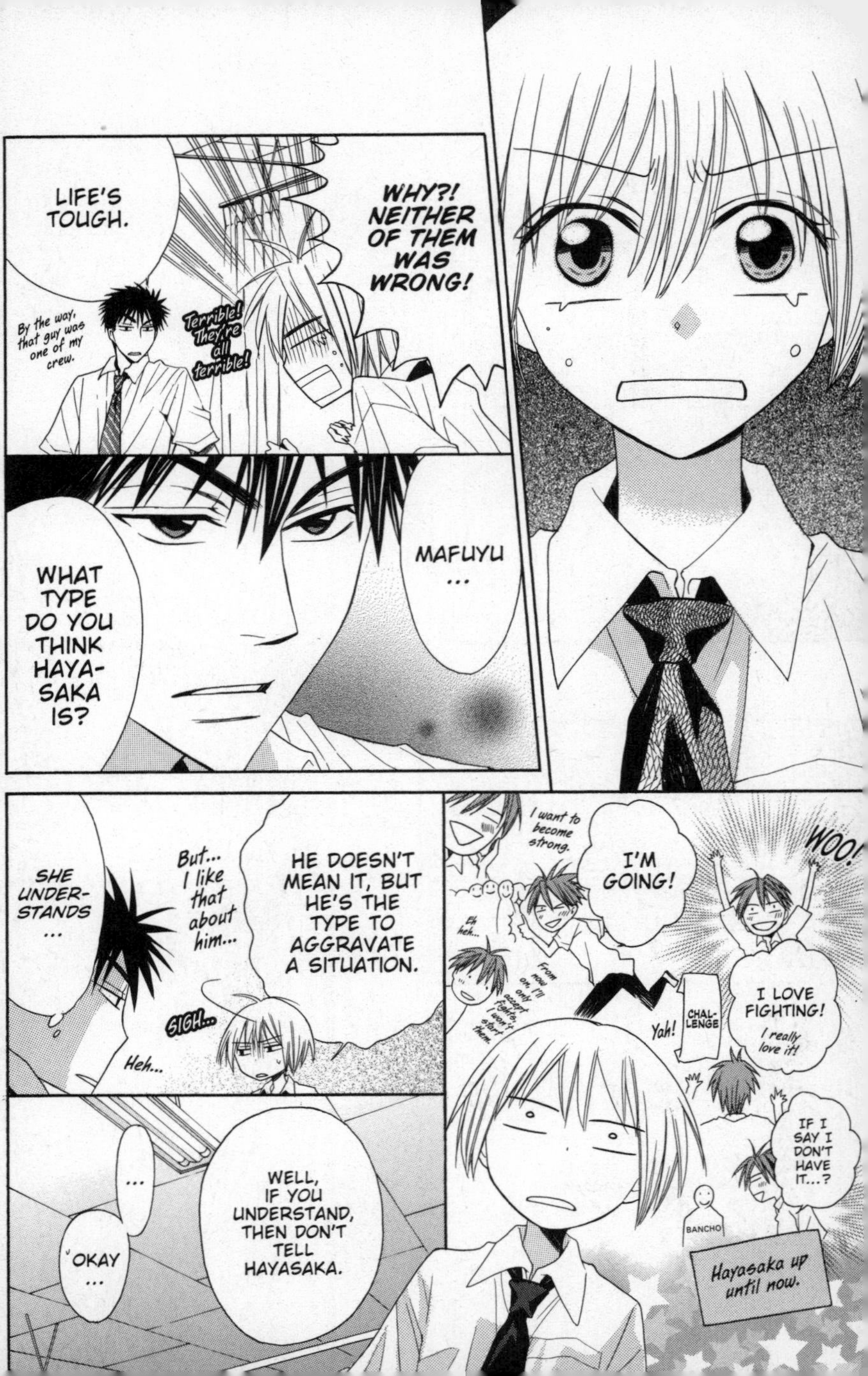
WHY?! NEITHER OF THEM WAS WRONG!
Terrible! They're all terrible!
LIFE'S TOUGH.
By the way, that guy was one of my crew.
MAFUYU ...
WHAT TYPE DO YOU THINK HAYA-SAKA IS?
WOO!
I'M GOING!
I want to become strong.
Eh heh...
I LOVE FIGHTING!
I really love it!
CHAL-LENGE
Yah!
From now on, I'll only accept fights. I won't start them.
IF I SAY I DON'T HAVE IT...?
BANCHO
Hayasaka up until now.
HE DOESN'T MEAN IT, BUT HE'S THE TYPE TO AGGRAVATE A SITUATION.
But... I like that about him...
SHE UNDER-STANDS ...
SIGH...
Heh...
WELL, IF YOU UNDERSTAND, THEN DON'T TELL HAYASAKA.
...
OKAY ...

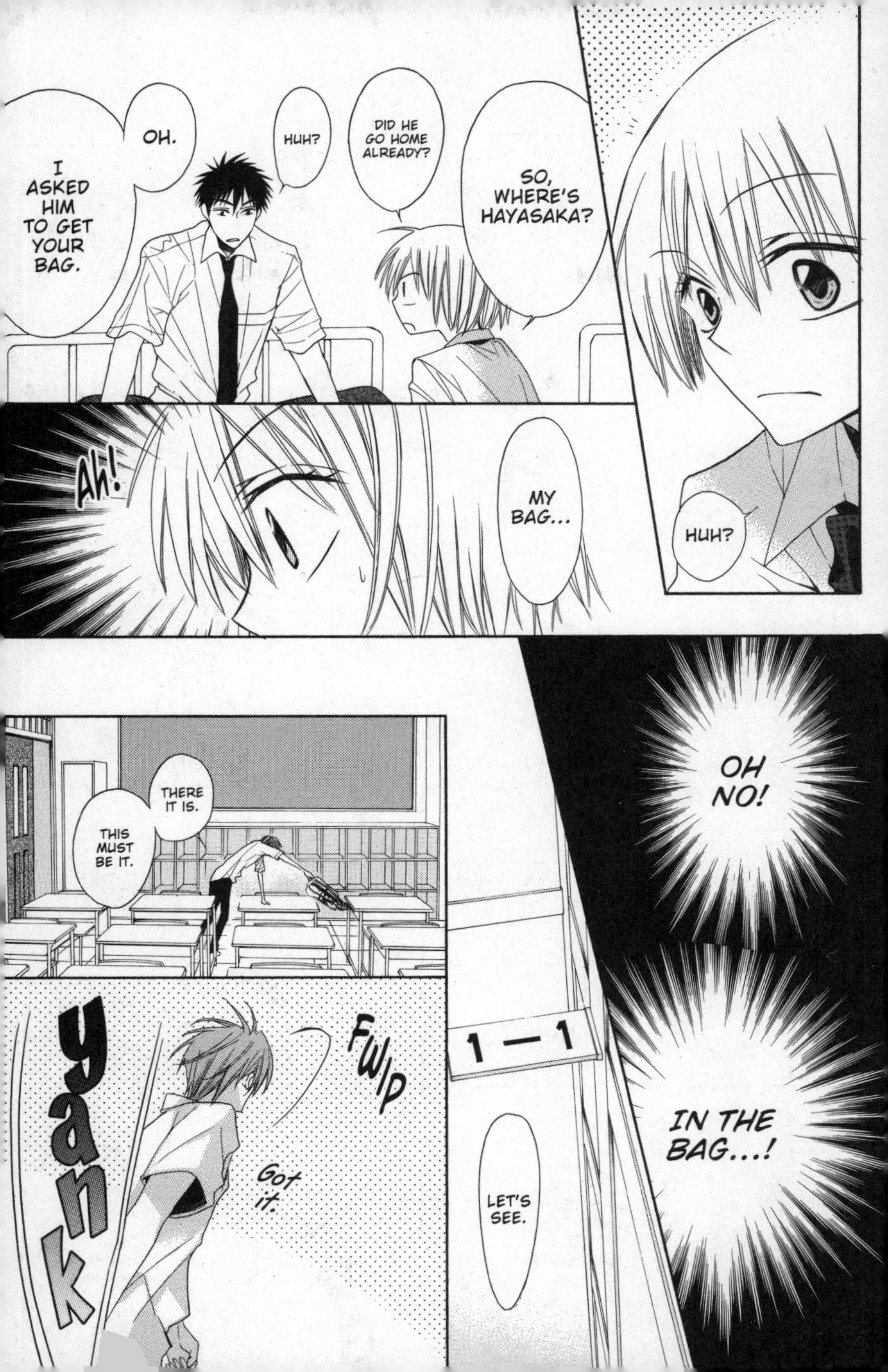
HUH?
SO, WHERE'S HAYASAKA?
DID HE GO HOME ALREADY?
HUH?
OH.
I ASKED HIM TO GET YOUR BAG.
MY BAG...
Ah!
OH NO!
IN THE BAG...!
1—1
LET'S SEE.
THERE IT IS.
THIS MUST BE IT.
FWIP
Got it.
yank

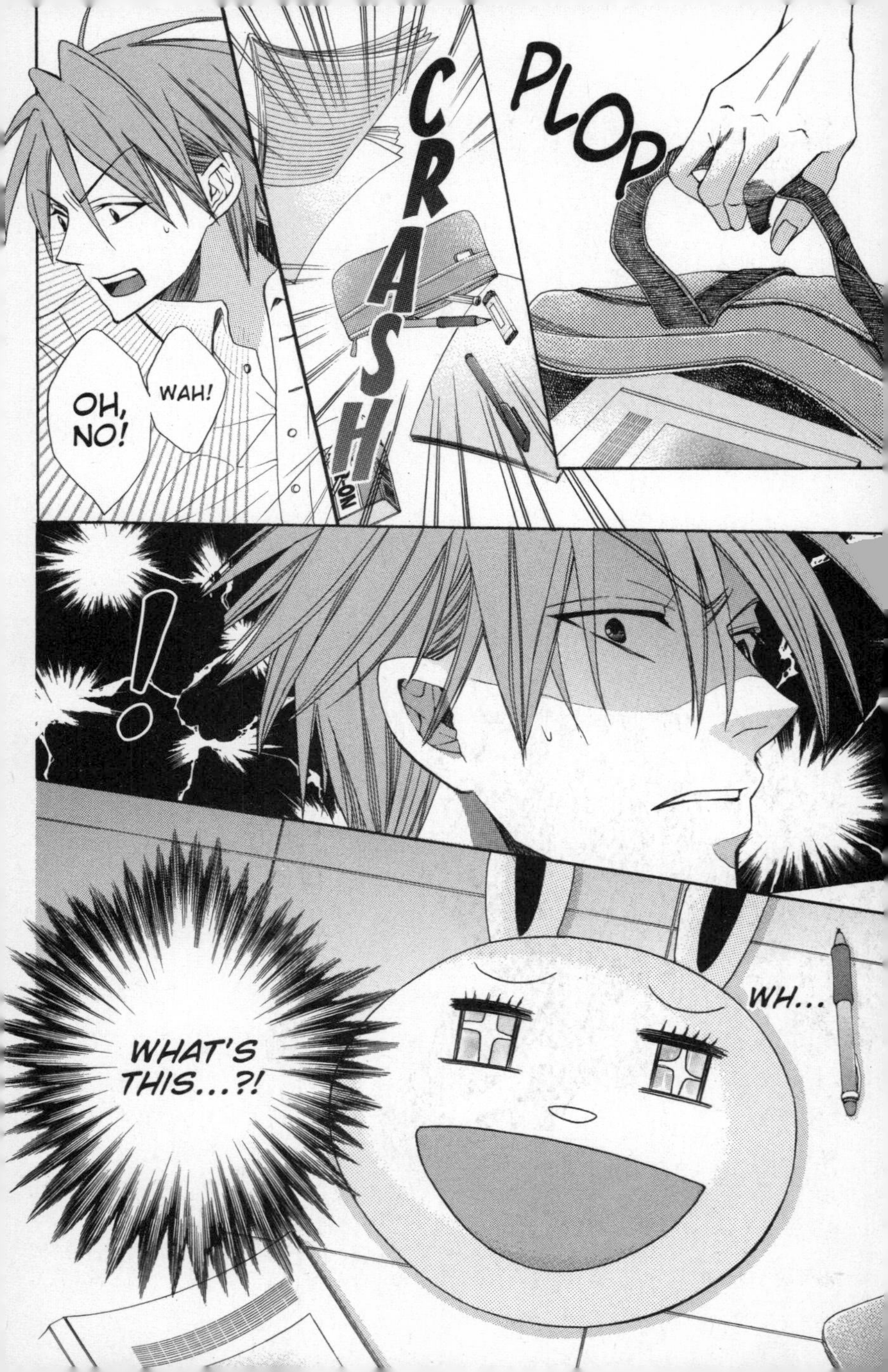
PLOP
CRASH
WAH!
OH, NO!
!
WH...
WHAT'S THIS...?!

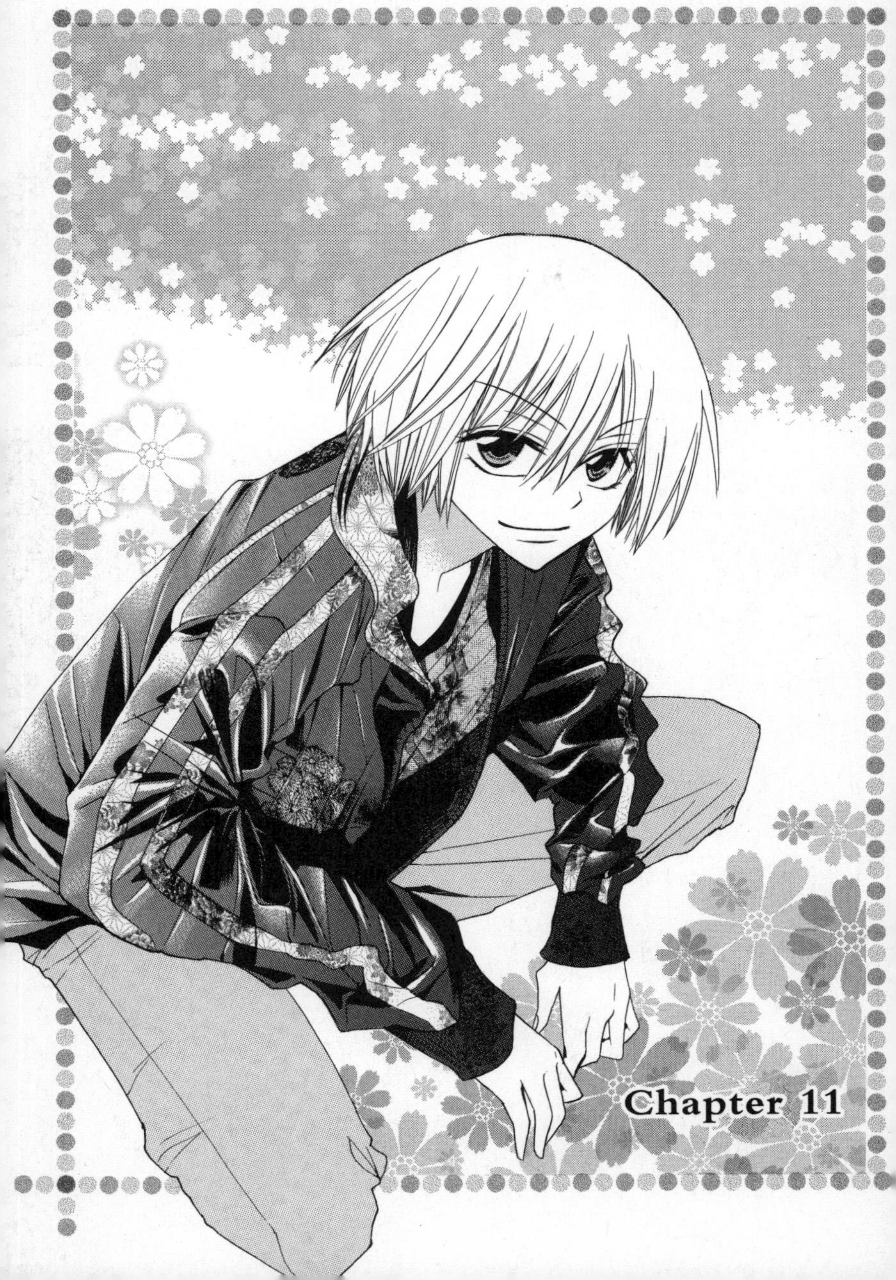
Chapter 11

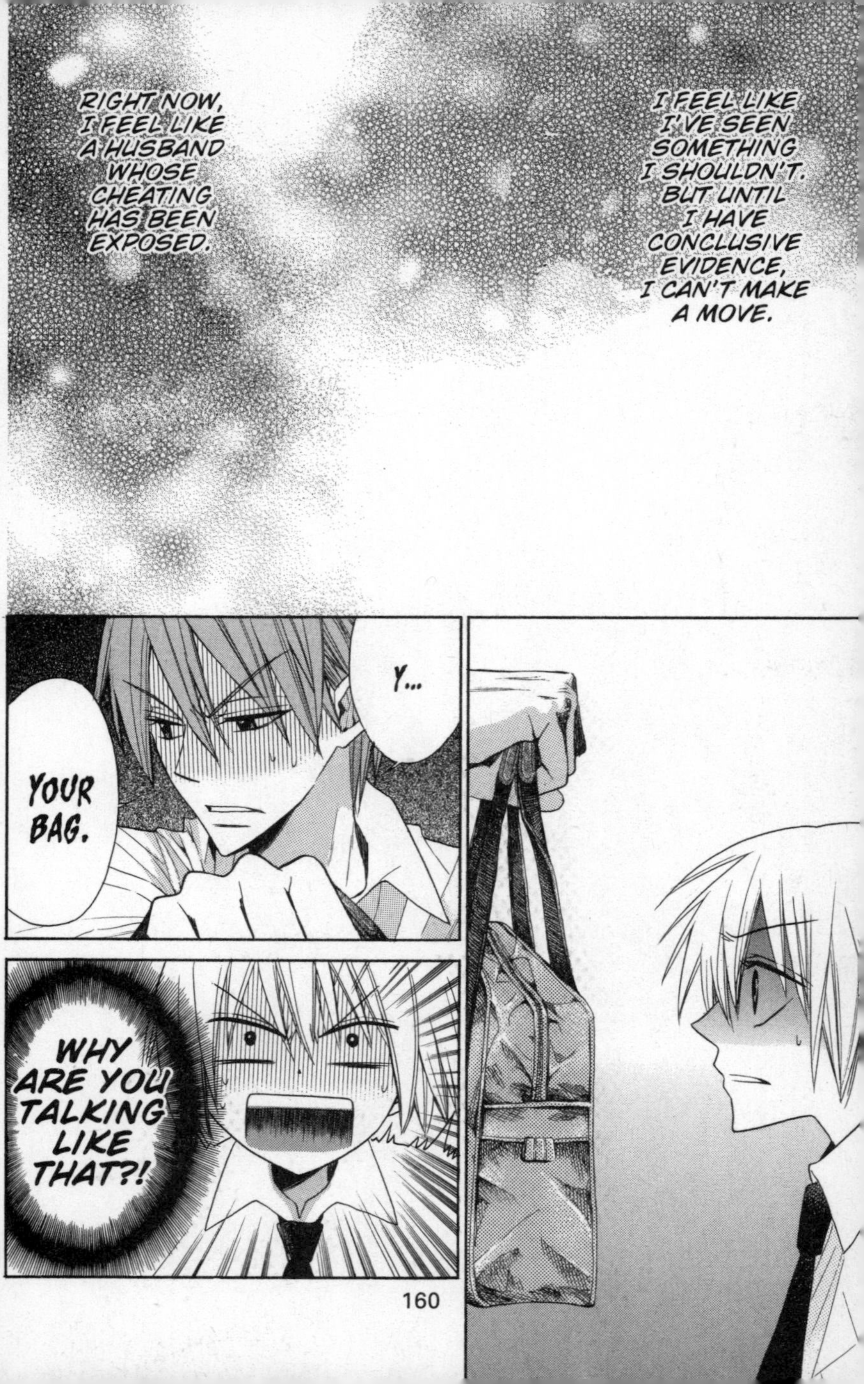
I FEEL LIKE I'VE SEEN SOMETHING I SHOULDN'T. BUT UNTIL I HAVE CONCLUSIVE EVIDENCE, I CAN'T MAKE A MOVE.
RIGHT NOW, I FEEL LIKE A HUSBAND WHOSE CHEATING HAS BEEN EXPOSED.
Y...
YOUR BAG.
WHY ARE YOU TALKING LIKE THAT?!

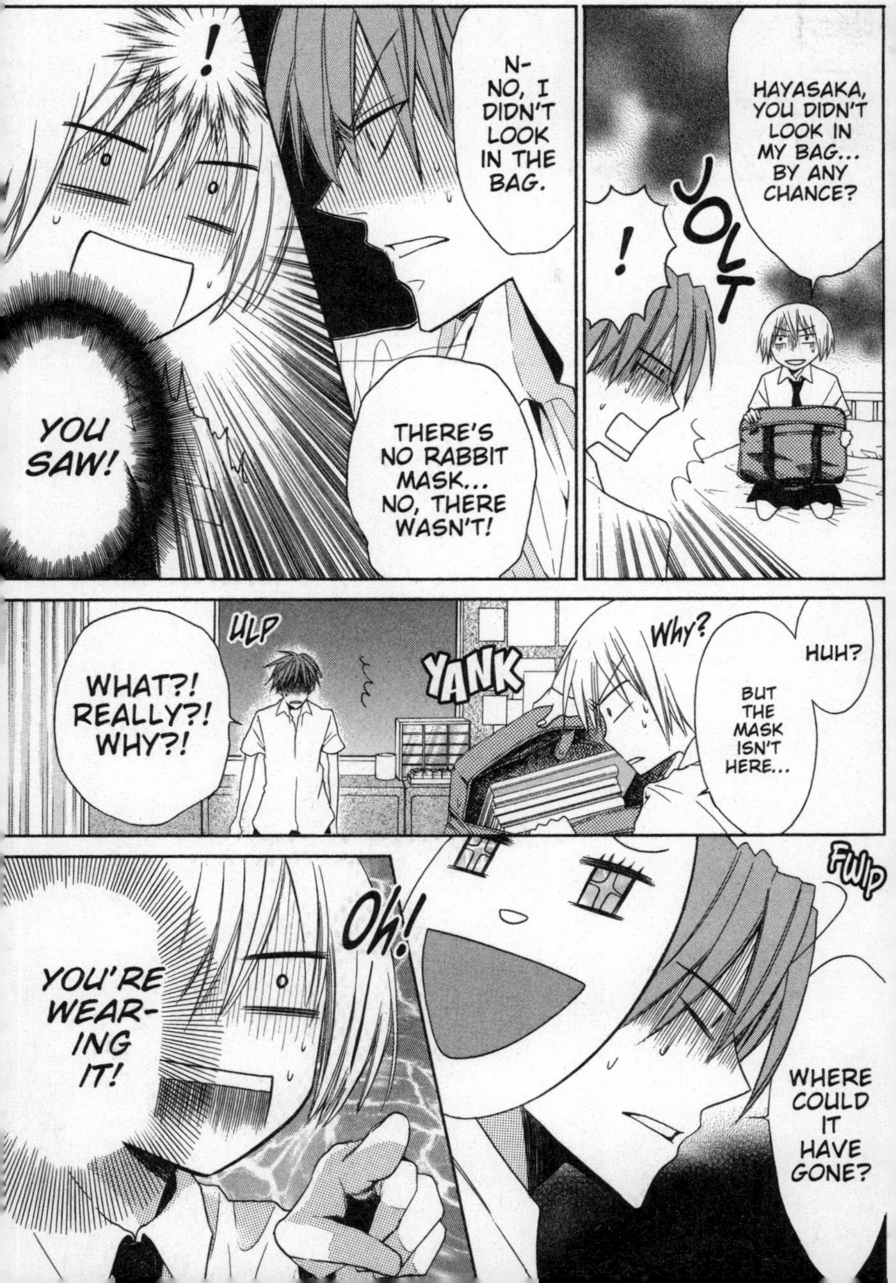
HAYASAKA, YOU DIDN'T LOOK IN MY BAG... BY ANY CHANCE?
JOLT
!
N-NO, I DIDN'T LOOK IN THE BAG.
THERE'S NO RABBIT MASK... NO, THERE WASN'T!
!
YOU SAW!
Why?
HUH?
BUT THE MASK ISN'T HERE...
YANK
ULP
WHAT?! REALLY?! WHY?!
FWIP
WHERE COULD IT HAVE GONE?
Oh!
YOU'RE WEAR-ING IT!

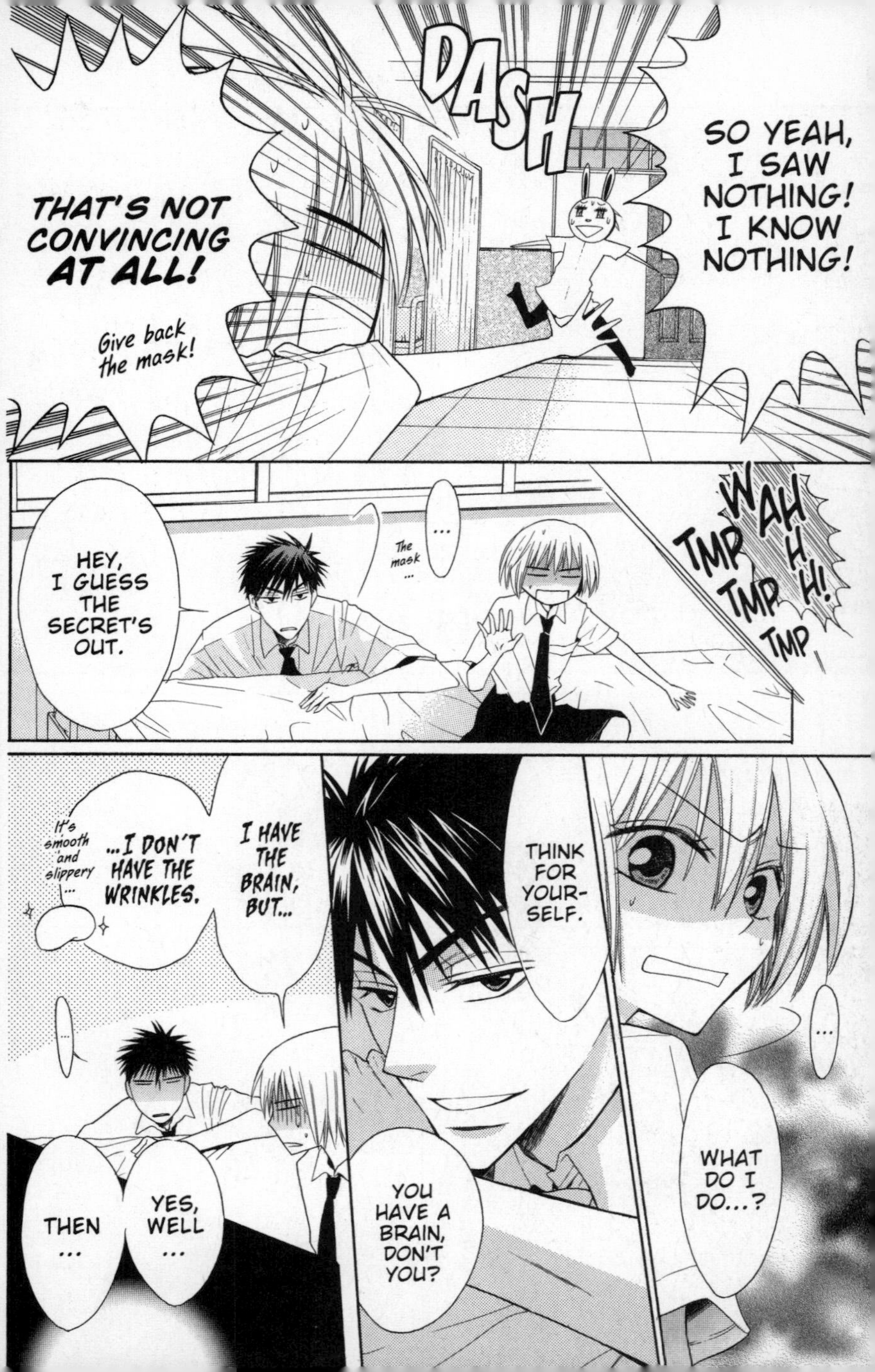
DASH
SO YEAH, I SAW NOTHING! I KNOW NOTHING!
THAT'S NOT CONVINCING AT ALL!
Give back the mask!
WAHHH!
TMP TMP TMP
...
The mask...
HEY, I GUESS THE SECRET'S OUT.
...
WHAT DO I DO...?
THINK FOR YOURSELF.
YOU HAVE A BRAIN, DON'T YOU?
I HAVE THE BRAIN, BUT...
...I DON'T HAVE THE WRINKLES.
It's smooth and slippery...
...
YES, WELL...
THEN...

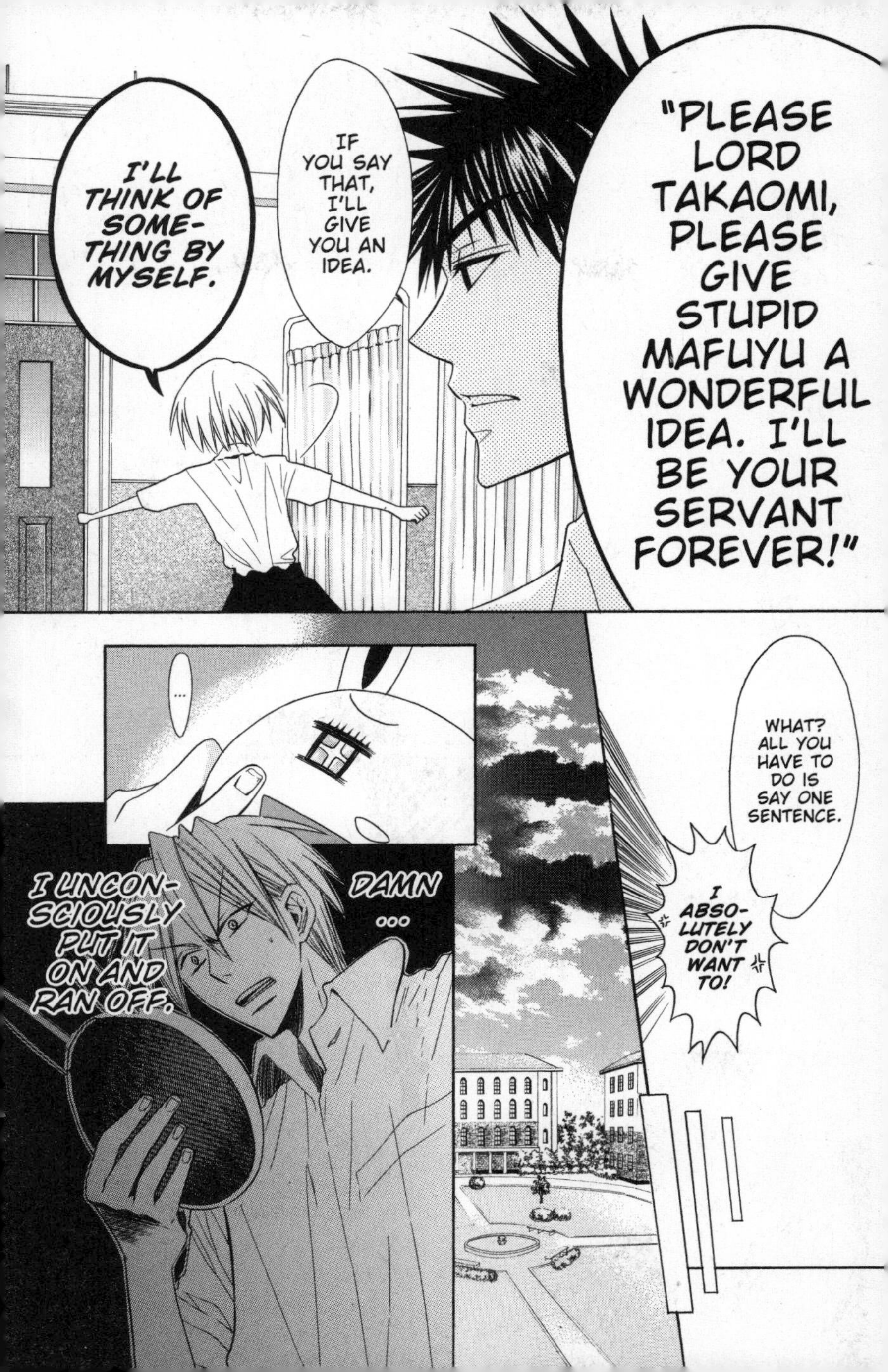
"PLEASE LORD TAKAOMI, PLEASE GIVE STUPID MAFUYU A WONDERFUL IDEA. I'LL BE YOUR SERVANT FOREVER!"
IF YOU SAY THAT, I'LL GIVE YOU AN IDEA.
I'LL THINK OF SOME-THING BY MYSELF.
WHAT? ALL YOU HAVE TO DO IS SAY ONE SENTENCE.
I ABSO-LUTELY DON'T WANT TO!
...
DAMN ...
I UNCON-SCIOUSLY PUT IT ON AND RAN OFF.

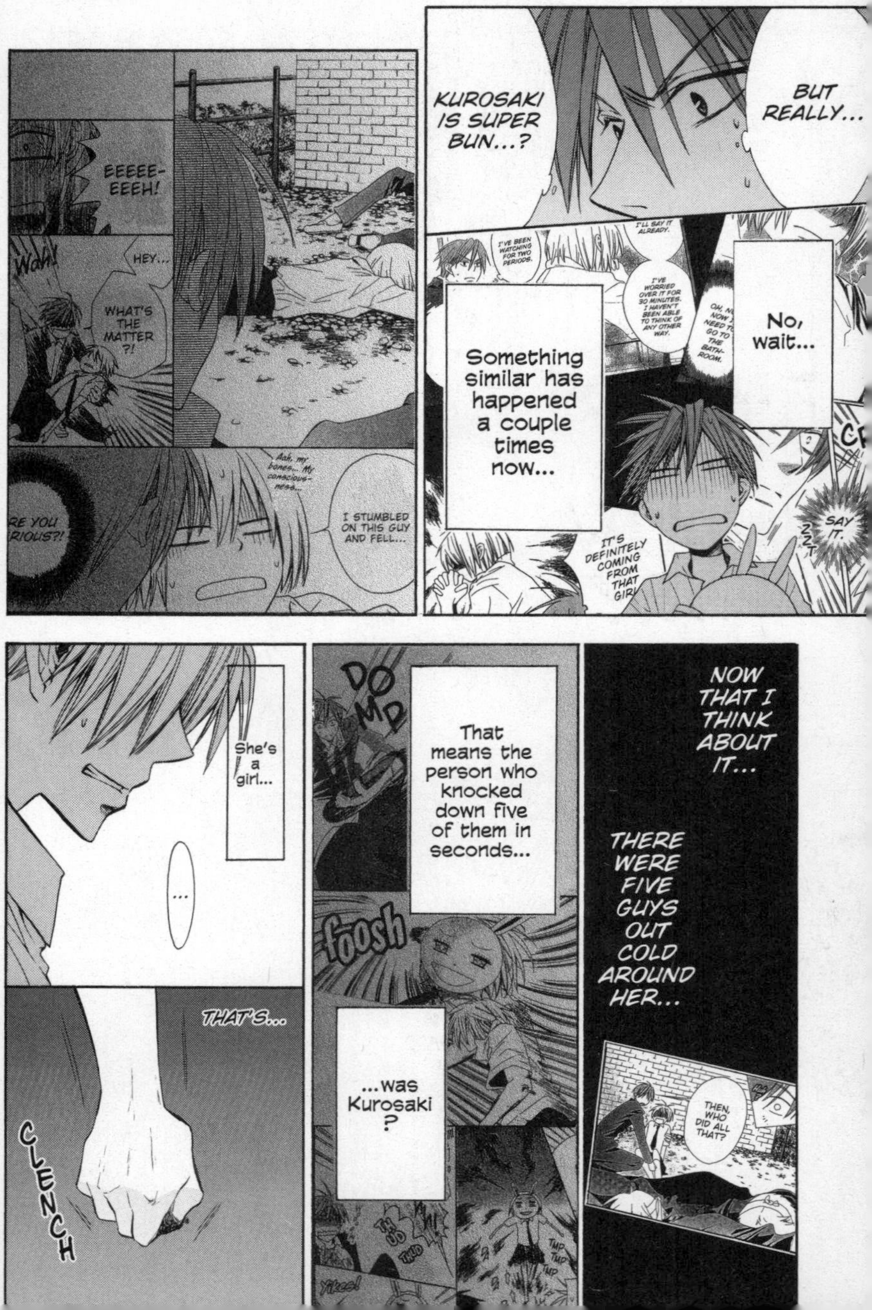
BUT REALLY...
KUROSAKI IS SUPER BUN...?
No, wait...
SAY IT.
I'LL SAY IT ALREADY.
I'VE BEEN WATCHING FOR TWO PERIODS.
I'VE WORRIED OVER IT FOR 30 MINUTES. I HAVEN'T BEEN ABLE TO THINK OF ANY OTHER WAY.
Something similar has happened a couple times now...
IT'S DEFINITELY COMING FROM THAT GIRL
EEEEE-EEEH!
HEY...
WHAT'S THE MATTER?!
Wah!
I STUMBLED ON THIS GUY AND FELL...
Aah, my bones... My consciousness...
NOW THAT I THINK ABOUT IT...
THERE WERE FIVE GUYS OUT COLD AROUND HER...
THEN, WHO DID ALL THAT?
DOMP
That means the person who knocked down five of them in seconds...
foosh
...was Kurosaki?
TMP TMP TMP
Yikes!
She's a girl...
...
THAT'S...
CLENCH

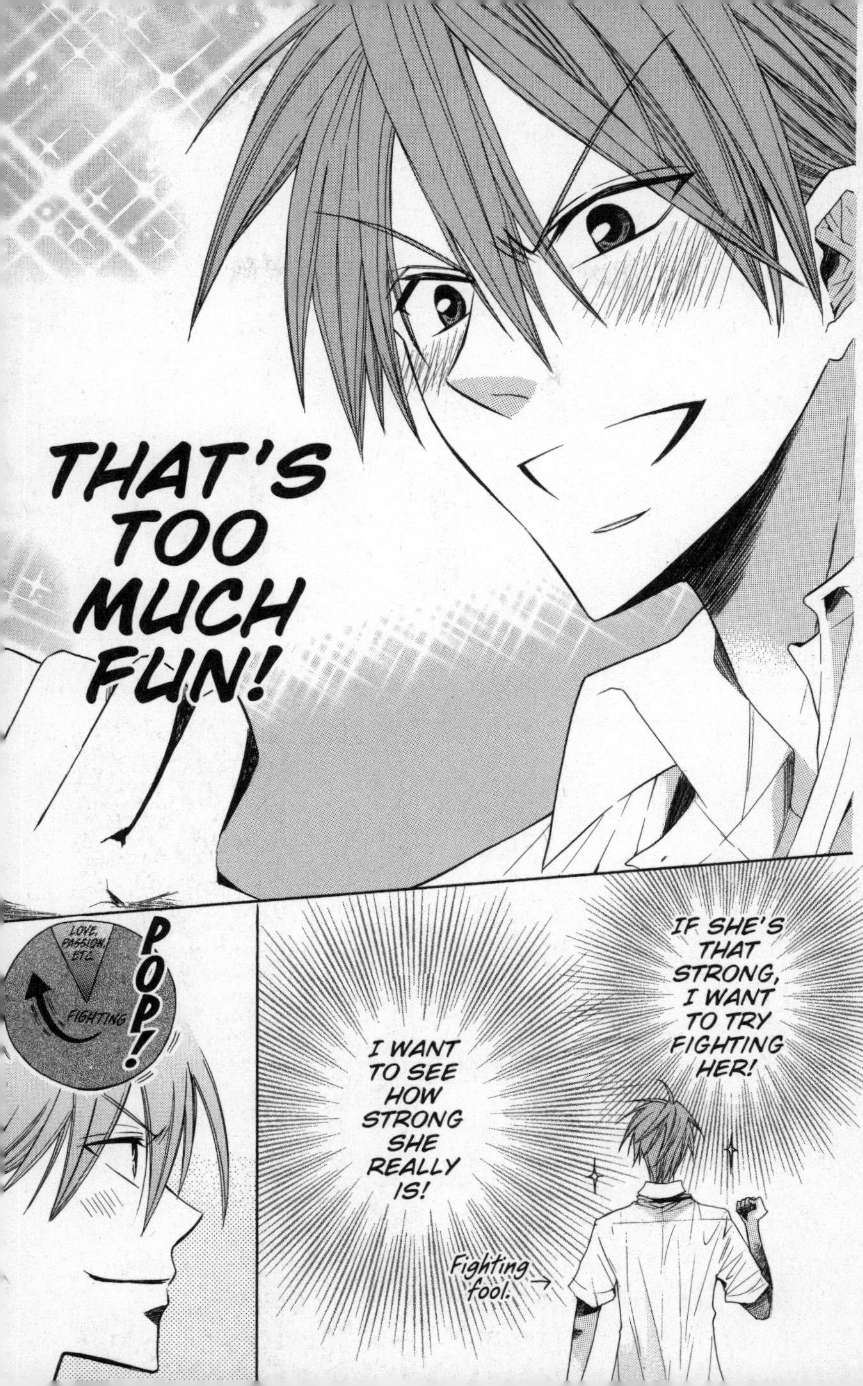
THAT'S TOO MUCH FUN!
IF SHE'S THAT STRONG, I WANT TO TRY FIGHTING HER!
I WANT TO SEE HOW STRONG SHE REALLY IS!
Fighting fool.
LOVE, PASSION, ETC.
FIGHTING
POP!

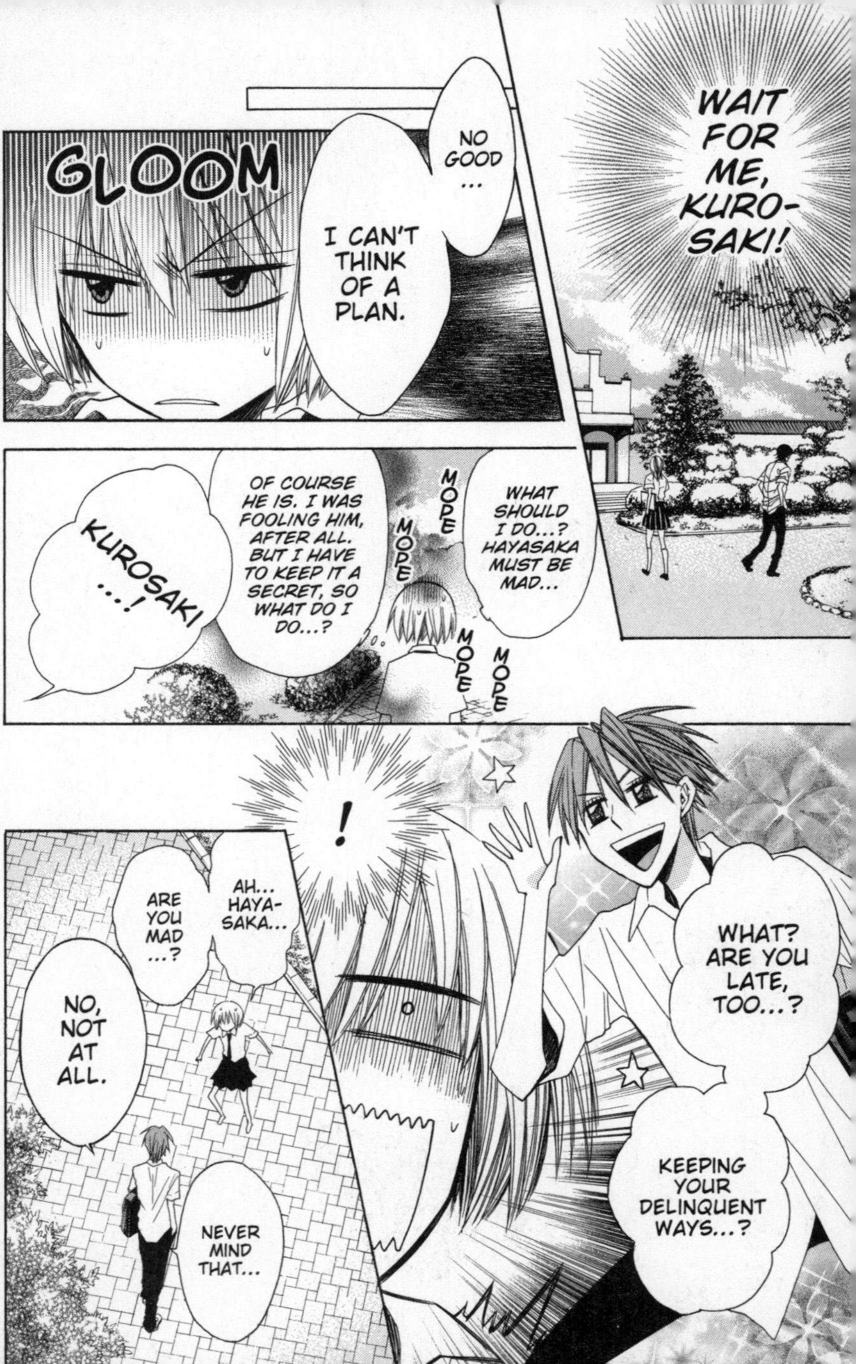
WAIT FOR ME, KURO-SAKI!
NO GOOD ...
I CAN'T THINK OF A PLAN.
GLOOM
MOPE
WHAT SHOULD I DO...? HAYASAKA MUST BE MAD...
MOPE
OF COURSE HE IS. I WAS FOOLING HIM, AFTER ALL. BUT I HAVE TO KEEP IT A SECRET, SO WHAT DO I DO...?
MOPE MOPE
KUROSAKI ...!
!
WHAT? ARE YOU LATE, TOO...?
KEEPING YOUR DELINQUENT WAYS...?
AH... HAYA-SAKA...
ARE YOU MAD ...?
NO, NOT AT ALL.
NEVER MIND THAT...

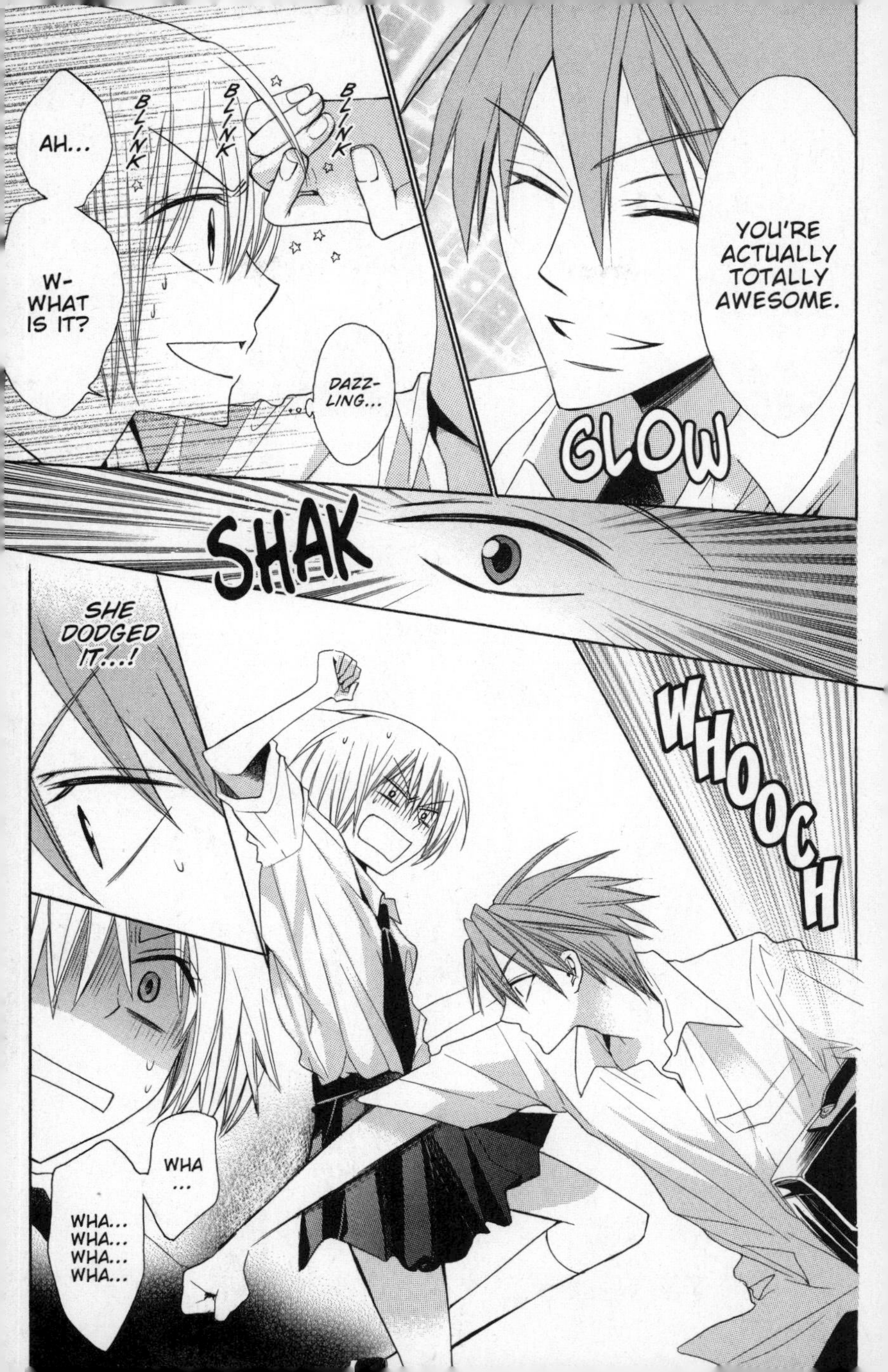
YOU'RE ACTUALLY TOTALLY AWESOME.
GLOW
BLINK
BLINK
BLINK
AH...
DAZZ-LING...
W- WHAT IS IT?
SHAK
WHOOOCH
SHE DODGED IT...!
WHA ...
WHA... WHA... WHA... WHA...

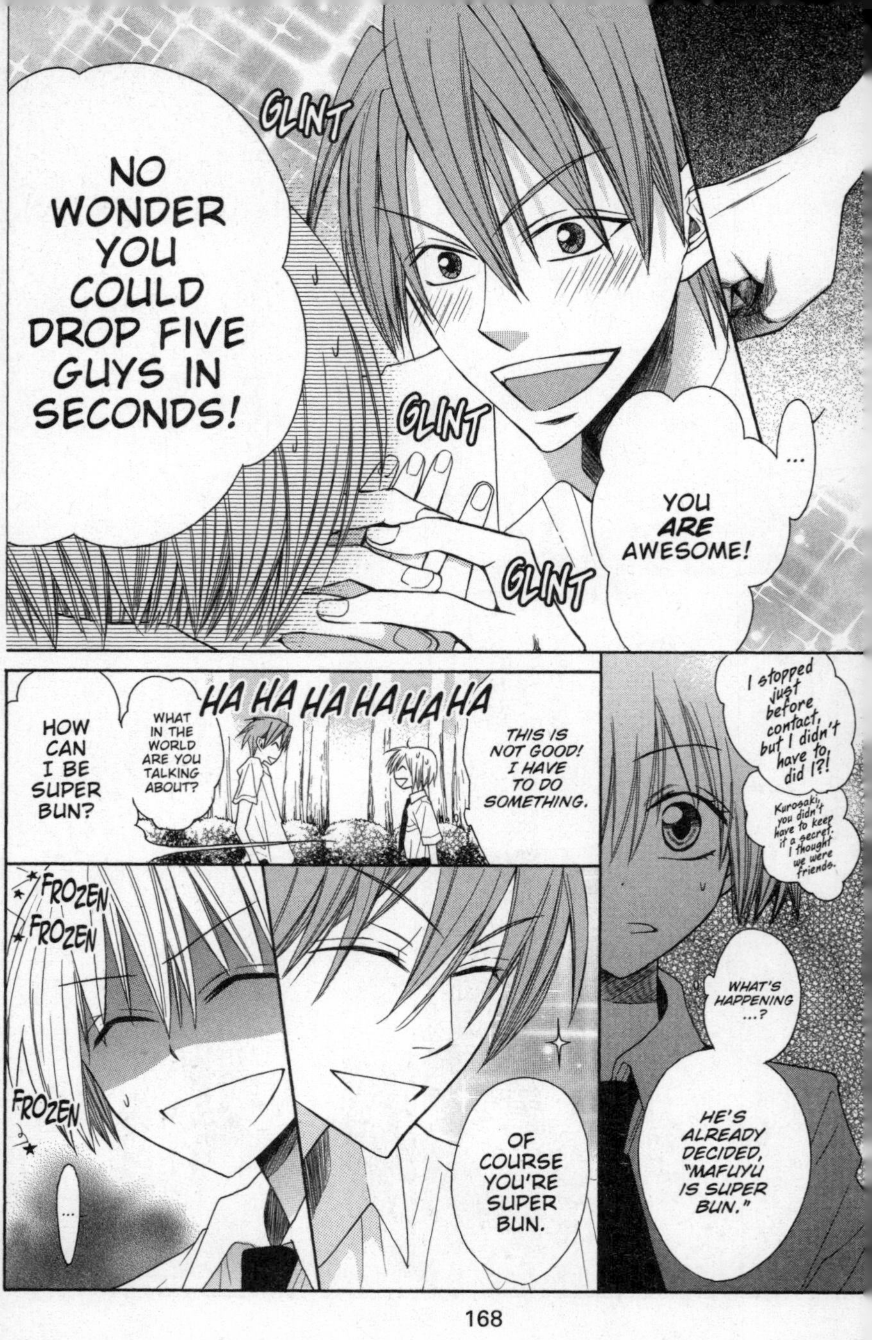

GLINT
NO WONDER YOU COULD DROP FIVE GUYS IN SECONDS!
GLINT
GLINT
...
YOU **ARE** AWESOME!
I stopped just before contact, but I didn't have to, did I?!
Kurosaki, you didn't have to keep it a secret. I thought we were friends.
WHAT'S HAPPENING ...?
HE'S ALREADY DECIDED, "MAFUYU IS SUPER BUN."
THIS IS NOT GOOD! I HAVE TO DO SOMETHING.
HA HA HA HA HA HA
WHAT IN THE WORLD ARE YOU TALKING ABOUT?
HOW CAN I BE SUPER BUN?
OF COURSE YOU'RE SUPER BUN.
FROZEN
FROZEN
FROZEN
...

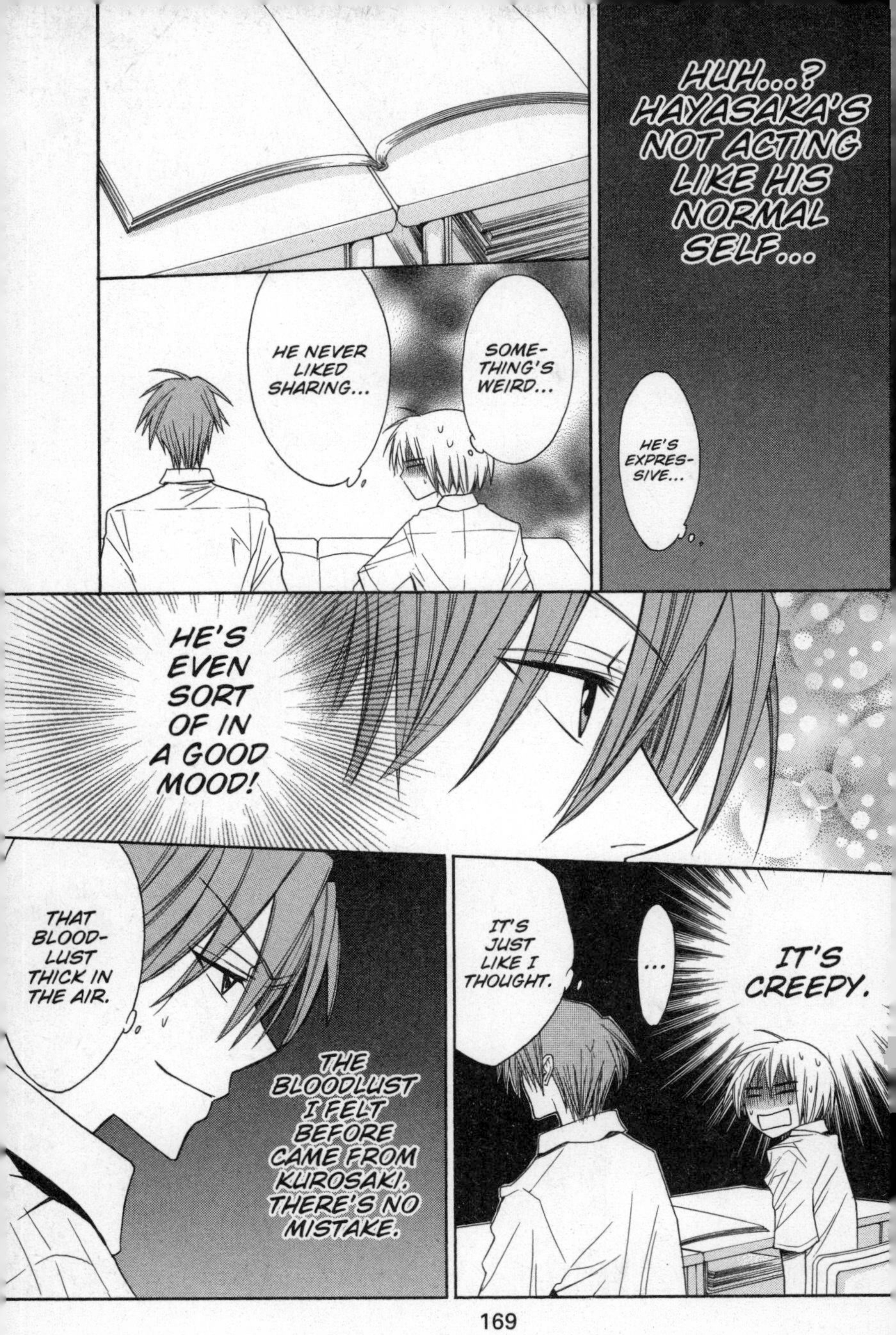
HUH...? HAYASAKA'S NOT ACTING LIKE HIS NORMAL SELF...
HE'S EXPRES-SIVE...
SOME-THING'S WEIRD...
HE NEVER LIKED SHARING...
HE'S EVEN SORT OF IN A GOOD MOOD!
IT'S CREEPY.
...
IT'S JUST LIKE I THOUGHT.
THAT BLOOD-LUST THICK IN THE AIR.
THE BLOODLUST I FELT BEFORE CAME FROM KUROSAKI. THERE'S NO MISTAKE.

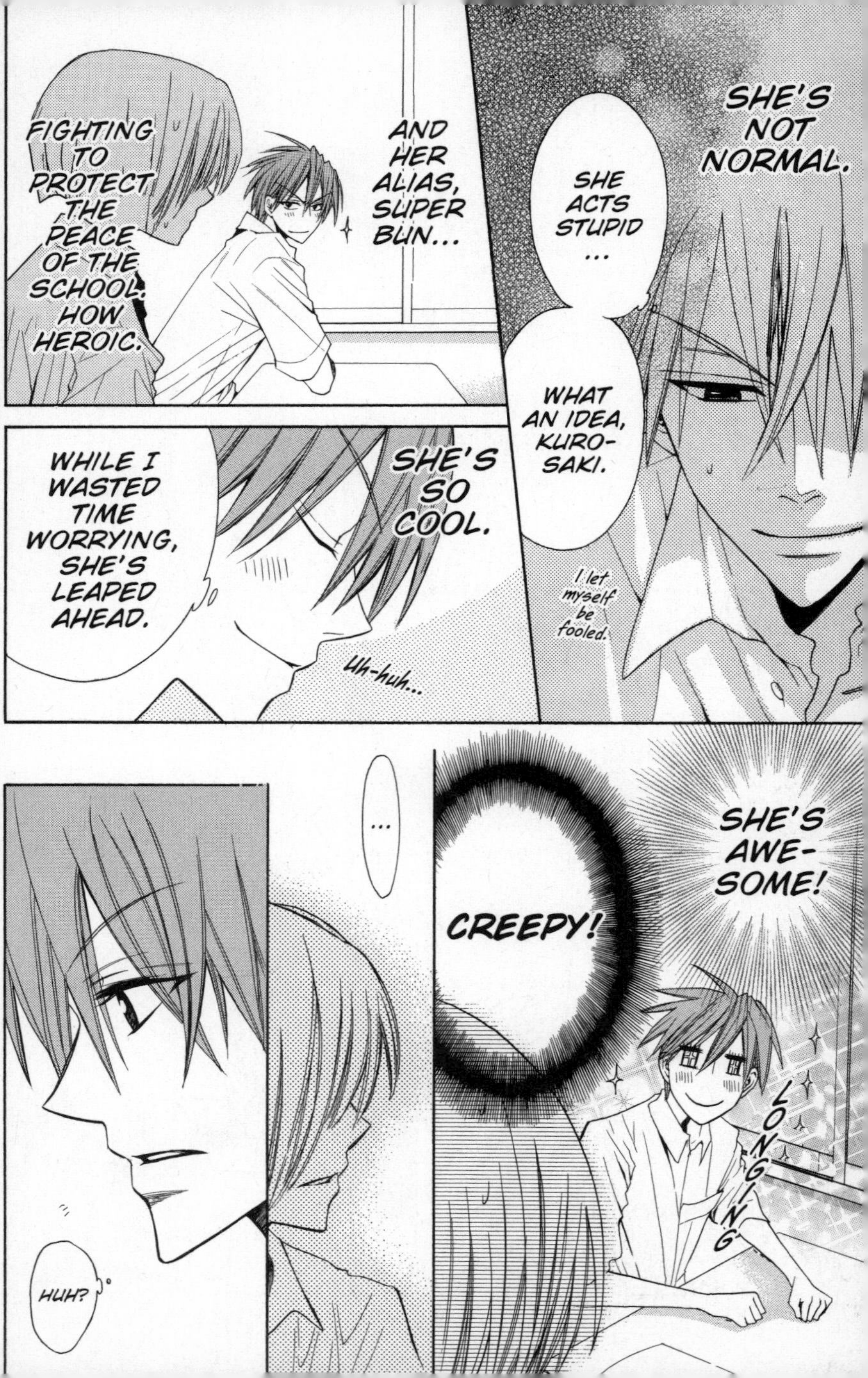
SHE'S NOT NORMAL.
SHE ACTS STUPID ...
WHAT AN IDEA, KUROSAKI.
I let myself be fooled.
AND HER ALIAS, SUPER BUN...
FIGHTING TO PROTECT THE PEACE OF THE SCHOOL. HOW HEROIC.
SHE'S SO COOL.
WHILE I WASTED TIME WORRYING, SHE'S LEAPED AHEAD.
Uh-huh...
SHE'S AWESOME!
LONGING
CREEPY!
...
HUH?

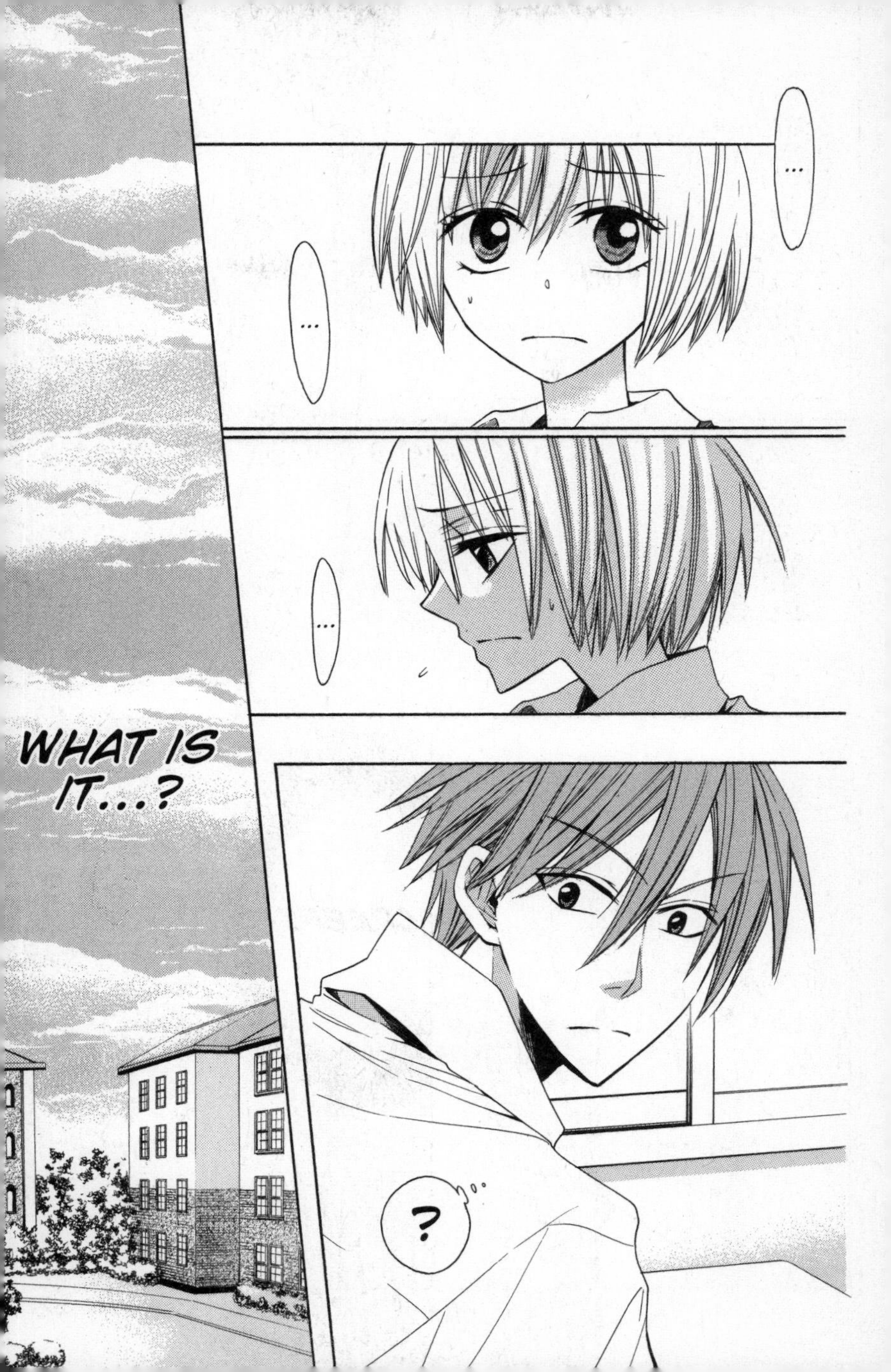
...
...
...
?
WHAT IS IT...?

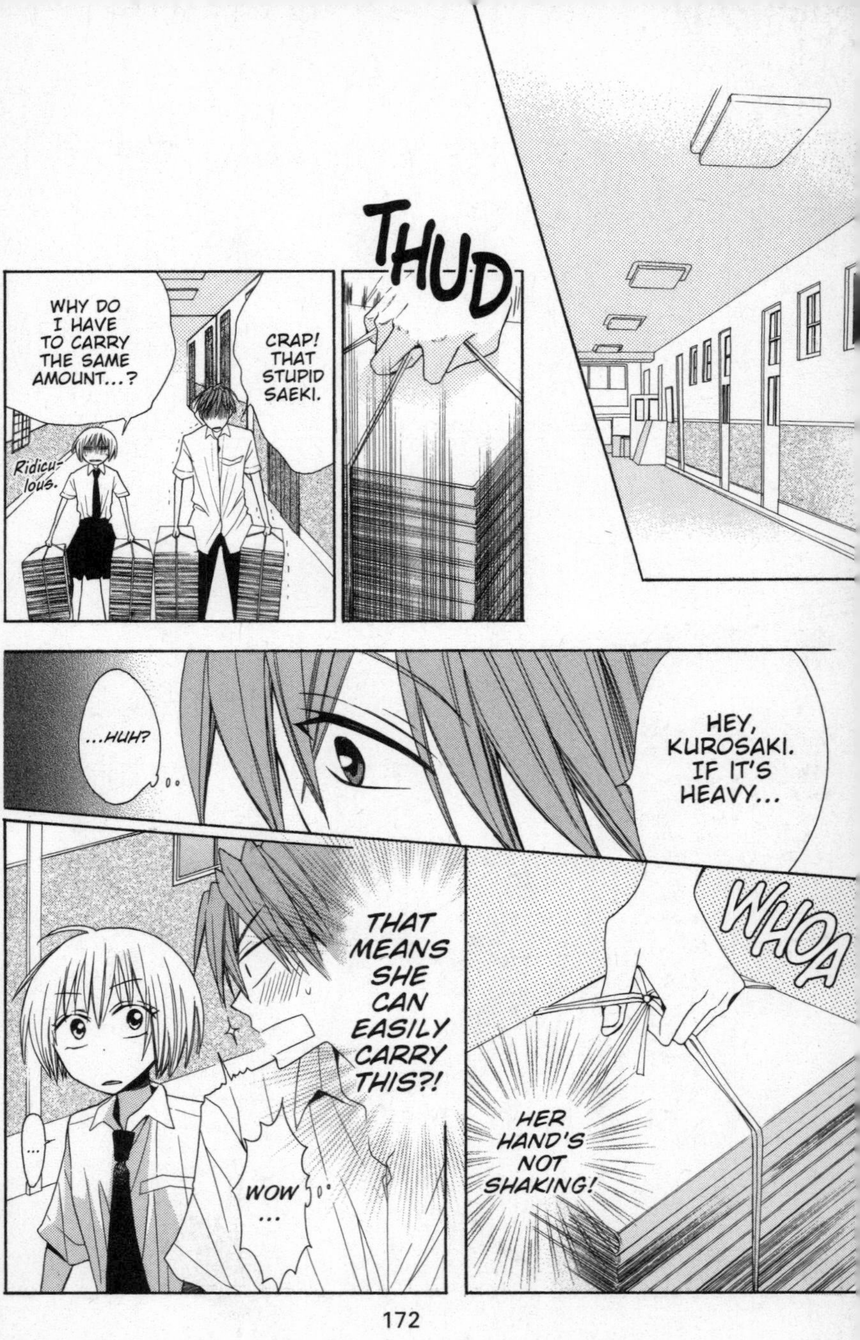
THUD
CRAP! THAT STUPID SAEKI.
WHY DO I HAVE TO CARRY THE SAME AMOUNT...?
Ridicu-lous.
HEY, KUROSAKI. IF IT'S HEAVY...
...HUH?
WHOA
HER HAND'S NOT SHAKING!
THAT MEANS SHE CAN EASILY CARRY THIS?!
WOW...
...

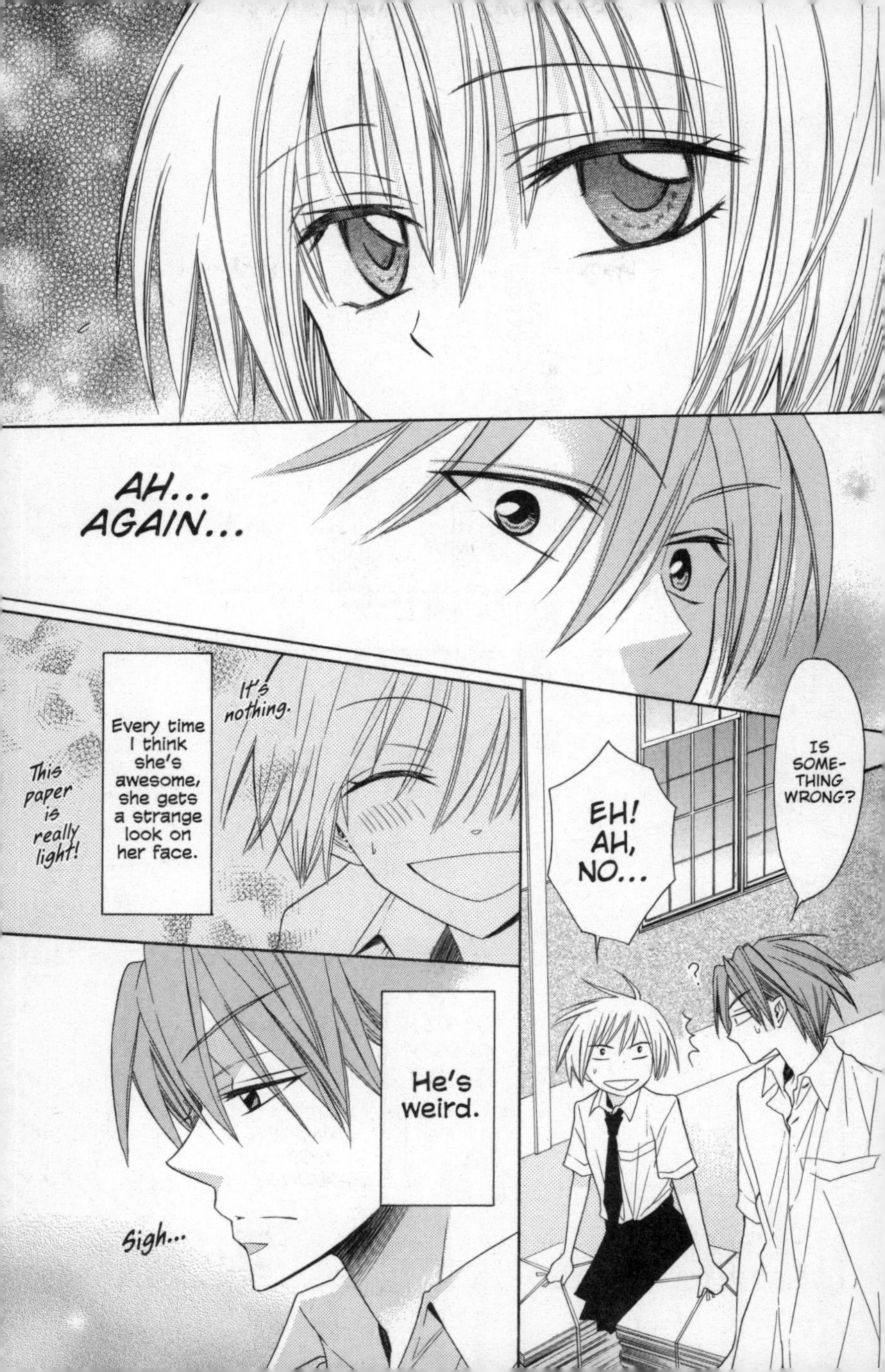
AH... AGAIN...
IS SOMETHING-THING WRONG?
EH! AH, NO...
It's nothing.
Every time I think she's awesome, she gets a strange look on her face.
This paper is really light!
He's weird.
Sigh...

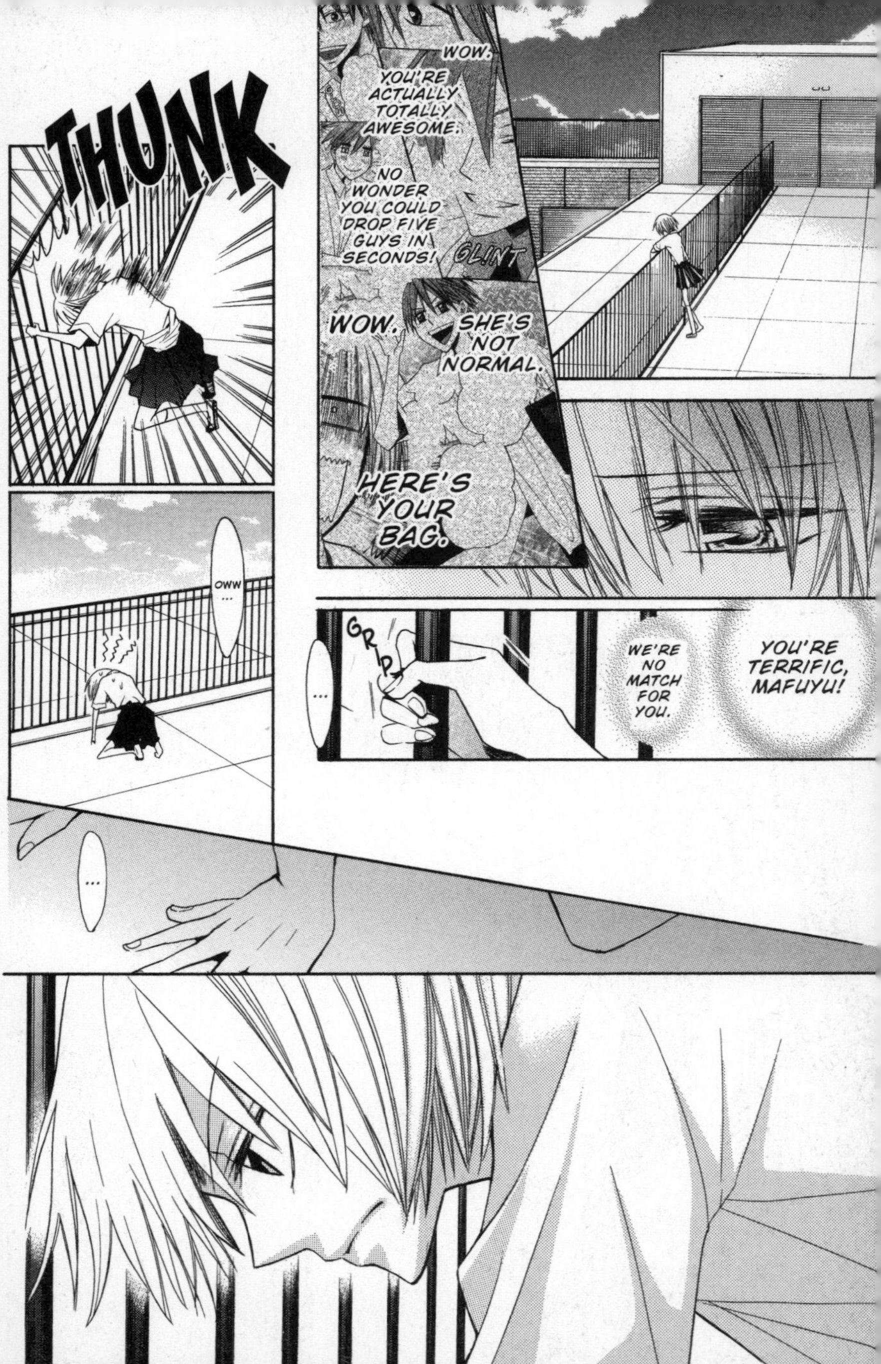
WOW.
YOU'RE ACTUALLY TOTALLY AWESOME.
NO WONDER YOU COULD DROP FIVE GUYS IN SECONDS!
GLINT
SHE'S NOT NORMAL.
WOW.
HERE'S YOUR BAG.
THUNK
OWW ...
YOU'RE TERRIFIC, MAFUYU!
WE'RE NO MATCH FOR YOU.
GRIP
...
...

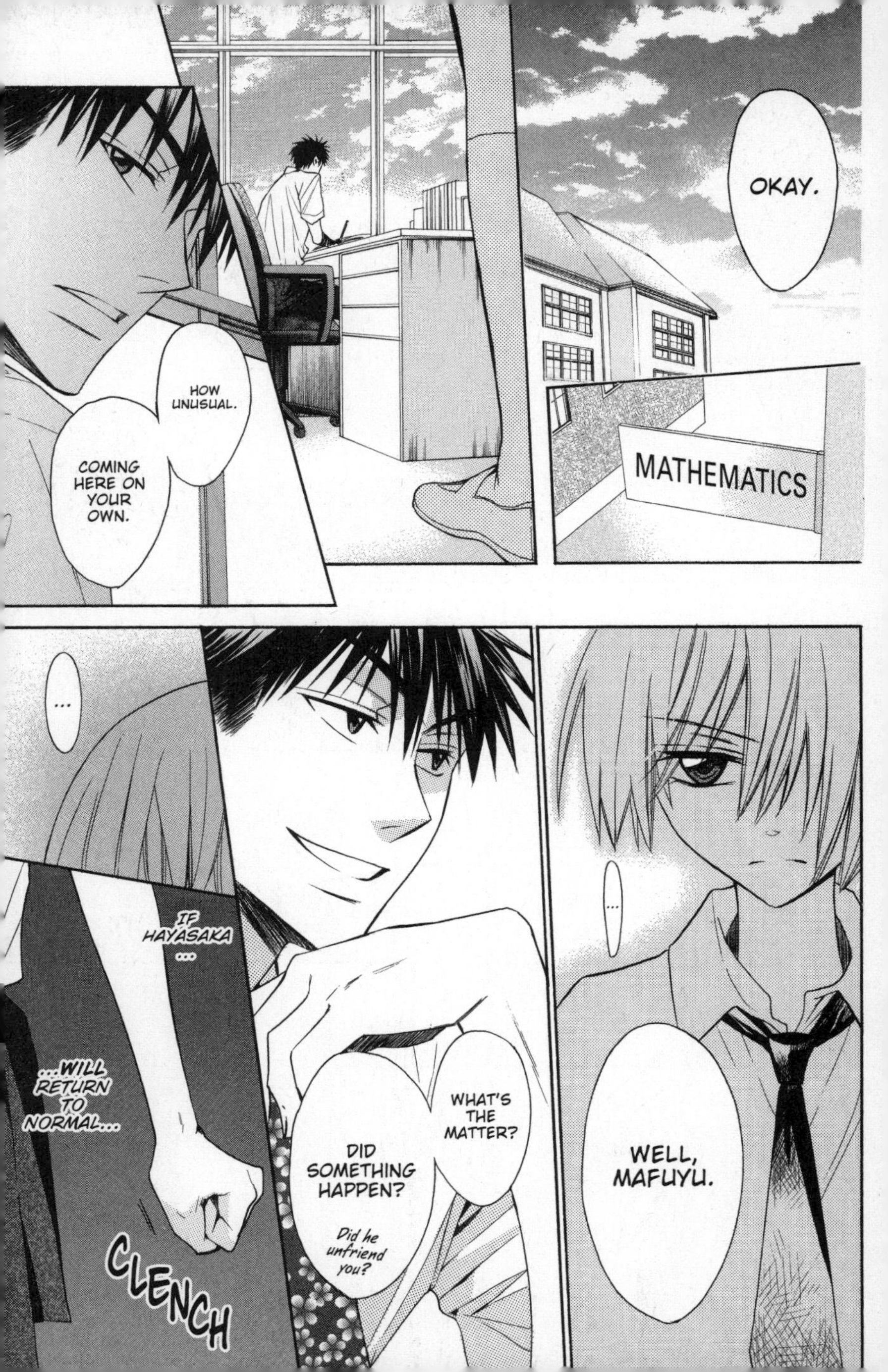
OKAY.
MATHEMATICS
HOW UNUSUAL.
COMING HERE ON YOUR OWN.
...
WELL, MAFUYU.
WHAT'S THE MATTER?
DID SOMETHING HAPPEN?
Did he unfriend you?
...
IF HAYASAKA...
...WILL RETURN TO NORMAL...
CLENCH

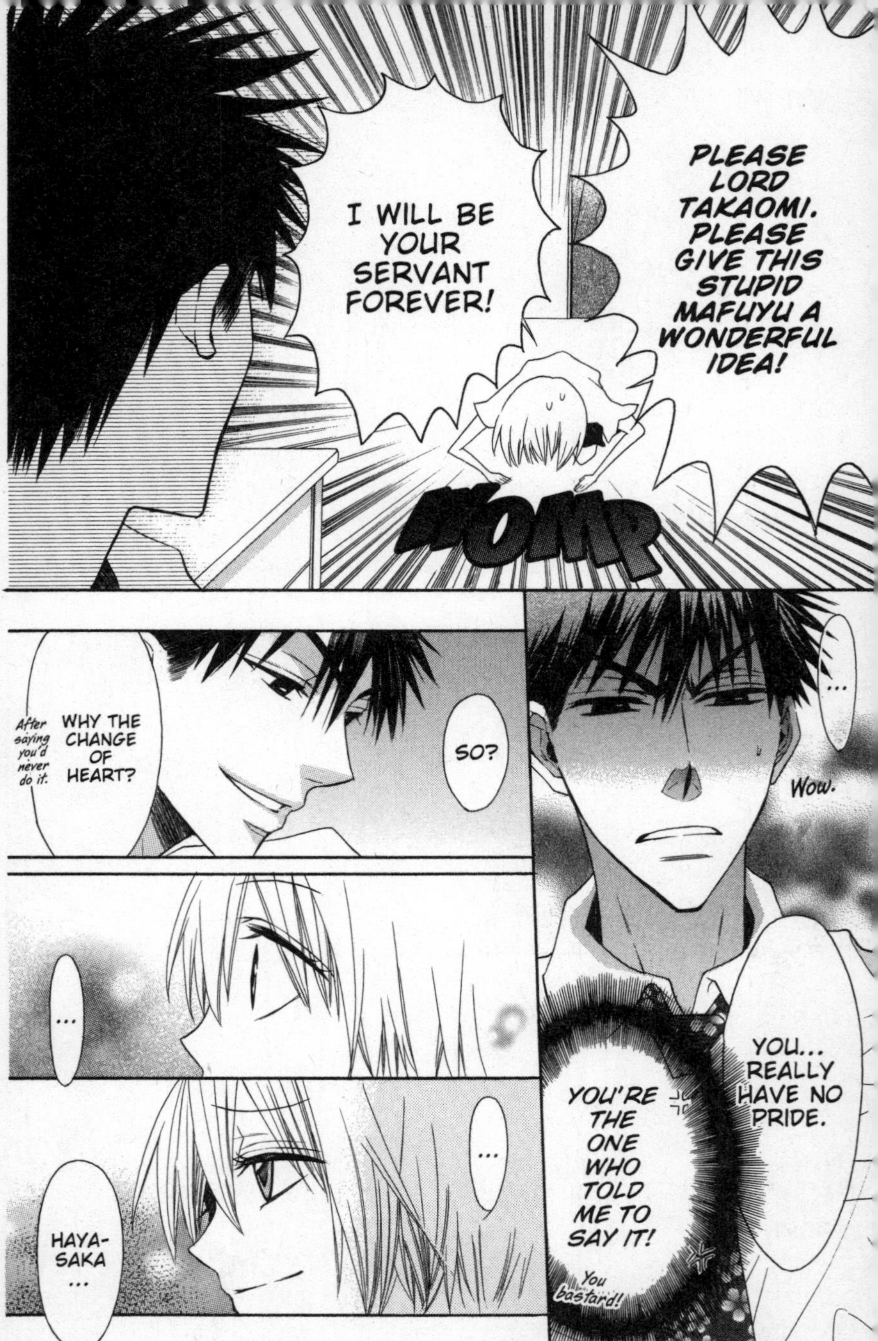
PLEASE LORD TAKAOMI. PLEASE GIVE THIS STUPID MAFUYU A WONDERFUL IDEA!
I WILL BE YOUR SERVANT FOREVER!
WOMP
...
Wow.
YOU... REALLY HAVE NO PRIDE.
YOU'RE THE ONE WHO TOLD ME TO SAY IT!
You bastard!
SO?
WHY THE CHANGE OF HEART?
After saying you'd never do it.
...
...
HAYA-SAKA ...

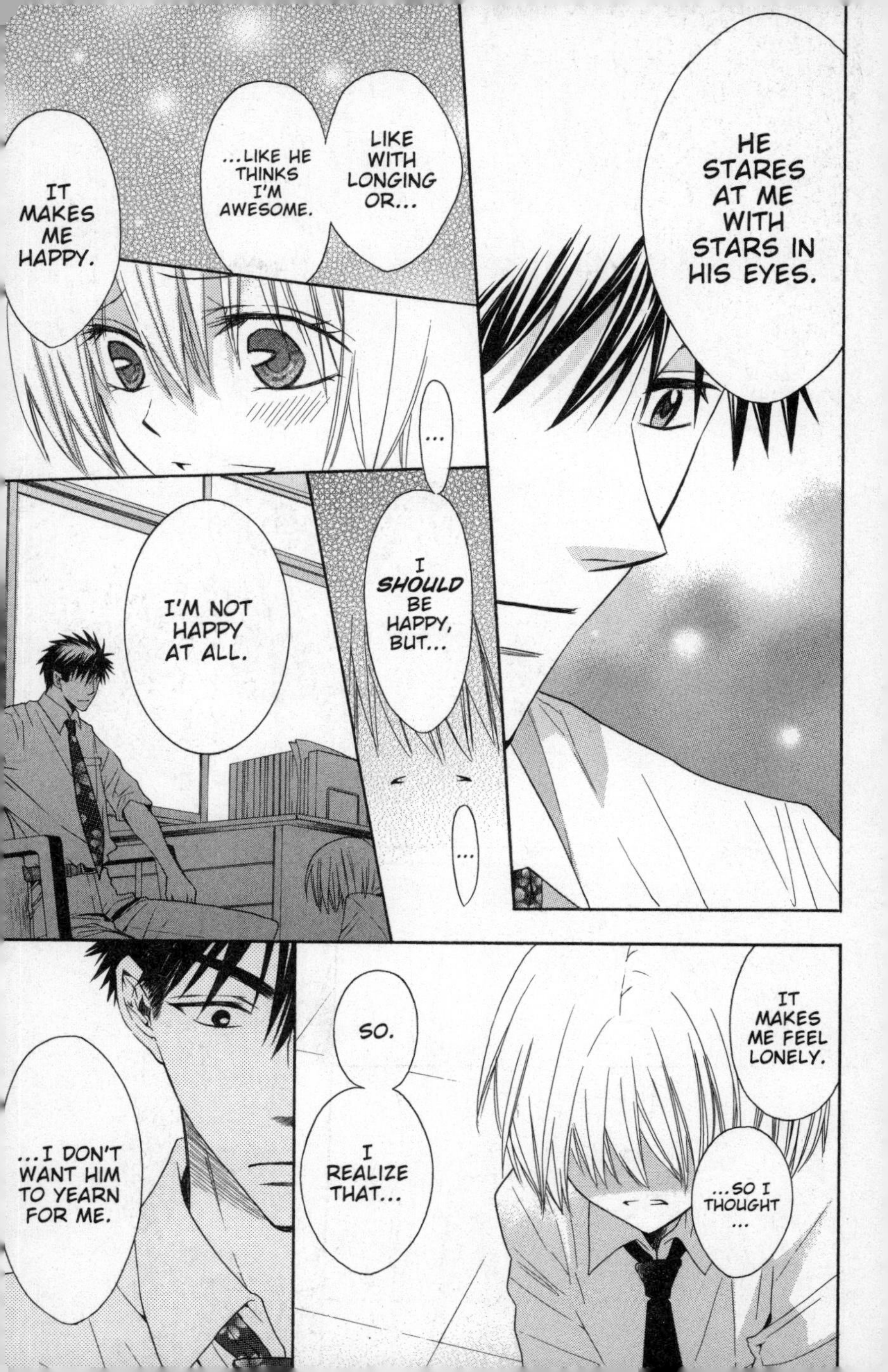
HE STARES AT ME WITH STARS IN HIS EYES.
LIKE WITH LONGING OR...
...LIKE HE THINKS I'M AWESOME.
IT MAKES ME HAPPY.
...
I *SHOULD* BE HAPPY, BUT...
...
I'M NOT HAPPY AT ALL.
IT MAKES ME FEEL LONELY.
...SO I THOUGHT ...
SO.
I REALIZE THAT...
...I DON'T WANT HIM TO YEARN FOR ME.

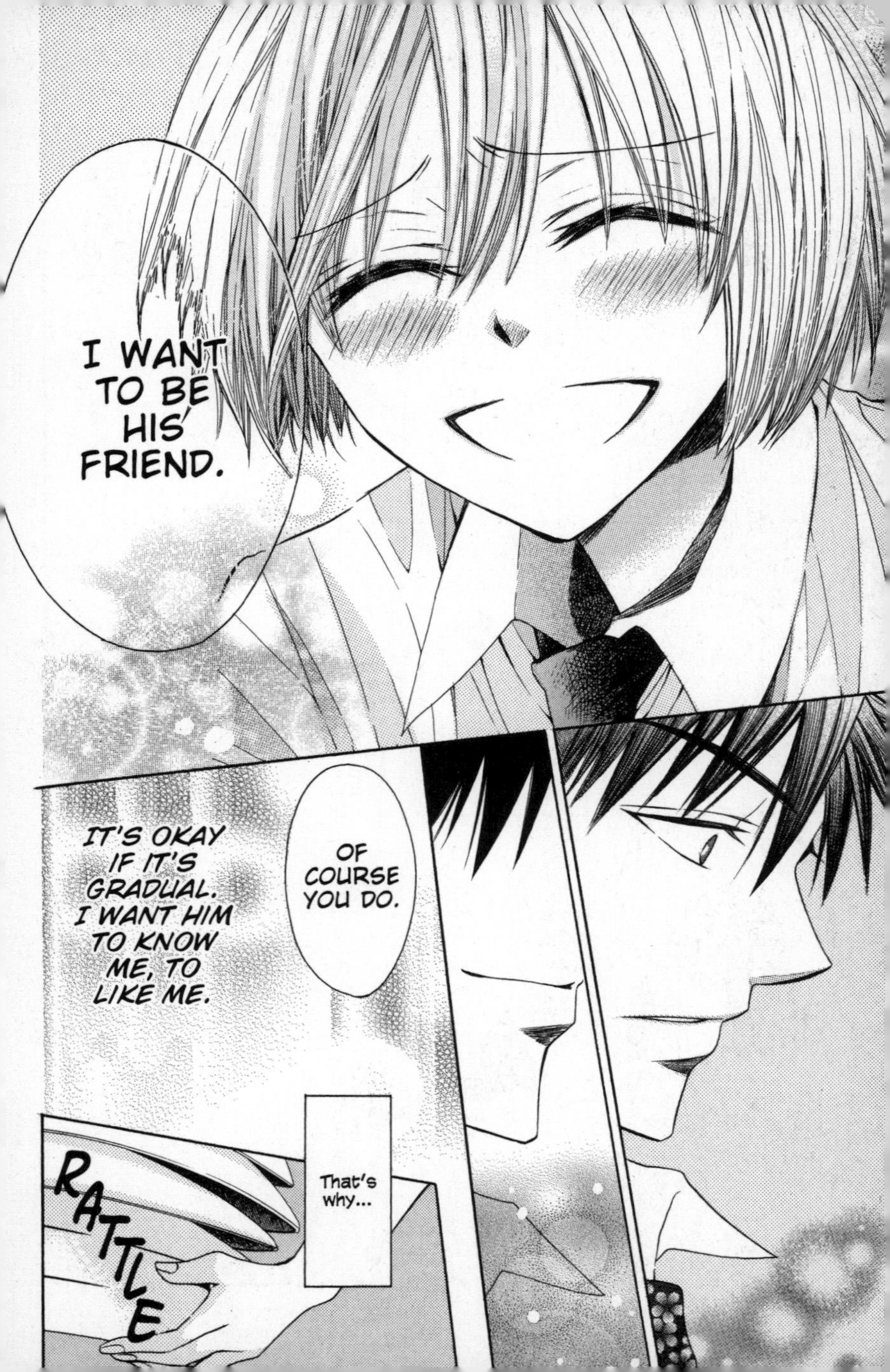

I WANT TO BE HIS FRIEND.
OF COURSE YOU DO.
IT'S OKAY IF IT'S GRADUAL. I WANT HIM TO KNOW ME, TO LIKE ME.
That's why...
RATTLE

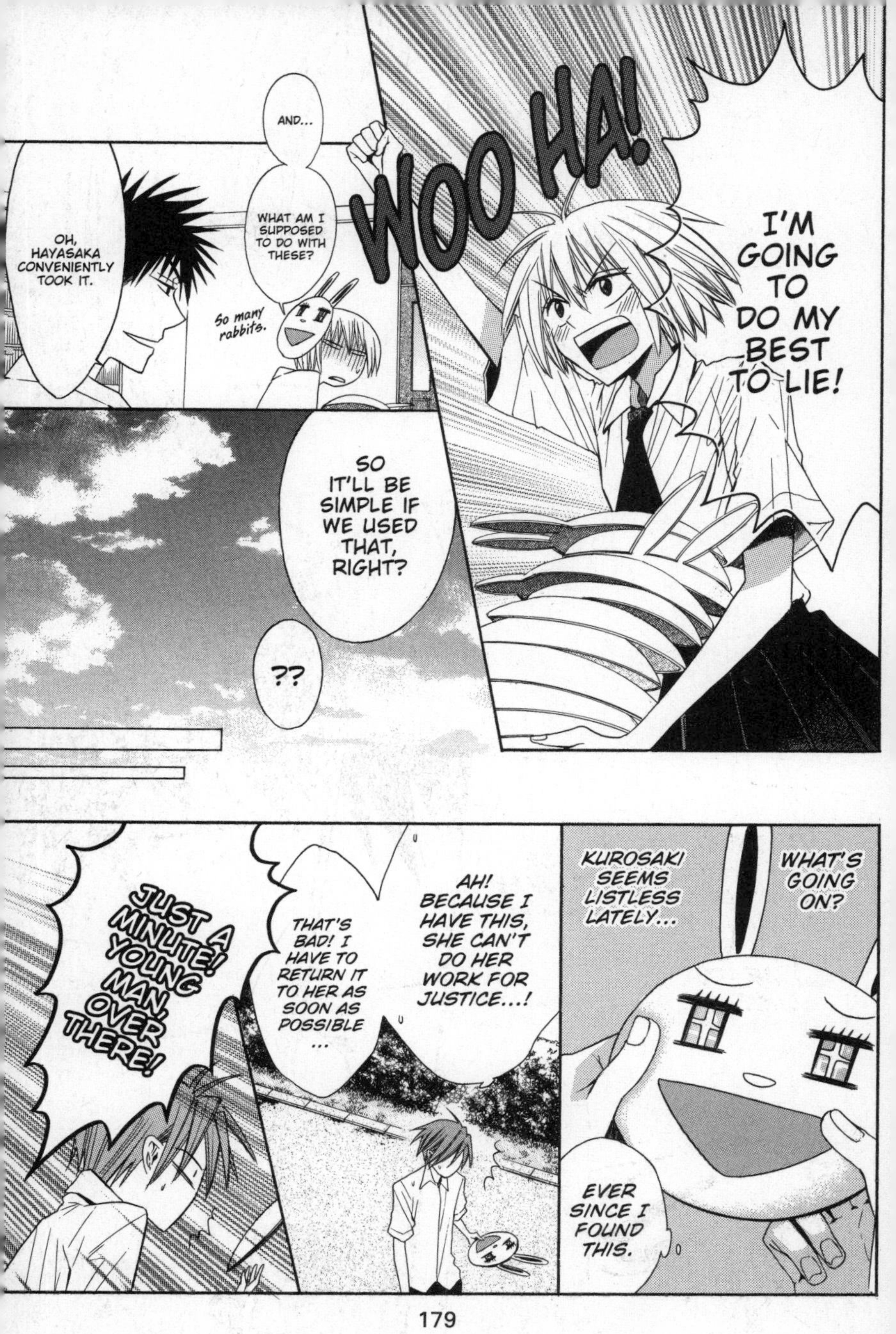
WOO HA!
I'M GOING TO DO MY BEST TO LIE!
AND...
WHAT AM I SUPPOSED TO DO WITH THESE?
So many rabbits.
OH, HAYASAKA CONVENIENTLY TOOK IT.
SO IT'LL BE SIMPLE IF WE USED THAT, RIGHT?
??
WHAT'S GOING ON?
KUROSAKI SEEMS LISTLESS LATELY...
EVER SINCE I FOUND THIS.
AH! BECAUSE I HAVE THIS, SHE CAN'T DO HER WORK FOR JUSTICE...!
THAT'S BAD! I HAVE TO RETURN IT TO HER AS SOON AS POSSIBLE...
JUST A MINUTE! YOUNG MAN, OVER THERE!

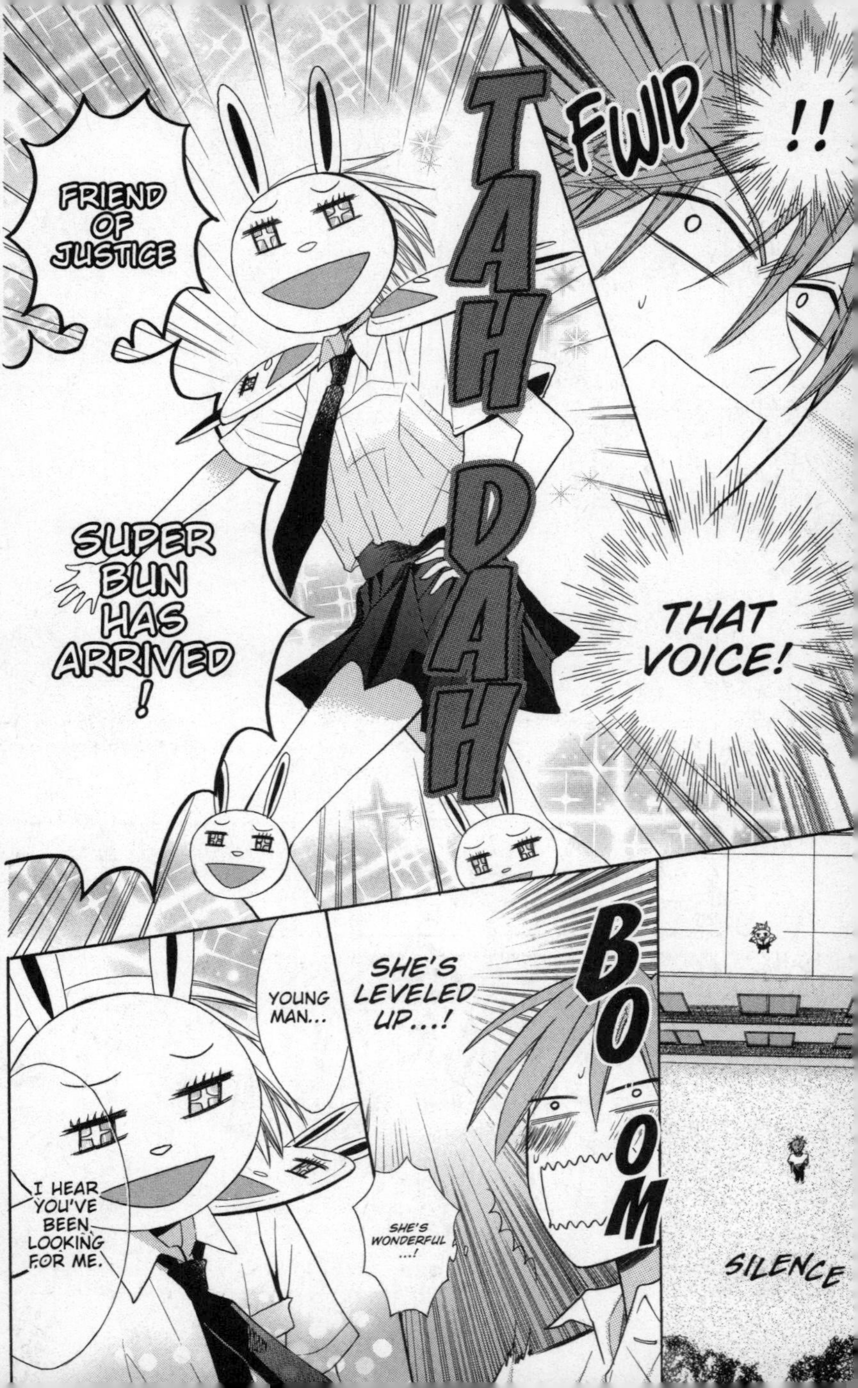
FWIP
!!
THAT VOICE!
TAHDAH
FRIEND OF JUSTICE
SUPER BUN HAS ARRIVED!
SILENCE
BOOM
SHE'S LEVELED UP...!
SHE'S WONDERFUL...!
YOUNG MAN...
I HEAR YOU'VE BEEN LOOKING FOR ME.

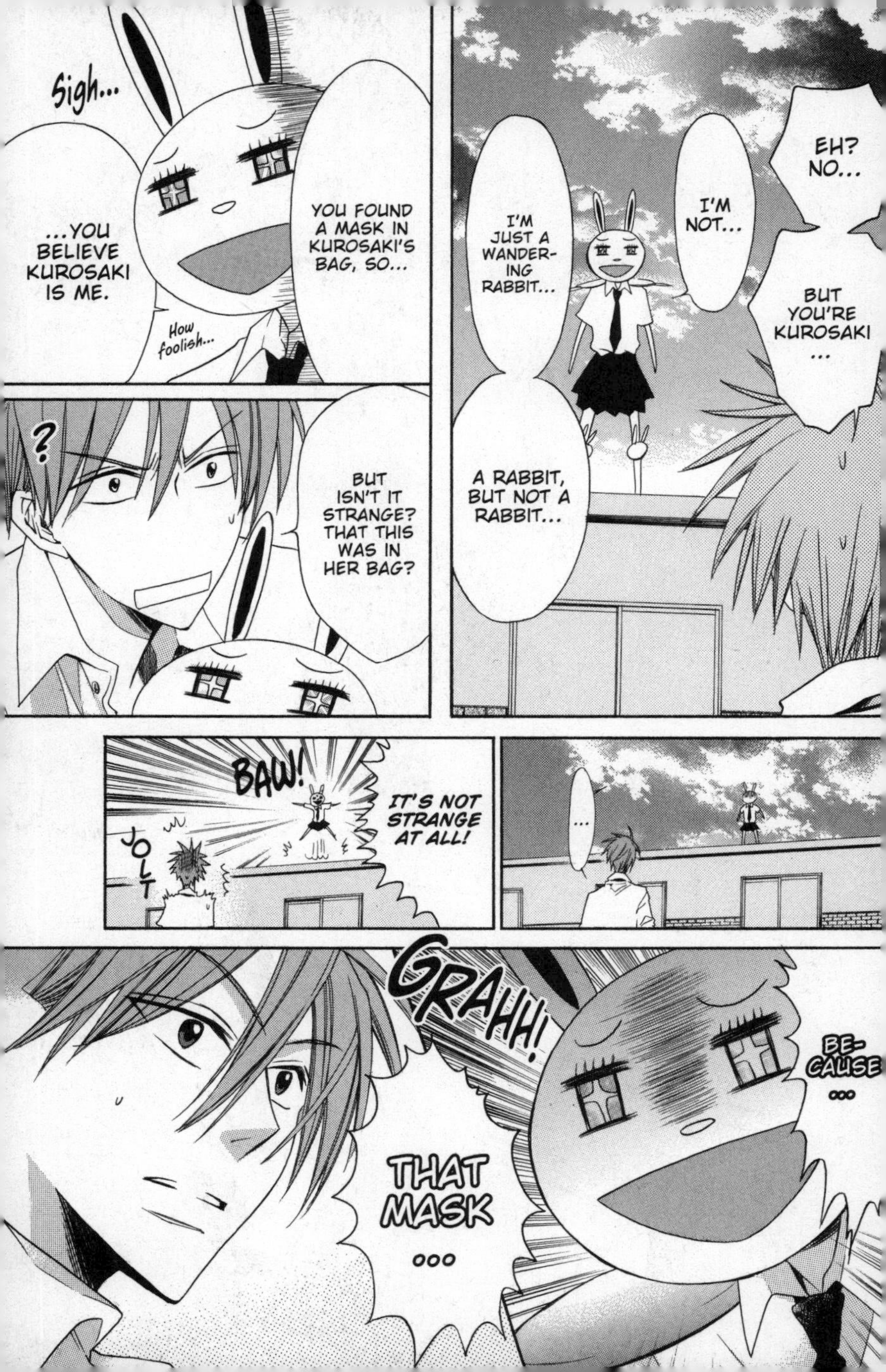

EH? NO...
BUT YOU'RE KUROSAKI...
I'M NOT...
I'M JUST A WANDERING RABBIT...
A RABBIT, BUT NOT A RABBIT...
YOU FOUND A MASK IN KUROSAKI'S BAG, SO...
Sigh...
...YOU BELIEVE KUROSAKI IS ME.
How foolish...
BUT ISN'T IT STRANGE? THAT THIS WAS IN HER BAG?
?
...
IT'S NOT STRANGE AT ALL!
BAW!
JOLT
BE-CAUSE...
GRAHH!
THAT MASK...

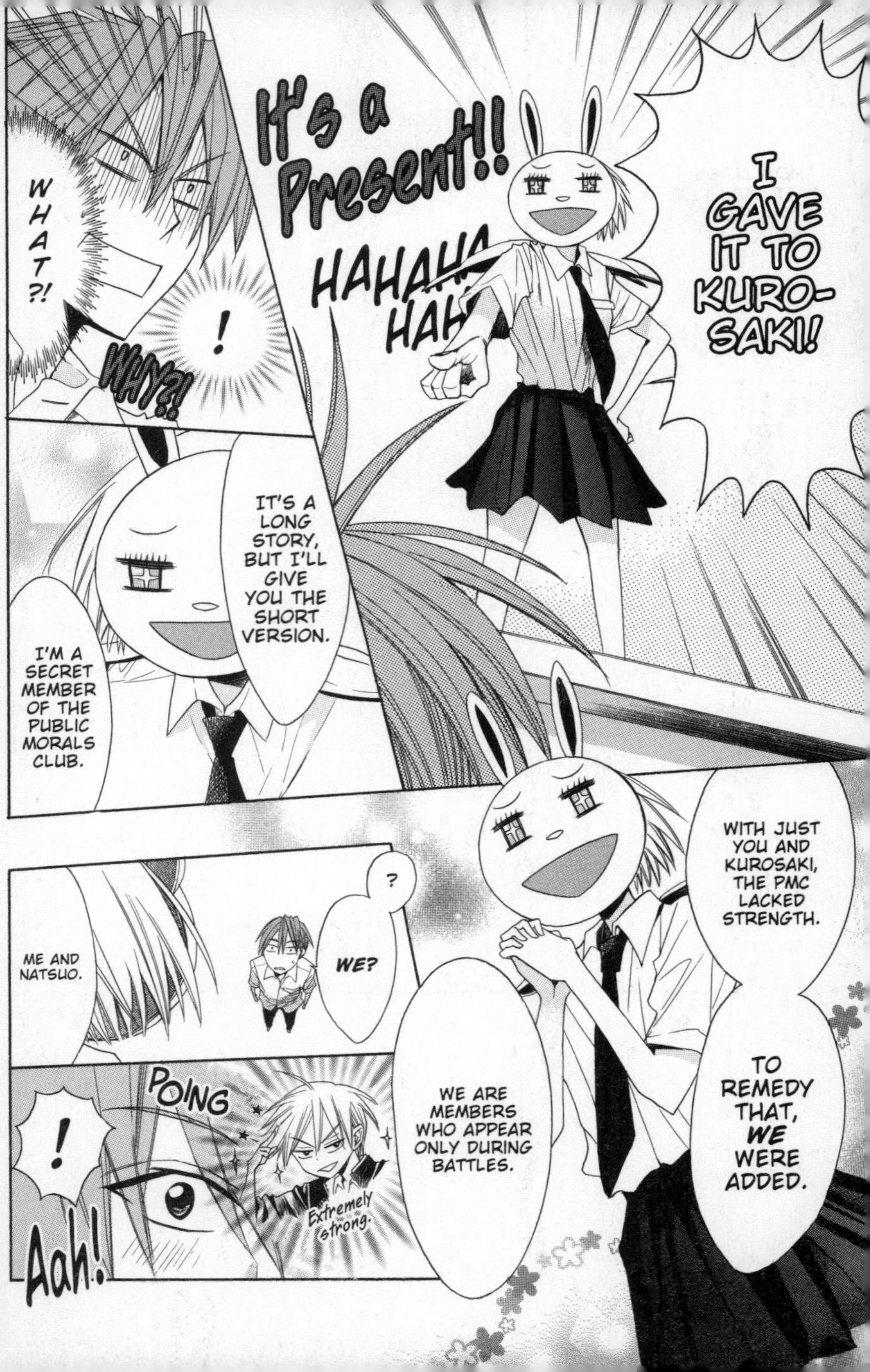
I GAVE IT TO KURO-SAKI!
It's a Present!!
HAHAHA HAH
!
WHAT?!
WHY?!
IT'S A LONG STORY, BUT I'LL GIVE YOU THE SHORT VERSION.
I'M A SECRET MEMBER OF THE PUBLIC MORALS CLUB.
WITH JUST YOU AND KUROSAKI, THE PMC LACKED STRENGTH.
TO REMEDY THAT, WE WERE ADDED.
?
WE?
ME AND NATSUO.
WE ARE MEMBERS WHO APPEAR ONLY DURING BATTLES.
POING
Extremely strong.
!
Aah!

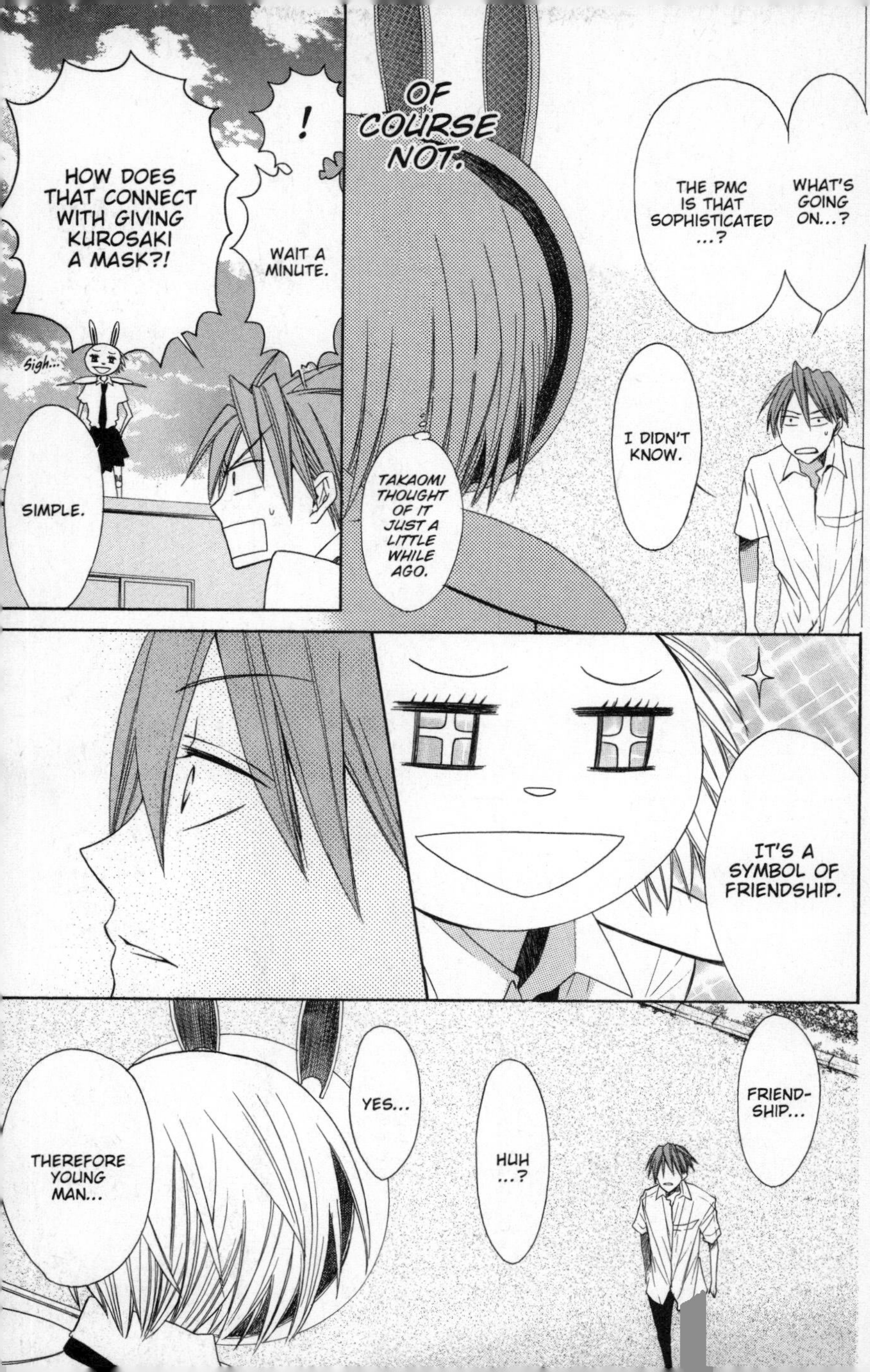
WHAT'S GOING ON...?
THE PMC IS THAT SOPHISTICATED ...?
OF COURSE NOT.
I DIDN'T KNOW.
TAKAOMI THOUGHT OF IT JUST A LITTLE WHILE AGO.
!
WAIT A MINUTE.
HOW DOES THAT CONNECT WITH GIVING KUROSAKI A MASK?!
Sigh...
SIMPLE.
IT'S A SYMBOL OF FRIENDSHIP.
FRIEND-SHIP...
YES...
HUH ...?
THEREFORE YOUNG MAN...

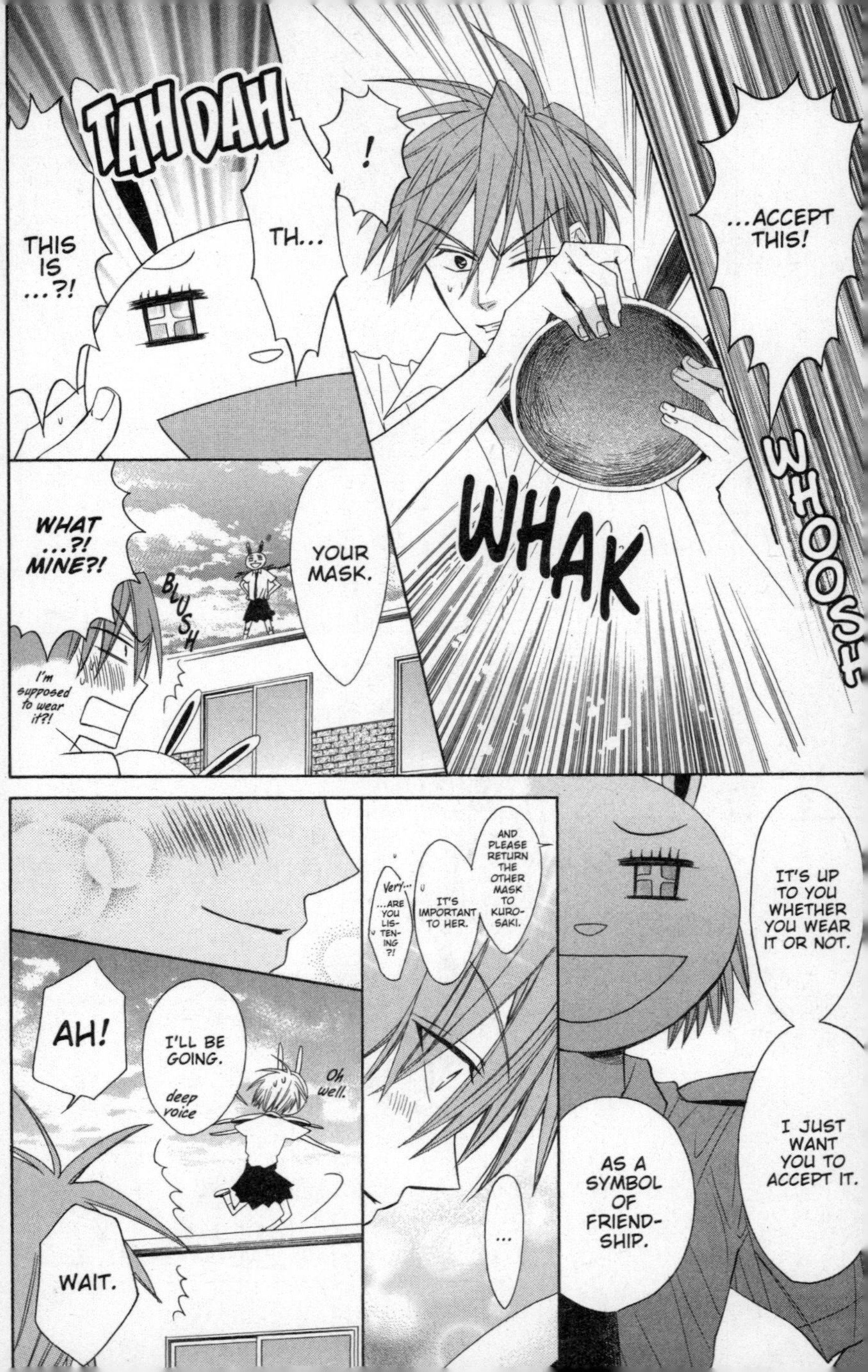
...ACCEPT THIS!
WHOOSH
WHAK
TAH DAH
!
TH...
THIS IS ...?!
YOUR MASK.
WHAT ...?! MINE?!
BLUSH
I'm supposed to wear it?!
IT'S UP TO YOU WHETHER YOU WEAR IT OR NOT.
I JUST WANT YOU TO ACCEPT IT.
AS A SYMBOL OF FRIEND-SHIP.
...
AND PLEASE RETURN THE OTHER MASK TO KURO-SAKI.
IT'S IMPORTANT TO HER.
Very... ...ARE YOU LIS-TEN-ING?!
I'LL BE GOING.
deep voice
Oh well.
AH!
WAIT.

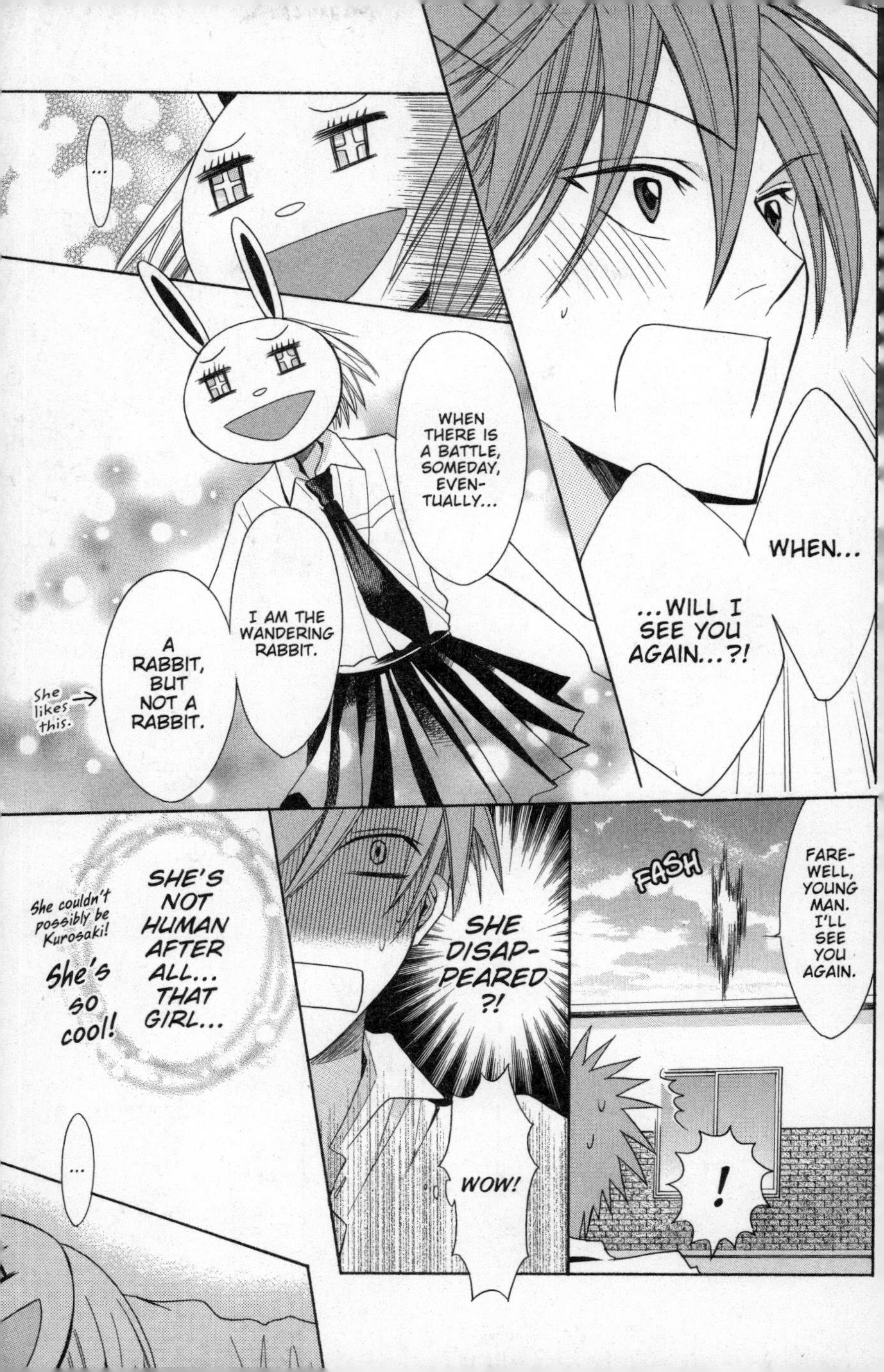
WHEN...
...WILL I SEE YOU AGAIN...?!
...
WHEN THERE IS A BATTLE, SOMEDAY, EVEN-TUALLY...
I AM THE WANDERING RABBIT.
A RABBIT, BUT NOT A RABBIT.
She likes this.
FARE-WELL, YOUNG MAN. I'LL SEE YOU AGAIN.
FASH
!
SHE DISAP-PEARED?!
WOW!
SHE'S NOT HUMAN AFTER ALL... THAT GIRL...
She couldn't possibly be Kurosaki!
She's so cool!
...

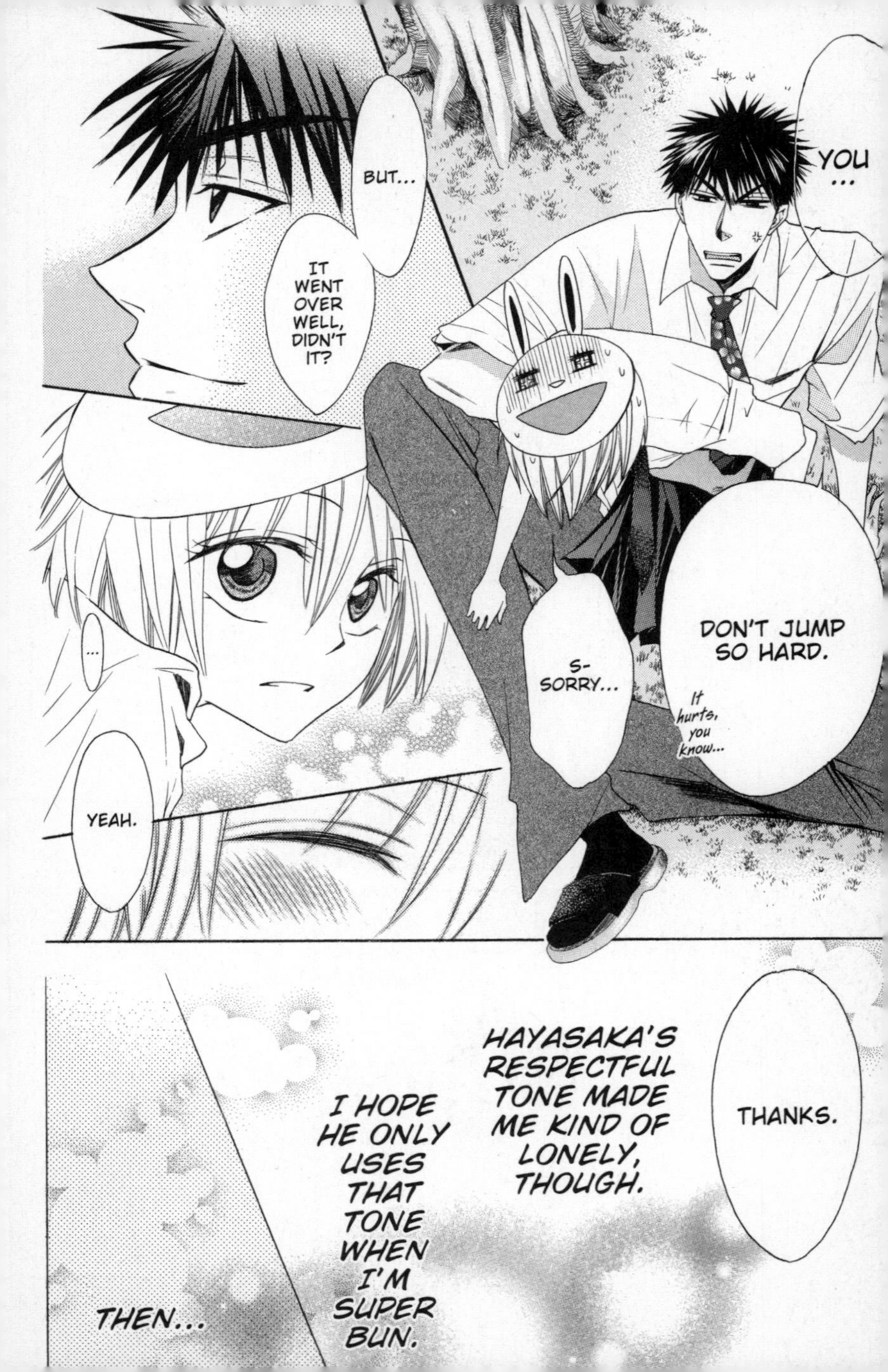
YOU...
DON'T JUMP SO HARD.
It hurts, you know...
S-SORRY...
BUT...
IT WENT OVER WELL, DIDN'T IT?
...
YEAH.
THANKS.
HAYASAKA'S RESPECTFUL TONE MADE ME KIND OF LONELY, THOUGH.
I HOPE HE ONLY USES THAT TONE WHEN I'M SUPER BUN.
THEN...

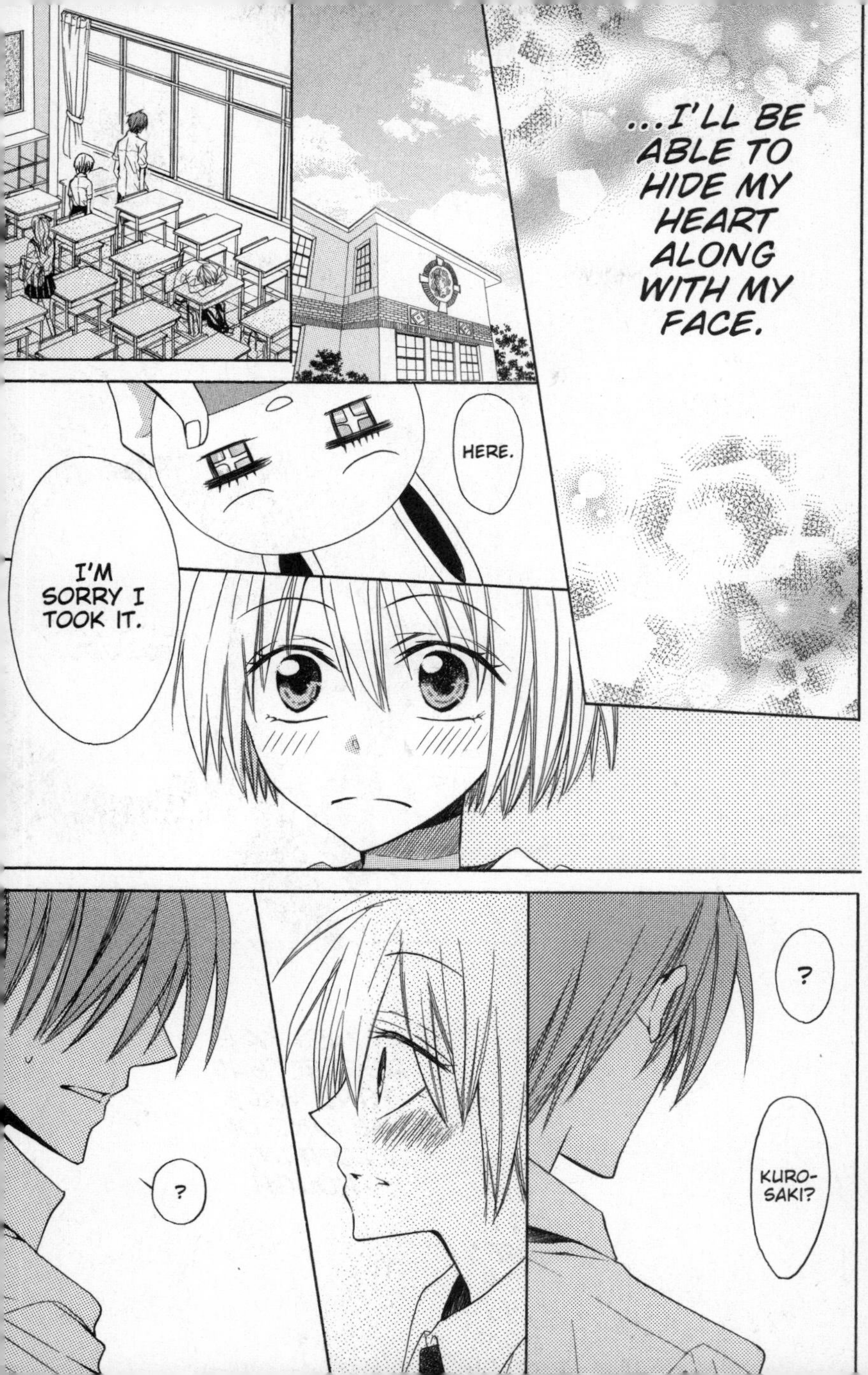
...I'LL BE ABLE TO HIDE MY HEART ALONG WITH MY FACE.
HERE.
I'M SORRY I TOOK IT.
?
KURO-SAKI?
?

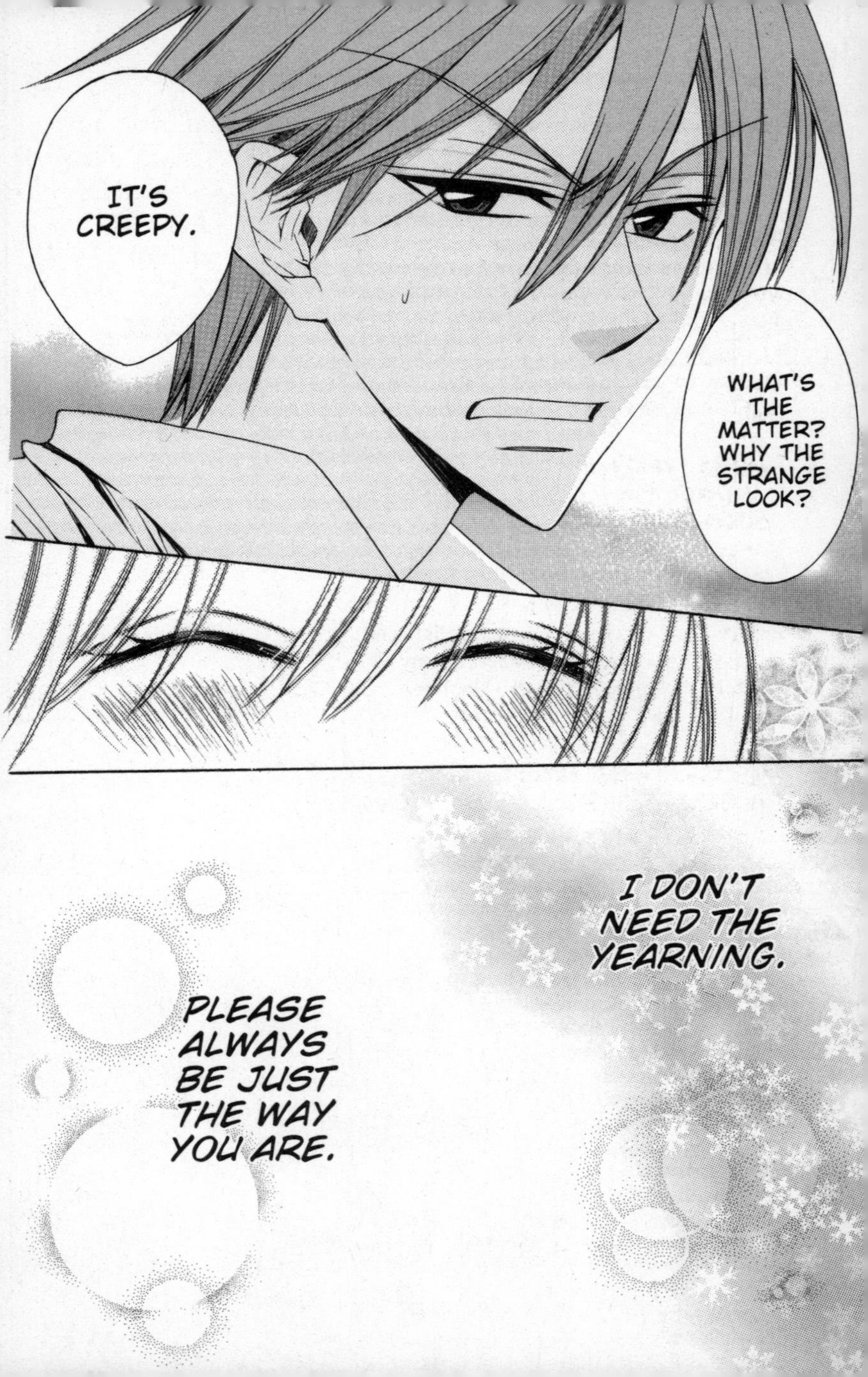
WHAT'S THE MATTER? WHY THE STRANGE LOOK?
IT'S CREEPY.
I DON'T NEED THE YEARNING.
PLEASE ALWAYS BE JUST THE WAY YOU ARE.

End Notes

Page 10, panel 1: Club
In Japan, school clubs are often treated
with the same seriousness given to
sports teams in the United States.
Although participation is not technically
mandatory to graduate, students are
highly encouraged to join a club.

Page 14, panel 1: Manager
In Japan, the team manager is a student
position. It is not unusual for a girl to be
manager of a boys' team.

Page 38, citation: Kojien
A Japanese dictionary first published in
1955. Its reputation in Japan is similar
to that of *Webster's* in the English-
speaking world.

Page 124, panel 4: Flight North
The German film *Flucht in Den Norden*.

Izumi Tsubaki began drawing manga in her first year of high school. She was soon selected to be in the top ten of *Hana to Yume's* HMC (*Hana to Yume* Mangaka Course), and subsequently won *Hana to Yume's* Big Challenge contest. Her debut title, *Chijimete Distance* (Shrink the Distance), ran in 2002 in *Hana to Yume* magazine, issue 17. In addition to *The Magic Touch* (originally published in Japan as *Oyayubi kara Romance*, or "Romance from the Thumbs"), she is currently working on the manga series *Oresama Teacher*.

ORESAMA TEACHER
Vol. 2
Shojo Beat Edition

STORY AND ART BY
Izumi Tsubaki

English Translation & Adaptation/JN Productions
Touch-up Art & Lettering/Jose Macasocol
Design/Yukiko Whitley
Editor/Pancha Diaz

Printed in Canada

Published by VIZ Media, LLC
P.O. Box 77010
San Francisco, CA 94107

10 9 8 7 6 5 4 3 2
First printing, May 2011
Second printing, June 2013

www.viz.com   www.shojobeat.com

You may be reading the wrong way!

It's true: In keeping with the original Japanese comic format, this book reads from right to left—so action, sound effects, and word balloons are completely reversed. This preserves the orientation of the original artwork—plus, it's fun! Check out the diagram shown here to get the hang of things, and then turn to the other side of the book to get started!

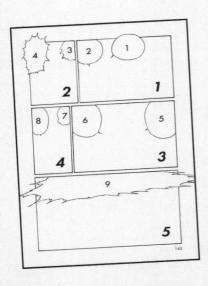